ADMINISTRATIVE DISCRETION

Problems of Decision-Making by Governmental Agencies

ADMINISTRATIVE DISCRETION

Problems of Decision-Making by Governmental Agencies

CLARK C. HAVIGHURST
Editor

OCEANA PUBLICATIONS, INC.

Dobbs Ferry, New York

1974

Library of Congress Cataloging in Publication Data
Main entry under title:

Administrative discretion.

(The Library of law and contemporary problems)
Issued also as Law and contemporary problems, v. 37, no. 1, winter
1972.
Includes bibliographical references.
1. Administrative discretion—United States—Addresses, essays, lec-
tures. I. Havighurst, Clark C., ed. II. Law and contemporary problems.
KF5407.A5A34   342'.73'06   73-11108
ISBN 0-379-11518-2

Originally published in Winter 1972

by

LAW AND CONTEMPORARY PROBLEMS
DUKE UNIVERSITY SCHOOL OF LAW

PRINTED IN THE UNITED STATES OF AMERICA

Titles Published in

The Library of Law and Contemporary Problems

POPULATION CONTROL. The Imminent World Crisis
Melvin G. Schimm, *Editor*

EUROPEAN REGIONAL COMMUNITIES
A New Era on the Old Continent
Melvin G. Shimm, *Editor*

AFRICAN LAW, New Law for New Nations
Hans W. Baade, *Editor*

ACADEMIC FREEDOM, The Scholar's Place
in Modern Society
Hans W. Baade, *Editor*

THE SOVIET IMPACT ON INTERNATIONAL LAW
Hans W. Baade, *Editor*

URBAN PROBLEMS AND PROSPECTS
Robinson O. Everett and Richard H. Leach, *Editors*

ANTIPOVERTY PROGRAMS
Robinson O. Everett, *Editor*

INTERNATIONAL CONTROL OF PROPAGANDA
Clark C. Havighurst, *Editor*

HOUSING
Robinson O. Everett and John D. Johnston, Jr., *Editors*

MEDICAL PROGRESS AND THE LAW
Clark C. Havighurst, *Editor*

THE MIDDLE EAST CRISIS: TEST OF INTERNATIONAL LAW
John W. Halderman, *Editor*

AIR POLLUTION CONTROL
Clark C. Havighurst, *Editor*

CONSUMER CREDIT REFORM
Clark C. Havighurst, *Editor*

THE INSTITUTIONALIZED PRESIDENCY
Norman C. Thomas and Hans W. Baade, *Special Editors*
John C. Weistart, *Series Editor*

HEALTH CARE
Clark C. Havighurst, *Special Editor*
John C. Weistart, *Series Editor*

COMMUNITY ECONOMIC DEVELOPMENT
John C. Weistart, *Editor*

POLICE PRACTICES
John C. Weistart, *Editor*

ADMINISTRATIVE DISCRETION
Clark C. Havighurst, *Editor*

CONTENTS

FOREWORD

Professor Kenneth Culp Davis's seminal book, *Discretionary Justice*, is subtitled "A Preliminary Inquiry."[1] Viewing this as an invitation for others to apply themselves to exploring the ramifications of administrative discretion, the editors of *Law and Contemporary Problems* have procured the papers in this symposium as expressions either of the authors' general views on discretion problems or of their observations on discretion issues in specific agencies or governmental activities. The articles were for the most part meant to examine, apply, and extend Davis's approach. The symposium on *Police Practices* contained in the last issue of *Law and Contemporary Problems* also addressed problems which Davis examines in his book.

Although addressing areas of intense concern to lawyers in his book, Professor Davis is seldom strictly lawyerlike in dealing with the issues which he raises. Often he suggests no means of rectifying by legal action the failure of agencies to correct the abuses which concern him, and he frequently appears instead merely to be appealing to administrators' better instincts. As an illustration of how he skimps on legalistics, what is perhaps the most important substantive legal point in the book, namely that the courts could compel much more extensive agency rule making by employing a variant of the nondelegation doctrine,[2] is made so briefly that Judge J. Skelly Wright, in a review, wrote as if it had been omitted altogether, criticizing Davis for not suggesting such a role for the courts.[3]

Although often omitting to clear legal pathways to achievement of the reforms he advocates, Davis nevertheless has given others some useful tools for breaking through the underbrush. The best agencies and conscientious commissioners have now been advised that there is more to good administration than the wise exercise of discretion and that it is also incumbent on them to establish procedures and practices which strengthen the guarantees of justice even in their informal, discretionary activities. Administrators can now be taxed by scholars, congressmen, litigants, and other critics—and occasionally, where a legal handle can be found, by judges—for failing to adopt the Davis prescriptions for "confining," "structuring," and "checking" discretion. The Administrative Conference of the United States, which stim-

---
[1] K.C. Davis, Discretionary Justice: A Preliminary Inquiry (1969).

[2] *Id.* at 57-59, 220-21. *See also* Davis, *A New Approach to Delegation*, 36 U. Chi. L. Rev. 713 (1969).

[3] Wright, *Beyond Discretionary Justice*, 81 Yale L.J. 575 (1972).

ulated some of the work reflected in articles in this symposium, has recently pushed several agencies in the direction of reform in discretion-related areas. Davis's work provided much of the impetus for these efforts.

Although Davis's book was concerned as much with public administration as with legal doctrine, legal developments calculated to advance the cause of confining, structuring, or checking discretion are beginning to pick up as courts begin to respond to the concerns which Davis voiced. In *Environmental Defense Fund, Inc. v. Ruckelshaus,*[4] the Court of Appeals for the District of Columbia required the Agriculture Department (and subsequently the EPA) to explain why they had failed to act to ban DDT widely in response to the documented demands of environmental groups. In another case establishing accountability for the exercise of previously unreviewable prosecutorial discretion, a U.S. district judge in Washington, D.C., recently ordered the Department of Health, Education, and Welfare to correct its nonenforcement of the Civil Rights Act.[5] Other decisions have also begun to reflect judicial scrutiny of prosecutorial decisions,[6] and many signs in the daily press point to further and even more fundamental courtroom confrontations between citizens and the federal executive. Impoundment of funds, which is dealt with in Dr. Fisher's article herein, is just one area of probable conflict.

Among other things, Davis succeeds dramatically, though perhaps inadvertently, in demonstrating the difficulty of bringing government under meaningful control. Many judges, like Judge Wright, would confidently expand the judiciary's oversight of administrative activities, but Davis's basic instinct that law alone, imposed from outside the agency, cannot right all wrongs, remains correct. Whether stronger traditions of openness, supervision and review, adherence to rules, and so forth can be established among civil servants remains to be seen, but bureaucrats as a species are probably no less likely than the rest of mankind to pursue self-interest more consistently than other goals.[7] Although implementation of Davis's reforms would often succeed in changing bureaucrats' perceptions of where their interests in fact lie, the inherent limitations of political institutions are so many that complete coincidence of interests between bureaucrats and the public is seldom likely. By facilitating more thoughtful consideration of the effectiveness of remedies involving large doses of governmental control, however, Davis's work should contribute to the devising of more nearly optimal forms of intervention. Students of the newly popular "policy sciences" should study *Discretionary Justice* with care.

April 1973   CLARK C. HAVIGHURST.

[4] 439 F.2d 584 (D.C. Cir. 1971).

[5] Washington Post, Nov. 17, 1972, p. 1.

[6] *E.g.,* United States v. Steele, 461 F.2d 1148 (9th Cir. 1972); American Public Health Ass'n v. Veneman, CCH FOOD, DRUG, & COSM. L. REP. paras. 40,723, 40,749 (D.C. Cir. 1972); Medical Committee on Human Rights v. SEC, 432 F.2d 659 (D.C. Cir. 1970). *See also* K.C. DAVIS, ADMINISTRATIVE LAW TEXT § 28.06 (1972).

[7] *Cf.* W.A. NISKANEN, BUREAUCRACY AND REPRESENTATIVE GOVERNMENT 36-42 (1971).

DECISIONS, DECISIONAL REFERENTS, AND ADMINISTRATIVE JUSTICE

DANIEL J. GIFFORD*

This article is an attempt to share some developing thoughts on the major problem of discretionary justice, which Professor Davis has brought to our attention. I first examine the contributions of the linguistic school of legal philosophy towards the development of our understanding of discretion. In that examination we find that informal and largely internal constraints may be operable upon decision-making, and we also find that many of these constraints may be invisible. Next (in Part II), from the inference that decisions are constrained or guided by factors which have hitherto tended to escape the sustained attention of lawyers, I attempt, in a preliminary way, to develop a conceptual structure in which to take cognizance of these factors. This structure, which I refer to as one of "decisional referents," I follow up (in Part III) by examining some examples of official decision-making, and by probing to find the effects of structure upon tendencies toward change and growth and upon countervailing tendencies toward stability. In Part IV, I pursue an examination of a decisional-referent conceptualization of official decision-making for its implications concerning the related factors of openness and substantive rationality. Finally (in Part V), I assess some of the recent developments in administrative standing in the light of this conceptual structure.

I

THE SIGNIFICANCE OF "INTERNAL" CONSTRAINTS ON THE EXERCISE OF DISCRETIONARY POWER

A. Discretion and Internal Constraints

Davis finds discretion present in any situation in which "the effective limits on . . . [an official's] power leave him free to make a choice among possible courses of action or inaction."[1] He includes within that concept power to make unauthorized decisions "because a good deal of discretion is illegal or of questionable legality."[2] In this article, I will depart from Davis's definition of the problem and confine myself largely to a consideration of "authorized" discretion. I will, however, return periodically to Davis's emphasis upon the "effective limits" of an official's power.

Davis's assertion that he is concerned with unauthorized as well as with authorized discretionary power and his stress upon the need for "effective limits" on decision-making power may be somewhat misleading. The critical factor is the meaning of

---

* Professor of Law, State University of New York at Buffalo.
[1] K. DAVIS, DISCRETIONARY JUSTICE 4 (1969).
[2] Id.

the "effective limits" phrase. Certainly, the implication of his writing is correct that limits upon the authorized discretion of an official are unimportant in those cases in which that official pays little heed to the limits of his authorized power. But, in the case of officials who have internalized the rules of the system within which they work, a latent ambiguity in Davis's phrasing appears: to the extent that officials have in fact internalized the system's rules, limitations on their authorized powers will be "effective." I am assuming here an empirical meaning for effectiveness, that is, that an "effective" limit is a limit which works.

Among those who have most recently directed their attention to an internalization of rules by officials are the legal philosophers Dworkin and Hart. Both men have drawn attention to the "binding" effect which externally made rules have upon a decision-maker who has internalized the legal system in which he functions as an official. Hart first made the point about the effectiveness of internal constraints when he pointed out that a judge in a court of last resort could be "bound" by prior cases or principles embodied in the legal system even though, were he to ignore those cases or principles, his decision would be irreversible.[3] Dworkin followed Hart's approach in a discussion of administrative and judicial discretion.[4] Dworkin there attributed discretion only in a "weak" sense to an official whose decisions are either a matter of judgment or unreviewable or both but discretion in a "strong" sense to an official who has been entrusted decision-making power but with no standards for the exercise of that power supplied to him by the authority vesting him with it.[5] In the case of "weak" discretion, the official is "bound" by standards supplied by the external authority although that authority may not, especially in the second case, enforce those standards against him. The official, however, is not free to decide any way he wishes. He is free only in case he decides to flaunt the imperatives of the system in which he acts. So long as he identifies with that system, he internalizes the "obligation" which the system imposes upon him to decide in accordance with its mandates; he is in effect "bound" by its rules.

It is tempting, at this point, to assert that effective limits on discretionary power exist when officials internalize the system's rules. But at least two difficulties inhere in this method of statement: first, officials probably are not separable solely into two categories composed, respectively, of those who accept the system's rules and of those who do not. Some officials will accept some of the system's rules but not others, and some rules will be accepted to a greater degree than will others—that is, more temptation or inducement to depart from some rules will be required before they are disregarded than in the case of other rules. This is merely to suggest that the degree to which the system's rules are internalized will vary with the rule and with the official.

But, second, this method of statement is overly "rule" oriented. In focusing upon

---

[3] H.L.A. HART, THE CONCEPT OF LAW 56, 141-42 (1961). *See also id.* at 56, 86-88, 139-44.
[4] Dworkin, *The Model of Rules*, 35 U. CHI. L. REV. 14, 32-40 (1967).
[5] *Id.* at 32-33.

an internally felt obligation to adhere to rules as a constraint upon an official's exercise of power, it leads us away from the discretion which is conveyed by rule ambiguity and imprecision. In cases in which the "rules"—if they are observed—do not determine the outcome of a case, the decison-maker appears to have discretion both in Davis's "effective limits" sense and in Dworkin's "strong" sense.[5a] It is to those cases, then, that our present inquiry is directed: where will we find the criteria which are or should be used for decision and what methods are available for improving the consistency and the quality of those criteria?

B. An Extrapolation of the Hart-Dworkin Insight: Conformity to Self-created Rules

Hart and Dworkin, in pointing out that an official might be effectively constrained in his decision-making by his recognition of the "obligations" which the legal system imposes upon him, have focused upon a situation in which an official is supplied with decisional criteria by an external authority and internalizes an obligation to apply those criteria. But the constraints which can be created by internalization may go further. Let us consider a situation in which a statute commits decisions of a certain kind to an agency and in which the agency redelegates the decision-making function to one official, who then develops rules governing his exercise of that power. And let us further suppose that this official does not publish or otherwise disseminate those rules to other persons within or without the agency. Davis has given us just such an example,[6] in his description of an official in the Justice Department who decided cases involving remission and mitigation of automobile forfeitures incurred for violating the narcotics laws.[7] His decisions were, so far as the governing statute was concerned, fully discretionary. Indeed, the statute expressly commits such decisions to administrative discretion.[8] Yet in Davis's description, the official had worked out a set of elaborate rules to govern the cases coming before him, with the result that he decided pursuant to that set of rules, and exercised little or no discretion in deciding individual cases.[9] Although his decisions invariably conformed to this set of rules, those rules were unknown not only outside of the agency but within it. Their content was known only to their creator, the official entrusted with the task of making the remission and mitigation decisions which, in practice, were governed by those rules. In such a situation, is it correct to assert that the decision-maker has discretion? Or is it more correct to assert that his action is so governed by rules that he has little or no discretion? Or, in this context, is the term "discretion" still useful? Observe that even Dworkin's three

---

[5a] Dworkin himself would deny that rule ambiguity often confers discretion in the strong sense. Rather, he would assert that an official who confronts rule ambiguity is most frequently obliged to resolve the ambiguity in accordance with "principles" or other guides furnished by the legal system in which he operates. Dworkin, *supra* note 4 at 36-46; Dworkin, *Social Rules and Legal Theory*, 81 YALE L.J. 855, 879 (1972).

[6] K. DAVIS, *supra* note 1, at 109-11.

[7] 19 U.S.C. §§ 1595a, 1618 (1970).

[8] 19 U.S.C. § 1618 (1970).

[9] K. DAVIS, *supra* note 1, at 109.

senses[10] of discretion are of little value in answering these questions. While the official has discretion in all three of Dworkin's senses, his actions are governed by rules, albeit not externally made rules. If he always decides in accordance with those rules, do not those rules in fact act as the "effective limits"[11] on his decision-making which Davis seeks?

Even if we conclude that it is accurate to describe the official who invariably conforms to his own set of unpublished rules as possessing discretionary power, it is also accurate to describe him as habitually failing to employ that discretion. Davis here, of course, would point out that the official may sometime actually employ the discretionary power which he now "possesses" but does not now "use." But even a conclusion that the official possesses unexercised discretionary power is not a simple statement. If the official never "uses" discretion which he is said to "possess," the reality of his asserted possession of discretionary power is at least questionable. Certainly, there are reasons why that power is not employed, and we need to inquire when, if at all, these reasons are likely to permit the employment of that power.[12]

Davis's actual criticism of the arrangement involving the official who created his own rules is centered on the secrecy of the rules and seems to be concerned primarily with the fact that no external constraints prevent the official from departing from his rules in individual instances.[13] But a focus upon external constraints tends to obscure the fact that the decision-maker himself decided to adopt his set of rules and has been applying them. Perhaps we should ask why the rules were created and the extent to which the decision-maker feels an obligation to apply those rules. If the decision-maker feels a sense of obligation or duty to apply the rules which is strong enough to overcome his personal desires in individual instances, then could we not conclude that his decisions are in fact constrained, even in the absence of external constraints? Could we not admit that some constraints on decision-making might be internal to the actor himself? Or, if the decision-maker could alter or

---

[10] See text accompanying notes 4-5 *supra.*

[11] See text acompanying note 1 *supra.*

[12] This inquiry began with the "legal realist" writers of a generation ago. Many of these writers directed their attention to the factors, psychological, political and other, which influence judges' decisions within the free scope provided by the ambiguities of the laws. See notes 21 and 25 *infra.* As suggested in text, an official may be effectively confined to a set of rules or to the use of a set of "referents" through a sense of "obligation." He also may experience external imperatives towards consistency of action from formal or informal bureaucratic controls. Again, a constraining influence may arise when decisions must be made in routine cases which occur in large numbers; consistency must be maintained to preserve the integrity of a set of rules which comprise the means by which an official copes with a voluminous caseload. Cf. Friedman, *On Legalistic Reasoning—A Footnote to Weber,* 1966 WIS. L. REV. 148, 157. Former Chairman Cary of the Securities and Exchange Commission has described how he was able to avoid some external constraints—consisting of pressures brought by business and political sources—by carefully choosing the manner of acting: adjudication rather than rule-making. See W. CARY, POLITICS AND THE REGULATORY AGENCIES 83-84 (1967).

The "costs" to an official or agency—in effectiveness, in organizational stability, in psychological satisfaction—of resisting external pressures would be a proper subject of study. The focus of this article, however, is largely upon the substantive inputs into the decisional structure, that is, upon the content of assertedly "discretionary" decisions.

[13] K. DAVIS, *supra* note 1, at 110.

waive his rules only at some cost, could we not admit that a constraint—measurable by the extent of the cost which would otherwise be incurred—was present and which operated to induce decisions in conformity with his rules? An affirmative answer to any one of these questions suggests a need to inquire whether all constraints on decision-making need be external to the actor. By implication, such an answer also suggests that we need to examine the existence and strength of internal constraints. This approach will also facilitate our inquiry into constraints (or constraining influences) external to the actor which are informal and which, therefore, may be easily overlooked by lawyers.

C. Internal Constraints and the Appearance of Nonexistent Discretion

The Hart-Dworkin insight into the relevance of rule-internalization for understanding discretion is useful in differentiating the appearance from the reality of discretion—a differentiation which is sometimes obscured under more-or-less traditional perceptions of administrative discretion. Thus, under the traditional view of administrative discretion, there tends to exist a negative correlation[14] between the predictability of a decision and the extent of the decision-maker's discretion: When the facts are clear or undisputed, the content of a decision is highly predictable in those cases which involve a governing rule in its "core"[15] area of application; and in this kind of case the decision-maker has little or no discretion. But when the case involves situations which depart from the governing rule's core area of application —or when it is uncertain which of several apparently conflicting rules govern— the decision becomes increasingly unpredictable, and the decision-maker's discretion is, accordingly, said to increase.[16]

This traditional description, however, is inaccurate in at least two respects: it neglects, first, the distinction between decisional ambiguity[17] perceived by the decision-maker and decisional ambiguity perceived by an observer. These perceptions

---

[14] *Cf.* H.L.A. HART, THE CONCEPT OF LAW 143 (1961); Cohen, *Transcendental Nonsense and the Functional Approach*, 35 COLUM. L. REV. 809, 843 (1935).

[15] On the distinction between a "core" area of word meaning or rule application and "pennumbral" areas, *see* Hart, *Positivism and the Separation of Law and Morals*, 71 HARV. L. REV. 593, 606-08 (1958); Fuller, *Positivism and Fidelity to Law—A Reply to Professor Hart*, 71 HARV. L. REV. 630, 661-69 (1958); Gifford, *Communication of Legal Standards, Policy Development, and Effective Conduct Regulation*, 56 CORNELL L. REV. 409, 426-30 (1971).

The distinction, in its current form, is derived from the preoccupation of British and American philosophers in recent decades with the open-texture of all language. *See, e.g.,* L. WITTGENSTEIN, PHILOSOPHICAL INVESTIGATIONS (G. Anscombe transl. 1953); Waismann, *Verifiability*, in ESSAYS IN LOGIC AND LANGUAGE 117 (1st ser., A. Flew ed. 1951). The impact of such open-texture for law has been pointed out, *inter alia*, in H.L.A. HART, THE CONCEPT OF LAW 121-32 (1961); Hart, *The Ascription of Responsibilities and Rights*, 49 PROCEEDINGS OF THE ARISTOTELIAN SOC'Y (n.s.) 171, 173-74 (1948-49). Kelsen long ago, however, pointed out that vagueness, ambiguity, or conflict in directives addressed to officials confers discretionary decision-making power upon those officials. Kelsen, *The Pure Theory of Law*, 50 L.Q. REV. 474 (1934).

[16] *See* note 15 *supra. See also* notes 20 & 21 *infra.*

[17] The phrase "decisional ambiguity," as used in the text, includes all situations in which the correct decisional result is uncertain. It includes cases in which that uncertainty results from ambiguity in the decisional norms, as well as cases in which that uncertainty results from vagueness or imprecision in those norms or from conflict among decisional norms.

are not always the same. An extreme example of a difference in such perceptions is presented by the situation in which an official appears to an outside observer to possess discretion because no statute or promulgated rules compel a decision one way or another but in which he actually has little or no discretion at all because his decisions are governed by a set of rules known and acted upon within that official's agency but unknown outside of it.[18] But the internal-rule situation is only an extreme form of a disparity in the perceptions of decisional freedom by a decision-maker and his onlookers. In other circumstances, the decision-maker will feel bound by prior practice, trade custom, analytical techniques, and so forth, all of which may be unknown to at least some onlookers. The obligation which he feels to utilize those factors in deciding may or may not be enforced by his superiors. His decisions may even be unreviewable. Yet he may feel that the decisional system in which he functions requires him to utilize these factors in deciding. He may be "bound" in the Hart-Dworkin sense. An observer, however, who is unaware of these factors and of the official's concomitant "obligation" to employ them sees discretion which the official does not see. Finally, even when both the decision-maker and the on-lookers perceive the same prospective decision in a similar analytical framework, they may differ in their respective assessments of the degree of decisional freedom present in that framework.[19] The degree to which a given set of rules and other constraints forecloses (or does not foreclose) a decision-maker's freedom is frequently a matter of perception and judgment, and persons differ in their capacities for both. And this, at least partially, explains why an observer may confidently expect a decision in a certain way and then be surprised to learn that the deciding official had decided in a way which the observer had thought impossible, or, again, why the official may consider himself bound by precedent in a case in which an observer sees large amounts of decisional discretion.

Second, the preceding description not only neglects the distinction between decisional ambiguity perceived by the decision-maker and decisional ambiguity perceived by an observer, but it also neglects the related distinction between the decisional ambiguity initially perceived by the decision-maker and the full or partial resolution of that ambiguity by him in the course of deciding. Here I focus upon a decisional situation which is initially perceived as ambiguous by the decision-maker (and perhaps by onlookers as well). But the need to decide compels the decision-maker to resolve that ambiguity.[20] He may resolve it by research, consultation, weighing alternatives, or other means, but resolve it he must. Because an observer may lack access to all of the information sources available to the decision-maker and because he necessarily lacks access to the later's mental processes in which judgments and evaluations are made, the observer cannot predict with

---

[18] *Cf.* text accompanying notes 6-9 *supra.*

[19] *See, e.g.,* J. FRANK, LAW AND THE MODERN MIND 164-65 (1963 ed.) and note 21 *infra.*

[20] Judge Hutcheson has described the perplexity of a judge facing a situation of decisional ambiguity and has noted the absence of predictability in those situations. Hutcheson, *Lawyer's Law and the Little, Small Dice,* 7 TULANE L. REV. 1, 6 (1932). See also note 21 *infra.*

assurance how that ambiguity will be resolved. He may thus see the decision as discretionary with the decision-maker. Yet the latter may feel no such discretion at all. The difference is due to the fact that the observer is not privy to the processes by which the initial ambiguity is resolved.[21] Thus, in a situation in which the relevant decisional norms appear ambiguous both to the deciding official and to an observer, the former may feel bound to resolve that ambiguity in accordance with the mandates of the legal system in which he is acting and, accordingly, to ferret out, if possible, the latent meaning of the governing rule or rules. In a very simple example, both the deciding official and an observer may initially perceive ambiguity in the decisional norms. But the deciding official may then resolve that ambiguity by reference to information sources, such as the legislative history of those norms. If these sources are not available to the observer, he cannot predict the official's decision.[22] That decision, if it is not explained on the basis of the legislative history resorted to, may even appear to the observer to have been completely discretionary with the deciding official. Yet, to the deciding official, after he had researched the legislative history of the statute or other rule in question, the decision appeared controlled by a statute or rule whose purpose was disclosed by that history.

But the problem is more complex than this. Decisional ambiguity is frequently the result of vague, ambiguous, or conflicting statutes or rules inhering against a background of principles—generally largely shared by the decision-maker—mandating, when at all possible, decisions which are, among other things, "just" and compassionate. Thus, when the statutory purpose seems to require one result while justice or compassion require a different one, or when several statutory or policy goals conflict in their application to the case at hand, decisional ambiguity results. Dworkin,[23] for one, has attempted to describe this process where judicial decision-makers struggle to apply correctly justice or equity or other "principles" supplied by the legal system in which they participate. In all of these situations, the system requires the official to find ways, if possible, of reconciling the apparent conflicts and, to the extent that this is impractical, to assign weights to the conflicting goals. In resolving the initial decisional ambiguity which confronts him, the decision-maker

---

[21] In his famous essay, *The Judgment Intuitive: The Function of the "Hunch" in Judicial Decision*, 14 CORNELL L. REV. 274 (1929), Hutcheson described the mental processes by which initial decisional ambiguity is often resolved, and he there differentiated those processes from the rationalization of the decision in the judge's written opinion. Hutcheson is not, however, describing processes in which a judge injects his personal whims which differ from his perception of the mandates of the legal system in which he participates. Rather, he appears to be describing processes in which the judge strives to resolve decisional ambiguity in accordance with a sense of justice which is seen as pervading that legal system. *Compare* J. FRANK, LAW AND THE MODERN MIND 164-65 (1963 ed.) where it is observed that most judges attempt to decide in accordance with their perceptions of the legal system's mandates. The less aware judges, however, deceive themselves into applying precedents and rules, unconscious of the discretion which existing formulations of these precedents and rules give them and oblivious to the policy choices which they are in fact making.

[22] *See, e.g.,* United States v. Public Util. Comm'n, 345 U.S. 295, 319-20 (1953) (Jackson, J., concurring); Schwegmann Bros. v. Calvert Distillers Corp., 341 U.S. 384, 396-97 (1951) (Jackson, J., concurring).

[23] Dworkin, *supra* note 4.

may not feel himself free to decide as he pleases. He may feel himself bound to decide in accordance with the principles, rules, goals, and so forth, which the system has supplied to him. His ability to reconcile apparent conflict will depend upon his own imagination; and the weights he accords to different goals and principles will often reflect his own perception of the system's priorities. His own preferences will also enter directly, as in some cases the system will entrust him with discretion in a "strong" sense.[24] But, for the most part, the official will be struggling to apply the system's priorities as he can best perceive them. His decisions will tend to be perceived by him as strongly constrained by the information at his disposal and by his perception of the decisions, policies, and goals of the system which he is administering.

In the type of situation described, an observer, as well as the decision-maker, may perceive the initial decisional ambiguity. But since it will be exceedingly difficult, if not impossible, for the observer accurately to predict the manner in which the official will resolve the ambiguity, he is tempted to assert that the decision is discretionary with the official. Indeed, this was suggested by some of the so-called "legal realist" writers earlier in this century.[25] But, as we have seen, such an assertion may not at all accord with the perceptions of the deciding official. Once he has re-solved the ambiguity in accordance with the system's mandates as he perceives them, the official feels bound to decide in accordance with that resolution. While the "binding" nature of the official's resolution is perceived by him as a result of his own struggle to accord to the relevant factors the priorities which the system demands of them, because an external observer has not participated in that struggle and because an external observer would not necessarily have arrived at the same balance of those competing factors, the observer will often rightly fail to preceive the "obligation" felt by the decision-maker to decide the way that he did. The result is an externally perceived decisional freedom which is not at all perceived by the decision-maker.

D. Summary

Constraints upon the exercise of discretion can be real, even though they are largely internal and self-imposed. But the range of constraints is not exhausted in a dichotomy between "internal" and "external" constraints. Some constraints fall intermediate between the poles of internality and externality. Illustrative of this middle ground are the constraints described by Hart and Dworkin which have an external origin but which bind only those officials who have internalized the authority of their legal system to impose such obligations. But even the Hart-Dworkin model of constraints must be extended because the perception and understanding by officials of the constraints imposed by the legal system will vary, and not all officials will

---

[24] Dworkin, *supra* note 4, at 33.

[25] *See, e.g.,* Haines, *General Observations on the Effects of Personal, Political, and Economic Influences in the Decisions of Judges,* 17 ILL. L. REV. 98 (1922). *Cf.* Schroder, *The Psychologic Study of Judicial Opinions,* 6 CALIF. L. REV. 89 (1918). *See also* note 21 *supra.*

internalize every constraint established by the system. Moreover, those who do internalize will not all internalize all obligations with the same degree of intensity.

Some types of internal constraints operable upon officials are invisible to observers. Other constraints which are now largely unnoticed by such observers would be more visible if the observers knew where to direct their attention. If constraints upon decision-making include a spectrum of constraints from those which are fully external (in the sense that they are fully visible and enforced through supervision or other formal checking device) through those which are completely internal, then it is incumbent upon lawyers concerned to understand official decision-making to develop a conceptual framework which will facilitate the recognition of constraints which are wholly or partially internal to the decision-maker and which will engender among lawyers abilities to cope with and even to utilize these constraints to advantage. Especially in the more structurally-oriented task of law reform, a developed understanding and appreciation of the roles performed by internal constraints are likely to be highly useful.

But perhaps here it is time to examine our use of the term "constraint." "Constraint" suggests that a decision-maker is compelled to act in a way which is against his will. Yet a decision-maker who internalizes to a high degree the mandates of the legal system may not perceive those mandates as constraints; for him they may be welcome "guides" or "aids" in the performance of what otherwise would be a hopelessly complex and difficult task. Perhaps, then, instead of focusing exclusively upon constraints or constraining influences, we should direct our attention toward the guides or factors which officials in fact utilize in their decisional processes. Such a focus would include within our inquiry those rules, standards, criteria, or factors which the legal system requires officials to use and hence which may be "constraints" upon officials who have not internalized those factors completely. But it will also include, as within our inquiry, factors which conscientious officials employ in their decisional processes out of a sense of propriety but which they may not perceive as "constraints." Such an expanded inquiry would be likely to improve our understanding of discretionary decisional powers and their exercise, to increase our sensitivity to factors which do affect or control decision-making, to enable us to utilize these factors to advantage in dialogue with administrators, and to perceive the directions toward which some changes in decisional structure may tend.

II

"REFERENTS" AND THE PROCESS OF DECIDING

One way of viewing the decisional process is to focus upon the needs of a deciding official, first, to ascertain the relevant facts and, second, to apply to those facts the appropriate decisional standard. The process is not always so straightforward, however, because the selection of those facts which are "relevant" depends upon the decisional standard to be applied, and the choice of the decisional standard depends, at least in part, upon the facts. Nonetheless, the relation between the facts and the decisional standard is not entirely circular: the totality of the concrete facts exerts an often controlling influence upon the choice of a decisional standard, and sometimes that choice is also influenced by the goals or other motives or sensitivities of the decision-maker. It is this latter aspect that I wish to focus upon in the present article. What determines the choice by a decision-maker of the standards which he will employ in deciding?

Two comments upon this question are immediately in order. First, observe that the question, as phrased, departs slightly from most inquiries into standards in administrative decision-making. Most such inquiries have focused upon the needs for standards as an aid to consistency. They have largely avoided asking why one standard is employed rather than another, and have instead asked why standards as such—regardless of the content of those standards—have not been forthcoming. Second, the term "standards" was used in the question in order to stress the connection between that question and the traditional inquiries into the needs for guides for consistency in administrative decision-making. Yet, in order properly to deal with the question, I would rephrase it slightly. I would rephrase it in terms of "decisional referents," a concept which I will explain below. Rephrased, the question now becomes: what determines the choice by a decision-maker of his decisional referents? And this question projects the further question: how can the decisional process be structured so as to improve the choice of decisional referents?

A. Decisional Referents in General

As I use the term, a decisional referent is whatever a decision-maker deems significant in deciding.[26] Thus an official, or for that matter anyone else, who decides anything at all can be conceived as deciding with reference to one or more factors which are the important considerations underlying his choice among the options available to him. In most situations, the major factors determining the outcome of any decision are a statute, regulation, or other rule which specifies the basis for decision and the deciding official's view of the facts. In such cases the decisional referents are the applicable rule (or statute or regulation) and the official's view of the facts to which the rule applies. If the rule is sufficiently precise in its formulation and if there is no dispute as to the facts or if the facts have already been decided (as they may be in some cases in which an official reviews the decision of a subordinate), then the decision is preordained; there is no choice, no discretion. Once the deciding official has determined or obtained a view of the facts, his decisional referent is the applicable rule. If the rule is sufficiently clear, the rule itself determines the outcome: it—and the facts to which it is applied—are the sole decisional referents.

But rules are not the only kind of referents. A rule (apart from the set of facts

---

[26] The "referent" terminology has long been utilized by scholars. *See, e.g.,* C. OGDEN & I. RICHARDS, THE MEANING OF MEANING 11 (1st ed. 1923). In legal literature similar terminology is found, *inter alia,* in M. GLUCKMAN, THE JUDICIAL PROCESS AMONG THE BAROTSE IN LAW AND WARFARE 59, 88 (P. Bohannan ed. 1967). *Cf.* Gifford, *supra* note 15, at 420.

to which it is applied) is a sole referent only where there are no conflicting rules and the terms of the rule speak precisely to the case at hand. Elsewhere than in these situations, referents other than the provisions of a single rule will come into play. The decision-maker necessarily must refer to matters outside of the rules themselves to resolve ambiguity in the rules. These nonrule referents may be guidelines, trade customs, social customs, analytical techniques, professional disciplines, prior practice, approaches shared or unshared with other persons, shared or unshared attitudes, values, understandings, the desires of superiors, political-party considerations—anything, in fact, which influences the decision-maker in his decision and to which he consciously adverts in deciding. This is an essential point of the present article: if we can broaden our focus from standards or rules to "referents" as just defined, we have a tool useful to lawyers interested in understanding, coping with, and improving administrative decision-making of both the formal and informal varieties.

B. Judicial and Administrative Referents Compared

When an appellate judge decides a question before him, his first look for decisional referents is to the statutes and to past decisions. A reference to what has gone before is likely to control, or to exert a heavy influence upon, the decision which he now must make. This search of the past may have contributed to the now-obsolescent conceptualization of the judge's function as one of "finding" a pre-existent law and of consequently underplaying the policy choices which the judge had to make. But even though judicial policy-making is now more clearly recognized, it is still circumscribed by the deference which the judge is expected to show the past. His opinions are expected to justify his present decisions largely in terms of these past referents, previously enacted statutes and prior cases.

Despite the primary orientation of judicial decision-making towards the past, a judge's decisional referents are not exclusively past events. They could not be, otherwise he would never be able to overrule a prior decision. In any event, these past referents, that is, statutes and cases, may be inclusive and open-ended. In this latter event, we have seen that when the "rules" or prior cases are inconclusive, the decision-maker must attempt to resolve the ambiguity by making reference to factors outside of those rules or prior cases. Not infrequently, in resolving cases of decisional ambiguity, courts employ future-oriented referents. They are moved by the new states of affairs which will be brought about by the policy choices which they embody in their decisions. These potential states of affairs are thus "referents" which assist the judge in deciding and which make his decision intelligible.[27]

---

[27] In deciding new questions, courts are frequently moved by the results—or new states of affairs— which will be brought about by their decisions. These new states of affairs to be brought about may be perceived by the court as not only furthering justice for the parties before the court but as furthering justice in other cases which may arise in the future. Again, the effect of the present decision on future conduct is also taken into account as a decisional referent. Will a decision in favor of a destitute widow against an overreaching mortgagee discourage the granting of credit to widows of modest means? Cf. R. WASSERSTROM, THE JUDICIAL DECISION 142-43 (1961). Cases in which courts have overruled the traditional doctrine of charitable immunity furnish an example of courts utilizing as referents their

In contrast to courts, agencies are often assigned a role which is openly recognized to be a more active one—and one which is less tied to the past. Their grants of power are sometimes made in statutory phrases which specifically refer to future —as yet unrealized—states of affairs which the agency is charged with bringing about. Thus the Civil Aeronautics Board is assigned the task of bringing about the development and prosperity of American air transportation.[28] The Federal Power Commission, whose assigned tasks consist partly in conserving and promoting an adequate power supply for the nation,[29] is perhaps typical of those agencies whose grants of power are phrased in present-oriented language but which are effectively charged with bringing about future states of affairs. Not only are agency charges phrased or understood in terms of future goals; they are also phrased in language which is often quite vague.[30] These two factors—the orientation toward the future and the vagueness of the terms themselves—suggest that the role which the agency is expected to play is an active one. Its attention is to be directed toward reaching a future state of affairs; and the lack of precise standards means that its efforts in reaching those goals are not to be circumscribed by the past in a manner analogous to the manner in which the past circumscribes the possibilities of judicial activism.

---

concern with present justice and a future, more desirable ordering of affairs. *See, e.g.*, Bing v. Thunig, 2 N.Y.2d 653, 143 N.E.2d 3, 163 N.Y.S.2d 3 (1957); President & Directors of Georgetown College v. Hughes, 130 F.2d 810 (D.C. Cir. 1942). In these cases, that future ordering would be one in which charitable institutions would possess incentives to encourage care by their employees and to insure against the consequences of their negligent acts. Indeed, sometimes, as in the prospective overruling cases, the courts' holdings have been based upon referents which were primarily future states of affairs which their decisions would bring about and, in order to avoid injustice to the defendants before them who had shaped their conduct in reliance upon preexisting legal doctrine, the cases before them have been exempted from their holdings. *Cf.* Great North. Ry. v. Sunburst Oil & Ref. Co., 287 U.S. 358 (1932).

[28] 49 U.S.C. § 1302 (1970). Judge Friendly has pointed out that the delegated grant is one which would have implicitly incorporated the Motor Carrier Act scheme of regulation were it not for the large measure of uncertainty injected by a command in section 2(d) that competition was to be fostered "to the extent necessary to assure the sound development of an air transportation system properly adapted to the needs of the foreign and domestic commerce of the United States, of the Postal Service, and of the national defense." H. FRIENDLY, THE FEDERAL ADMINISTRATIVE AGENCIES: THE NEED FOR A BETTER DEFINITION OF STANDARDS 75-76 (1962).

[29] At least as construed. FPC v. Union Elec. Co., 381 U.S. 90, 98-99 (1965); First Iowa Hydro-Elec. Coop. v. FPC, 328 U.S. 152, 180 (1946). *See also* N.Y. EXECUTIVE LAW § 294 (McKinney Supp. 1971) (Division Against Discrimination charged with formulating policies designed to bring about a state of affairs in which discrimination is reduced).

[30] In the examples of the Civil Aeronautics Board and the Federal Power Commission, the referents supplied by the Congress are phrased in language which appears extremely vague when considered as a standard for decision in a case. But vagueness is a relative matter, and it may be that the statutorily-supplied referents, while aiding little in the decision of any particular case, yet may be helpful in the formulation of a general approach towards ultimate policy goals. Thus Davis and others have pointed out the error of expecting agency decisional standards to be supplied by the legislature and have suggested that recognition be given to the responsibility of the agency itself for the development of such standards. K. DAVIS, DISCRETIONARY JUSTICE 49-51 (1969); Davis, *A New Approach to Delegation*, 36 U. CHI. L. REV. 713 (1969); H. FRIENDLY, THE FEDERAL ADMINISTRATIVE AGENCIES— THE NEED FOR A BETTER DEFINITION OF STANDARDS 10-18, 142-47 (1962). *Compare*, H. FRIENDLY, *supra* at 10, 163-75. This approach thus implicitly acknowledges that language vagueness is relative to the purpose for which that language is employed, and that statutory language which describes ends or goals of administration is adequate for its purpose even though it is unworkable as a criterion for decision in an individual case. *Cf.* L. WITTGENSTEIN, PHILOSOPHICAL INVESTIGATIONS § 88, at 41 (G. Anscombe transl. 1953); 1 K. DAVIS, ADMINISTRATIVE LAW TREATISE § 2.03, at 82 (1958).

Operationally, this means that the major policy decisions of an agency which has been legislatively instructed to bring about a new state of affairs will be oriented primarily to the future rather than to the past. And since the agency has been left relatively free about the methods of arriving at the future goal which is itself described only imprecisely, the agency will require information about the subjects and subject-matter which it regulates so that it will be able to employ its freedom intelligently. It needs information about the probable consequences of various changes in the legal and regulatory environment which it is capable of bringing about. It will require knowledge about, or access to, analytical techniques or professional disciplines concerned with the subject matter of its regulation. In short, it is the task of the agency concerned to formulate as guides for its everyday operations decisional criteria and other decisional referents which will assist it in looking to the future. And these decisional referents, to be useful, must possess more content than the vaguely-phrased goals or directives contained in the statutory grant of power to the agency.

C. Particular Kinds of Decisional Referents

1. Studies and Analyses

Since it is the task of an agency to formulate usable decisional referents and since the agency requires knowledge to perform this task, it is critically important for the agency to learn about the subject-matter which it is regulating. One method for an agency to increase its knowledge about a problematic subject-matter is by studying it.[31] The leader in large-scale, planned studies of regulated subject-matter has probably been the Securities and Exchange Commission. Its studies[32] of the stock exchanges and of mutual funds have supplied a host of information useful to the Commission in making decisions, about major policy approaches.[33] But in-

---

[31] In the Federal Communication Commission decisions allocating the electromagnetic spectrum among users, Commissioner Johnson has pointed out the Commission's lack of planning and its tendency to move in the direction of the greatest current pressure for use. Johnson, *Tower of Babel: The Chaos in Radio Spectrum Utilization and Allocation*, 35 LAW & CONTEMP. PROB. 505 (1969). He noted that one of the greatest impediments to planning is the Commission's present ignorance about the "actual use" of radio spectrum in the various bands. Suggesting the desirability of a sophisticated decisional-referent system in which the net marginal social benefits of each use would be compared with benefits of alternative uses, Johnson saw a need for "data concerning actual use and economic value to the user—and modern data processing procedures" *Id.* at 530. He asserted, in short, a primary need for knowledge—for information collection—and for processing that information into usable categories. Only when information is collected and made available in usable form can the Commission operate on a meaningful system of decisional referents and thereby routinize its decisions in a way which will further the goals achievement of which is its delegated responsibility.

[32] See SEC REPORT, SPECIAL STUDY OF SECURITIES MARKETS, H.R. Doc. No. 95, 88th Cong., 1st Sess. (1963); SEC, A STUDY OF MUTUAL FUNDS, H.R. REP. No. 2274, 87th Cong., 2d Sess. (1962).

[33] Action by which major new policies are adopted necessarily utilizes different decisional referents from the more modest alternative form of agency action which proceeds incrementally along a path of small policy choices. In the latter case, information which facilitates each new step is gathered from prior experience. In the former case, information justifying a major new policy commitment is supplied from information sources, such as studies, other than the agency's prior experience. *See, e.g.,* Lindblom, *The Science of "Muddling Through,"* 19 PUB. AD. REV. 79 (1959); Dror, Lindblom, Jones & McCleery, *Symposium on Governmental Decision Making*, 24 PUB. AD. REV. 153 (1964). *See also,* A. ETZIONI, THE

formation and the evaluations of information contained in those studies also furnish referents for Commission decisions about matters of lesser import, including some cases involving the rights of particular parties. Dialogue within the Commission and its staff—and with outsiders when it occurs—will frequently make reference to material contained in these studies.

In the complaint-issuance decisions of the Federal Trade Commission, the studies and recommendations of its Economic Bureau seem, in the past, to have furnished important decisional referents. Thus, for example, the Economic Bureau's 1955 *Report on Corporate Mergers and Acquisitions*[34] seems to have been instrumental in the Commission's decision to issue complaints against a number of mergers in the dairy industry.[35] By keeping informed about mergers and merger trends, the Bureau can bring to the attention of the Commission information which may be crucial to the Commission's choice of respondents. The decisional processes of the Justice Department's Antitrust Division, which enforces the same antimerger statute, furnishes an instructive comparison of rule-referents with non-rule referents as significant decisional factors. The Antitrust Division's guidelines[36]—issued after prolonged study during the Turner administration of the Division—announce Division policy with respect to cases against which proceedings will be brought for merger-law violations. These guidelines thus become decisional referents[37] for the Division's complaint-issuance decisions. The specificity of the guidelines and the form in which they are couched makes them appear as rules. But the Trade Commission, in acting upon information and recommendations supplied by its Economic Bureau, is acting no less than the Justice Department upon the basis of decisional referents. Because the Commission's referents may not take the form of rules (and because Economic Bureau recommendations may not always be contained in published documents and hence sometimes may be less visible than the Department's guidelines) is no reason to ignore the essential similarity of the decisional processes of the two agencies. Dialogue within both agencies preliminary to a complaint-issuance decision would properly address itself to the coverage of the case under consideration by the guidelines or the recommendations of the Economic Bureau and the extent to which the studies and information supplied by the latter indicated the propriety of a complaint-issuance. Officials advocating positions for and against

---

ACTIVE SOCIETY ch. 12 (1968) on a composite or so-called "mixed-scanning" approach to decision-making. Pursuit of a mixed-scanning approach would involve the use of both prior experience and in-depth studies as prime decisional referents.

[34] FTC, REPORT ON CORPORATE MERGERS AND ACQUISITIONS (1955). *See* 3 TRADE REG. REP. ¶ 10,365 (FTC 1955).

[35] In the year subsequent to the issuance of the 1955 *Report on Corporate Mergers and Acquisitions*, the Commission issued anti-merger complaints against four concerns in the dairy industry, two of which were identified in the report as the first and third most active acquiring firms in the nation. *See* Beatrice Foods Co., 67 F.T.C. 473, 704 (1965). *See* note 34 *supra*.

[36] 1 TRADE REG. REP. ¶ 4510 (1968).

[37] It has been suggested, however, that referents other than the guidelines or those factors expressly incorporated in the guidelines occasionally are employed by the Justice Department. *See* M. GREEN, B. MOORE, JR. & B. WASSERSTEIN, THE CLOSED ENTERPRISE SYSTEM 110-11 (1972).

complaint issuance would attempt to justify their respective positions largely in terms of the guidelines or the Bureau's recommendations and studies. And the decision to issue or not to issue a complaint would be made in large part upon a judgment of the extent to which the guidelines or the Bureau studies so indicated.

In addition to their role in complaint-issuance decisions, the studies of the Economic Bureau may form an important referent in the Commission's decision-making about other enforcement steps which it may take in the battle against anti-competitive mergers. Thus, the Bureau's study of vertical mergers in the cement industry led the Commission to institute rule-making proceedings to counter that trend,[38] and the bureau's early study of the post-World War II merger movement was the Commission's main referent when it decided to ask Congress for legislation amending the original Clayton Act.[39]

2. Specialized Disciplines

Decisional referents, especially in connection with the decisions of routine issues, are often specialized bodies of knowledge.[40] Thus in its enforcement of the Robinson-Patman Act, the Federal Trade Commission must evaluate cost-justification defenses raised by respondents. These defenses are generally based upon fixed and other cost allocations whose propriety turns upon the application of principles accepted by the accounting profession. This is to say that specialized knowledge of the accounting profession and its methods of analysis are proper referents in assessing the validity of an asserted cost-justification defense. Properly performed, the Commission's decisions upholding or rejecting asserted cost-justification defenses would utilize accounting concepts as referents, and those decisions would be motivated by and explainable in terms of accounting concepts. Similarly, the Federal Power Commission, in licensing proceedings, often makes use of knowledge and methods of analysis which belong to the economics and engineering professions.[41] Prosecutorial decisions of the Justice Department and Federal Trade Commission use, or should use, the concepts and techniques of economic analysis as referents,[42] and court decisions on antitrust questions have openly employed such concepts as referents in a number of cases.[43] Decisions of various public utility commissions should employ as decisional referents, perhaps more frequently than they do, concepts drawn from economic analysis, such as marginal-cost pricing and consumer surplus.[44]

---

[38] See 1 TRADE REG. REP. ¶ 4520 (1967); 3 TRADE REG. REP. ¶ 10,122 (1966).

[39] FTC, REPORT ON THE MERGER MOVEMENT: A SUMMARY REPORT (1948).

[40] Cf. H. SIMON, ADMINISTRATIVE BEHAVIOR 169-70 (2d ed. 1957).

[41] See, e.g., Consolidated Edison Co., 33 F.P.C. 428 (1965).

[42] See D. GIFFORD, A LEGAL AND ECONOMIC ANALYSIS OF SECTION 2(A) OF THE ROBINSON-PATMAN ACT AS APPLIED TO SELECTED FORMS OF BUSINESS ORGANIZATION (forthcoming).

[43] E.g., United States v. E. I. DuPont deNemours & Co., 351 U.S. 377 (1956) (cross-elasticity of demand); United States v. Columbia Steel Corp., 334 U.S. 495 (1948) (cross-elasticity of production facilities).

[44] See note 102 infra. Compare, e.g., 3-B I. SHARFMAN, THE INTERSTATE COMMERCE COMMISSION 446-63 (1936). Cf. Hotelling, The General Welfare in Relation to Problems of Taxation and of Railway and Utility Rates, 6 ECONOMETRICA 242 (1938).

3. Cost Analysis and Program Planning

An assessement of the full resources of almost any regulatory agency in terms of manpower, budget, and perhaps special skills available to it and an assessment of the agency's delegated responsibilities would probably indicate that the agency lacks the resources to perform fully every function delegated to it.[45] Such a situation calls upon the agency to structure a system of priorities and to allocate its resources on the basis of those priorities.[46] Budget allocation upon the basis of a priority system created in this way would tend to promote resource allocation by functions or goals.[47] And such a function or goal-oriented budget would, in turn, be best performed when the functions or goals were seen in their operations over an extended period, since it is only over an extended period that the budgetary claims of alternative programs competing for the agency's dollars can be assessed in their full light. This, in turn, suggests that budgetary decisions for the current year can best be made when the agency's various programs are planned in advance for a several year period. When the agency's programs are planned in this fashion, the current year's budgetary decisions are made in the light of, and as a part of, the projected several year plan.

The present relevance of cost analysis and program planning[48] is that once the agency's resources are allocated by program, many agency decisions and especially those with major budgetary impact will be reached in the light of their cost and the agency's program plan. Whether to proceed by rule or by adjudication in connection with particular kinds of undesirable conduct,[49] whether to proceed through precisely formulated rules issued in advance or to proceed by restructuring objectionable transactions,[50] whether to issue complaints in certain categories of cases are all questions whose discussion within the agency and resolution by the agency will, or should, use cost analysis and the agency's programmed budget as referents. In order properly to decide a particular issue such as a complaint-issuance or effectively to argue within the agency for or against a particular resolution of such a decision, an agency official would have to be familiar with the grounds upon which that decision should or would be reached. When the grounds are program cost and program-budget allocations, he would need to know the content of the program-

---

[45] *See, e.g.,* Elman, *Administrative Reform of the Federal Trade Commission,* 59 GEO. L.J. 777 (1971); Dixon, *Program Planning at the Federal Trade Commission,* 19 AD. L. REV. 408 (1967).

[46] *See, e.g.,* Smithies, *Conceptual Framework for the Program Budget,* in PROGRAM BUDGETING 2, 19 (D. Novick ed. 1964-65). *Cf. Developments in the Law—Deceptive Advertising,* 80 HARV. L. REV. 1005, 1099-1101 (1967); Note, *Program Budgeting for Police Departments,* 76 YALE L.J. 822 (1967).

[47] Smithies, *supra* note 46.

[48] By relating costs to functions, the way is paved for the exercise of a cost-benefit type of control over the priorities accorded to each function. This, in turn, facilitates advance planning of the agency's various functions. Comparative judgments can now be made about how much emphasis is to be placed upon each function in the light of its costs and alternative uses for the money involved. *Cf.* Dixon, *supra* note 45. *See generally* notes 45 & 46.

[49] *See, e.g.,* FTC, TRADE REGULATION RULE FOR THE PREVENTION OF UNFAIR OR DECEPTIVE ADVERTISING AND LABELING OF CIGARETTES IN RELATION TO THE HEALTH HAZARDS OF SMOKING AND ACCOMPANYING STATEMENT OF BASIS AND PURPOSE OF RULE 137 (1964).

[50] On *post hoc* restructuring of objectionable transactions, see Gifford, *supra* note 15, at 440-42.

budget allocation decisions in order, first, to evaluate for himself which way such a decision should go and, then, when he himself is not the decision-maker, to make a presentation which is meaningful to the officials who are the decision-makers. He would have to be able to explain, first, to himself and, second, in cases in which he participates in the decisional process as a subordinate or is otherwise accountable to others, how the decision he is supporting meets the terms or rationale of those budgeting allocations. And, while the budgeting decisions might not be the only relevant factor, an advocate of a position would have to connect his arguments with those factors in order to be convincing when they are significant or major elements in the decisional process.

D. The Significance of Decisional Referents

The concept of a decisional referent as a factor consciously taken into account by a decision-maker is an old one. Statutes listing factors to be considered and weighed by agency decision-makers have not been infrequent in the past.[51] Nor has it been unusual for agencies themselves to promulgate lists of factors which they assert are the major ones which they consider in deciding cases.[52] Moreover, judicial review of agency action for arbitrariness or abuse of discretion proceeds, at least at times, on the basis of an analysis implicitly in terms of the appropriateness or inappropriateness of the decisional referents employed by the agency.[53] Jaffe's analysis of judicial review, for example, explicitly embodies the concept of decisional referents.[54]

Yet, despite its familiarity, the close relationship between rules and all decisional referents[55] has gone largely unexplored and perhaps has been recognized only superficially by many observers of administrative behavior. There has been a continuing outcry against secret administrative rules,[56] but little outcry against secret decisional referents. In his recent book, Davis stretches the concept of "rules" to embody advisory opinions, including advisory opinions on hypothetical facts,[57] and in this manner he hopes both to encourage agencies to disclose their policies and to encourage them to act consistently (by complying with the policies so disclosed). But even Davis fails to focus upon the need to conceptualize agency decisional processes in terms of

---

[51] *See, e.g.,* TENN. CODE ANN. § 56-602 (repl. 1968) (listing factors to be considered by state insurance commissioner in approving or rejecting applications for rate increases). *See* Long v. National Bureau of Casualty Underwriters, 209 Tenn. 435, 442-46, 354 S.W.2d 255, 259-60 (1961).

[52] WHDH, Inc., 22 F.C.C. 767 (1957).

[53] *See* text accompanying notes 75-82 infra.

[54] L. JAFFE, JUDICIAL CONTROL OF ADMINISTRATIVE ACTION 181 (1965) ("nearly all powers to act, however numerous and broad the considerations relevant to choice, exclude and deny the legality of other elements as factors of choice.")

[55] *See* text accompanying note 26 *supra.*

[56] *E.g.,* U.S. COMM'N ON ORGANIZATION OF THE EXECUTIVE BRANCH OF THE GOV'T, REPORT OF THE TASK FORCE ON LEGAL SERVICE AND PROCEDURE 150 (1955); ATTORNEY GENERAL'S COMMITTEE ON ADMINISTRATIVE PROCEDURE, FINAL REPORT, S. Doc. No. 8, 77th Cong., 1st Sess. 29 (1941). *Cf.* Newman, *Government and Ignorance—A Progress Report on Publication of Federal Regulations,* 63 HARV. L. REV. 929, 936-37 (1950).

[57] K. DAVIS, DISCRETIONARY JUSTICE 59-64 (1969).

decisional referents. By so doing we would see the blurring of rules into other decisional referents—compare "rules" with "guidelines," for example—and the need to apply many of the approaches which we now apply to rules to the latter as well. More precisely, in dealing with any government official, lawyers would be more conscious of their need to learn the official's major decisional referents in order to carry on an effective dialogue or to present their cases in their most favorable light; they would be more conscious of their need to address their arguments to those referents, or to cast them in terms of those referents; and they would be more conscious of their need to seek out the particular supervisory official who has power to change a referent or to waive its application.

Let me make these points in a more concrete fashion. Suppose, for example, that one decisional referent of a public service commission in setting freight rates consists in the application of "the usual and ordinary ratio of distribution of freight charges according to the value of the product carried."[58] In rate negotiations with the commission—to say nothing of his conduct in a formal rate proceeding— counsel for a carrier would be handicapped to the extent that he was ignorant of the use of a ratio as a tool in the setting of a freight rate and would be further handicapped if he did not know what the "usual and ordinary" ratio was. Suppose, for instance, that good reasons could be shown why the usual and ordinary ratio ought not to be applied to the rates for the particular commodity in question. An attorney ignorant of the decisional referent would never make that showing. But it will be said that counsel for a carrier would have learned about that referent and its significance from his experience and associations with others involved in rate regulation. Maybe. But would counsel for a firm engaged in large but occasional shipments? Would his greater distance from rate regulation as a central concern deprive him of knowledge of referents which would be critical in rate negotiations with the commission or with a carrier?

Let us consider another example. Is a lawyer for an applicant to the Small Business Administration always aware of the fact that a decisional referent for the Administration is the applicant's record with the Federal Bureau of Investigation and with the House Un-American Activities Committee?[59] If not, might not his client's application be rejected on a ground which the lawyer could have met had he been aware of it? I am thinking here, of course, of a case in which the client's activities which brought him to the attention of these investigating bodies could be shown by the lawyer to be completely innocuous. Perhaps, also, the lawyer might be able to persuade the Small Business Administration that the use of such a referent was improper. But, again, he could never do this so long as he remained unaware of the referent.

---

[58] Chicago & N.W. Ry. v. Railroad Comm'n, 156 Wis. 47, 56, 145 N.W. 216, 218 (1914).
[59] HOUSE COMM. ON GOVERNMENT OPERATIONS, 85th Cong., 1st Sess., SURVEY AND STUDY OF ADMIN-ISTRATIVE ORGANIZATION, PROCEDURE AND PRACTICE IN THE FEDERAL AGENCIES 2011 (Comm. Print 1959).

An analysis in terms of rules, as commonly understood, is not helpful in either of these situations if we assume (1) that the public service commission does not always apply a ratio in its calculations nor in those cases in which a ratio is employed is the ratio always the same, and (2) that the Small Business Administration does not always reject applicants whose names appear in the investigatory files of the FBI and the House Committee but that it takes such a factor into consideration as a negative element in deciding whether to grant an application. A requirement of rule disclosure would not help. And an attorney who was conscious of a need to master the agency's rules and to present his case in terms of those rules would still be likely to miss the point. Here Davis's concept of reconceptualizing the meaning of a "rule" to include an advisory opinion on hypothetical facts might be of some assistance, especially in the example of the public service commission. If the agencies accepted Davis's suggestion about reconceptualizing rules and if they then formulated advisory opinions on hypothetical facts and promulgated those opinions, lawyers in the first example might receive the information they require to present their cases adequately. But in the second example, where factors are weighed which are not deemed controlling, even the agency which adopted the suggestion to promulgate hypothetical advisory opinions might not be led to inform interested and affected persons about the manner in which it reaches its decisions, namely, that in deciding, it weighs in the balance investigators' files on criminal and subversive behavior.

More to the point, however, is that Davis's suggestion is one directed at agencies. It is an admonition to officials and to agencies to disclose their standards for decision, however undeveloped those standards may be. The suggestion in this section of the article is that the concept of a decisional referent is useful not only to agencies thinking about disclosing their decisional standards but also to lawyers attempting to cope with a bureaucracy. By focusing upon the decisional referents of the officials with whom he is dealing, the lawyer will be better prepared—to look for and to discover relevant decisional referents, to present his case in its most favorable light, to negotiate effectively, to appeal within the administrative hierarchy the application of improper referents or the improper application of generally proper referents. He will be better equipped to assess the level in the administrative hierarchy at which he can find the relief he requires. Normally, for example, a lower-echelon official will be unable to respond to an argument which attacks the basic validity of a referent widely used in his department. Yet a presentation which undercuts the validity of such a referent may gain the time and attention of an upper-echelon official who does have power to grant relief. And—here the analogy between rule and nonrule referents is apt—the very widespread use of the referent within the department may make the challenge sufficiently important to merit that official's attention. Again, the analogy between rule and nonrule referents indicates that the lawyer who seeks the nonapplicability of a nonrule referent to his case will have a better chance of succeeding if he can show why the nonapplication which he seeks will have very little consequence for the overall administrative routine—that the uniqueness of his case would enable a consistent administration to grant the relief which he seeks without affecting the disposition of a significant number of other cases. But the concept is not limited in its usefulness to the practitioner. An analysis in terms of decisional referents may uncover, or direct attention upon, other aspects of administrative action which have been unnoticed or neglected. The beginnings of such an attempt are contained in this article.

III

Human Interaction and the Choice of Decisional Referents

The process of interaction among the participants in a decisional process seems likely to influence the choice, by each participant, of the referents which will underlie his decisions. As more fully developed below, this interaction process seems to have both dynamic and stabilizing dimensions in the sense that it may affect the information upon which each decision-maker acts and it may reenforce a natural inclination on the part of each decision-maker to repeat prior solutions.

In situations in which officials employ rules supplied to them by an external authority to reach solutions anticipated in the rules and described with precision in those rules, the impact of personal interaction among the participants in the decisional process is minimized. (Of course, even here the interaction between the decision-maker(s) and a claimant or his representative and witnesses may significantly affect the content of the decision.) When an external authority supplies the deciding officials with their major decisional referents (rules, studies, budgetary allocations, and so on), interaction among the decision-makers is not needed to ensure that those externally-supplied referents are employed by them. But interaction may have a significant impact upon the weights accorded to each referent and in the selection and development of new decisional referents.

A. Dynamic Aspects of Human Interaction in Decisional Processes

The dynamic dimension of human interaction comes into play when a decision-maker or other participant in a decisional process (such as an advisor) alters his approach as a result of his contact with another person. Such a situation would occur when a decision-maker's contact with another person brings him new information or acquaints him with new ways of perceiving the matter before him or makes him aware of criticism of his own position to which he had previously not been exposed.[60] Thus, for example, in a program[61] utilized by the federal district court judges for the Eastern District of Michigan, judges meet in groups of three to discuss the sentences which each intends to impose in cases coming before him. Each judge reports to the other two on a number of cases, describes the relevant factors as he sees them, and states his own evaluation and the sentence which he has initially decided upon. Each of the other two judges then states his own perceptions of those

---

[60] Indeed, the performance of this function of collecting information and criticisms has always been perceived as the primary goal of agency rule-making proceedings.

[61] See Levin, *Toward a More Enlightened Sentencing Procedure*, 45 Neb. L. Rev. 499 (1966).

cases and of the relevant factors in them, his evaluations, and the sentences which he would impose. The procedure thus exposes each judge to insights and to criticisms of his own positions of which he otherwise would have been unaware. In that sense, the final sentencing decision of each judge is better informed. The exposure of his decision and the reasoning behind it to his colleagues also influences each judge "to examine his own prejudices and motivations underlying his conclusions."[62] The procedure thus is an aid to each judge in uncovering factors personal to himself which ought not to influence his decision, but which might do so in a manner hidden even to himself. In this sense, the procedure seems useful in helping each decision to reflect the conscious choice of the deciding judge. The procedure does not divest the assigned judge of the responsibility for deciding. Indeed, as noted, it heightens that responsibility. It enables each judge assigned to render a sentencing decision to exercise that responsibility in a more informed manner. The procedure thus encourages self-criticism and openness to change. It also appears to have influenced a significant number of judges to rethink and to change the sentencing decision which they had initially reached. Judge Levin informs us that the Sentencing Council has tended

> to create a consensus among the judges on which factors are most relevant in sentencing and the weight to be accorded to each of them. . . . The factors presently considered most significant are the offender's prior record, family responsibility, work record, the likelihood that the defendant will respond to probation, and whether custody is required for either rehabilitation or for the protection of the public.[63]

He thus describes a situation in which interaction among the judges has produced a growth process in which the original set of decisional referents of each participant has developed and has been modified in the light of the insights, comments, experiences, and criticisms of the others. The result has been a developing convergence toward a commonly held set of referents.[64]

In a very different context, a similar process may be at work in the Office of the General Counsel of the National Labor Relations Board. That office supervises the enforcement of the National Labor-Management Relations Act by the several Regional Directors located throughout the nation. New policy questions may arise within the General Counsel's office or they may be referred there by a Regional Director who seeks advice on a novel issue. Such new policy questions are usually resolved in that office in a meeting of several officials called an "agenda."[65] Par-

---

[62] *Id.* at 505.

[63] *Id.*

[64] *Cf.* Carp, *The Scope and Function of Intra-Circuit Judicial Communication: A Case Study of the Eighth Circuit,* 6 LAW & SOC'Y REV. 405, 407 (1972). Carp hypothesizes that "differences in the judicial behavior of U.S. trial judges from circuit to circuit persist because for these judges the circuit is a semi-closed system, a nearly self-contained organizational unit within which there is considerable interaction among its members and almost no interaction between members of one unit (circuit) and another." *See also id.* at 421-22.

[65] CCH LAB. L. REP., 1 LAB REL. ¶ 1150.01, at 3076 (1961).

ticipating in the agenda are a staff attorney who has researched the problem under consideration (and who has uncovered the relevant prior advice which the office has rendered in other cases), his supervisor, the Assistant General Counsel in Charge of Advice, the Associate Branch Chief, the Assistant General Counsel in Charge of District Court Litigation, the Special Assistant to the General Counsel, and, in some instances, the Associate General Counsel in Charge of the Division of Litigation. The agenda device brings about the exposure of each of the several participating officials to the insights and criticisms of the others. As in the case of the Sentencing Council, it is possible that such exposure would induce a participant to alter the position which he originally espoused. Indeed, the resemblance of the agenda device to committee decision-making appears close. And it has been at least my own experience that the insights and criticisms of other committee members will persuade me to reevaluate and to modify or to alter my original position. In any event, the decision reached by the agenda is informed by the considerations brought out in the research of the staff attorney and in the group discussion of the agenda participants. Since most of the participating officials are involved in various aspects of enforcement administration, each can draw upon his own special area of administration for insights on the ramifications of the new policy positions which the office might adopt.[66]

In the two examples, the agenda is more formally a group or collective decision-making or decision-recommending body[67] than the Sentencing Council, which explicitly recognizes that decision-making remains with each of the participating judges acting individually. Yet in each example the structure of interaction is designed to expose the participants to the insights, attitudes, experiences, and information of the others. When such exposure does occur, it is not unlikely that an individual's position will be affected.[68] By contrast, and as a third example of agency decisional processes, the United States Parole Board, at least in the past, never met in group deliberations about individual cases.[69] It thus seems to have structured its operations in just the kind of way which would avoid the interaction process described in connection with the Sentencing Council and the General Counsel's agendas. As we have been informed by Judge Levin,[70] the effects of the interaction process upon individual participants in the Sentencing Council have been dramatic. In the agenda, we might expect that similar dramatic shifts would occur in the case of individuals who are newly appointed to agenda positions and who previously have not been exposed in a prolonged manner to some significant factors or attitudes which recur in agenda deliberations. As an institution, however, we might expect that the agenda would be relatively stable in its collective approaches, because its

---

[66] *Cf.* J. GALBRAITH, THE NEW INDUSTRIAL STATE 61-67 (1967).

[67] The agenda's decisions are recommendations to the General Counsel.

[68] Levin reported that a change in the proposed decisions of each participating judge occurred at least eight times in 1965. Levin, *supra* note 61, at 507.

[69] K. DAVIS, *supra* note 57, at 126.

[70] Levin, *supra* note 61, at 505-06, 511-12.

relatively stable membership should produce a relatively constant mix of attitudes and information in the agenda dialogues. Indeed, as we have seen, such an ultimate stability—in the form of a group consensus—seems to be developing in the Sentencing Council.[71] Nevertheless, this stabilizing quality ought not to obscure the fact that the Council and the agenda—in contrast to the procedures of the Parole Board— are designed to bring to the attention of the participants factors, that is, decisional referents, of which they were previously unaware and, in that light, to promote changes of individual positions. Implicit in such a statement is the suggestion that a broader exposure of the participants might, by acquainting them with additional relevant decisional factors, affect their decisions even more. The potential for administrative dynamism in this suggestion is explored more fully in the next section.

B. The Stabilizing Aspects

When a decision-maker decides, not in isolation, but in the presence of one or more other people who are aware of the positions which he is taking, he is acting in a significantly different context from the official who acts in isolation. In the non-isolated situation, the deciding official is exposed to pressure to justify departures from his own prior practice not only to himself but, since his earlier decisions have been seen by other officials who will observe his present decisions, to other officials as well. Moreover, not only may the decision itself be observed by other officials, but the considerations underlying those decisions—the decisional referents—may be exposed to the gaze of those officials. In these circumstances, the official who feels a need to justify a departure from his prior practice must explain his justification in the light of the decisional referents used by him in his earlier decisions. He must explain how these referents justify apparent departure or, alternatively, if new or different referents are used to justify his present decision, why these latter referents are appropriate for present use but were inappropriate for use in the earlier decisions.

It should be observed that the officials whose presence induces the decision-maker to explain his departures from his prior practice need not be superiors. They may be colleagues or even subordinates. The important factor is that the deciding officials act, and have acted, in the presence of these same individuals and that those same individuals are aware of the decisions which are being made and of the factors underlying them. Thus, for example, decisions about remitting or mitigating forfeitures are currently made in the Justice Department's Bureau of Narcotics and Dangerous Drugs by two officials and reviewed by their superior.[72] The two officials

---

[71] *Id.* at 505, quoted in text accompanying note 63 *supra*.

[72] This description of the Justice Department's decisional structure for mitigation and remission cases is different from that which was described by Davis and to which reference was made earlier. *See* text at note 6 *supra*. Davis, *supra* note 57, at 109-11. The present description is drawn from my own work on behalf of the Administrative Conference of the United States in the late 1960's while Davis's description is that of the Justice Department's organization of the early and mid-1960's. *See* Gifford, *Remission and Mitigation of Forfeitures in the Justice Department*, in 1 RECOMMENDATIONS AND REPORTS OF THE ADMINISTRATIVE CONFERENCE OF THE UNITED STATES 697 (Jan. 8, 1968-June 30, 1970).

share the same office, and frequently discuss their decisions with each other. They spend about a quarter of their time making remission decisions and each has been involved in this work for a number of years. In such circumstances, it is apparent that decisional criteria are worked out by the two officials together; that the hard cases are discussed by each with the other and with their superior; that common approaches worked out together will probably be followed by each of them. But more is apparent also. It is apparent that when either of the two is tempted to depart from the commonly worked-out path, he feels a pressure to justify any departure, not only to himself, but also to his colleague. Initially, the pressure is not that which is exerted by any formal rule—or any binding obligation. Rather, it is a pressure which arises from human interaction. Having once explained what I thought was a well-considered position to my colleagues, I feel uncomfortable in deviating from that position in future cases without explaining the reasons for my departure to those colleagues.

The preceding discussion is not meant to suggest that a responsible person will refuse to change his approach in the light of new factors brought to his attention.[73] It is meant to suggest that when such a person does change he may feel called upon to justify that apparent deviation. Moreover, as the Sentencing Council experience seems to illustrate, a person may feel pressure to justify (to himself and to others) not only deviations from his prior patterns of action, but also to justify (to himself and to others) deviations from norms or other decisional referents shared by other members of the group in which he is acting.[74]

IV
IDENTIFYING PERMISSIBLE AND IMPERMISSIBLE REFERENTS

A. "Arbitrary" Administrative Action as the Use of Impermissible Referents

It is hornbook law that agency action which is "arbitrary" or "capricious" generally may be set aside by the courts.[75] Sometimes the term "arbitrary" has been equated by the courts with "irrational."[76] But this cannot really be the meaning of "arbitrary" when it is used in connection with judicial disapproval of agency action. It cannot, because very little governmental or other action is really irrational in the normal meaning of that term. Indeed, even in the case of an official who awards a contract to a firm which has paid him a bribe (rather than on the basis of a judgment about the quality of the contractor's work), the contract award would probably be set aside as arbitrary. But the official was not acting irrationally at all; he knew what he wanted and used effective means to realize that end. A second meaning of "arbitrary" is "based on or subject to individual judgment or dis-

---

[73] See, e.g., Levin, supra note 61, at 507.
[74] Id. at 505.
[75] See 2 F. COOPER, STATE ADMINISTRATIVE LAW 758-65 (1965).
[76] See R. BENJAMIN, ADMINISTRATIVE ADJUDICATION IN THE STATE OF NEW YORK 346 (1942). Cf. 2 F. COOPER, supra note 75, at 764.

cretion."[77] But, again, this meaning cannot explain its use by the courts in describing agency action which ought to be set aside: much agency action is properly a matter of judgment (that is, discretionary in Dworkin's first, weak sense),[78] and some agency action is explicitly made discretionary in the strong sense by the legislature. And such authorized discretionary action is not subject to judicial invalidation.

The significant part of the latter definition, rather, is the adjective "individual" modifying "judgment." "Individual" throws light upon the equation of "arbitrary" with "irrational" in the former usage. When a characterization of arbitrariness is used by a court as a justification for invalidating administrative action, the court's objection to that action is not that one or more individuals have utilized their judgment, but rather that in utilizing their judgment their decisional referents were their own in a context where the legal system within which they operated demanded the use of other referents; in other words, their referents were "individual" rather than "system" ones where the two conflicted: the contract was awarded on the basis of a bribe rather than on the basis of the quality of the contractor's work. A similar explanation is available for the usage of the term "irrational": a test of rationality is the adaptation of means to a desired end or goal.[79] When action is characterized as irrational in a legal context, it means that the action is not designed to reach the goals of the legal system, that it is designed to reach other, "individual" goals instead. In short, the test of arbitrariness has largely been whether the agency decision was based upon permissible or impermissible referents. And the test of the permissibility of the referents employed has been their relation to a recognized end or goal of administration.

This perception of arbitrary versus rational action—a largely traditional perception—has developmental possibilities that embrace the whole of administrative action. If it is correct, as suggested,[80] to explain the difference between "arbitrary" and "rational" action as action based, respectively, upon "impermissible" and "permissible" referents,[81] then we can use this analysis to probe further into both formal and informal decision-making. Remembering that judicial invalidation of agency action characterized as arbitrary has depended upon the exposure of the underlying decisional referents to the court which makes the judgment about the permissibility

---

[77] AMERICAN HERITAGE DICTIONARY.

[78] See Dworkin, supra note 4, at 32, and accompanying text.

[79] See, e.g., H. SIMON, ADMINISTRATIVE BEHAVIOR 76-77 (2d ed. 1957). Compare Davis's use of the term "irrational" in DISCRETIONARY JUSTICE 91 (1969) ("cases are often selected for enforcement on irrational grounds").

[80] See text accompanying notes 75-79 supra.

[81] A similar approach is followed in L. JAFFE, JUDICIAL CONTROL OF ADMINISTRATIVE ACTION 181 (1965). Cf. Friendly, Chenery Revisited: Reflections on Reversal and Remand of Administrative Orders, 1969 DUKE L.J. 199, 211-12. Friendly properly distinguishes between incorrect reasons and findings, id. at 205, while pointing out that either incorrect reasons or incorrect findings are a basis for court reversal of administrative action. In the text I have generally utilized the term "decisional referent" in preference to "reasons" because the term "referent," while sometimes including "reasons," is broader and includes motives and matters which Davis might characterize as "legislative facts" or "adjudicative facts" present or absent from the record. 1 K. DAVIS, ADMINISTRATIVE LAW TREATISE § 7.02 (1958).

of the referent, we might ask whether exposure[82] of the underlying decisional referents—to persons other than the decision makers—could become a prime tool in preserving or changing decisional referents and their contents.

B. The Limitations of Judicial Review

Before exploring referent exposure further, let us, for purposes of perspective, focus upon the limitations of judicial review for administrative arbitrariness. It is obviously true that a court cannot deem a referent employed by an administrator to be "impermissible" unless the court can perceive the referent and judge its use to be in conflict with the goals of the statute which the agency is administering. Two factors thus are necessary: first, exposure of the referent to the court and, second, a court evaluation that use of the referent in question is inconsistent with statutory goals. Yet the second factor itself requires further analysis: an analysis which distinguishes between (a) a judicial judgment whether the agency employed the referent in question in a good-faith attempt to reach statutory goals and (b) a court evaluation of the adequacy of the referent for the purposes for which it was used by the agency. A court will not be reluctant to strike down agency action which employed a referent whose use was inconsistent with statutory goals. But those courts which are sensitive to a need for a functional division of labor between courts and agencies will inquire into the adequacy of the agency's decisional referents for the purposes for which they were employed, if at all, only with trepidation. It would be too much to say that courts will not substitute their own referents for those employed by the agency whose action they are reviewing. They will and do when the issues are sufficiently important. It remains true, however, that an area surrounding the routine, the everyday operations of the agency, is an area which courts are reluctant to enter. Within this area, judicial inquiry would normally be perceived as an unwarranted interference in agency policy-making.[83]

The last distinction made in the preceding paragraph is somewhat reminiscent of one employed by Herbert Simon in a discussion of administrative behavior.[84] Simon's distinction is between "subjective" and "objective" rationality. A decision is subjectively rational if it "maximizes attainment relative to the actual knowledge of the subject"; it is objectively rational "if *in fact* it is the correct behavior for maximizing given values in a given situation."[85] Simon proceeds to assert that few, if any, decisions can be consciously objectively rational because full information is rarely available when a decision must be made. But, since some decisions can be more accurately informed than others, it is perhaps acceptable to say that de-

---

[82] The cutting edge of the administrative "openness" for which Davis has long argued, K. Davis, Discretionary Justice 97-141 (1969); K. Davis, 1 Administrative Law Treatise § 4.14 (Supp. 1965), §§ 4.14-4.18 (Supp. 1970), consists in exposure of administrative decisions to persons who have the competence and time to evaluate those decisions.

[83] *Cf.* L. Jaffe, *supra* note 81, at 182.

[84] H. Simon, Administrative Behavior 76 (2d ed. 1957).

[85] *Id.*

cisions can differ in the degree to which they approach an ideal of objective rationality. So stated, Simon's distinction is useful to our present analysis of decisional processes: judicial review is concerned with the subjective rationality of decision-making. Exposure, as I will argue below, is capable of improving the "objective" rationality of agency decision-making.

C. Exposure of Agency Referents as a Force for Increasing the Objective Rationality of Administrative Decision-Making

Now let us direct our focus away from judicial review and toward other ways, including less formal ways, of controlling agency action. As we have already observed in connection with the Sentencing Council,[86] the exposure of an official's decisional referents to the critical scrutiny of others may disclose the inadequacy of those referents and create pressures to bring about their change. This type of constraint upon agency action will tend not to be limited—as is judicial review—to overseeing the good faith of agency policy choices. Rather, exposure of the agency's decisional referents to the critical scrutiny of others possesses a potential for promoting the selection of decisional referents which are adequate for the purposes for which they are employed, that is, for improving the degree of objective rationality of agency decisions.

Earlier we asked whether exposure of decisional referents to superiors or to subordinates or to colleagues would exert pressures upon a decision-maker to act consistently.[87] Now we ask whether exposure of decisional referents to superiors or to subordinates or to colleagues or to others will generate pressures to improve the choice of substance of the referents themselves. In support of an affirmative answer to this question is the point that the exposure of decisional referents to others gives those others the opportunity to examine those referents critically. When, for example, a colleague knowledgeable in matters of economic theory observes a trial attorney in the Federal Trade Commission utilize as a decisional referent a misconception of pricing theory,[88] he may be able to explain to the trial attorney the correct conception. In such event the trial attorney acquires the knowledge which he needs to improve the quality of a decisional referent. The more the trial attorney's referent is exposed to numbers of observers with some degree of sophistication in economic theory and the more those persons strive to point out to him his erroneous conception, the more difficult will it be for the attorney to persist in the use of his original referent. Again, the exposure, if only to his superior, of the set of rules used by the official exercising remission power[89] would bring that set of decisional referents under a new source of critical scrutiny, and, in so doing, the

---

[86] *See* text accompanying notes 60-64 *supra.*

[87] *See* text accompanying notes 72-74 *supra.*

[88] *Cf.* Forster Mfg. Co., 62 F.T.C. 856, 902 (1963) *vacated and remanded,* 335 F.2d 47 (1st Cir. 1964). *Compare* Atlas Bldg. Prod. Co. v. Diamond Block & Gravel Co., 269 F.2d 950, 956 (10th Cir. 1959), *cert. denied,* 363 U.S. 843 (1960).

[89] *See* text accompanying notes 6-11 *supra.*

content of those rules might be affected. Exposure of those rules to a wider circle, including those affected by them—such as, for example, banks and other credit institutions which hold large numbers of security interests in automobiles[90]—would subject those rules to a wider range of critical scrutiny which, in turn, again might affect their content.

Exposure, thus, is a relative rather than an all-or-nothing matter. Exposure of referents employed by an official to other officials working in close proximity to him may exert pressure upon him to employ referents which can withstand their critical scrutiny. But exposure of those referents to larger circles of officials within the agency structure (who have time and motivation to see those referents and to reflect upon the propriety of their use)[91] and to persons outside of the agency structure (including persons adversely affected by the use of those referents who are likely to have both the time and the motivation to reflect upon the propriety of their use)[92] will subject them to increased amounts of scrutiny. And the potential or resulting criticisms may affect the kinds of referents which will be employed.

The significance which attaches to exposure thus turns upon the ability and the motivation of the onlookers to criticize the referents and to convey that criticism to the decision-maker. Besides the degree of the onlooker's competence to evaluate the referent's content, his ability to make meaningful criticisms of its use depends upon his familiarity with the decisional content in which the referent is employed,[93] the time which he has to devote to criticism[94] and to communication of that criticism, and the ease with which that criticism can be conveyed.[95]

D. Implications for the Decisional Structure

We have concluded that the exposure of referents (including non-rule referents) to increased critical scrutiny has potential for improving the quality of decisions, that is, for increasing their objective rationality. The publication of the Securities and Exchange Commission studies[96] exposes their content to experts and others knowledgeable in the securities field and thereby facilitates the correction of errors in those studies. If, and to the extent that, substantial errors are shown to exist in them, the

[90] Gifford, *supra* note 72.

[91] Exposure to others is not alone sufficient. Those others must understand the context in which the referent is employed and possess the requisite time and motivation to make a judgment about the propriety of its use. The considerations raised here are analogous to those which the courts have raised in conjunction with the grant of judicial and administrative standing to so-called "public-interest" representatives. *See* text accompanying notes 106-175 *infra*.

[92] The adverse effects may themselves be helpful in engendering the motivation. *See* text accompanying note 113 *infra*.

[93] That is to say, familiarity with a particular body of specialized knowledge (such as engineering, economic theory, or regulatory law) is requisite to understanding the context in which the referent is employed.

[94] Cf. J. MARSH & H. SIMON, ORGANIZATIONS 169 (1958).

[95] In order to complete the feedback loop, the understanding observer must be able to communicate his criticism. But the greater the impediments to his doing so (such as access barriers to the person whose acts are being criticized), the greater his motivation must be to overcome those impediments.

[96] *See* note 32 *supra*.

Commission and its officials will learn that some of the contents of those reports cannot be accepted as accurate, and, hence, are to that extent improper referents for decision. By contrast, the reports of the Federal Trade Commission's economic bureau—especially those which focus upon assertedly dangerously developing anti-competitive situations—are not always public documents. Errors or deficiencies in those reports, therefore, cannot so easily be uncovered, and the Commission and its officials may use these reports as referents in ignorance of their defects. Examples of administrative secrecy protecting a referent-system from critical scrutiny abound.[97] Thus, for example, an early study of the then New York State Commission Against Discrimination complained that the Commission's work could not be accurately evaluated because of the secrecy shrouding its settlement policies and the criteria underlying them.[98]

Again, the handling of the Federal Trade Commission of cost-justification defenses by firms charged with Robinson-Patman violations has been criticized for demanding precision which cost-accounting principles cannot supply. I make no attempt here to determine the extent to which this criticism is valid or the extent to which the Commission's insistence upon precision is necessary to prevent business-men from abusing the permission which the statute accords them.[99] The relevant point is that the best decisions about the cost-justification defense would be made when the decisional process was designed to include professional accounting advice. Auerbach's study of Commission organization was critical of the Commission on just that point. He asserted that by making the Commission's accounting division a component of the bureau of restraint of trade, the Commission tended to deprive itself and its hearing officers of accounting advice which is not proffered from an adversary source.[100] This, of course, does not have to occur, even under the existing organizational structure, and the Commission has full access to accounting advice on questions of complaint issuance and settlement. The only point I would make here is that the decisional referents which are brought to bear on agency decisions are frequently a function of the agency's procedural organization.

What is required is the conceptualization of principles and analyses used in

---

[97] See Sperry & Hutchinson Co., 69 F.T.C. 1112, 1115-16 (1966) (Elman, dissenting).

[98] M. BERGER, EQUALITY BY STATUTE 193 (Rev. ed. 1968).

[99] See the discussion of the stringent approach to cost-justification questions which the Commission has employed in M. ADELMAN, A & P: A STUDY IN PRICE-COST BEHAVIOR AND PUBLIC POLICY 164-71 (1959). Adelman here criticizes Commission disallowance of cost studies which appeared to have evident validity but which contain cost elements some of which may be unprovable. Accord, U.S. ATTORNEY GENERAL'S NATIONAL COMMITTEE TO STUDY THE ANTITRUST LAWS, REPORT 170-76 (1955). Although cost-accounting data appear to be important tools of management, businessmen do not appear to base their actions on cost-accounting data which would prove acceptable to the Commission. See M. ADELMAN, supra at 165 n.24. See also C. EDWARDS, THE PRICE DISCRIMINATION LAW 600 (1959). Cf. A. SAWYER, BUSINESSS ASPECTS OF PRICING UNDER THE ROBINSON-PATMAN ACT 123 (1963).

[100] Auerbach, The Federal Trade Commission: Internal Organization and Procedure, 48 MINN. L. REV. 383, 498-500 (1964). Even under existing organization, accounting advice could be proffered by an accountant to the hearing officer or to the Commission so long as the individual proferring that advice had not participated in the investigation or prosecution of the case (and, by extension, so long as his supervisor had not so participated).

the specialized disciplines and, where appropriate, in other areas of collective social or business experience, as decisional referents in a way not very different from the way in which rules are used as decisional referents. Today many decisional referents employed by officials purport to be based upon specialized disciplines but could not withstand critical scrutiny from professionals of those disciplines. Thus, for example, many decisions of the courts and of the Federal Trade Commission which attempt to determine the competitive effects of discriminatory pricing grossly misapply microeconomic theory.[101] And the decisions of public utility regulatory bodies often seem to operate in ignorance of the concepts of demand elasticity and of marginal-cost-pricing, concepts that seemingly ought to constitute important decisional referents for them.[102] Yet these and other referents escape correction because they come to light only in their ad hoc application. If and when the suggested reconceptualization begins to occur, we will perhaps more fully appreciate that an economic or social misconception in one case sometimes may be symptomatic of a chronic use of decisional referents which are based upon ignorance or misinformation.

The discussion of the use of specialized disciplines as decision referents thus points up the fact that exposure—or openness—is not the only factor required. To the extent that specialized disciplines are, or should be, the decisional referents, the decision-making process must in some way bring in those who possess the requisite skills in those disciplines.[103] Otherwise outside criticisms that the agency officials have misapplied or misunderstood the disciplines will necessarily go unheeded.[104] Unless persons possessing the requisite skills are themselves utilized in the decisional process, the decision cannot reflect those skills. The moral, then, in the situations we have referred to is for the Federal Trade Commission to utilize its accounting and economic staff in decisions dealing with cost-justification and the competitive effects of pricing and for public utility commissions to utilize the services of skilled economic technicians in their rate-regulation decisional processes.

The point—not just of exposure—but of exposure to critical persons within the agency structure and, in some situations, the incorporation of those persons in the decisional process is especially important in connection with agency decisions whose referents cannot be fully exposed to public view. Thus, for example, budget allocation decisions which substantially restrict resources available for specific kinds of enforcement activities often cannot be fully disclosed to the public without impairing the deterrent effects of agency enforcement.[105] Yet complaint-issuance and other decisions within the agency structure ought to utilize the budget decisions as referents. They can do this, however, only if persons fully acquainted with the

---

[101] See note 88 supra.

[102] See J. BONBRIGHT, PRINCIPLES OF PUBLIC UTILITY RATES 315-16 (1961).

[103] H. SIMON, ADMINISTRATIVE BEHAVIOR 82 (2d ed. 1957).

[104] Because they will not be understood. Competence in a discipline is a prerequisite for understanding criticisms made in the language of that discipline.

[105] See, e.g., Gifford, Communication of Legal Standards, Policy Development, and Effective Conduct Regulation, 56 CORNELL L. REV. 409, 436 (1971).

implications of the budgetary decisions are involved, either as participants in complaint-issuance and related kinds of decision-making, or as participants in the review of those decisions.

V

The Impact of Recent Developments in Judicial and Administrative "Standing" Upon the Choice of Decisional Referents

Recent developments in the law of standing have as their ultimate effect the designation of new or preferred referents for administrative decision-making. Let me trace the major outlines of that development in an effort to show the interaction of standing and the designation of new decision-making referents. In order to do this I must first describe certain aspects of the *Sanders*[106] and *Associated Industries*[107] cases, cases which are familiar to all students of administrative law. This description will enable me to make some points about the post-*Scenic Hudson I*[108] developments in standing and the relation of those developments to the designation of new decisional referents for administrative bodies.

In *Sanders*, the Supreme Court displayed a willingness to differentiate between the subject-matter of a claim and the motivation for bringing suit. It is true that it had previously displayed such a willingness at times,[109] but in *Sanders* it began a radical expansion of standing to obtain judicial review of administrative action by reading this differentiation into the judicial review provisions of the Communications Act. The Communications Act provided for judicial review of decisions of the Federal Communications Commission at the instance of any person aggrieved or adversely affected by that decision.[110] In *Sanders*, the Court construed the terms "aggrieved" and "adversely affected" as they appeared in the Communications Act as conferring standing upon an existing radio station to challenge in court a Commission decision granting a new license to a rival station.[111] The Court, in reaching this result, differentiated between the substance of the claim being asserted and the grounds upon which the objecting radio station was permitted to assert that claim. The claim was that the issuance of the license was inconsistent with the public's right to quality radio service. A public right was being asserted and the issues and

---

[106] FCC v. Sanders Bros. Radio Station, 309 U.S. 470 (1940).

[107] Associated Indus. of N.Y. State, Inc. v. Ickes, 134 F.2d 694 (2d Cir. 1943).

[108] Scenic Hudson Preservation Conference v. FPC, 354 F.2d 608 (2d Cir. 1965), *cert. denied*, 384 U.S. 941 (1966).

[109] Thus, for example, in Pierce v. Society of Sisters, 268 U.S. 510 (1925), the Court permitted affected and motivated persons to assert the rights of others. In *Pierce* a religious organization which operated a private school was permitted to assert the rights of parents to send their children to a school of their choice against a state law which interfered with that right. See also the later case of Barrows v. Jackson, 346 U.S. 249 (1953), in which a white defendant was permitted to assert the rights of unidentified blacks in a defense to an action for damages for breach of a restrictive covenant.

[110] Under § 402(b) of the Communications Act, an appeal of a Commission decision could be taken by an applicant for a license or permit or "by any other person aggrieved or whose interests are adversely affected by any decision of the Commission granting or refusing any such application."

[111] 309 U.S. at 476-77.

arguments were required to be directed to the vindication of the public interest.[112] Implicit in the Court's reasoning is the assumption that for the public right to quality radio service to be effectively maintained, that right—and the need for Commission consideration of factors underlying the preservation of that right—had to be pressed upon the courts. Indeed, since the judicial system works within an adversary framework, it is necessary that an advocate press the public right to quality radio service before the courts if the judiciary is to be able to accord it meaningful protection.

Since the existing radio station would be economically injured by the grant of a license to a second, competing station (because the available advertising revenues would now be shared between the two stations), the existing station would have a strong motive to try to prevent the licensing of a rival.[113] That motive, the competence of the existing station to bring forward the appropriate legal arguments bearing on the public interest, and the absence[114] of other persons or firms able, willing, and as strongly motivated, to present the public case against Commission action, gave the Court the basis for recognizing the standing of the existing station. Later, the provision allowing standing to persons "aggrieved" or "adversely affected" within the meaning of the Communications Act was construed to allow public-interest standing to an existing station to raise public interest arguments challenging the issuance of a license to another station, when the operation of the second station would allegedly cause electrical interference with the existing station's operations.[115] The potential electrical interference was seen as ensuring that the existing station would be sufficiently motivated to press the requisite public interest arguments against the Commission's licensing decision before the court. Apart from the different source of motivation, the other factors justifying standing were the same as in *Sanders*.

Prior to *Sanders*, the meaning of the term "aggrieved" was unclear.[116] After that decision the term "aggrieved" in the Communications Act was understood to confer standing upon existing radio stations whose economic interests would suffer when licenses were issued to rivals, although the standing conferred by that Act was understood as allowing existing stations to present only public interest arguments on the public's behalf. But the implications of *Sanders* ran deeper. The term "aggrieved" appeared also in other statutes. Especially in statutes using that term to confer standing which were enacted subsequent to the *Sanders* decision, it could now be

---

[112] The Court concluded that no person could have a "property right" in the airwaves as a result of a license grant and that the Act was not designed "to protect a licensee against competition." 309 U.S. at 475. Nonetheless, the Court concluded that Congress could properly confer standing upon one likely to be financially injured by the issuance of a license "to bring to the attention of the appellate courts errors of law in the action of the Commission in granting the license." *Id.* at 477. Consistent with these two conclusions, the Court's opinion suggests that the rights vindicated by the appeal would be not those of the appellant but those of the public. *See id.* at 475-76.

[113] 309 U.S. at 477.

[114] *Id.*

[115] NBC v. FCC, 132 F.2d 545 (D.C. Cir. 1942), *aff'd*, 319 U.S. 239 (1943).

[116] *Cf.* L. JAFFE, JUDICIAL CONTROL OF ADMINISTRATIVE ACTION 516 (1965).

inferred that Congress used that word advisedly.[117] The word could be seen as a legislative attempt to incorporate the expanded conception of standing which *Sanders* read into the term "aggrieved."

In the mid-1940's Judge Frank's imaginative opinion in *Associated Industries v. Ickes*[118] gave further conceptual form to the new public-interest standing doctrine begun in *Sanders*. There the court confronted a challenge to a decision by the Department of the Interior's Bituminous Coal Division raising coal prices. The challenge was made by an association whose members collectively consumed large amounts of bituminous coal. In granting standing to the association, the court observed that the Bituminous Coal Act conferred standing upon persons "aggrieved" by decisions of the Bituminous Coal Board[119] and that the term "aggrieved," as used in the Communications Act, had been interpreted in *Sanders* and *KOA*[120] to confer standing upon radio stations suffering economic injury or electrical interference as a result of administrative action to address legal arguments on behalf of the public to the court against that administrative action. The court then concluded that the standing provision in the Bituminous Coal Act, by employing the term "aggrieved," incorporated the *Sanders* doctrine of expanded public-interest standing.[121] It concluded that the standing conferred upon radio stations to challenge FCC decisions exposing them to new competition or to electrical interference were explainable on the ground that their subjection to that competition or interference gave them a strong motive to press public interest arguments. Since the association challenging the Bituminous Coal Division decision represented firms economically injured by the Division's action, the court found that the association and its members had the same kind of motivation to make public-interest arguments as had the radio station in *Sanders*. On this basis the court granted the association standing to make legal interest arguments against the division action.

In support of his decision granting standing, Judge Frank developed his now-famous characterization of the position of the association, or, indeed, of any *Sanders*-type plaintiff, as private attorneys general.[122] In this way Judge Frank laid to rest serious constitutional challenges to the then-emergent public-interest type of standing. Since Congress could authorize the Attorney General to seek judicial relief against commission action extending beyond its statutory mandate, it could as easily confer standing on others to challenge such action by, in effect, creating private or ad hoc attorneys general to vindicate the public interest in lawful commission action in particular cases. In order to ensure that these private attorneys general effectively represented the public interest, *Sanders* required that the private person have a strong

---

[117] *See, e.g.*, Associated Indus. of N.Y. State, Inc. v. Ickes, 134 F.2d 694, 705 (2d Cir. 1943).
[118] 134 F.2d 694 (2d Cir. 1943).
[119] Bituminous Coal Act of 1937, ch. 127, § 6(b), 50 Stat. 72.
[120] NBC v. FCC, 132 F.2d 545 (D.C. Cir. 1942), *aff'd*, 319 U.S. 239 (1943).
[121] 134 F.2d at 705.
[122] *Id.* at 703.

objective motivation.[123] That motivation was found here and in *Sanders* in economic injury which the challenged agency action caused the objector.[124]

But while standing in *Associated Industries* could be established relatively easily from *Sanders* once the court focused upon the factors of economic injury, the public interest need for unlawful commission action to be challenged, and the scarcity of effective private challengers other than consumers of coal or their representatives, *Associated Industries* itself is an important milestone in the evolution of the law of standing. First, the economic injury recognized as a basis for standing was injury to a consumer interest.[125] While the felt harm may be just as great whether the injury occurs in the form of increased costs of fuel or a decrease in advertising revenues, the recognition of the consumer class as possessing an interest capable of conferring standing opened the gates to a vast increase in the number of persons potentially capable of challenging agency action.[126] Second, while the Court struggled in *Sanders* to differentiate the interest conferring standing from the arguments which could appropriately be made by the station accorded standing,[127] that distinction became less clear in *Associated Industries*. In *Sanders*, there was an overlap: the public interest did extend to the economic well-being of the radio station, but only insofar as a degree of well-being was essential to ensure adequate service to the public.[128] In *Associated Industries*, the public interest in bituminous coal prices which are not unduly high appears almost co-extensive with the interest of consumers in preventing such price increases.[129] Later cases recognized consumer interests as a basis for challenging agency action increasing prices under a number of price or rate-regulating statutes.[130] In most of these cases the objectors were industrial consumers. The liberalization of the law of standing which began in *Sanders* and

---

[123] 309 U.S. at 477.

[124] 134 F.2d at 705.

[125] *Id.*

[126] *Cf.* 134 F.2d at 707.

[127] 309 U.S. at 475-77.

[128] *Id.* at 476.

[129] The differentiation of the public interest claim from the grounds which give rise to standing to assert that claim made sense in *Sanders* where the public interest was in quality broadcasting service —and implicitly in conformity by the Federal Communications Commission to procedures designed to vindicate that public interest—and the grounds which gave rise to standing consisted of economic injury to an existing licensee. Even though some economic injury to an existing licensee would impair service, not every such economic injury had that potentiality: economic injury which diminishes the licensee's profits but which leaves him with a revenue margin sufficient to maintain service lacks that potentiality. And service can be impaired otherwise than by impairing the revenue margins of existing licensees. In *Associated Industries*, however, the ground giving rise to standing is that the approved price increase economically injures the consumers granted standing. And a public right to be asserted is that the rates must not be unreasonably high. A situation in which the ground giving rise to standing and the public-interest claim would not overlap would be that in which a consumer was injured as the result of a rate increase which was a reasonable one. In that case the consumer who would be granted standing would lose his case on the merits. This is not, of course, to say that the grant of standing in such a case would be useless, for it is only after the standee litigates his public-interest claim that the claim is officially determined to be lacking in merit.

[130] *E.g.*, City of Pittsburgh v. FPC, 237 F.2d 741 (D.C. Cir. 1956).

was extended in *Associated Industries* had consequences that by and large were confined to the industrial and commercial sectors of American life.

But in 1965 the United States Court of Appeals for the Second Circuit rendered its decision in *Scenic Hudson Preservation Committee v. FPC*.[131] That case involved the issuance of a license by the Federal Power Commission to Consolidated Edison Company for the construction of a pumped storage hydroelectric project on the Hudson River. After the Commission's decision, an association of neighboring landowners which had been a party to the licensing proceedings before the Commission asked the court of appeals to invalidate the Commission's license grant. The court accepted the case and reversed the Commission's decision largely because the Commission had made its licensing decision primarily on engineering grounds and had neglected to consider esthetic and environmental factors in its decision.[132] Yet in order to do this, the court had to come to grips with the standing issue raised by the association's petition to the court. The Federal Power Act conferred standing upon "aggrieved" parties,[133] and the court found standing in the association under the *Sanders* and *Associated Industries* rationales.[134] Here, however, the court indicated that a personal economic interest was not a prerequisite to suit.[135] It thus differentiated *Scenic Hudson* from the consumer cases symbolized by *Associated Industries*. The court then went on to say that "those who by their activities and conduct have exhibited a special interest" in the "aesthetic, conservational, and recreational aspects of power development" would be held to be within the class of "aggrieved" parties under the Federal Power Act.[136] In this way the court solved the motivational problem: it found proof of strong motivation from the plaintiffs' actions, especially their actions in contesting the license in question. It is difficult to fault the court for this: the logic of *Sanders* and *Associated Industries* requires strong motivation in the plaintiff. And motivation can be strong even if it is not economically grounded. And since the court felt that the public interest included the "aesthetic, conservational and recreational" factors pressed by the associa-

---

[131] 354 F.2d 608 (2d Cir. 1965), *cert. denied*, 384 U.S. 941 (1966).

[132] 354 F.2d at 620, 624-25.

[133] Federal Power Act, 16 U.S.C. § 825*l*(b) (1970).

[134] 354 F.2d at 615.

[135] It so indicated in its rejection of the Federal Power Commission's contention that the association lacked standing because it made "no claim of any personal economic injury resulting from the Commission's action." In that rejection the court asserted that the Federal Power Act seeks to protect noneconomic as well as economic interests and observed that the Supreme Court "has not made economic injury a prerequisite where the plaintiffs have shown a direct personal interest." 354 F.2d at 615. The court reenforced its decision on standing, however, by finding that such an economic interest was possessed by one of the member organizations of the plaintiff association in its ownership of seventeen miles of trailways which would be flooded by the project's reservoir. It also found that towns which were co-petitioners with the association had standing because the transmission lines connected with the project "would cause a decrease in the proprietary value of publicly held land, reduce tax revenues collected from privately held land, and significantly interfere with long-range community planning." *Id.* at 616.

[136] 354 F.2d at 616.

tion[137] and since others were not likely to press those factors, the rationales of *Sanders* and *Associated Industries* indicated that the association should be given standing to assert these factors on behalf of the public.

In *Scenic Hudson*, however, the latent implications of the earlier cases are exposed. *Sanders* and *Associated Industries* granted standing "to vindicate the interest of the public." But there is no one public interest. Both cases implicitly acknowledge this when they note that standing is granted in order that needed "legal" arguments[138] may be brought to the court's attention. If the public interest is conceived as one concerned with correcting any illegal action by an agency, then anyone who can point out an error of law which would otherwise go unnoticed should be given standing. The existing broadcast licensee and the industrial association will bring needed arguments to the court's attention, but so will the new licensee, the Federal Communications Commission, and the Bituminous Coal Division. The existing licensee and the industrial association have a motive to point out some errors of law by the agency; they have no motive at all to point out errors of law in their favor. The public-interest characterization thus tends to obscure the fact that the public-interest plaintiff brings to the court's attention only some of the arguments which the court requires to understand the case and to decide it correctly. In *Scenic Hudson* the administrative illegality which the public-interest plaintiff is pressing the court to consider consists in the Federal Power Commission's neglect, in its decisional processes, of "aesthetic, conservational and recreational" factors, factors which constitute only a portion of the factors which the Commission must consider. Since the public-interest plaintiff apparently was prepared to challenge the legality of the administrative proceeding only on the ground of the Commission's failure to grant adequate consideration to "aesthetic, conservational and recreational" factors, the grant of public-interest standing in the *Scenic Hudson* case is transparently a grant of standing to vindicate only a part of the public interest. The association supplied the mechanism for pressing the need to consider the "aesthetic, conservational and recreational" factors, but it would play no role at all in ensuring that other factors were properly taken into account. Public-interest standing now clearly appears as standing to press particular factors or values or points of view.

But this statement of the case is incomplete because we are dealing with a decisional process which takes place on two levels: at the agency level and in the courts. At the court level, the grant of standing to the association served the *Sanders* purpose of enabling the court to be informed why the Commission decision was

---

[137] *Id.*

[138] The Court's reference in *Sanders*, as well as in much of its progeny, to undefined—and hence more-or-less abstract—"errors of law" in the action of the agency which the public-interest standee will bring to the attention of the appellate court tends to gloss over the fact, which clearly appears in *Scenic Hudson*, that the errors of law which a standee raises may be limited to those connected with a particular concern of the standee such as the agency's insufficient attention to aesthetic factors in *Scenic Hudson* or to nondiscriminatory programming in Office of Communication of United Church of Christ v. FCC, 359 F.2d 994 (D.C. Cir. 1966).

wrong. But the case is different from *Sanders* because it was assumed that the objecting radio station would muster all of the "public interest" arguments available to defeat the FCC's licensing. The grounds for standing were conceived to be different from the substantive grounds urged before the court for invalidating the agency decision. In *Scenic Hudson*, by contrast, the grounds for recognizing standing are activities and conduct in the very areas which are pressed before the court. The court's grant of standing to the association is seen not so much as a general charge to bring forward any and all "public interest" arguments against the agency's action, but as a charge to bring forward arguments in the area in which the association has demonstrated its interest and competence—in presenting the aesthetic, conservational, and recreational arguments against licensing.[139] At the court level, therefore, our earlier conclusion thus remains true: public interest standing as it appears in *Scenic Hudson* is standing to press particular factors or values or points of view. But in deciding *Scenic Hudson*, the court perceived the association not only as pressing aesthetic, conservational, and recreational factors before it—in the sense of urging the court to command agency attention to those factors—but as pressing them at the agency level as well. Indeed, the court saw standing in court as a necessary adjunct to standing at the administrative level. Because these aesthetic, conservational, and recreational factors should be considered by the Commission, it was necessary to grant judicial standing to the association in order to enable the association to alert the court when the Commission has inadequately attended to these factors.[140] Public interest standing in *Scenic Hudson*, therefore, necessarily involves the pressing of particular factors or values or points of view at the administrative level as well as on the level of court review.

In its total effect, then, *Scenic Hudson* uses the pre-existing standing law as a base for deciding that aesthetic, conservational, and recreational factors should be taken into account by the Commission—that (in our earlier terminology)[141] they should be made "referents" for Commission decisions. In remanding the proceeding to the Commission, the court utilized the association as a mechanism for pressing these referents upon the Commission and for bringing out before the Commission information and arguments geared to the utilization of these referents in the licensing proceeding. In summary, then, (*i*) *Scenic Hudson* saw public interest standing as a device to bring some factors or values or points of view into the decisional process; (*ii*) these factors or values or viewpoints are made "referents" in the sense that they must be taken into account, although here, at least, they constitute some, but not all, of the "referents" which the decision-making body must take into account; (*iii*) judicial standing is employed as a device to enable the court to compel agency attention to those referents; but (*iv*) the mechanism which carries through—which presses these judicially articulated referents upon the agency—is the association

---

[139] 354 F.2d at 616.
[140] *Id. Compare* Sierra Club v. Morton, 405 U.S. 727 (1972).
[141] *See* text accompanying note 26 *supra*.

itself.[142] Judicial standing, therefore, is the tip of the iceberg through which the court reshapes the decisional process at the agency level. But, it will be asked, does this summary accurately describe a process through which the decisional process can be reshaped in other cases as well? The review provisions involved in such cases may—as did the review provisions of section 13 of the Federal Power Act,[143] which was involved in *Scenic Hudson*—require that the "aggrieved" person seeking review must be a party to the agency proceeding. And in *Scenic Hudson*, the court expressly recognized the agency's power to limit intervention.[144] Here the answer must be that the court which wishes to reshape the decisional structure in the manner outlined will have to require[145] that the agency admit as an intervenor a proponent of the factors which the court thinks should be considered in such a restructured decisional process.

From this point, the *Church of Christ* cases[146] follow naturally. In these cases the primary facet of decision was the standing of a church and others to intervene in agency proceedings. The court applied the *Sanders* arguments to grant administrative standing to a church which sought to represent viewers in television-license-renewal proceedings before the Federal Communications Commission.[147] The court observed—as in *Sanders*—that unless the church or other listener representatives were given standing, arguments and information which the Commission needed in order to make a well-informed decision would be lacking.[148] But although the court spoke of the church as a "listeners" representative, it is also true that the church was primarily the representative of the black population which objected to the television station's racially discriminatory broadcasts.[149] The court thus saw the church as pressing, not "public interest" arguments in general nor even "listeners" arguments in general, but a concern primarily with racially nondiscriminatory pro-

---

[142] This is what the court contemplated in *Scenic Hudson* and what did in fact happen. *Cf., e.g.,* 354 F.2d 617 where the court refers approvingly to representation of common interests at the administrative level by an organization such as Scenic Hudson which, by reducing the need for intervention by others with similar concerns, will "expedite the administrative process." *Compare* Norwalk CORE v. Norwalk Redevelopment Agency, 395 F.2d 920, 937-38 (2d Cir. 1968). In *Norwalk* the court, in treating judicial standing, indicated that the standing of an association of minority-group persons (adversely affected by a redevelopment agency's failure to relocate them on terms as satisfactory as those on which displaced white tenants were relocated) would depend upon whether individual members of the affected class could adequately represent the claims of the whole class before the court.

[143] 16 U.S.C. § 825*l*(b) (1970).

[144] 354 F.2d at 617.

[145] *See, e.g.,* Office of Communication of United Church of Chirst v. FCC, 359 F.2d 995 (D.C. Cir. 1966).

[146] Office of Communication of United Church of Christ v. FCC, 425 F.2d 543 (D.C. Cir. 1969); Office of Communication of United Church of Christ v. FCC, 359 F.2d 994 (D.C. Cir. 1966).

[147] 359 F.2d at 1004-05.

[148] *Id.*

[149] The court was conscious that the kind of public-interest administrative standing with which it was concerned involved representation of different groups in the listening community, and that, in ruling on petitions for public-interest intervention, the Commission would have to judge the usefulness for arriving at a correct licensing decision of adjudicating the claims asserted by the potential intervenors. 359 F.2d at 1005, 1006.

gramming.[150] Racially nondiscriminatory programming, a goal which the court saw as important, was also the special goal of the church and the black population which it represented. In order to make racially nondiscriminatory programming an effective referent for decision-making in the license-renewal proceedings, the court perceived a need for a greater input in the decision-making process of information and arguments addressed to the goal of racially nondiscriminatory programming. This need, the court saw, could be fulfilled in part by granting administrative standing to the church. By combining its own command to the agency to use the goal of racially nondiscriminatory programming as a referent with a grant of administrative standing to the church or to another listener representative associated with it,[151] the court ensured that the Commission would be continually reminded of that referent and that it would be pressed with information and arguments directed to the application of that referent.[152] Again, then, the court utilized the spokesmen for a group of citizens having a particular interest or concern as a device for impressing a decision-making referent on an agency. This procedure was especially useful here because the Commission had continually acknowledged verbally its adherence to the same referent and, indeed, had used that acknowledgment as a reason for urging that the church's intervention to press that referent upon it was unnecessary.[153] The decision thus emphasizes the court's felt differentiation between a verbal acknowledgement of a referent and decisions which in fact are made in the light of that referent.

In *Scenic Hudson* the court's utilization of the association as a device for pressing a referent upon a licensing agency was perhaps seen—even by the court—as entrusting the association with the primary responsibility for bringing forward before the agency information and arguments relating to the application of the aesthetic, conservational, and recreational referents which the court had approved. But in the second *Church of Christ* case where the Commission appeared to have seen the church-intervenor as primarily responsible for developing the case for applying the court-approved referent of racially nondiscriminatory programming, the court insisted that the implementation of that referent was primarily the responsibility of the Commission.[154] The church-intervenor was cast by the court in the role of a complaining witness and the Commission as a prosecutor whose duty it is to ascertain whether probable cause exists for the complaint—here against the station—and, if so, vigorously to develop a case based upon such cause.[155] In context, it seems that the court is demanding that the Commission not only (*i*) accept the referent of racially nondiscriminatory programming verbally (which it had previously done) and

---

[150] Other claims of the church and associated parties were some elements of religious discrimination, oppressive overcommercialization, and fairness doctrine violations. 359 F.2d at 1006.

[151] 359 F.2d at 1006, 1009.

[152] *Id.* at 1006, 1007, 1009.

[153] *Id.* at 1004, 1007-08.

[154] 425 F.2d at 546.

[155] *Id.*

(*ii*) be receptive to a case developed by the church-intervenor based upon that referent (in the manner of the *Scenic Hudson* procedure),[156] but (*iii*) also take steps on its own to implement that referent, using the church-intervenor not as an advocate before it but as an aid for its own investigation and case-development.[157] The referent thus becomes not merely one to which the agency must be receptive and which the agency will apply if others supply information and arguments requisite for its effective utilization, but one which the agency itself has the affirmative duty to employ. The "public interest" standee remains as the agency's "conscience," if you will, in applying the referent. It keeps the agency forcefully reminded of the referent and calls incidents and approaches to the agency's attention for exploration and investigation. The affirmative duty imposed on the agency is perhaps intended to magnify the agency's responsiveness to the standee's suggestions, a state of affairs which, if brought about, will heighten the importance of the referent in the agency decision-making process.

The law of public interest standing has thus developed from a tool for informing the judiciary of any or all available public-interest arguments which the standee wishes to make[158] into a device for restructuring agency decision-making by impressing new referents upon the agency and ensuring that those new referents are heeded. *Church of Christ II*[159] gives referents to the decision-making agency in a dynamic form. They are imposed upon the agency together with a standee who presses the agency to relate to the referents. The standee's function is the agency's conscience and helper in applying the referent. And his role is both eased and strengthened by the magnified voice which he is given when the court makes the implementation of the referent in question an affirmative duty of the agency.

One way of viewing these cases would be to say that the courts are merely applying to agencies their long-standing rule of ensuring that judicial decisions are based upon adequate information. In this view the courts would be seen as enlarging judicial standing as a means of enlarging administrative standing. And they would be seen as enlarging administrative standing in order to ensure that information needed by agency decision-makers is brought before them. But one difficulty with such a narrow view is that agencies almost always have access to the information which they need to make informed decisions. The courts are saying something more. They are saying that the decisional perspective from which the agency in question approached its problem was too narrow, that its decisional frame of reference needs to be broadened, and that it needs exposure not only to additional

---

[156] *But cf.* notes 157 & 162 *infra*.

[157] *Cf.* Scenic Hudson Preservation Conference v. FPC, 354 F.2d 608, 620 (2d Cir. 1965), *cert. denied*, 384 U.S. 941 (1966): ("the Commission has claimed to be the representative of the public interest. This role does not permit it to act as an umpire blandly calling balls and strikes for adversaries appearing before it; the right of the public must receive active and affirmative protection at the hands of the Commission."). *Accord*, Calvert Cliffs' Coordinating Comm., Inc. v. AEC, 449 F.2d 1109, 1119 (D.C. Cir. 1971).

[158] FCC v. Sanders Bros. Radio Station, 309 U.S. 470, 477 (1940).

[159] 425 F.2d 543 (D.C. Cir. 1969).

information but that it needs to utilize new decisional referents. The choice of the kinds of information which the agency will employ and the factors which it will consider, these courts are saying, is not entirely the agency's to make. But this, of course, is nothing new. Courts have long exerted a power of review over agency choices of decisional referents, either rejecting some as improper or requiring agency consideration or use of other referents.[160] What is new in these cases is the combination of the judicial imposition of referents with the grant of administrative standing to proponents of the referent which is imposed. These courts are thus saying that the information to be acquired by the agency in question and the referents to be used by it need not only to be approved judicially but also to be vigorously pressed upon the agency by a proponent of the enlarged frame of reference.

The referent-proponent is thus cast in a two-fold role which corresponds to the changes in agency decision-making which these decisions are designed to achieve. First, the proponent is cast by the court in the role of pressing the agency to orient its processes in line with the new or previously unheeded—but generally phrased—referents which it is championing. The proponent must continually exert pressure upon the agency to consider these referents in its own decisional processes, and, if it fails, the proponent is given standing to seek judicial review on the ground that these referents have been neglected. The proponent's function here is partly one of reenforcing the court's orders about the frame of reference in which agency decisions are to be made. Thus *Church of Christ II* utilizes the analogy of a complaining witness and the prosecutor[161] in order to compel the agency staff not only to take seriously the new decisional referent (the furtherance of racially nondiscriminatory programming as a conduct norm for radio and television licensees) but to develop the case which active employment of that referent requires. Judge Wright in *National Welfare Rights Organization v. Finch*[162] seeks to accomplish the same result by forcing the Department of Health, Education, and Welfare to accept the NWRO as a party to compliance proceedings which the Department had instituted against two states. The court is saying that the best insurance that the administrators take into account the attitudes, views, and information which welfare recipients have to contribute consists in making their representatives parties to those administrative proceedings which decide policies affecting them. Again, the court is not merely helping HEW obtain the information it requires. HEW, if it has the interest and motivation, undoubtedly has the capacity to collect all of the information which it will get in the court-mandated procedure. But Judge Wright's point is just that it may lack that motivation. The rigidities in approaches to decisions imposed or fostered by its own bureaucratic organization may create inertia

---

[160] *E.g.*, NLRB v. Hearst Publications, Inc., 322 U.S. 111 (1944) (inapplicability of respondent-superior and workmen's compensation principles for decision-making under the National Labor Relations Act). Congress later took a different view as to the relevancy of these sources as referents for labor board decisions. *See* 29 U.S.C. § 152(3) (1971).

[161] 425 F.2d at 546.

[162] 429 F.2d 725 (D.C. Cir. 1970).

to changes in its selection of decisional referents unless new decisional foci are pressed vigorously upon it.[163] And the granting of administrative standing to NWRO was apparently designed to do just that. Although here the agency organization was not made part of the mechanism by which the application of the decisional referents were applied as in *Church of Christ II*, the court recognized[164] the need to alter the decisional process at the administrative level in such a way as to make it both open and receptive to new decisional referents supplied by welfare recipients' representatives.

The referent-proponent is given a second role under the recent cases. Because the judicially-approved referents are often phrased in general and, hence, open-ended language—such as the "aesthetic, conservational and recreational" factors referred to by the court in *Scenic Hudson*[165]—the referent-proponent is charged not only with a reenforcing function at the agency level but with a development function as well. It is charged with the function of pressing the agency to come to grips with the concerns which the court has approved in generalized language in the specifics of a concrete case. This calls for imagination, initiative, and perseverance. It may be easier to concretize the concerns of the welfare recipients involved in the *NWRO* case than to concretize the environmental concerns involved in cases like *Scenic Hudson*. In cases of the latter type the interplay between a broad concern with environmental quality and engineering considerations may require the public-interest representative to possess technical skill if his representation is to be effective.[166]

The Supreme Court's twin decisions on standing under the Administrative Procedure Act—*Association of Data Processing Service Organizations, Inc. v. Camp*[167] and *Barlow v. Collins*[168]— expand the standing rights of persons injured or potentially injured by agency action. These cases create the mechanism through which questions as to the types and extent of protections created by statute can be judicially resolved. And in that resolution, agencies will be at least verbally required to develop the decisional referents necessary to accord those protections. Taken by themselves, the apparent weaknesses of these cases appear to lie in the absence of a mechanism—discussed in those cases—through which the judicially determined referents will be reenforced and developed at the administrative level. But in combination with Judge Wright's decision in *NWRO*, they may exert a growing impact upon the choice of decisional referents by officials and agencies. In *NWRO*, Judge Wright

---

[163] Cf. Elman, *Administrative Reform of the Federal Trade Commission*, 59 GEO. L.J. 777, 789-92 (1971) (pointing out that in the absence of consumer representation before it, the Commission, itself a consumer-protection agency, may neglect the consumer interests in its decisions).

[164] 429 F.2d at 736-39.

[165] 354 F.2d at 616.

[166] Cramton, *The Why, Where and How of Broadened Public Participation in the Administrative Process*, 60 GEO. L.J. 525, 526-27 (1972).

[167] 397 U.S. 150 (1970).

[168] 397 U.S. 159 (1970).

granted judicial standing—under the *Data Processing* and *Barlow* cases[169]—to the National Welfare Rights Organization to seek judicial review of compliance proceedings which HEW had brought against two state welfare departments. But he then reasoned that judicial standing, to be meaningful, presupposed standing at the administrative level.[170] To the extent that Judge Wright's gloss on *Data Processing* and *Barlow* is followed, the dynamic characteristics of the *Scenic Hudson* and *Church of Christ* cases will be imparted to a wide range of administrative action.

Other recent cases—such as *Citizens to Preserve Overton Park, Inc. v. Volpe*[171] and *Medical Committee for Human Rights v. SEC*[172]—have broadened vastly the scope of administrative horizons by insisting that the agencies whose action was under review utilize decisional referents which they had theretofore neglected or openly refused to employ or consider. Where the new referents can be forcefully urged and developed by competent "public-interest" representatives in agency-level proceedings, they carry the potential for dynamic referent development and reenforcement illustrated in the *Scenic Hudson, Church of Christ*, and *NWRO* litigation. But where the new referents are judicially ordered in a context which lacks a mechanism for their development and reenforcement at the agency level, as for example, where the absence of formal administrative proceedings precludes intervention of a public-interest representative,[173] their promise appears not quite so bright as in the circumstances where that possibility is present. In this regard, legislatively-imposed procedures under the National Environmental Policy Act of 1969[174] appear to be designed to impel the agencies governed by that Act to utilize environmental concerns as referents in ways that are meaningful. While the Act's mandates were forcefully imposed upon a reluctant Atomic Energy Commission at the insistence of a public-interest plaintiff in *Calvert Cliffs*,[175] it is possible that even without the involvement of a public-interest representative the Act's mandated procedures (as construed in *Calvert Cliffs*) may themselves play the reenforcing role which is needed if the externally imposed referents are to be accepted and actively employed by the agencies.

SUMMARY AND CONCLUSIONS

I have tried to articulate a conception of agency decision-making which uses the concept of "decisional referents." As developed in the article, referents include, but are not limited to, "rules," criteria, factors, considerations, principles, policies, goals, and reasons. These all have their proper places in analyses of administrative decision-making, and the distinctions which can be made among them must not be lost. Agency-disclosed "reasons," for example, may sometimes be reviewed by

---

[169] 429 F.2d at 733-35.
[170] 429 F.2d at 736-37.
[171] 401 U.S. 402 (1971).
[172] 432 F.2d 659 (D.C. Cir. 1970), *vacated as moot*, 92 S.Ct. 577 (1972).
[173] *Cf.* Citizens to Preserve Overton Park, Inc. v. Volpe, 401 U.S. 402, 420-21 (1971).
[174] 42 U.S.C. § 4321-47 (1970).
[175] Calvert Cliffs' Coordinating Comm., Inc. v. AEC, 449 F.2d 1109 (D.C. Cir. 1971).

the courts under a standard different from that under which agency "rules" are reviewed. But I have attempted to find an inclusive concept in order to provide a tool by which the likenesses and the similarities in agency employment of these various factors can be assessed. The lawyer, conscious of the similarity in an agency's use of "goals" and "reasons" in its decisional processes, may be stimulated to look for each, rather than to rest after he is assured that the agency matter in which he is concerned is within the "discretionary" decision-making power of the agency. After he uncovers the relevant referent and notes the similarity in the ways in which "rule" and nonrule referents are employed, he will negotiate with agency officials in terms of the relevant decisional referent. He will present his case in terms of the governing referents and will take cognizance of those referents in shaping his arguments. This is how negotiation would be conducted when the case in question was governed by a "rule," and the negotiation process would seem to be essentially the same when the case is governed by a nonrule referent. The analogy to rule-referents may carry the lawyer further. Conceptualizing nonrule referents as analogous to rules, he would immediately sense the fact that somewhere in the administrative hierarchy is an official with power to change a referent or to waive its application. By facilitating the lawyer's perception of an appeal of the use of a nonrule referent, the lawyer may be stimulated to seek out and to find the particular official to whom he must address his arguments for the non-application of a referent to which the lawyer objects.

The usefulness of the "referent" concept must not be overstated. A perceptive lawyer would act in the ways just described, regardless of how he conceptualized the factors utilized by agency officials in deciding. A less perceptive lawyer, however, might not. The value of the concept, therefore, consists, first, in its capacity for demonstrating the manner in which "rules" blur into nonrule decisional factors. The analogy to rules may help further in assessing the likelihood (i) of obtaining relief from lower-echelon officials and (ii) of obtaining the time and attention of higher-echelon officials. Referents widely applied by numerous officials as a matter of course to large numbers of cases can be revoked, if at all, only by officials in the upper echelons of administration. For the same reason, higher echelon officials who might lack the time to review a routine case may make time to consider a major objection to a referent widely used by their subordinates. Again, officials will be reluctant to interfere unnecessarily with normal administration. The lawyer who can point out why a widely-used referent ought to be inapplicable to his case may be more successful than the lawyer who makes a broadside attack upon the basic propriety of the referent. The decisional-referent concept is offered for whatever stimulus it may afford to persons concerned with administrative decision-making to search out similarities among the ways in which various decisional factors are employed.

Second, the decisional referent concept is useful in illustrating the manner in which ad hoc or tentative decisional criteria blur into more fixed criteria. Davis, for example, has referred to the desirability of "rule" issuances by administrators who have arrived at "firm" answers to significant hypothetical cases.[176] But long before an administrator has arrived at "firm" answers, he may have arrived at "tentative" answers. As time progresses these answers may become increasingly less "tentative" and more "firm." Yet the dividing line between tentative and firm answers may not be sharp. Davis's rule-issuance suggestion is a praiseworthy admonition directed to agencies; it is only indirectly addressed to the problem of a lawyer grappling with agency officials. The lawyer needs to learn the officials' decisional referents, even though they be "tentative" ones. The referent concept may aid him in perceiving the dimensions of his problem and in organizing his negotiation strategy.

Third, the referent concept is useful in demonstrating the manner in which the factors employed by individual officials blur into decisional factors employed by the subunits, units, bureaus, or agencies in which those officials work. Referents—whether of the rule or nonrule variety—differ in their authority bases. We have taken cognizance of this point above when we referred to the possibility of a lawyer appealing the application of a decisional referent to his case. This leads us to the fourth manner in which the referent concept may be useful. A focus upon the referents actually employed focuses attention upon informal rule and nonrule referents which arise from personal interaction among officials and which have often been the subject of inquiry by social scientists.[177] These informal referents may "fill in" or "complete" open-ended formal rules, or, at times, may even effectively countermand them. The perceptive lawyer must be alert to the possibility that his client will be denied benefits to which he might otherwise be entitled because of the operation of such an informal decisional-referent structure.

Not only may the referent concept be helpful in engendering sensitivity to the existence of informal decisional referents, but, fifth, it may aid in understanding the processes through which such referents develop, change, and are reenforced. While, again, this is presently the domain of social scientists, I have, with some trepidation, tentatively expressed some of my own reflections on that subject in this article. Since the interaction of officials may affect the kind and quality of decisions, lawyers involved with administrative-law reform will, in the future, be increasingly concerned with the studies of complex organizations and with other findings of social scientists. In this article I have also made use of Davis's focus upon "openness," but as a factor affecting the degree of "substantive rationality" of the referents employed in deciding cases.

In connection with the foregoing approach, I have attempted to relate some contributions of legal philosophy. The probings of the legal realists are obviously relevant to a conceptualization of decision-making in terms of decisional referents. But the current linguistic school is also helpful in contributing to our understanding of referent-internalization. By focusing upon the contributions of Profesosrs H. L. A.

---

[176] K. DAVIS, DISCRETIONARY JUSTICE 60 (1969).
[177] E.g., P. BLAU, THE DYNAMICS OF BUREAUCRACY (2d ed. 1963).

Hart and Dworkin in Part I, I have attempted to lay the foundations for an analysis of decision-making in terms of decisional referents where those referents are often internalized by the official or sub-departmental group utilizing them. This initial focus upon internalization also prepared the way for a perception of the possibility that decisional referents might be generated by the personal interaction of officials involved in the decisional process. Finally, I have speculated as to the extent to which the more recent administrative-standing cases may work to expand the frame of reference in which agency decisions are made. Will agencies which are exposed to greater input from heretofore unrepresented interests become more responsive to those interests? And if they do become more responsive in formal proceedings in which these groups are represented, will the phenomenon of referent internalization carry over into informal actions by those agencies?

In summary, then, the article has utilized a conceptualization of decision-making in terms of decisional referents, and has attempted to explore the usefulness of this framework in increasing understanding or awareness of various types of administrative decision-making.

ON *DAVIS* ON CONFINING, STRUCTURING, AND CHECKING ADMINISTRATIVE DISCRETION

Victor G. Rosenblum*

I

Davis and Discretionary Justice

Although he subtitled *Discretionary Justice* a "preliminary" inquiry, Kenneth Culp Davis made a definitive addition to the literature and public understanding of the administrative process through his Edward Douglass White Lectures that engendered the volume.[1]

In reviewing Davis's *Administrative Law Treatise*[2] a decade earlier, I had thought it a remarkable compilation and evaluation of court cases dealing with administrative agency practices and procedures, as well as the most comprehensive examination of the relationship to administrative law of such central legal concepts as stare decisis, res judicata, estoppel, official notice, ripeness, primary jurisdiction, and exhaustion of remedies.[3] Although he recognized that many principles of administrative law, because of confusing or conflicting authorities, could not be asserted with certainty, Davis's objective as author of the *Treatise* was to make a systematic statement of principles derived from the huge mass of administrative law that had sprung up in recent decades. The data he examined were primarily Supreme Court decisions and lower court opinions that were based on agency rules, adjudications, and practices related to them. Unsurprisingly, the evaluations he made consisted primarily of learned observations and incisive critiques of what the courts had said and done in response to what agencies had said and done.

My principal reservation about the *Treatise* was that it focused much more on formal law than on administration, more on the delineation of legal principles than on processes of decision-making. As a consequence, little was done to meet the concern of practitioners, administrators, and students about *how* administrative law develops and functions in reality. To the extent that Davis was then concerned with discretion at all, his emphasis was on judicial rather than on administrative discretion. Even in his examination of institutional decisions, Davis dealt mainly with the formal aspects of administrative problems. He discussed, for example, the extent to which deciding officers must personally consider evidence, the consultation of staff by examiners and agency heads, and the absences of or substitutions for officers and agency heads in decision sessions.[4] Implicit in his analysis was the view that

* Director of the Program in Law and the Social Sciences and Professor of Law at Northwestern University; President, Law and Society Association.

[1] K. Davis, Discretionary Justice: A Preliminary Inquiry (1969) [hereinafter cited as Discretionary Justice].

[2] 1-4 K. Davis, Administrative Law Treatise (1958) [hereinafter cited as Treatise].

[3] Rosenblum, *Realities of Regulation*, 20 Pub. Ad. Rev. 219 (1960).

[4] 2 Treatise 36-129.

the universe of administrative law was hierarchical, with the judiciary at its apex. He supported judicial discretion in applying rules such as exhaustion of administrative remedies because he believed the quest for "a neat word formula" that could eliminate discretion in determining when to grant judicial relief to be futile, if not undesirable. To channel the judiciary's discretion, he proposed consideration of such factors as the extent of injury a petitioner might suffer through delay, the degree of apparent clarity or doubt of administrative jurisdiction, and the significance of specialized administrative understanding.[5]

Discretion became a central, rather than a peripheral, concern to Davis during the 1960's, and *Discretionary Justice* was a major product of the broadening of his insights and inquiries. His objective shifted from a predominant effort to codify the law of the past and admonish judges about the law of the future to an emphasis on the primacy of discretion in administration at all levels. He sought "to dispel the virtually universal impression that discretionary justice is too elusive for study, . . . to open up problems that seem susceptible of further research and thinking, and . . . to formulate a framework for further study."[6] No longer preoccupied with the quest for *judge-made* principles of administrative law, Davis focused on the quality of justice in all facets of the administrative process and stressed that the strongest need and greatest promise for improving that quality for individuals "are in the areas where decisions necessarily depend more upon discretion than upon rules and principles and where formal hearings and judicial review are mostly irrelevant."[7]

The key question he now posed was, how can we reduce injustice to individuals from the exercise of discretionary power? His framework for developing an answer was simple: unnecessary discretionary power should be cut back and the discretionary power that is found to be necessary should be properly confined, structured, and checked. Since this formulation constitutes an approach to an answer, rather than the answer itself, a critic would have to yield to cavil at this stage to denigrate Davis's contribution by attacking the vagaries of meaning of "necessary." One could draw on Justice Marshall in *McCulloch v. Maryland* to argue that necessary means convenient, or one could insist on confining the term to essentiality or indispensability to a goal or achievement.[8] The point is that Davis did not stop with enunciation of the "necessary" and "properly confined" criteria. He rejected

---

[5] 3 TREATISE 67-69.

[6] DISCRETIONARY JUSTICE vii.

[7] *Id.* at 216 (emphasis omitted).

[8] McCulloch v. Maryland, 17 U.S. (4 Wheat.) 316, 413 (1819). In construing the meaning of "necessary" as used in the "necessary and proper" clause of the Constitution, Marshall observed that "[t]he word 'necessary,' is considered as controlling the whole sentence, and as limiting the right to pass laws for the execution of the granted powers, to such as are indispensable, and without which the power would be nugatory . . . . Is it true, that this is the sense in which the word 'necessary' is always used? Does it always import an absolute physical necessity, so strong, that one thing, to which another may be termed necessary, cannot exist without that other? We think it does not. If reference be had to its use, in the common affairs of the world, or in approved authors, we find that it frequently imports no more than that one thing is convenient, or useful, or essential to another."

as a false hope the sharper delineation of statutory standards and pointed out the incongruity of the non-delegation doctrine in light of the reality of the common-place power of selective enforcement. Instead, he espoused administrative rule-making as the key to proper confinement and control of discretion. He insisted that "agencies through rule-making can often move from vague or absent statutory standards to reasonably definite standards, and then, as experience and understanding develop, to guiding principles, and finally, when the subject matter permits, to precise and detailed rules."[9]

Concomitantly with his proposal for enlarged rule-making, he urged openness as a means for structuring discretionary power. He saw openness as a natural enemy of arbitrariness and called for open plans, open policy statements, and open findings and reasons in situations warranting informal discretionary action as well as in more formal realms of decision-making.[10] With regard to the bearing of appeals on checking discretion, he noted that the natural system of administrative appeals from subordinates to superiors is less desirable than appeals to independent officers. An independent ombudsman could be a more effective critic of administration than a superior officer or a legislator. Davis was especially concerned about reducing powers of lenience and privilege since "the inescapable reality" is that the discretion of public officers to confer privileges or to be lenient, is power susceptible to abuses including the most egregious forms of discrimination, favoritism and caprice.[11]

The Davis of the *White Lectures* was more sensitive to and perceptive of realities of regulation than the Davis of the *Treatise*. It would have been unthinkable for the author of the *Treatise* to conclude, as Davis does in *Discretionary Justice*, that "our jurisprudence of statutes and of judge-made law is overdeveloped; our jurisprudence of administrative justice, of police justice, of prosecutor justice—of discretionary justice—is underdeveloped. *We need a new jurisprudence that will encompass all of justice, not just the easy half of it.*"[12]

Without claiming that all that has been done in administrative law and process research since the publication of *Discretionary Justice* is rooted in Davis, one can still justifiably credit him with commencing, inspiring, and spurring significant new probes of the nuances of administrative discretion that would otherwise have been neglected or discarded. Several prototypes of projects that are at least compatible with Davis's observations and admonitions are worth considering. Lest the reader conclude that my response to the "Discretionary" Davis is 100 per cent encomium, it should be added that I am not yet persuaded that too little discretion is not as often to blame for denials of justice as too much discretion. In developing projects and in planning and allocating funds for research, I think it essential that we devote equal amounts of intellectual energy and tangible resources to probing positive

[9] Discretionary Justice 219.
[10] *Id.* at 99-116.
[11] *Id.* at 170-76, 231-32.
[12] *Id.* at 233 (author's emphasis).

relationships between discretion and justice as we do to their dysfunctional interactions.

II
PROTOTYPES OF PROJECTS ON POLICE DISCRETION

Davis observed that the police constitute one of the most important policy making
agencies of our society since "they make far more discretionary determinations in
individual cases than any other class of administrators."[13] He also found the amount
of police activity measured in man hours to be more than forty times as great
as the amount of governmental activity through all seven of the major independent
regulatory agencies. Although he was not the discoverer of the discretionary dimensions of police work, Davis's work has shown the suitability and feasibility of
intensive research on policies, procedures, and programs of the police.[14] A current
project at Northwestern University and an emergent one at Arizona State University
help to illustrate the potentialities, if not yet the benefits, of implementing Davis's
proposals.

In an attempt to discern patterns in the conduct of police toward civilians in
Chicago, the Law Enforcement Study Group, a joint research project of the Center
for Urban Affairs at Northwestern University and a dozen other Chicago area
organizations, undertook to examine policies and practices governing the use of
fatal force by police officers. Little data of record was available prior to this study.
Even when complaints were solicited or registered the information was usually
considered too sensitive and controversial for public examination. A basic objective
of the study was to determine the adequacy of institutions and mechanisms for
reviewing incidents involving fatal force.

Through the Police Weapons Center of the International Association of Chiefs
of Police, comparative statistical information on killings of and by police was collected on each of the five largest U.S. cities according to the 1970 census. The death
rate of civilians from police actions per 100,000 population was found to be highest
in Chicago—0.95 from July 1970 to March 1971 as compared to 0.27 in New York,
0.28 in Los Angeles, 0.26 in Detroit, and 0.67 in Philadelphia.[15] Chicago also scored
highest on the civilian death rate per 1000 police officers—2.53 compared with 0.66 in
New York, 1.18 in Los Angeles, 0.77 in Detroit, and 1.67 in Philadelphia.[16] With

---

[13] *Id.* at 222-23, 81.

[14] An excellent selected bibliography of both early and recent research into police roles, functions
and discretion is found in AMERICAN BAR ASSOCIATION PROJECT ON STANDARDS FOR CRIMINAL JUSTICE,
THE URBAN POLICE FUNCTION 296-303 (1972) (tentative draft). This comprehensive report draws heavily
on Davis in developing and supporting its recommendations that "[p]olice discretion can best be structured
and controlled through the process of administrative rule-making by police agencies. Police administrators
should, therefore, give the highest priority to the formulation of administrative rules governing the
exercise of discretion, particularly in the areas of selective enforcement, investigative techniques and
enforcement methods." *Id.* at 125-133.

[15] Law Enforcement Study Group, The Police and Their Use of Fatal Force in Chicago, 6 (1972).

[16] *Id.* at 10.

regard to police fatalities during the same period, Chicago was the highest with 7 and second highest in ratio of police deaths to department size.

Although the researchers could obtain statistical summaries and other aggregate data from the International Association of Chiefs of Police, individual departments, including the Chicago Police Department, were reluctant to make available their data on individual cases involving civilian deaths. As a consequence, one of the investigative research techniques employed was to identify incidents of civilian deaths at the hands of police reported in Chicago newspaper files. This information was then used to locate transcripts of inquests at the Cook County Coroner's office. Selected characteristics of the civilians who died were recorded by race, age, and sex; the locations of the fatal incidents were plotted on a map of Chicago; and whatever information was available on the characteristics of the policemen involved was analyzed. 70.9% of the civilians who died were black males, 3.9% were black females, 24% were white males and 1.3% were unidentified.[17] The death rate by race per 100,000 population was found to be 5.35 for blacks and 0.86 for whites. The authors noted that during 1969 and 1970, a black person in Chicago was more than six times as likely to die at the hands of police than a white person.[18] Comparing the death rate with arrests, they found that blacks had a 2.01 death rate per 10,000 arrests of blacks, whereas whites had a 1.00 rate per 10,000 arrests of whites.[19]

The researchers next analyzed the standards governing police use of fatal force and the structures and mechanisms for review of such force. Statutory standards of the state criminal law and administrative standards of the police department both govern review. The administrative standards showed that officers are specifically prohibited from firing into crowds; firing over the heads of crowds, except on specific order of a member of the Department above the rank of Captain; firing at a fleeing car, except one in which a person who has attempted or committed a forcible felony is riding; firing warning shots in the case of individuals where the use of deadly force is not permitted; and firing into a building or through doors when the person fired at is not clearly visible.[20] In addition, an official Chicago police training bulletin cautions the officer to use "every possible means at his disposal" to avoid a killing and reminds him of the possibility of prosecution for voluntary manslaughter.[21]

Several different public bodies, including the internal division of the police department, the Cook County coroner, and the State's Attorney, were found to have authority and formal responsibility in review of cases of civilian death. Of 76 cases examined that involved fatal police force, the police pressed charges in two, the state's attorney presented charges to a grand jury in four, and a grand jury indicted a policeman and a trial was conducted in one. The coroner's office exonerated

---

[17] *Id.* at 19.
[18] *Id.* at 20.
[19] *Id.* at 21.
[20] *Id.* at 30-32.
[21] *Id.* at 32.

the police in all but two of the 76 cases, the same two in which the police department pressed charges. The authors of the report found that in 28 of the cases
the evidence showed violations of administrative guidelines during the fatal incident.
Ten of the 28 indicated substantial likelihood of criminal misconduct by the
police.[22] No administrative discipline measures were found to have been taken in
any of these 28 cases. The researchers concluded that the public cannot be assured
of the integrity of the police review process. As a result of the wide disparity between
cases warranting official action and those in which action actually was taken, the
authors called for a re-examination of the review system to determine whether and
how structural defects contribute to the inadequacy of the examination of police
use of fatal force.[23] Two defects in the system of reviewing police use of fatal
force—both of them consistent with Davis's critique—were cited for combining to
compromise the integrity of the review process: "The agencies in the system have
a close working relationship, an arrangement which precludes independent examination within the system; the review proceedings are conducted almost entirely
out of view of the public, an arrangement which precludes independent examination
from without."[24]

The Chicago report was obviously controversial and could be transformed wholly
into political fodder in an election year. Needless to say, performance of such a
project by the faculty and students of a university requires exceptional stress on
objectivity, depth, and fairness. At the same time, the capacity of a university
to accept leadership in research that has immediate public policy implications has
added significantly to the checks and balances over arbitrary uses of discretion.

A more direct implementation of Davis's urgings about research into police
discretion may be found in the Center recently established at Arizona State University Law School for study and research into police administrative law. Directed
by Professor Gerald Caplan, previously general counsel of the District of Columbia
Police Department, the first project of the Center will be a study of rule-making
in law enforcement agencies. Davis's observation that "no other agency, so far as
I know, does so little supervising of vital policy determinations which directly involve
justice or injustice to individuals"[25] was invoked as a demonstration of the need for
the new Center, along with the exhortation of the President's Commission on
Law Enforcement and Administration of Justice to police to develop and articulate
concrete policies.[26] The objective of the Center is not simply to survey and report
on police policies and practices. Its active goal will be "to transform law enforcement agencies from comparatively passive and lethargic bodies, ever responding to

---

[22] *Id.* at 62.

[23] *Id.* at 63-64.

[24] *Id.* at 72.

[25] DISCRETIONARY JUSTICE 88.

[26] U.S. PRESIDENT'S COMMISSION ON LAW ENFORCEMENT AND ADMINISTRATION OF JUSTICE, THE CHAL-
LENGE OF CRIME IN A FREE SOCIETY 103-06 (1967).

the cues or dictates of others, most notably the judiciary, into active initiators of policies reflective of their own goals."[27]

Discussions Caplan has had with police chiefs, legal advisors, and other police officials have re-enforced Davis's contentions and shown a need for comprehensive updating of existing police manuals. For example, one police chief told Caplan that community concern over a recent shooting might have been alleviated had the department had written statements of its rules and policies to present to the city council and other concerned groups.

The Center will endeavor to fashion model administrative orders for law enforcement agencies in such specific areas as service of arrest and search warrants, problems associated with stop and frisk and field interrogation, finger-printing policies, the settlement of minor disputes among neighbors and within the family, development of a citation and summons system, problems associated with vagrancy and disorderly conduct statutes, and policies relating to freedom of assembly and grievance procedures. The Center hopes to involve in its efforts groups often critical of the police, such as the American Civil Liberties Union, Urban Coalition, legal services organizations and anti-poverty organizations. Interest in participation in the work of the Center has been manifested by a number of major city police departments including Kansas City, Phoenix, Dallas, San Antonio, San Diego, Oakland, New York, and Washington, D.C. Students at the Arizona State Law School will assist in the research along with the director, deputy director, junior attorney and participating consultants.

As prototypes of university involvement in appraising and assisting community needs, the Law Enforcement Study Group and the Center for Police Administrative Law are not expected to produce panaceas for the problems of police discretion. They can, however, help to institutionalize, channel and direct discretion toward constructive ends by giving visibility to basic information otherwise submerged or secreted and by developing proposals that can be weighed in politically neutral settings.

III

Research About Potential Participants in Ombudsmen's Roles

Like the university researcher, the ombudsman is usually outside the system he examines and his only real power is that which prestige and public opinion may accord him. A recent proposal to experiment with ombudsman-like roles for social workers and a report on performance of such roles by state lieutenant governors suggest the feasibility of additional checks on administrative discretion, implementing Davis's proposals, from inside operative administrative systems.

---

[27] Caplan, Rulemaking in Law Enforcement Agencies: A Proposal for a Police Administrative Law Center 1-2 (1972) (mimeo). Professor Caplan has expanded the proposal for the Center into a law review article, *The Case for Rulemaking by Law Enforcement Agencies*, 36 Law & Contemp. Prob. 500 (1971).

A professor of social work at the University of Texas, for example, has considered the potential effectiveness of social workers as ombudsmen in the areas of mental retardation, crime, delinquency, housing, and welfare administration.[28] While cognizant of Cloward's conclusion that there is no public commitment to justice, equity, or dignity in the social welfare system, Professor Payne insists that there are many opportunities for an ombudsman to help welfare department staffs improve at least the administrative fairness of their programs even if they can't eliminate public antipathy toward the poor.[29] Payne does not feel that the social worker's position as an advocate of client interests in some instances would jeopardize the objectivity deemed a hallmark of the ombudsman, for he believes that any ombudsman must take on some dimensions of an advocate whenever he finds a citizen's complaint is justified and seeks to have the government rectify the error.[30] Payne is especially enthusiastic about the capacity of social workers to perform as ombudsmen through impartial arbitration or neutral mediation in disputes between client groups and public agencies. The social worker's opportunity and task in such situations would be "to promote the public consensus that people-serving institutions should in fact serve people and to facilitate the implementation of such service."[31] To protect impartiality and objectivity, Payne recommends that the social worker-ombudsman be designated an employee of a public legislative body or a private council of social agencies with funding authority, such as the United Fund, rather than an employee of any of the agencies in whose disputes he will be called upon to intervene. The relevance of law and public policy to ombudsmanship leads Payne to propose curricular changes in social work education that would emphasize legal doctrines and practices and also enable would-be ombudsmen to understand bureaucratic structure and organization beyond what is taught in the traditional social work administration courses. Whether ombudsman's roles can be effectively performed by social workers is conjectural of course. The obvious problem with Payne's proposal is that public legislative bodies and private councils of agencies have no guaranteed immunity against becoming partisans in conflict themselves. As Payne suggests, however, the feasibility of social worker-ombudsmen could well be the subject of active experimentation that could help, at the same time as it tested the new role, to enhance social work's professional purpose and philosophy.[32]

In his study of lieutenant governors as political ombudsmen, Alan Wyner noted at the outset that lieutenant governors differ from the traditional model of the

---

[28] Payne, *Ombudsman Roles for Social Workers*, 17 Social Work, January, 1972, 94. Earlier discussions of potentialities of social workers as ombudsmen were contained in Cloward, *An Ombudsman for Whom?*, 12 Social Work, April, 1967, at 117; Zweig, *The Social Worker as Legislative Ombudsman*, 14 Social Work, January, 1969, at 25; and Payne, *An Ombudsman for the Retarded?*, 8 Mental Retardation, October, 1970, at 45.

[29] Cloward, *supra* note 29. *See also* Cloward & Elman, *Poverty, Injustice and the Welfare State*, 202 The Nation 230 (1966).

[30] Payne, *Ombudsman Roles for Social Workers*, *supra* note 28, at 98.

[31] *Id.* at 99.

[32] *Id.* at 100.

ombudsman in two major ways.[33] Whereas traditional ombudsmen cannot hold another public office during their terms and are rarely interested in future political office, lieutenant governors are elected politicians with major responsibilities as well as continuing political aspirations. Furthermore, whereas ombudsmen traditionally owe their ultimate allegiance to the legislature, lieutenant governors are generally executive officers with at least as much identification with the executive branch as with the legislature. For lieutenant governors, "opportunities for conflict of interest abound."[34] Perhaps surprisingly, Wyner found that, in strictly quantitative terms at least, such conflicts have not arisen in' the vast majority of instances thus far.[35]

Focusing on the ombudsman experiences of Lieutenant Governors Mark Hogan of Colorado, Paul Simon of Illinois, and Roberto Mondragon of New Mexico, Wyner's study showed that the office of ombudsman had no indigenous attributes that ordained it with any natural affinity for lieutenant governors. Each of the state officials voluntarily and independently sought out the responsibility and established his role as ombudsman—Simon and Mondragon in their platforms for office and Hogan in the course of his inaugural speech. In Wyner's appraisal, "a combination of personal political ambition, plus a genuine interest in resolving people's grievances against administrative agencies provided the motivation for Hogan, Simon and Mondragon to adopt political ombudsman roles."[36] The public seemed to welcome a new avenue of possible redress.

Welfare, employment, and licensing cases led in all three states for ombudsman attention—the typical welfare complaint alleging wrongful diminution or inadequacy of benefits, the typical employment case alleging unfair personnel practices by the state or a need and desire for a job, and the typical licensing case alleging excessive delays or mistakes in handling automobile registration certificates and drivers' licenses. The most common causes underlying complaints were delays because of excessive paperwork, buck-passing, and inadequate understanding by citizens of the law.[37]

Office efficiency was not a hallmark of the lieutenant governors' ombudsman roles. Procedures for complaint handling were developed ad hoc, staffing was sparse, and formal records almost nonexistent. Yet office inefficiencies did not lead to operational ineffectiveness. Thousands of citizens did receive hearings, and significant reductions of friction between agencies and the public were achieved. Moreover, the political ombudsmen were not politically embarrassed when they found that up to fifty per cent of the submitted complaints were unjustified. They reported that they received as many expressions of appreciation from initiators of complaints found after investigation to be unjustified as from those whose complaints were found justified

---

[33] Wyner, Lieutenant Governors as Political Ombudsmen, 12 Bulletin of the Institute of Governmental Studies of the University of California, No. 6 (1971).

[34] *Id.* at 2.

[35] *Id.*

[36] *Id.*

[37] *Id.* at 3.

and were remedied.[38] One of the reasons for the high reported level of efficacy of the lieutenant governors as ombudsmen stemmed from the routine, non-sensational nature of the cases brought to their attention. The substance of the problems had no major ramifications for political survival or advancement.

Wyner concluded that traditional ombudsmen probably enjoy greater public credibility than the lieutenant governors since many citizens view the lieutenant governor-ombudsman as a public relations gimmick to win votes. Nonetheless, "it remains to be seen" whether traditional ombudsmen are more effective in the American polity. In any event, Wyner found the political ombudsman's role viable as long as he does not seek to perform his tasks for political advantage, has an adequate staff, has at least tacit support from the chief executive, and has the cooperation of agency personnel.[39]

IV

TOO MUCH V. TOO LITTLE DISCRETION

Consistent with Payne's stress on mediational aspects of the proposed social worker-ombudsman role, Wyner found that relatively few cases pit the lieutenant governor-ombudsman against agencies in an adversary position. Simply hearing the two sides often allowed the lieutenant governor "to clear the air by informing both parties of his findings."[40] If a dominant need in effectuating redress for citizens is for heightened mediational roles and if the great majority of complaints submitted to the lieutenant governors concerned paperwork, buck-passing and inadequate understanding of the law, it should be apparent that, without detracting from the importance of Davis's emphasis on confining discretion, we need to go beyond seeking better checks and controls. We need equally to determine ways to stimulate imaginativeness, creativity and efficiency in the performance of administrative functions and the delivery of services.

A research project to be undertaken by Professor Larry Hill of the University of Oklahoma will help us to learn, with regard to the federal agencies at least, how much of the problem of administrative discretion is arbitrariness through too much discretion and how much of the problem is indecision and buck-passing because of too little discretion.[41] In his project prospectus Hill notes the evidence of growing public distrust of bureaucracy and comments that, although some citizens complain about their treatment by administrative agencies, we still don't know enough about the nature and subject of the complaints or about the processes and devices for their resolution. In a comprehensive examination of what he terms "the consumption-complaints subsystem" of the American political system, Hill will identify com-

---

[38] *Id.* at 5.

[39] *Id.* at 5, 6.

[40] *Id.* at 4.

[41] Hill, Relationships Between the Rulers and the Ruled: The Consumption of Government and the Processing of Federal Complaints (mimeo) (1972).

plainants and their complaints through analysis of the files of major agencies.[42]
Through interviews with samples of that population, as well as a random sample
of others who may or may not have been complainants, he will seek to measure
and interpret attitudes toward governmental agencies and to correlate experiences
and attitudes of his informants with their pertinent sociological, psychological, and
economic attributes.

Hill will also endeavor to evaluate relationships between ranges of agency discretion and their procedures and practices in responding to complaints.[43] Building
on *Discretionary Justice* as well as on Gellhorn's *When Americans Complain,* he
will be able to speak authoritatively about which Americans complain about what
to whom and with what consequences in their relationships with the federal
bureaucracy.[44] Of course, this assumes wholehearted cooperation by the agencies
with Hill, a state of affairs not invariably borne out by experience—as researchers
from Indiana University and the University of Illinois had occasion to learn recently.

Professors Julius Getman and Stephen Goldberg had to take their case to court
before the high degree of cooperation they thought had been assured by the National
Labor Relations Board reached that level in fact. Getman and Goldberg, both former
NLRB attorneys, had a grant from the National Science Foundation to study voting
in elections ordered by the NLRB. Proposing to question willing employees about
their attitudes toward the bargaining-agent election process and especially about
the impact on their votes of campaign tactics utilized by employers and unions, the
professors asked the agency for the names and home addresses of employees eligible
to vote in the elections they were studying. The Board had established a structure
of rules governing the behavior of parties during a campaign, and the specific purpose
of the Getman-Goldberg study was to provide an empirical foundation for evaluating
these regulations.[45] In April, 1970, the Board denied them the voter lists on the
ground that their study could upset the "laboratory conditions" necessary for conducting a fair election. In August, after negotiations for the lists proved unfruitful,
the professors filed suit in the District Court, claiming that they were entitled to
the lists under the Freedom of Information Act.[46] In January, 1971, the District
Court ruled that the NLRB had failed to establish that it had the authority or
discretion to withhold the requested information, a judgment that was stayed pending appeal.[47] On August 31, 1971, the Court of Appeals for the District of Columbia
Circuit upheld the professors' position and commented that "the Board's position
suffers from the obvious self-justifying tendency of an institution which in over
30 years has itself never engaged in the kind of much needed systematic empirical

[42] *Id.* at 4.
[43] *Id.* at 4-7.
[44] W. GELLHORN, WHEN AMERICANS COMPLAIN: GOVERNMENTAL GRIEVANCE PROCEDURES (1966).
[45] Getman v. NLRB, 450 F.2d 670, 671-72 (D.C. Cir. 1971).
[46] 5 U.S.C. § 552 (1970).
[47] Judge J. Skelly Wright reviewed the history of the case in the course of his Court of Appeals opinion in Getman v. NLRB, 450 F.2d 670, 671-72 (D.C. Cir. 1971).

effort to determine the dynamics of an election campaign or the type of conduct which actually has a coercive impact."[48]

The experience of Getman and Goldberg, even with the delay of almost a year and a half occasioned by the agency's intransigence and the time required for judicial review, shows that redress through the adversary system may still, on occasion, be the most effective means for coping with agency arbitrariness. Regardless of the ultimate contribution of the Getman-Goldberg voting study, countless academic researchers, including Professor Hill, may have occasion to be grateful to the two law professors for establishing so stunningly the right to agency information in the conduct of research.

Side by side with the glow of satisfaction left by the Court of Appeals ruling in the Getman case, there is a malaise engendered by one aspect of the case. The facts suggest that formulation of rules—which the NLRB had prescribed in abundant detail for the conduct of elections—may freeze requirements into a time-worn and dysfunctional mold that stifles innovation and change and evokes blatant arbitrariness in its defense. In channeling and controlling discretion, rule-making must not prevent or discourage reappraisals and revisions of rules. On the contrary, there ought to be built-in provisions in rule-making proceedings for testing and evaluating the functions and consequences of rules at regular intervals. Otherwise, the danger is that the rules may vest, rust, and atrophy, but still be followed rigorously for perhaps no other reason than that often cited by mountain climbers to explain their urges to ascend, "because they're there." How to update and energize administrative practices, how to transcend the administrative syndrome of "I don't make the rules, buddy, I just have to follow them" when the rules have become outmoded, and how to achieve interactions between the public and administrators that deliver justice in individual cases through allocation and channeling of discretion are at least as worthy of attention as how to keep administrators from exercising discretion in whimsical, arbitrary, and unjust ways.

In his discussion in the *Treatise* of interpretations of the rule that no one is entitled to judicial relief until the prescribed administrative remedy has been exhausted, Davis pointed out that the Supreme Court's holdings were often irreconcilable and that "the word formulations in the opinions are inadequate, conflicting and usually affirmatively misleading."[49] He preferred the frank statement by the Court of Claims in *Adler v. U.S.*[50] to the "Supreme Court's absolutes in either one direction or the other."[51] The Court of Claims had asserted that there is no absolute requirement that a party exhaust his administrative remedies before coming into court. "The court may entertain his suit before he has done so, if in its discretion it thinks the circumstances make it appropriate to do so."[52] Just as a "neat word formula"

---

[48] *Id.* at 675.
[49] 3 TREATISE 67.
[50] 146 F. Supp. 956 (Ct. Cl. 1956).
[51] 3 TREATISE 69 n. 9.
[52] 146 F. Supp. 956, 957 (Ct. Cl. 1956).

for exercising such judicial discretion probably is not feasible,[53] there are equal limits and drawbacks to precise formulae for checking administrative discretion. Davis, of course, recognizes this fact in *Discretionary Justice* when he rejects "the extravagant version of the rule of law" that declares that legal rights may be finally determined only by regularly constituted courts and reminds us that "eliminating discretionary power would paralyze governmental processes and would stifle individualized justice."[54] Nonetheless, his stress in striving to reduce injustice to individuals is on cutting back, confining, and checking discretionary power. He does not delineate a framework for coping with categories of cases in which injustice stems from paucity of discretion.

Davis's use of "structure" may provide a solution to this seeming overemphasis on restricting discretion. Although he generally sandwiches references to structuring discretionary power between calls for confining and checking it, thereby fostering the impression that it is another limitation, Davis's proposed instruments for structuring discretion could actually help to invoke and apply it in appropriate cases where it currently lies dormant. He notes that "structuring discretionary power is different from confining it, although the two may overlap"; and his call for open plans, open policy statements, open rules, open findings and reasons, and open precedents can protect against arbitrariness from *failure* to exercise discretion as well as against arbitrariness from its use.[55] Proper structuring of discretion, like the constitutional principle of checks and balances, could pluralize planning and initiative while at the same time facilitating controls over the boundaries of power.

Conclusion

In *Discretionary Justice*, Kenneth Culp Davis added a new dimension to his already monumental contribution to the formulation, analysis, and critique of legal facets of the administrative process. His probe and presentation of a framework for future research into the nuances of discretion, a topic that did not qualify for listing in the index to his *Treatise* a decade earlier, have been instrumental in setting agendas for policy makers, scholars, and practitioners that will enhance the capacity of the administrative process to be both just and fair. In the course of this article, we have examined prototypes of projects and proposals toward these ends, such as the Law Enforcement Study Group at Northwestern University, the Center for Police Administration at Arizona State, Payne's observations about social workers and Wyner's study of lieutenant governors as ombudsmen, Hill's design for determining the nature and consequences of citizen complaints, and Getman's and Goldberg's tests both of the validity of the NLRB's rules for elections and of the NLRB's discretion to withhold information from researchers. Works such as these will assist in resolving the massive problems of administrative regulation today.

---

[53] 3 Treatise 69.
[54] Discretionary Justice 28-44, 217.
[55] *Id.* at 97.

Marver Bernstein recently decried the fact that "after nearly a century of regulatory experience in an industrial economy, we are unable to identify, on the basis of rigorous analysis rather than impressionistic judgments, the requisites of acceptable administrative performance."[56] He urged that the talent and energy devoted to protecting the regulated from unfair procedures and to minimizing effects adverse to regulated clienteles now be targeted on the problem of "designing and improving systems of regulation that have a fighting chance of achieving some useful public result."[57] Perhaps Professor Davis, having completed in *Discretionary Justice* the journey to the second dimension of his professional role, just might be prepared to lead the rest of us into administrative law's Consciousness III.

---

[56] Bernstein, *Independent Regulatory Agencies: A Perspective on Their Reform*, 400 Annals 14, 26 (1972).

[57] *Id.*

JUDICIAL AND ADMINISTRATIVE REVIEW OF GOVERNMENT CONTRACT AWARDS

Richard E. Speidel*

The government, as representative of the community as a whole, cannot be stopped in its tracks by any plaintiff who presents a disputed question of property or contract right.

—Chief Justice Fred M. Vinson[1]

The public interest is not necessarily in the solution adopted by the agency. . . . [I]ndeed . . . the public interest is often identified with settling an issue right rather than settling it quickly.

—Louis L. Jaffe[2]

The basic issue [involves] balancing the public interest in preventing undue judicial interference with ongoing governmental programs against the desire to provide judicial review to individuals claiming that the government has harmed or threatens to harm them . . . .

—Roger C. Cramton[3]

I

THE PROBLEM STATED

Government contracts for supplies, construction, research and development, personal services, and the like are awarded to private business concerns through two basic techniques, formal advertising and negotiation. The standards for choice between and the basic controls upon each of these techniques are set forth in such legislation as the Armed Services Procurement Act and the Federal Property and Administrative Services Act and implemented by complex procurement regulations, such as the Armed Services Procurement Regulation (ASPR) and the Federal Procurement Regulation (FPR),[4] promulgated by the various executive agencies

* Doherty Professor of Law, University of Virginia. I have served as a member of the Remedies Study Group of the Commission on Government Procurement, and as a consultant to the Administrative Conference of the United States. Though owing much to this experience, the views expressed in this article are my own and do not necessarily represent the views or conclusions of the Administrative Conference, the Remedies Study Group, the Commission on Procurement Law, or any other person connected with the Commission. I wish to thank Mr. Carl Eastwick, University of Virginia School of Law, Class of 1972, for his valuable assistance in the preparation of this article. I am also indebted to my colleague, Ernest Gellhorn, whose perceptive comments eased my uncertain passage from commercial to administrative law.

[1] Larson v. Domestic & Foreign Commerce Corp., 337 U.S. 682, 704 (1949).
[2] L. JAFFE, JUDICIAL CONTROL OF ADMINISTRATIVE ACTION 693 (1965).
[3] Cramton, *Nonstatutory Review of Federal Administrative Action: The Need for Statutory Reform of Sovereign Immunity, Subject Matter Jurisdiction, and Parties Defendant*, 68 MICH. L. REV. 387, 400 (1970).
[4] Armed Services Procurement Act, 10 U.S.C. §§ 2304-05 (1970); Armed Services Procurement Regulations, 32 C.F.R. pts. 2-3 (1971); Federal Property and Administrative Services Act, 41 U.S.C. §§ 252-53 (1970); Federal Procurement Regulations, 41 C.F.R. pts. 1-2, 1-3 (1972). For some purposes, these implementing regulations have the force of law. *See*, Grossbaum, *Procedural Fairness in Public Contracts: The Procurement Regulations*, 57 VA. L. REV. 171, 185-209 (1971).

and departments. In addition, each agency has its own set of internal procurement regulations and operating instructions which further delegate and define the power of agents to bind the United States by contract.[5]

Formal advertising is, by statute, the preferred method of procurement.[6] This highly structured method is administered under a set of detailed and tightly drawn standard forms and regulations which are designed, in the words of the Court of Claims, "to give everyone an equal right to compete for Government business . . . ."[7] Negotiation, whereby roughly eighty-five per cent of the total government expenditure for procurement is obligated, is conducted with much less formality but, in theory at least, with the same concern for competitive pricing.[8] Under both methods of procurement, bids or offers are solicited from a pool of prospective contractors and are evaluated on the grounds of price, responsiveness to the invitation for bids or request for proposals, and the responsibility—that is, the capacity, credit, and integrity—of the potential contractor. A critical difference between the two methods of procurement is the degree of control imposed by statute and regulation upon contracting officers. In formal advertising, Congress, to obtain competitive prices and equality of access, relies upon a system within which contracting officers have relatively little discretion. If the system works, basic legislative policies are supposedly achieved. In negotiation, Congress relies more upon executive judgment and discretion to achieve similar objectives in procurements where formal advertising is not practical or feasible, either because of urgency, the complexity or experimental nature of what is being purchased, or the absence of multiple sources of supply.[9] The constant tension between these methods of procurement mirrors a deeper conflict between two different kinds of public interests in the procurement process.

---

[5] It is well established that, without more, executive officers have a "capacity . . . to contract" that is "co-extensive with the duties and powers of government." More specifically, there is power to contract "in every case where it is necessary to the execution of a public duty." United States v. Maurice, 26 F. Cas. 1211, 1217 (No. 15,747) (C.C.D. Va. 1823). See United States v. Tingey, 30 U.S. (5 Pet.) 248 (1831); United States v. Salon, 182 F.2d 110 (7th Cir. 1950). Professor Whelan has provided two interesting studies of the process whereby authority is delegated and limited within a particular agency and the legal effect when an executive officer exceeds his actual authority in the contracting process: Whelan & Phillips, Government Contracts: Emphasis on Government, 29 LAW & CONTEMP. PROB. 315, 331-42 (1964); Whelan & Dunigan, Government Contracts: Apparent Authority and Estoppel, 55 GEO. L.J. 830 (1967).

[6] "Purchases of and contracts for property or services covered by this chapter shall be made by formal advertising in all cases in which the use of such method is feasible and practicable under the existing conditions and circumstances." 10 U.S.C. § 2304(a) (1970); 32 C.F.R. § 2.102-1(a) (1971).

[7] Prestex, Inc. v. United States, 320 F.2d 367, 372 (Ct. Cl. 1963).

[8] See 10 U.S.C. § 2304(g) (1970), as amended, Pub. L. No. 90-500 (Sept. 20, 1968); 32 C.F.R. § 3.101 (1971); Schoenbrod v. United States, 410 F.2d 400 (Ct. Cl. 1969) (competitive negotiation policy). It has been suggested that truly open competition for advanced technical systems is not possible and that such competition as does exist "is not a significant factor in controlling costs, nor does it affect efficiency directly." Drake, Major DOD Procurements at War with Reality, HARV. BUS. REV., Jan.-Feb., 1970, at 119, 120. See Moore, Efficiency and Public Policy in Defense Procurement, 29 LAW & CONTEMP. PROB. 3 (1964).

[9] 10 U.S.C. § 2304(a) (1970). See Pierson, Standing to Seek Judicial Review of Government Contract Awards: Its Origins, Rationale and Effect on the Procurement Process, 12 B.C. IND. & COM. L. REV. 1, 26-41 (1970).

The first is the practical need for executive officers to have power effectively to implement public programs or satisfy agency needs from private sources of supply. This need is implicit in Professor Mitchell's theory of governmental effectiveness[10] and may be the primary justification for what remains of the sovereign immunity doctrine.[11] The second is a broader and perhaps overriding Congressional concern that the award process achieve competitive pricing and insure equality of access to the procurement dollar. In addition, there are diverse social and economic policies, rooted in statute and Executive Order, which are to be implemented through the contracting process. These policies, which are somewhat collateral to the business of getting timely supplies and quality services at fair prices, include preferences for small business and economically disadvantaged areas, a condition that government contractors and subcontractors provide equal employment opportunities, and a requirement that contractors "buy American."[12] The potential for collision between the ongoing procurement process and these restraints upon eligibility for award is great indeed. A contracting officer may honestly and correctly believe that the procurement could be accomplished more efficiently if the agency is permitted to deal quickly and exclusively with a reliable supplier who charges a bit more and is neither a small business concern nor an equal opportunity employer. Yet action according to this belief could exceed or abuse the limited authority actually delegated to him.

---

[10] J. MITCHELL, THE CONTRACTS OF PUBLIC AUTHORITIES: A COMPARATIVE STUDY 6-7 (1954); Mitchell, *A General Theory of Public Contracts*, 63 JURIDICAL REV. 60 (1951). For discussions of this theory in other contexts, see Frenzen, *The Administrative Contract in the United States*, 37 GEO. WASH. L. REV. 270 (1968); Speidel, *Implied Duties of Cooperation and the Defense of Sovereign Acts in Government Contracts*, 51 GEO. L.J. 516 (1963).

[11] While speaking about intergovernmental tax immunity, Mr. Justice Frankfurter caught the essence of governmental effectiveness:

". . . The distinction [between direct and indirect taxes] embodies a considered judgment as to the minimum safeguard necessary for the National Government to carry on its essential functions without hindrance from the exercise of power by another sovereign within the same territory. That in a particular case there may in fact be no conflict in the exercise of the two governmental powers is not to the point. It is in avoiding the potentialities of friction and furthering the smooth operation of complicated governmental machinery that the constitutional doctrine of immunity finds its explanation and justification." City of Detroit v. Murray Corp., 355 U.S. 489, 504 (1958) (dissenting opinion). Compare Perkins v. Lukens Steel Co., 310 U.S. 113, 130 (1940), where the Court, speaking through Mr. Justice Black, stated,

"Courts should not . . . subject purchasing agencies of Government to the delays necessarily incident to judicial scrutiny at the instance of potential sellers, which would be contrary to traditional governmental practice and would create a new concept of judicial controversies. A like restraint applied to purchasing by private business would be widely condemned as an intolerable business handicap. It is . . . essential to the even and expeditious functioning of Government that the administration of the purchasing machinery be unhampered."

[12] For the classic study, see Miller & Pierson, *Observations on the Consistency of Federal Procurement Policies with Other Governmental Policies*, 29 LAW & CONTEMP. PROB. 277 (1964). For recent developments, see Contractors Ass'n of E. Pa. v. Shultz, 442 F.2d 159 (3d Cir. 1971), *cert. denied*, 92 S. Ct. 98 (1971) (Philadelphia Plan upheld); Leiken, *Preferential Treatment in the Skilled Building Trades: An Analysis of the Philadelphia Plan*, 56 CORNELL L. REV. 84 (1970); Sky, *Defense Procurement Preferences as a Remedy for Subemployment: A Comment*, 82 HARV. L. REV. 1266 (1969) (while price differentials magnify departures from traditional procurement aims, costs are outweighed by gains achieved in the ghetto). For another perspective, see *DOD Irked at Growing Social Responsibilities*, AIR FORCE MANAGEMENT, Jan., 1970, at 48.

There are, of course, substantial private interests involved in this public award process. The United States does not rely upon "in-house" sources, condemnation, requisition, or mandatory orders to implement public programs. Rather, private concerns must be induced by the prospect of profitable contracts to invest the often substantial sums necessary to be in a position to compete with other bidders. While this undertaking is replete with business risks, it is the opportunity to compete and the prospect of profitable awards that holds the public contracting system together.[13]

Profit, in this context, is a broad concept. The failure to receive an expected award could mean the loss of net gains on the particular contract or the loss of valuable experience needed to compete for and earn future awards. Both are important to the firm's long-range profit picture. Losses other than of net gains are also involved. At the very least, the expenses incurred in preparing to compete may be wasted.[14] At the other extreme, losing the award of a contract destined to be a "sure loser" may mean the difference between business survival and bankruptcy. At a time of economic instability where there is fierce competition for scarce awards, the paradigm of the healthy government contractor who wins some and loses others and yet is still willing and able to compete is suspect.[15] This suspicion is reinforced by the increasing dependence of business concerns upon government spending through contracts and the disruptive impact of spending cutbacks upon the communities in which these businesses are located. As in other areas of governmental operations, the reality of dependence has eroded the traditional right-privilege distinction[16] and has stimulated remarkable candor by some courts:

---

[13] Professor Reich has pointed out that the "opportunity for private profit is intended to serve as a lure to make private operators serve the public" and that only a contractor's "right to profits and his control over how the job is done distinguish his private status." Reich, *The New Property*, 73 YALE L.J. 733, 745 (1964). The same point has been made about public contracts in Great Britain, another economy which features a blurring or fusion of public and private interests. *See* Turpin, *Government Contracts: A Study of Methods of Contracting*, 31 MOD. L. REV. 241 (1968). Apparently agreeing that public contracts are "undoubtedly" located in the "area too large to be comfortable, in which the market economy does not automatically look after the public interest," H. CATHERWOOD, THE CHRISTIAN IN INDUSTRIAL SOCIETY 35 (2d ed. 1966), Mr. Donald Frenzen has urged that the theories which underlie private contracts be replaced by an administrative contract. Frenzen, *supra* note 10. *See also* Mewett, *The Theory of Government Contracts*, 5 McGILL L.J. 222 (1959). For a particularly stimulating discussion of these and other developments, see Smith, *Accountability and Independence in the Contract State*, in THE DILEMMA OF ACCOUNTABILITY IN MODERN GOVERNMENT 3-69 (B. Smith & D. Hague eds. 1971). For discussions of the business risks and strategies of competitive bidding, see Stark & Mayer, *Some Multi-Contract Decision-Theoretic Competitive Bidding Models*, 19 OPERATIONS RESEARCH 469 (1971); Anderson, *Handling Risk in Defense Contracting*, HARV. BUS. REV., July-Aug., 1969, at 90.

[14] These expenses are, however, deductible as "ordinary and necessary" business expenses, INT. REV. CODE of 1954 § 162(a), unless the business is on a "completed contract" method of accounting, whereupon they are treated as business losses under INT. REV. CODE of 1954 § 165(a).

[15] Even more suspicious is Professor Reich's assertion that it is "virtually impossible to lose money" on government contracts. Reich, *supra* note 13, at 735. See *Contractors Claw at the Money Door*, BUS. WEEK, Jan. 2, 1971, at 14, where it is stated that inflation and the substantial drop in defense spending has changed contractor behavior patterns. Where previously they tended to minimize and settle disputes at the lowest possible level, they now protest more frequently and visibly, risk ire by filing claims for extras, and ask to be declared essential to maintenance of the mobilization base.

[16] The "right-privilege" distinction in government contracts reached its zenith in Perkins v. Lukens

The consequences of administrative termination of all right to bid or contract, colloquially called "blacklisting" and formally called suspension or debarment, will vary, depending upon multiple factors: the size and prominence of the contractor; the ratio of his government business to non-governmet business; the length of his contractual relationship with government; his dependence on that business; his ability to secure other business as a substitute for government business. These are some of the basic factors involved. The impact of debarment on a contractor may be a sudden contraction of bank credit, adverse impact on market price of shares of listed stock, if any, and critical uneasiness of creditors generally, to say nothing of "loss of face" in the business community. These consequences are in addition to the loss of specific profits from the business denied as a result of debarment. We need not resort to a colorful term such as "stigma" to characterize the consequences of such governmental action, for labels may blur the issues. But we strain no concept of judicial notice to acknowledge these basic facts of economic life.[17]

The critical question, therefore, is how much protection this private economic interest should receive against award decisions which exceed or abuse the actual authority delegated to contracting officers.[18] In approaching this question, the

---

Steel Co., 310 U.S. 113 (1940), where the Court stressed that procurement statutes and regulations were managerial and conferred no rights upon prospective contractors to whom no contract had been awarded. *See also* Cafeteria Workers Union v. McElroy, 367 U.S. 886, 896 (1961) (summary dismissal of federal employee upheld because in its "proprietary military capacity, the Federal Government . . . has traditionally exercised unfettered control" and because the action involved the government's "dispatch of its own internal affairs.") The decline of the distinction in other areas of governmental operations, principally welfare spending, has been notable. *See* Goldberg v. Kelly, 397 U.S. 254 (1970); R. O'NEIL, THE PRICE OF DEPENDENCY 251-318 (1970); Van Alstyne, *Demise of the Right-Privilege Distinction in Constitutional Law*, 81 HARV. L. REV. 1439 (1968); Note, *Another Look at Unconstitutional Conditions*, 117 U. PA. L. REV. 144 (1968). *Cf.* Summers, *The Technique Element in Law*, 59 CALIF. L. REV. 733, 739-41 (1971) (legal ordering and control are essential elements when public benefits are conferred). The attack on the distinction in government contracts has been persistent, *see, e.g.*, K. DAVIS, DISCRETIONARY JUSTICE: A PRELIMINARY INQUIRY 177-80 (1969); JAFFE, *supra* note 2, at 369-71; Schwartz, *Crucial Areas in Administrative Law*, 34 GEO. WASH. L. REV. 401, 430-42 (1966); Miller, *Administrative Discretion in the Award of Federal Contracts*, 53 MICH. L. REV. 781, 803 (1955), and not without some impact in the courts. As the distinction continues to erode, the ultimate questions are, what are the "rights" of disappointed bidders, and how can they best be protected in a system of broad standards, wide discretion, and, because of the fact of dependency upon government spending, a relationship that is fundamentally coercive.

[17] Gonzalez v. Freeman, 334 F.2d 570, 574 (D.C. Cir. 1964) (Burger, J.).

[18] A number of questions about the propriety of contract award decisions are raised by those competing for government business. In one category is the prospective contractor who complains that he and perhaps others similarly situated have improperly been excluded from competing for government business. The actions complained of may include debarment or suspension, bidding conditions which he is unable or unwilling to meet, an inadequate solicitation for bids, or unduly restrictive specifications. Parties in this category normally have a continuing interest in and a general investment in a capacity to compete for government contracts, but have not actually made any expenditures toward a particular contract. For a recent example, see Ballerina Pen Co. v. Kunzig, 433 F.2d 1204 (D.C. Cir. 1970). A second and larger category includes actual but disappointed bidders on particular contracts who complain about decisions made in the award process. These complaints take two basic forms, either that the opportunity fairly to compete has been impaired and should be restored or that the disappointed bidder was entitled to a contract which went to someone else. The substance of the complaint might involve one or more of the following: (a) the contract should have been awarded through formal advertising rather than negotiation (or vice versa); (b) the invitation for bids or the proposed specifications were so defective or ambiguous as to preclude competition on an equal basis;

reciprocal dependence of the government upon the private sector of the economy must be taken into account. Both agency effectiveness and overriding Congressional policies would seem to depend, in the long run, upon a broad base of willing and able prospective contractors. Usual business risks aside, if a pattern of award decisions exists which seem to deviate from the "rules of the game" and there is no effective way to improve or reverse the pattern, a realistic cost-benefit analysis might induce many firms to stop or cut back competition for government business and reallocate resources to other commerical markets.[19] Given this possibility, the loss to and of particular contractors would not necessarily be offset by the assertion that the award process works well most of the time and that occasional defects will be corrected in the next procurement.

Assuming the importance of the private interest and the need for balancing

---

(c) one or more bidders had an unfair opportunity after the time for bid opening had passed to withdraw or modify his bid; (d) the contracting officer erroneously determined that a bid was or was not responsive to the invitation or that a bidder was or was not responsible; (e) the decision to prefer one bidder over another, made after evaluating complex, technical proposals, was erroneous; or (f) the decision to cancel an advertisement or solicitation and try again was improper.

There are an infinite number of variations on these themes, all of which are complicated by the degree of discretion given by statute and regulation to the contracting officer. Consider, for example, what is involved in the decision to cancel the invitation and try again. The Armed Services Procurement Act provides that "all bids may be rejected if the head of the agency determines that rejection is in the public interest." 10 U.S.C. § 2305(c) (1970). The head of the agency, however, may delegate this power to a subordinate officer, and there is no statutory requirement that the decision to reject all bids be reduced to a writing containing the findings which justify it. The Armed Services Procurement Regulation (ASPR), 32 C.F.R. § 2.404-1 (1971), however, states that "the preservation of the integrity of the competitive bid system dictates that after bids have been opened, award must be made to that responsible bidder who submitted the lowest responsible bid, unless there is a compelling reason to reject all bids and cancel the invitation." To cancel an invitation after opening but before award, the contracting officer, to whom the cancellation power is delegated, must determine in writing that one or more of eight possible justifying conditions exist, including that the "supplies or services being provided are no longer required," or "all acceptable bids received were at unreasonable prices" or "for other reasons, cancellation is clearly in the best interest of the Government." As might be expected, both GAO and the courts have been reluctant to overturn decisions to cancel an invitation unless there was a clear abuse of discretion. 49 Comp. Gen. 683 (1970); M. Steinthal & Co. v. Seamans, 455 F.2d 1289 (D.C. Cir. 1971). Cf. Citizens to Preserve Overton Park v. Volpe, 401 U.S. 402, 413-16 (1971); Comment, The Supreme Court, 1970 Term, 85 Harv. L. Rev. 38, 315-25 (1971).

[19] In an earlier article I stated:

"In an enlightened public purchasing process, both the public and private interests should be identified, evaluated and given protection commensurate with the actual needs of that process. On the Government's side, one such basic need is for a broad base of capable contractors who are willing and able to satisfy the Government's purchasing requirements; another is for efficient and economical operation. The inherent difficulty, however, is that if, in the name of the public interest in economy, a broad imposition of risk is made on private contractors, the public interest in a broad base of capable producers may be impaired. Without reasonable assurance of a fair profit the capable, responsible contractor may divert his productive energy to private commercial undertakings." Speidel, supra note 10 at 516-7.

I would only add that whether the contractor will divert his productive energy depends upon the transaction costs incurred in preparing to deal in another or different market or reorganizing the firm. If because of size, specialization, or other variations on the dependence theme, the rearrangement is excessively costly, the contractor may decide to forego the activity altogether or continue to compete despite the harmful effect complained of. This latter point is well made in Drake, supra note 8, at 120: "A company that has prepared itself to compete in this market cannot readily redirect its energies into the commercial market place. Competition requires a deep and relatively inflexible commitment to serving the needs of the DOD." See also Coase, The Problem of Social Cost, 3 J. Law & Econ. 1 (1960).

it with the often conflicting public interests in the award process, the more particular inquiry becomes when and how can a disappointed bidder insist that a decision be right rather than quick. In almost every case, the most effective way to protect the private and the overriding public interest will be for the contracting officer to stop, reverse the wrong decision, and continue the award process according to the rules.[20] There are, of course, costs to governmental effectiveness in this approach, primarily in delay and the effort to undertake a reconsideration. But who is to tell the contracting officer to stop and for how long? Who has power to order the contracting officer to play the game according to the rules and when should this power be exercised? The complexity of these questions is obvious—a price to be paid for a government of separate powers and a procurement process that has evolved as a pragmatic, unplanned response to governmental needs.[21] The answers are not made easier by the plain fact that if a court is the body empowered to act, the relief most appropriate from the plaintiff's perspective—a temporary or preliminary injunction pending a decision on the merits followed by a mandatory injunction—poses the greatest threat to governmental effectiveness. Yet anything short of this permits the award process in the particular procurement to continue at the discretion of contracting officials. If the decision complained of was in fact wrong, the agency will be reluctant to cancel the contract and start over. Thus, protection of the private interest will be left to the remote prospect of damages in the Court of Claims, and protection of the overriding public interest in an award system operating in accordance with law will depend on the uncertain pressures of the political process.

With these problems in mind, let us next examine the extent to which a disappointed and protesting bidder can, through either administrative or judicial review, stop the award process "in its tracks" pending an authoritative determination of the validity of the proposed action.

II

ADMINISTRATIVE REVIEW

Disappointed bidders have two primary administrative channels within which to protest an award decision. The first is within the procuring agency itself, the protest being lodged with the contracting officer or his superiors. The second is to

---

[20] Another cost of this action may be to the competitor unfortunate enough to have received an allegedly erroneous award. If the contract is cancelled and the award was illegal, the contractor's recovery is limited to restitution. *See* Campbell v. Tennessee Valley Authority, 421 F.2d 293 (5th Cir. 1969). If the award was not illegal, the contractor's recovery for the improper cancellation is limited to actual expenses incurred plus profit on any work done. *See* G. C. Casebolt Co. v. United States, 421 F.2d 710 (Ct. Cl. 1970). Ironically, the contractor's position improves if, after a protest, performance is permitted to continue while a decision on legality is being reached. The Comptroller General is reluctant to direct cancellation, *see* 49 COMP. GEN. 639 (1970), and the courts, seemingly, require a more egregious error before willing to enjoin performance. *See* Keco Indus., Inc. v. Laird, 318 F. Supp. 1361 (D.D.C. 1970). This, of course, works to the disadvantage of the protesting bidder.

[21] This point is made in Stover, *The Government Contract System as a Problem in Public Policy*, 32 GEO. WASH. L. REV. 701 (1964).

the General Accounting Office (GAO), the protest being lodged with the Comptroller General. Frequently, a protest will be made in both channels, with a Congressman or Secretary thrown in for good measure. Despite procedures designed to facilitate administrative review, these channels have been relatively unsuccessful in stopping the award process or contract performance until a decision on the merits has been reached. Let us briefly consider why this is so.

A. Within the Procuring Agency

Most executive departments or agencies have some published procedures for internal review of contracting officer decisions in the award process.[22] Despite wide variances, all can be triggered by a protest from a disappointed bidder. How the protest is processed depends, in turn, upon whether it is made before or after award and whether the GAO has become involved.[23] Assuming for a moment that GAO is not involved, what chance might a bidder on an Air Force contract have to stop the award process pending internal review? More specifically, suppose that the Aeronautical Systems Division (ASD) at Wright-Patterson Air Force Base has been negotiating a complex contract and, after extensive evaluation, has decided to award the contract to Bidder A. Bidder B, who learns of the decision before the award is made, files a written protest with the contracting officer, claiming that the evaluation was erroneous and that he was entitled to the award.

Armed Services Procurement Regulation (ASPR) 2-407.8 provides that the contracting officer "shall consider all protests . . . to the award of a contract" and requires that notice of the protest be given to "other persons . . . involved in or affected by the protest" so that they may submit their views and supply relevant information. A general policy is stated in ASPR 2-407.8(a)(4): "Timely action on protests is essential to avoid undue delay in procurements and to assure fair treatment to protesting firms or individuals. Accordingly, protests should be handled on a priority basis." While ASPR and the implementing Air Force regulations state what shall be in the protest file and who shall decide the protest, they provide no procedures or standards for internal review.[24]

---

[22] Basic regulations governing bid protests are found in the Armed Services Procurement Regulation (ASPR), 32 C.F.R. §§ 2.407.8, 3-509 (1971) (military procurement), and the Federal Procurement Regulation (FPR), 41 C.F.R. § 1-2.407-8 (1971) (non-military procurement). Supplementary procedures for different agencies and departments exist. *See, e.g.,* Army Procurement Procedure (APP) 2-407.8 (1 Apr. 1970), 5 CCH Gov't Cont. Rep. ¶ 38,235; Navy Procurement Directives (NPD) 2-407.9 (Mar. 1971), 6 CCH Gov't Cont. Rep. ¶ 63,330; General Services Procurement Regulation (GSPR), 41 C.F.R. §§ 5-2.407-8, 5-2.408 (1971); National Aeronautics and Space Administration Procurement Regulation (NASAPR), 41 C.F.R. §§ 18-2.407-8, 3.111 (1971); Atomic Energy Comm'n Procurement Regulation (AECPR), 41 C.F.R. § 9-2.407-8 (1971).

[23] A direct protest to GAO shifts the responsibility for decision from the agency to the Comptroller General. In any case, the agency must prepare a file and report on the protest for GAO. See ASPR, 32 C.F.R. § 2-407.8(a)(2), (4) & (5) (1971). If protest is made to GAO before award, the contracting officer's decision to continue the award process must be approved by superior officers after GAO advice is given regarding the status of the protest. ASPR, 32 C.F.R. § 2-407.8(b)(2) (1971); Headquarters United States Air Force, ASPR Supp. (HQ USAF ASPR Supp.) ₂-407.9(b)(3), 5 CCH Gov't Cont. Rep. ¶ 41,542.20 (1970).

[24] *See* HQ USAF ASPR Supp. 2.407.9, 5 CCH Gov't Cont. Rep. ¶ 41,542.20 (1970).

In most cases, the final decision on the protest will be made at a major command headquarters, such as the Air Force Systems Command (AFSC), rather than by the contracting officer.[25] However, the primary decision to stop the procurement process or make the award to Bidder A remains with the contracting officer, subject to ASPR 2-407.8(b)(3). This subsection provides that when a written protest prior to award is made, "award shall not be made until the matter is resolved, unless the contracting officer determines that: (i) the items to be procured are urgently required; or (ii) delivery or performance will be unduly delayed by failure to make award promptly; or (iii) a prompt award will otherwise be advantageous to the government." In sharp contrast, if the protest is made after award, ASPR 2-407.8(c) provides that the contracting officer "should seek a mutual agreement with the successful offeror to suspend performance on a no-cost basis" when it "appears likely that an award may be invalidated" and a delay is not prejudicial to the government's interest.[26] Finally, a decision to award the contract to Bidder A after a protest from Bidder B need not be approved by superior officers unless a protest has also been filed with GAO.[27]

A charitable cynic might observe that the deck is stacked against the protesting bidder. In the absence of an early debriefing, he will be lucky to know enough to protest before award is made, and timing is obviously critical in this situation. Even with a protest before award, the decision to suspend the award process is left to the contracting officer from whose decision the bidder is appealing. If the contracting officer has consulted extensively with his "team" of experts before making the decision and considerations of urgency are present, the probabilities of achieving a suspension pending review seem slim indeed.

Unfortunately, there is little persuasive data available on the effectiveness of internal bid protests procedures in the Air Force or other executive departments. A synopsis of forty-seven bid protests involving AFSC during fiscal year 1970,[28] for example, shows that thirty-one protests were made prior to award and that relief of some sort was granted in seven of these cases. In the sixteen post-award protests, the requested relief of cancellation was granted in two cases. However, there is no indication in the synopsis in which cases the award process was actually suspended or for what reasons or for how long. Further, in thirty-four of the forty-seven protests and eight of the nine cases where some relief was granted, a direct protest to the GAO was also filed thereby preempting the internal review process. This data may confirm that many bidders believe that even the Air Force protest pro-

---

[25] An Air Force contracting officer decides a protest filed with him "only if he is satisfied that the protest is without any reasonable degree of foundation." HQ USAF ASPR Supp. 2.407.9(b)(2)(iv), 5 CCH Gov't Cont. Rep. ¶ 41,542.20 (1970). Otherwise, the protest is resolved at a major command level or higher. HQ USAF ASPR Supp. 2-407.9(a), 5 CCH Gov't Cont. Rep. ¶ 41,542.20 (1970).

[26] The critical importance of a timely protest is illustrated in Comp. Gen. B-169754 (23 Dec. 1970), where the protest was filed within minutes after award, performance under the awarded contract was not suspended and a final GAO decision was made 7 months later.

[27] See note 23 supra.

[28] The synopsis was prepared for the Commission on Government Procurement by the AFSC.

cedures, reputed to be among the best, offer little opportunity to stop the award process pending review. On the other hand, the ready availability of GAO bid protest procedures and the prospect of an independent review may be viewed as impairing the development of effective internal procedures and undermining the efforts of procurement officials to avoid and settle protests as quickly and fairly as possible.[29] However one reads the equivocal data, the potential for effective internal administrative review remains largely unrealized.

B. The General Accounting Office

Under interim GAO rules on "Bid Protest Procedures and Standards,"[30] an "interested party" may protest the award or proposed award of a contract by letter or telegram to GAO. The protest should identify the procurement and agency involved and state "the specific grounds upon which the protest is based." The contracting officer involved is provided with a copy of the protest. The popularity of the direct protest is attested by the fact that GAO received 1054 protests in fiscal year 1971—a thirty-seven per cent increase over fiscal year 1970.[31]

If the protest is not withdrawn, current procedures permit the protestor and others who have "a substantial and reasonable" prospect of receiving the award to have a "reasonable opportunity to present views," including a conference with a GAO attorney who has been assigned primary responsibility for handling the protest. The procuring agency's case is contained in the file and report submitted to GAO after the direct protest is filed. A written decision, often lengthy, is then made on this record but without a formal hearing or efforts to subpoena witnesses or documents.[32] These decisions review the challenged exercise of agency discretion under standards similar to those employed by courts and tend, when the evidence is balanced, to uphold rather than to reverse the agency action.[33] Nevertheless, of the

---

[29] According to Cibinic and Lasken, this "may be unfortunate since the operating agencies are probably better equipped by reason of practical experience, to determine which course of action would be in the Government's best interest." Cibinic & Lasken, *The Comptroller General and Government Contracts*, 38 GEO. WASH. L. REV. 349, 383 (1970). Informal discussions with Air Force procurement officials reveal that a stated objective is to avoid or minimize protests in the award process. Suggested methods for accomplishing this include: (a) develop incentives for contracting officers to follow more completely purchasing policies and procedures; (b) better preparation of solicitations for bids and more clarity and completeness in the criteria for evaluation; (c) earlier and more complete briefings— that is, information to unsuccessful bidders as to what happened and why; (d) more centralized administration of internal bid protest activities; (e) a more systematic collection of bid protest data.

[30] 4 C.F.R. pt. 20 (1972).

[31] For a discussion of these statistics, see 13 GOVERNMENT CONTRACTOR ¶ 411 (1971).

[32] A concise discussion of GAO practice and procedure is found in Schnitzer, Handling Bid Protests Before GAO (Briefing Paper No. 70-3, Federal Publications, Inc. 1970).

[33] Since GAO usually does not have any independent means of deciding disputed issues of fact, it adopts a presumption in favor of the contracting agency's version of disputed facts and this prevails unless the protestor can clearly prove facts to the contrary. *See* 49 COMP. GEN. 463, 469 (1970); 42 COMP. GEN. 346, 352-53 (1963). As for the standards of review, "it is a responsibility of our Office to insure that Government procurements are made in accordance with applicable law, and this necessarily involves review of the administrative discretion to the extent necessary to insure that such discretion has been exercised within proper limits. . . . In this regard, we have adopted the general rule that we will not substitute our judgment for that of the contracting officer, unless it is shown by

715 protests actually decided in fiscal year 1971, some relief was granted in seventy-four, or eleven per cent.

Several objections to the GAO role are frequently made, including alleged lack of statutory power, substandard procedures, and doubts about the propriety of an auditing agency lodged in the legislative branch being involved in what appears to be the adjudication of private protests against executive action.[34] From the protestor's perpective, however, the loudest complaints are against the time required to resolve a protest and the inability or unwillingness of GAO to direct the contracting officer to suspend the award process pending decision or cancel an award once made.[35] In fiscal year 1971, the average time to resolve a protest was 106 days. Given this delay, the probabilities are that the contract will be awarded and performance will be underway at the time of decision, even though the contracting officer's decision to proceed must be approved by superior officers. Here the fiscal year 1971 statistics show that of the seventy-four protests where some relief was granted, only four decisions, or five per cent, recommended cancellation of a contract. Notwithstanding the conceded beneficial impact of these decisions on the award process as a whole, disappointed bidders have been known to complain about pyrrhic victories where protests are sustained without either the award or damages being obtained.[36]

---

convincing evidence that a determination was arbitrary, or not based on substantial evidence." 48 COMP. GEN. 689, 696-97 (1969). For variations on this theme, see 49 COMP. GEN. 683, 685-86 (1970) (technical evaluation is matter of administrative discretion which will not be disturbed in absence of clear showing that determination was arbitrary); 49 COMP. GEN. 463, 471 (1970). In a decision of major importance, the Supreme Court has decided, *inter alia*, that GAO's power to review final agency post-award decisions under the contract disputes procedure is limited to allegations of fraud or bad faith. S&E Contractors, Inc. v. United States, 406 U.S. 1 (1972).

[34] *See* Cibinic & Lasken, *The Comptroller General and Government Contracts*, 38 GEO. WASH. L. REV. 349, 372-84 (1970). For discussion of the GAO functions of auditing and claims settlement, see S. Doc. No. 96, 87th Cong., 2d Sess. (1962); Note, 70 HARV. L. REV. 350 (1956). A complete collection of the various complaints about the GAO bid protest role can be found in the ABA SECTION ON PUBLIC CONTRACT LAW, REPORT OF THE COMMITTEE ON BIDS AND PROTESTS (1971).

[35] GAO takes the position that it cannot require the agency to withhold contract award pending a decision on the protest. *See* Schnitzer, *supra* note 32, at 4. However, GAO does, upon occasion, direct the agency to cancel a contract award which was improperly made. *See* 48 COMP. GEN. 589 (1969). If this direction is followed, the terminated contractor may sue for damages in the Court of Claims. *See* discussion accompanying note 47 *infra*. The basis for this direction to cancel is, according to the Comptroller General, his responsibility to "recommend or direct such action as we believe is required by the public policy expressed in applicable statutory enactments to preserve the integrity of the competitive bidding system" and his power under the Budget and Accounting Act of 1921 to "disallow credit in the accounts of the Government's fiscal officers for any payments out of appropriated funds made pursuant to an illegal contract." 44 COMP. GEN. 221, 223 (1964). *See* Meyer, *The Role of the Comptroller General in Awarding Formally Advertised Contracts*, 18 AD. L. REV. 39 (1966); Schnitzer, *Changing Concepts in Government Procurement—The Role and Influence of the Comptroller General on Contracting Officer's Operations*, 23 FED. B.J. 90 (1963). *But see* Keco Indus., Inc. v. Laird, 318 F. Supp. 1361 (D.D.C. 1970) (a Comptroller General opinion on the legality of a contract is not binding on the courts and the Comptroller General cannot order award or termination of a contract).

[36] SELECT SENATE COMMITTEE ON SMALL BUSINESS, SELECTED PROBLEMS OF SMALL BUSINESS IN THE AREA OF FEDERAL PROCUREMENT, S. REP. No. 1671, 90th Cong., 2d Sess. (1968) (GAO remedies too little and too late).

In summary, while GAO exists as an eager alternative to internal agency review and is quite capable of catching and exposing agency impropriety, its primary impact has been upon the ongoing award system rather than protecting private interests in particular protests. The agency frequently is told to correct a deficiency the next time, but nothing is done to disturb actions already taken.[37] Given the strong private economic interests involved and the inability of administrative review in either channel consistently to stop the award process pending a decision on the merits, it is not surprising that disappointed bidders and their attorneys have turned with renewed vigor to the courts.

III

Judicial Review: The Rise and Fall of Injunctive Relief

A. Prior to *Scanwell*

Prior to January 1970, the date of *Scanwell Laboratories, Inc. v. Shaffer*,[38] unsuccessful bidders seeking declaratory or injunctive relief were rarely able to obtain judicial review of contract award decisions. The primary reason was that the plaintiff had no standing to sue because he had no "right" to a government contract which could be invaded by improper governmental action. This was reinforced by the notion that procurement statutes were enacted and regulations were promulgated for the benefit of the public as a whole and that deviations by executive officers must be rectified through the political rather than the judicial process.[39] A secondary reason was rooted in the doctrine of sovereign immunity. Since Congress had not expressly consented to suits of this sort, the United States was immune unless the officer sued had acted beyond his actual authority or in an unconstitutional manner.[40] Otherwise, the suit and its invariable request for equitable relief was against the United States and barred under *Larson v. Domestic & Foreign Commerce Corp.*[41]

Beneath the labels "standing," "sovereign immunity," and "proprietary functions" invoked to deny review was a fear that judicial review backed by injunctive relief would impair governmental effectiveness in implementing public programs through contracts:

---

[37] "Corrective action (cancellation) at this date would be impracticable and inconsistent with the government's interest. We strongly recommend the procurement procedures at the buying activity be reviewed in the light of this protest and decision." 49 Comp. Gen. 639, 646 (1970). For more "hand slapping," see 49 Comp. Gen. 772, 779 (1970); 49 Comp. Gen. 764, 768 (1970).

[38] 424 F.2d 859 (D.C. Cir. 1970).

[39] Perkins v. Lukens Steel Co., 310 U.S. 113 (1940). *See* Woolridge Mfg. Co. v. United States, 235 F.2d 513 (D.C. Cir. 1956); Friend v. Lee, 221 F.2d 96 (D.C. Cir. 1955); Robert Hawthorne, Inc. v. United States, 160 F. Supp. 417 (E.D. Pa. 1958); O'Brien v. Carney, 6 F. Supp. 761 (D. Mass. 1934).

[40] United States v. Stewart, 234 F. Supp. 94 (D.D.C. 1964), *aff'd per curiam*, 339 F.2d 753 (D.C. Cir. 1964). *See* Cotter Corp. v. Seaborg, 370 F.2d 686 (10th Cir. 1966); Walter P. Villere Co. v. Blinn, 156 F.2d 914 (5th Cir. 1946).

[41] 337 U.S. 682 (1949). For a critical discussion of *Larson* and its progeny, see Cramton, *supra* note 3, at 404-17 (the vice of *Larson* is that it permits and even encourages courts to avoid the hard task of determining the limits of official power).

The relief sought by plaintiffs creates great policy problems and brings into play the distinctions between powers of government. It does not require much imagination to anticipate the chaos which would be caused if the bidding procedure under every government contract was subject to review by court to ascertain if it was fairly and properly done, and the corresponding damage and delay which would be done to government business if the injunctive power of the court was used to stay contractual activities pending judicial decision.[42]

Similar concerns were expressed in *Perkins v. Lukens Steel Co.* and the *Larson* case, two Supreme Court decisions frequently cited to support the "no-review" rule.[43]

These no-review decisions, in effect, minimized the importance of private legal interests in the bidding process and, by inference at least, preferred the public interest in effective procurement over the broader public interest in an award system operating in conformance with congressional policy. Protection of the latter public interest was first left to internal administrative review and, as time passed, was assumed by the General Accounting Office.

Three exceptions to the "no-review" rule evolved in the courts, each in its own way preserving the sanctity of government effectiveness:

1. In public land cases, disappointed competitors have been able to obtain both judicial review of award decisions and, where appropriate, the award itself through mandatory injunction.[44] These cases, which fail to confront the knotty problems of standing and sovereign immunity, may be partially explained by an historical exception in public land cases to the sovereign immunity doctrine.[45] In any event, the availability of injunctive relief where the government is a lessor or seller would seem to have a less adverse effect on effectiveness than where the government seeks to meet basic needs by procurement.

2. Where potential bidders have, by administrative action, been debarred or suspended from participating in the bidding process, the Court of Appeals for the District of Columbia has permitted judicial review under section 10 of the Administrative Procedure Act. These decisions hold, in essence, that the debarred bidder has standing to test the authority of the officer imposing the restraint or to attack the quality of the procedures used in the debarment and may, in appropriate cases, obtain injunctive relief. This result was justified in *Gonzalez v. Freeman*:

---

[42] Lind v. Statts, 289 F. Supp. 182, 186 (N.D. Cal. 1968).

[43] In Larson v. Domestic & Foreign Commerce Corp., 337 U.S. 682 (1949), the Court stated: "But in the absence of a claim of constitutional limitation, the necessity of permitting the Government to carry out its functions unhampered by direct judicial intervention outweighs the possible disadvantage to the citizen in being relegated to the recovery of money damages after the event." 337 U.S. at 704. *See* Perkins v. Lukens Steel Co., 310 U.S. 113, 130 (1940) (quoted in note 11 *supra*). *But see* Noce v. Edward E. Morgan Co., 106 F.2d 746 (8th Cir. 1939).

[44] Superior Oil Co. v. Udall, 409 F.2d 115 (D.C. Cir. 1969); McKay v. Wahlenmaier, 226 F.2d 35 (D.C. Cir. 1955).

[45] *See* Scalia, *Sovereign Immunity and Nonstatutory Review of Federal Administrative Action: Some Conclusions from the Public-Lands Cases*, 68 MICH. L. REV. 867 (1970).

There can be no doubt that the invasion of some legally protected right is the predicate upon which any exercise of judicial power must rest. . . . It is equally correct, broadly speaking, to say that no citizen has a "right," in the sense of a legal right, to do business with the government. . . . But use of such terms as "right" or "privilege" tends to confuse the issues presented by debarment action. Interruption of an existing relationship between the government and a contractor places the latter in a different posture from one initially seeking government contracts and can carry with it grave economic consequences.

. . . .

Thus to say that there is no "right" to government contracts does not resolve the question of justiciability. Of course there is no such *right*; but that cannot mean that the government can act arbitrarily, either substantively or procedurally, against a person or that such person is not entitled to challenge the processes and the evidence before he is officially declared ineligible for government contracts. An allegation of facts which reveal an absence of legal authority or basic fairness in the method of imposing debarment presents a justiciable controversy in our view. The injury to appellants alleged in their complaint gives them standing to challenge the debarment processes by which such injury was imposed.[46]

3. The Court of Claims has heard suits both by disappointed bidders and by plaintiffs to whom a contract was awarded but later terminated on the ground that the award was improper. In the latter cases, the plaintiff seeks damages for breach of contract under the Tucker Act.[47] Recovery is probable unless the termination was justified by the plain illegality of the award. Put another way: "If the contracting officer acts in good faith and his award of the contract is reasonable under the law and regulations, his action should be upheld. In other words, a determination should not be made that a contract is invalid unless its illegality is palpable."[48] The standard "termination for convenience" clause, however, has been held applicable to wrongful terminations, thus limiting the plaintiff's recovery to expenses incurred plus profit on work done up to the termination—anticipated profits are not recoverable.[49] Since the contested cancellation is usually prompted by a GAO recommendation made after a bid protest has been upheld, the Court of Claims is, in effect, reviewing a pressured reversal by the contracting officer of an earlier award decision.

---

[46] 334 F.2d 570, 574-75 (D.C. Cir. 1964). In Copper Plumbing & Heating Co. v. Campbell, 290 F.2d 368, 371 (D.C. Cir. 1961), the court stated that a prospective contractor had a "right not to be invalidly denied equal opportunity under applicable law to seek contracts on government projects." *See* Overseas Media Corp. v. McNamara, 385 F.2d 308 (D.C. Cir. 1967).

[47] "The Court of Claims shall have jurisdiction to render judgment upon any claim against the United States founded either upon . . . any express or implied contract with the United States . . . ." 28 U.S.C. § 1491 (1970). The district courts have concurrent jurisdiction on contract claims "not exceeding $10,000." 28 U.S.C. § 1346(2) (1970).

[48] Warren Bros. Rds. Co. v. United States, 355 F.2d 612, 615 (Ct. Cl. 1965); John Reiner & Co. v. United States, 325 F.2d 438 (Ct. Cl. 1963), *cert. denied*, 383 U.S. 931 (1964). If the award is found to be palpably illegal, the former contractor's recovery is limited to *quantum meruit* for work done and accepted by the United States. Prestex, Inc. v. United States, 320 F.2d 367 (Ct. Cl. 1963). *See* Campbell v. Tennessee Valley Authority, 421 F.2d 293 (5th Cir. 1969).

[49] *See* G. C. Casebolt Co. v. United States, 421 F.2d 710 (Ct. Cl. 1970), and cases cited therein.

The disappointed bidder to whom no contract has been awarded has been successful in obtaining review when his petition supports an inference that his bid was not "fairly and honestly" considered by contracting officials.[50] This implied condition of fair and honest treatment, by whatever process imposed, seems to square matters with the Court of Claims jurisdictional statute, the Tucker Act, and to support the view that the plaintiff without a contract has some "rights" in the process.[51] On the other hand, the theoretical limit of recovery is stated to be damages measured by lost bid preparation costs, not lost profits.[52] To date, no plaintiff has been able to prove that his bid was not fairly and honestly considered. This practical problem coupled with clear holdings that the Court of Claims has no power to grant declaratory or equitable relief[53] tends to produce minimal rights with illusory remedies.

In short, while the cumulative effect of the three exceptions is to recognize and justify some private "rights" in the award process, the remedies, when granted, have not interfered in any way with the on-going procurement process or adequately protected the bidder's competitive opportunity in particular cases. The twin reluctance on the part of the courts to "stop the government in its tracks" or to award damages based upon lost profits left disappointed bidders with no effective way to obtain judicial protection of substantial economic interests.

B. *Scanwell* and the Aftermath

In early 1970, the door to judicial review of award decisions seemed to burst open. In *Scanwell*, the Federal Aviation Authority (FAA) had solicited bids for an instrument landing system and limited eligibility for award to those producers who had operational systems already installed and tested in at least one location. Scanwell, the second low bidder, met this condition. Scanwell alleged, however, that

---

[50] Keco Indus., Inc. v. United States, 428 F.2d 1233 (Ct. Cl. 1970). *See* Note, *An Expanded Cause of Action Under the Tucker Act for an Unsuccessful Bidder*, 44 TEMP. L.Q. 552 (1971). The *Keco* test was reaffirmed in Continental Business Enterprises, Inc. v. United States, 452 F.2d 1016 (Ct. Cl. 1971).

[51] The implied condition theory originated in Heyer Prods. Co. v. United States, 140 F. Supp. 409 (Ct. Cl. 1956), which stressed that the plaintiff must show "by clear and convincing proof that there has been a fraudulent inducement for bids, with the intention, before the bids were invited . . . to disregard them all except the ones from bidders to one of whom it was intended to let the contract, whether he was the lowest responsible bidder or not." 140 F. Supp. at 414. The plaintiff was unable to sustain this burden before the Trial Commissioner. Heyer Prods. Co. v. United States, 177 F. Supp. 251 (Ct. Cl. 1959). *See* Robert F. Simmons & Associates v. United States, 360 F.2d 962 (Ct. Cl. 1966); Trans Int'l Airlines, Inc. v. United States, 351 F.2d 1001 (Ct. Cl. 1965). This test was relaxed in Keco Indus., Inc. v. United States, 428 F.2d 1233 (Ct. Cl. 1970).

[52] "Plaintiff claims that it is entitled to recover both bid preparation costs and lost profits. We find, however, that it would be improper for this court to award plaintiff lost profits since the contract under which plaintiff would have made such profits never actually came into existence. . . . Also, there is no way that it could be said for certain that had Acme's bid been rejected, the award would have been made to plaintiff. Consequently, if it should be determined subsequently by the commissioner that plaintiff's bid was not treated honestly and fairly by the Government, then plaintiff should be allowed to recover only those costs incurred in preparing its technical proposals and bid." Keco Indus., Inc. v. United States, 428 F.2d 1233, 1240 (Ct. Cl. 1970).

[53] United States v. King, 395 U.S. 1 (1969).

the low bidder to whom the contract was awarded did not and that the FAA's decision to accept a nonresponsive bid was arbitrary, capricious, and in violation of the statutory and regulatory provisions governing FAA procurement.[54] Suing in the United States District Court for the District of Columbia, Scanwell sought to have the decision reviewed and the award declared illegal. The District Court dismissed the petition on the ground that the plaintiff had no standing to sue. Upon appeal, the Court of Appeals, speaking through Judge Tamm, reversed and remanded the case for a hearing on the merits.

In the course of the long and complicated opinion, a number of propositions emerged. First, Scanwell had standing to obtain judicial review because its prospective beneficial relationship with the government had been adversely affected in fact by an allegedly illegal award to another. To the court, this conclusion was supported by the legislative history rather than the language of section 10 of the Administrative Procedure Act[55] and by the presumption in favor of judicial review unless there is "clear and convincing evidence" of a contrary legislative intent.[56] Conceding that Scanwell had suffered injury from governmental action, the court stressed that it "had no right . . . to have the contract awarded to it" and that the suit was "brought in the public interest by one acting essentially as a 'private attorney general' . . . ." Since Scanwell had a sufficient stake in the matter to insure a "case or controversy" under article III of the Constitution and to minimize the risk of a completely frivolous law suit, it had standing even though the injury was caused by governmental action in an area to which no constitutional protection attached.[57] Second, section 10 of the Administrative Procedure Act was also relied

---

[54] 41 U.S.C. § 253(b) (1970) provides that the award "shall" be made to the bidder whose "conforming" bid is most advantageous to the United States, price and other factors considered. The Federal Procurement Regulation which governs FAA procurement, however, provides that a bid, to be considered, "must comply in all material respects with the invitation for bids" and that "any bid which fails to conform to the essential requirements of the invitation . . . shall be rejected as non-responsive . . . ." 41 C.F.R. §§ 1-2.301(a), 1-2.404-2(a) (1971).

[55] Section 10 provides, in part, that "A person suffering legal wrong because of agency action, or adversely affected or aggrieved by agency action within the meaning of a relevant statute, is entitled to judicial review thereof." 5 U.S.C. § 702 (1970). The adversely affect "in fact" language appears in the legislative history but not in the statute. For further discussion, see note 57 infra.

[56] Abbott Laboratories v. Gardner, 387 U.S. 136, 139-48 (1967). See generally Vining, Direct Judicial Review and the Doctrine of Ripeness in Administrative Law, 69 MICH. L. REV. 1443, 1483-87, 1491-1500 (1971). Judge Tamm's lengthy effort at 424 F.2d at 866-68 to distinguish Perkins v. Lukens Steel Co., 310 U.S. 113 (1940), is criticized in Pierson, supra note 9, at 13-14.

[57] Relying on Flast v. Cohen, 392 U.S. 83 (1968), Judge Tamm stated that a "person injured by governmental activity which goes to non-constitutional areas of his well-being is just as interested in judicial review of that activity as one whose constitutional rights are being trammeled . . . ." 424 F.2d at 872. More recent Supreme Court decisions such as Ass'n of Data Processing Serv. Organizations, Inc. v. Camp, 397 U.S. 150 (1970), and Barlow v. Collins, 397 U.S. 159 (1970), both reinforce this point and cast doubt upon Scanwell's total reliance upon section 10 of the APA to confer standing. See note 55 supra. Under these decisions, three conditions must be met for standing: (1) the plaintiff must have a personal stake or interest imparting the concrete adverseness required by article III of the Constitution; (2) the plaintiff must "arguably" be within the zone of interests protected by the Constitution or any relevant statute; and (3) Congress must not have precluded judicial review of the decision involved. See Arnold Tours, Inc. v. Camp, 400 U.S. 45 (1970). The "zone of interest test," while going to standing rather than the merits, is tied to the "adversely affected or aggrieved by agency

upon to circumvent the defense of sovereign immunity, an interpretation frequently advocated but not fully supported in the primary materials.[58] Third, the award decision was not committed to agency discretion because the plaintiff had made a *prima facie* showing of illegality. Since that question was uniquely appropriate for judicial determination, judicial review could not be denied. Fourth, for similar reasons, Scanwell was not required first to exhaust administrative remedies by protesting to the GAO, a procedure which might be useful but was not a prerequisite to court review.[59] Finally, on remand the plaintiff was given an opportunity to prove either that the decision was illegal because there was no discretion to ignore the regulations or, if there was discretion, that it was not properly exercised. This concluded what proved to be an eventful day in the uneasy relationship between administrative law and the government contracting process.

Shortly thereafter, two decisions by the Court of Appeals for the District of Columbia reinforced the *Scanwell* conclusion on standing even though the plaintiffs there sought injunctive rather than declaratory relief.[60] In one case, however, the public interest in governmental effectiveness began to emerge in the question of how best to "weed out" frivolous law suits. The court, again speaking through Judge Tamm, used the summary judgment device where issues of illegality were

---

action within the meaning of a relevant statute" language of section 10 of the APA—there must be a "relevant statute" other than the APA which creates the zone of interest within which the plaintiff must "arguably be." *See* Ass'n of Data Processing Serv. Organizations, Inc. v. Camp, 397 U.S. 150, 153-54; Barlow v. Collins, 397 U.S. 159, 164-65; Vining, *supra* note 56, at 1473-82. Decisions of the District of Columbia Court of Appeals subsequent to *Scanwell* have applied the Supreme Court's "3 point" standing test to suits by disappointed bidders, concluding, *inter alia*, that an allegation that the award decision was illegal was required to show injury to an interest of the plaintiff that was "arguably within the zone of interests to be protected or regulated by the statute . . . in question." Ballerina Pen Co. v. Kunzig, 433 F.2d 1204, 1207 (D.C. Cir. 1970); Blackhawk Heating & Plumbing Co. v. Driver, 433 F.2d 1137, 1140-41 (D.C. Cir. 1970). This could be a shift from total reliance upon section 10 of the APA, although a recent decision states that standing is under the Administrative Procedure Act and rests upon "two interrelated principles: (1) the losing bidder's substantive interest as an aggrieved party in asserting that it was denied the contract because of arbitrary or capricious agency action . . . and (2) the public interest in policing governmental action through frustrated bidders serving as 'private attorney generals.'" M. Steinthal & Co. v. Seamans, 455 F.2d 1289, 1291 n. 2 (D.C. Cir. 1971). If disappointed bidders have any distinct private rights created and protected by procurement statutes, they have not clearly emerged in the efforts to find standing. *But see* Perkins v. Lukens Steel Co., 310 U.S. 113, 126-27 (1940); Edelman v. Federal Housing Administration, 382 F.2d 594, 597 (2d Cir. 1967); United States v. Gray Line Water Tours, 311 F.2d 779 (4th Cir. 1962) (bidding procedures are for the public generally and confer no private rights on bidders). At least one district court apears to have rejected *Scanwell* altogether. Gary Aircraft Corp. v. Seamans, 342 F. Supp. 473 (W.D. Tex. 1972).

[58] This is consistent with a proposal by the Administrative Conference of the United States made to Congress but not yet enacted into law. *See* Cramton, *supra* note 3, at 428-36. The accuracy if not the wisdom of this conclusion, however, has been doubted. *See* Byse & Fiocca, *Section 1361 of the Mandamus and Venue Act of 1962 and "Nonstatutory" Judicial Review of Federal Administrative Action*, 81 HARV. L. REV. 308, 326-31 (1967), and there is authority to the contrary. Cotter Corp. v. Seaborg, 370 F.2d 686, 692 n. 15 (10th Cir. 1966). The cases are discussed in Scalia, *supra* note 45, at 920-24.

[59] Unknown to the court, GAO had upheld the award against the protest of another participant in the procurement. 49 COMP. GEN. 9 (1969).

[60] Blackhawk Heating & Plumbing Co. v. Driver, 433 F.2d 1137 (D.C. 1970); Ballerina Pen Co. v. Kunzig, 433 F.2d 1204 (D.C. Cir. 1970). *See* note 57 *supra*.

raised by the pleadings but where there were no genuine issues of material fact and stated:

> Fortunately, the inquiry does not end with a determination that the plaintiff has standing; rather, the inquiry begins in more relevant detail at that point. As we noted in Scanwell . . . the mere fact that a party has standing to sue does not entitle him to render uncertain for a prolonged period of time government contracts which are vital to the functions performed by the sovereign. The recent decisions in this court and in the Supreme Court have served to eliminate the artificial barrier created by the concept of standing, but that does not mean that the traditional legitimate bars to frivolous lawsuits have also been abrogated.[61]

Despite this note of caution, the case stressed the importance of the "public interest in having agencies follow the regulations which control government contracting"[62] and determined that review on the merits would be governed by standards more or less consistent with those provided in the Administrative Procedure Act.[63] In neither case did the fact of internal administrative review or a protest before GAO figure in the decision.

Meanwhile, the corridors of the federal district court in the District of Columbia were seemingly swarming with disappointed bidders alleging illegality in award decisions and seeking to stop the government in its tracks. In these suits, the court was typically asked to restrain agency action in the particular procurement until a decision on the merits could be reached, declare that the award decision was improper, and order the government either to correct a defect in the process of competition or order the award of the contract to the plaintiff. While not present in every case, some plaintiffs sought to restrain agency action to preserve a protest then pending before GAO.[64] In exercising discretion whether to issue temporary restraining orders and grant preliminary injunctions in particular cases, the courts purported to balance four closely related factors: "the relative

---

[61] Blackhawk Heating & Plumbing Co. v. Driver, 433 F.2d 1137, 1141 (D.C. Cir. 1970).

[62] Scanwell Laboratories, Inc. v. Shaffer, 424 F.2d 859, 864 (D.C. Cir. 1970).

[63] Section 10(e) of the Administrative Procedure Act provides that the "reviewing court shall . . . (2) hold unlawful and set aside agency action, findings, and conclusions found to be (A) arbitrary, capricious, an abuse of discretion, or otherwise not in accordance with law; . . . (C) in excess of statutory jurisdiction, authority, or limitations, or short of statutory right . . . ." 5 U.S.C. § 706 (1970).
In the Scanwell line of cases, there is some confusion over what the plaintiff must allege to insure standing and what standards the court will apply to determine the merits. In Scanwell, the court held that standing turned, in part, on an allegation of illegality and suggested that the merits turned on whether the contracting officer "properly exercised discretion in awarding the contract" or, if no discretion was confided to ignore the regulations, whether the award was illegal. 424 F.2d at 873. In Ballerina Pen Co. v. Kunzig, 433 F.2d 1204, 1207 (D.C. Cir. 1970), the court stated that the plaintiff must allege that the "agency has acted arbitrarily, capriciously, or in excess of its statutory authority" to secure standing and suggested that the same standard governed the merits. Blackhawk Heating & Plumbing Co. v. Driver, 433 F.2d 1137 (D.C. Cir. 1970) is in accord. In M. Steinthal & Co. v. Seamans, 455 F.2d 1289 (D.C. Cir. 1971), the court, speaking through Judge Leventhal, stated that standing depended upon an allegation that the award decision was arbitrary and capricious and that the courts "should not overturn any procurement determination unless the aggrieved bidder demonstrates that there was no rational basis for the agency's decision."

[64] See, e.g., Keco Indus., Inc. v. Laird, 318 F. Supp. 1361 (D.D.C. 1970) (injunction denied); Law Bros. Contracting Corp. v. Resor, No. 2137-70 (D.D.C. 1970).

importance of the rights asserted and the acts sought to be enjoined, the irreparable nature of the injury allegedly flowing from the denial of preliminary relief, the probability of the ultimate success or failure of the suit, [and] the balancing of damage and convenience generally."[65]

Initially, the balancing permitted disappointed bidders to obtain the temporary or preliminary relief requested. The highwater mark in the district court was the celebrated case of *A. G. Schoonmaker Co. v. Resor*,[66] where a permanent injunction enjoining the award of the contract to anyone else and a mandatory injunction requiring the award of the contract to the plaintiff was issued.

In *Schoonmaker*, the plaintiff Libby and the intervenor Bogue Electric were determined to have acceptable proposals in step one of an Army generator procurement to be awarded by "two-step" formal advertising.[67] Both plaintiff and intervenor spent substantial time and money in preparing the technical proposal for step one and the pricing bid for step two. Prior to submission of bids in step two, however, a question of interpretation arose, and, after extensive discussion among Army and Air Force officials (who were also interested in generators), it was determined that identical prices should be bid for the pre-production and production models. This information was communicated to intervenor but not to plaintiff, even though defendant knew that plaintiff interpreted the invitation as requiring different prices for the models. When the bids were opened, plaintiff was low bidder by some $570,000 over intervenor. Intervenor protested to the GAO that plaintiff's bid was not responsive because of different pricing. Plaintiff then protested against the award to anyone but itself. On May 22, 1970, almost three months after intervenor's protest was filed, the GAO decided that, while plaintiff's bid was responsive to the invitation (the Army's interpretation of the invitation was "clearly erroneous"), intervenor was prejudiced by receipt of the Army's interpretation.[68] Accordingly, the defendant was directed to cancel the invitation and solicit new bids. The defendant, on May 27, 1970, cancelled the invitation and solicited new bids in step two, which provided for identical pricing of models. On June 11, plaintiff filed suit alleging

---

[65] Perry v. Perry, 190 F.2d 601, 602 (D.C. Cir. 1951), *quoting* Communist Party of the United States v. McGrath, 96 F. Supp. 47, 48 (D.D.C. 1951). *See* JAFFE, *supra* note 2, at 687-708; Semmes Motors, Inc. v. Ford Motor Co., 429 F.2d 1197 (2d Cir. 1970); Note, 71 COLUM. L. REV. 165 (1971).

[66] No. 1760-70 (D.D.C. 1970), *rev'd*, Nos. 24,706 & 24,708 (D.C. Cir. 1971). *See* note 70 *infra*. Other cases where a TRO or preliminary injunction was granted are Forera Corp. v. Avco Economic Sys. Corp., No. 1509-70 (D.D.C. 1970); Harry Winston, Inc. v. Kunzig, No. 1894-70 (D.D.C. 1970); Big Four Mechanical Contractors, Inc. v. Small Business Administration, No. 70-312 (W.D. Okla. 1970); Aero-Jet Gen. Corp. v. Thiokol Chem. Corp., No. C.70-1493-LHB (N.D. Cal. 1970).

[67] Two-step formal advertising was developed to increase the use of advertising in procurements where, due to inadequate specifications, negotiation had previously been employed. In step one, an attempt is made through negotiation to develop realistic specifications against which price competition can occur. In step two, the developed specifications form the basis for competition among some of those involved in step one under the usual procedures for formal advertising. *See* ASPR, subpt. E, 32 C.F.R. §§ 2.501-2.503 (1971); Cuneo & Crowell, *Negotiated Contracts—Two-Step Procurement, Cost and Pricing Data Requirements and Protests to the Comptroller General*, 5 B.C. IND. & COM. L. REV. 43 (1963).

[68] Ms. Comp. Gen. B-170268 (November 9, 1970), 50 COMP. GEN. — (1970).

the defendant had acted "arbitrarily, capriciously and unlawfully" and sought declaratory and injunctive relief prohibiting the award to anyone other than the plaintiff and requiring that a contract be awarded to it under the first invitation. On June 12, a temporary restraining order enjoining the opening of bids was issued, and, on June 26, a preliminary injunction was issued. The case then was heard on the merits, whereupon the court issued, on September 24, 1970, a permanent injunction enjoining award of the contract to anyone else and a mandatory injunction requiring the award of the contract to plaintiff.

In a cryptic opinion by Judge Waddy, the court first concluded by citing *Scanwell* that it had jurisdiction, that the plaintiff had standing, and that the action was not barred by the doctrine of sovereign immunity. On the merits, the court held that the defendant's *ex parte* communication to intervenor alone "undermined the integrity of the competitive bidding process" and that intervenor's reliance on such information was unjustified. Thus, cancellation of the invitation for bids was "arbitrary, capricious and unlawful," and the new invitation and any action taken thereunder was null and void. Second, the court concluded that the plaintiff rather than intervenor was the lowest responsive, responsible bidder and that the defendants had "a duty under the circumstances of this case" to award the contract to plaintiff under the original invitation. Finally, the permanent relief granted was justified as preventing irreparable injury to the plaintiff, who "does not have an adequate remedy at law," and as protecting the public interest "in the integrity of the bidding and procurement processes and procedures of the government."

Almost immediately, however, the balance seemingly struck in favor of the private interest and the broader public interest in having "agencies follow the regulations which control government contracting" over governmental effectiveness was reversed. The issue focused upon when temporary or preliminary restraints upon agency action pending judicial review should be granted. A key district court decision in this reversal was *Simpson Electric Co. v. Seamans*,[69] where the court exercised its discretion against injunctive relief.

In *Simpson*, the plaintiff submitted a bid modification which, if timely, would have entitled it to award. Bruno, a competing bidder, protested the contracting officer's determination that the bid was timely to the GAO, which decided that the modification was not timely and directed an award to Bruno. The plaintiff, seeking injunctive relief, sought review of final agency action under the Administrative Procedure Act and alleged that the contracting officer's decision, although pressured by the GAO, was "arbitrary, capricious, an abuse of discretion, or otherwise not in accordance with law." The court, speaking through Judge Gesell, first decided that the final decision to be reviewed was that of the contracting officer rather than the GAO, although the GAO's reasoning, which compelled the contracting officer "against his better judgment" to change his mind, was critical in the review. Rely-

---

[69] 317 F. Supp. 684 (D.D.C. 1970).

ing on *Scanwell* as authority for standing and jurisdiction, the court noted that *Scanwell* did not deal with the standard that should govern review or the scope of available relief. Stating that the standard for review was whether the contracting officer acted "arbitrarily, capriciously, or in violation of law," the court concluded that the refusal to accept plaintiff's bid modification was "arbitrary and irrational"— the GAO failed to consider a course of dealing between the parties which justified the communication device employed by the plaintiff.

On the question of appropriate relief, the court noted that the contract had been awarded to Bruno, "which is not before the court and the extent of whose performance to date is unknown but undoubtedly substantial." Rejecting the government's argument that the court had no power, under the APA, to "require the government to enter into a contract or enjoin it from proceeding with a contract,"[70] the question was posed by the court as whether injunctive relief, which is discretionary and to be used sparingly, was appropriate here. Classifying the transaction as a "routine, short-term procurement where performance has already begun" and suggesting that both parties could perfect their claim to damages, if any, in the Court of Claims, the court concluded that "[m]andatory relief by way of injunction is not required to preserve the integrity of the bid process since a declaration of rights with the liability for damages that will flow therefrom will suffice."[71] Further:

> The Court is hesitant to utilize its injunctive powers for yet another reason. Neither the Administrative Procedure Act nor *Scanwell Laboratories, supra,* can be responsibly read, whether singly or together, as contemplating that the Court in all disputed cases will direct the course of Government contracting. As already indicated, the scope of review is narrow, and once the rights of litigants are declared, the Government should in the normal case be free to make choices as to whether it will run the risk of damages, open the contract for rebidding, resolve the dispute by negotiation, or meet its needs, if they still exist, in some other fashion. The variety and complexity of situations that will be presented make it abundantly apparent that in the usual case the courts have only a limited function in this area.[72]

Finally, the court declared that the plaintiff was the lowest bidder, that he was admittedly qualified in all other respects and that it was illegal to award the contract to anyone else. Injunctive relief, however, was denied.[73]

---

[70] The court construed the statement by Judge Tamm in *Scanwell*, 424 F.2d at 864, that there was "no right in Scanwell to have the contract to it" to be "merely . . . recognition that Scanwell had not established facts which would compel award of the contract to itself in the event the award . . . should be declared void." 317 F. Supp. at 687.

[71] 317 F. Supp. at 687, 688.

[72] 317 F. Supp. at 688.

[73] In Keco Indus., Inc. v. Laird, 318 F. Supp. 1361 (D.D.C. 1970), the court stressed that the "appropriateness of injunctive relief turns, in some measure on the final relief this court will grant" and that "injunctive relief is discretionary and its exercise should be determined according to the circumstances of the particular case in question." In denying a request for a preliminary injunction against continued performance of a contract awarded by negotiation pending determination of a protest filed with GAO, the court relied upon three factors: (1) since procurement officials have more discretion in the award of contracts by negotiation than by formal advertising, the standards for judicial review

While the result in *Simpson* cast a pall over the corridors of the district court, a glimmer of hope remained. *Schoonmaker*, where permanent and mandatory injunctions had been issued, was on appeal to the Court of Appeals, as were two cases, *Wheelabrator Corp. v. Chafee*[74] and *M. Steinthal & Co. v. Seamans*,[75] where the district court had issued injunctions against making a protested award pending judicial review. The bad news, however, was not long in coming. *Schoonmaker* was reversed with a rather disappointing opinion,[76] and the injunctions issued in *Wheelabrator* and *Steinthal* were vacated with opinions that left no doubt that the interest in governmental effectiveness had returned with a vengeance.[77]

The critical case was *M. Steinthal & Co. v. Seamans*,[78] where the overlapping provinces of administrative and judicial review collided, with adverse vibrations for

should differ and protection may be achieved by "actions less than the directed award of a contract and preliminary injunctive relief"; (2) since the contract had been awarded, performance commenced, and the successful contractor was not before the court, only serious governmental irregularity would support injunctive relief; and (3) there was no serious irregularity. *Accord*, American Standard, Inc. v. Laird, No. 2653-70 (D.D.C. 1970); Lombard Corp. v. Resor, No. 2200-70 (D.D.C. 1970).

[74] No. 2437-70 (D.D.C. 1970).

[75] No. 2422-70 (D.D.C. 1970).

[76] A. G. Schoonmaker Co. v. Resor, Nos. 24,706 & 24,708 (D.C. Cir. 1971). The court ducked the question of power to order a contract award and, seemingly, assumed that the decision under review was that of the Comptroller General rather than the contracting officer. This decision was not arbitrary, capricious, abusive of discretion, or in violation of law, and the district court erred in not considering what GAO had done before issuing the injunction. That *Schoonmaker* reviewed the decision of the Comptroller General is confirmed in M. Steinthal & Co. v. Seamans, 455 F.2d 1289, 1305 (D.C. Cir. 1971), although the court noted that GAO's decision is "not necessarily dispositive" and that there "certainly may be instances where the District Court will find procurement illegality that the GAO failed to recognize, or at any event failed to correct."

[77] At issue in Wheelabrator Corp. v. Chafee, 455 F.2d 1306 (D.C. Cir. 1971), was the propriety of a Navy decision to use two-step formal advertising rather than negotiation. The plaintiff claimed that because of a 12 year research and development program costing over $100,000 it had developed a "new and unique" device and was thereby qualified as a sole source contractor. Plaintiff protested to GAO and submitted a proposal in step one. While that protest was pending, the Navy proceeded to step two, whereupon plaintiff first obtained a temporary restraining order and, later, a preliminary injunction against opening the bids in step two and making an award. *See* note 74 *supra*. The grounds were that the plaintiff would otherwise suffer irreparable loss, the Navy would be deprived of special skills, a meaningful protest to GAO would be abridged and there was a substantial likelihood of success on the merits. The court of appeals, speaking through Judge Leventhal, held that plaintiff had failed to establish the prima facie case of illegality needed to support the preliminary injunction. In seeking to force the Navy to negotiate the contract, plaintiff ran counter to the congressional policy favoring advertising and was requesting the court to order the Secretary to make a decision which under the statute, 10 U.S.C. § 2304(a)(14) (1970), was permissive rather than mandatory and was, therefore, "committed to agency discretion by law" within the meaning of the Administrative Procedure Act, 5 U.S.C. § 701(a)(2) (1970). According to the court, plaintiff failed to show that the Navy's decision violated a "clear command of governing law" or that "no state of facts may reasonably be conceived that would justify the administrative action." Given the nature of the question involved and the need for exceptional circumstances to justify a preliminary restraint upon the award process, the plaintiff had failed to show probability of success on the merits.

Regarding an injunction pending resolution of the GAO protest, the court, while stressing that it had primary jurisdiction and had the final say on any GAO decision, recognized that it might defer to an agency with special competence by issuing an injunction pendente lite. Without deciding whether GAO had authority to resolve bid protests, the court held that the plaintiff's request for relief pendente lite was too broad in this case—it had not limited its request for relief necessary to preserve the protest for GAO decision.

[78] 455 F.2d 1289 (D.C. Cir. 1971).

disappointed bidders seeking equitable relief. The plaintiff was low bidder on an Air Force advertised procurement for parachutes. Claiming an ambiguity in the specifications, the second low bidder protested to the contracting officer against the proposed award and claimed that under a correct interpretation of the specifications it was entitled to the contract. The contracting officer denied this protest but, after a careful internal review by the Air Force Logistical Command, re-evaluated and reversed his decision, cancelled the invitation, and readvertised under a revised invitation for bids. The plaintiff and the second low bidder both protested to GAO, and these protests were denied the day before the scheduled opening of bids on the new invitation. The plaintiff, with the second low bidder intervening, then obtained a permanent injunction against bid opening, the district court concluding that there was no basis for the cancellation and that the plaintiff would be unduly prejudiced if the new bids were opened.[79] Upon appeal, the court of appeals, speaking through Judge Leventhal, vacated the injunction and dismissed the complaint.

The essence of a long and complicated opinion is this. The court reaffirmed that two interrelated principles supported the plaintiff's standing under the Administrative Procedure Act to seek judicial review—his substantive interest as an aggrieved party denied a contract because of allegedly illegal action and the public interest in policing the award system as a private attorney general. However, a strong public policy exists in avoiding disruptions in the free flow of the contracting process. Thus, while there is a general public interest in having executive officers follow the statutes and regulations governing advertised procurement, the plaintiff, when asserting this interest as a private attorney general, bears a heavy burden when seeking to overturn executive action and obtain injunctive relief. This is especially true where the final decision complained of was made after careful internal administrative review and was sustained by GAO.[80] Thus, when "emergency challenges" to determinations of procurement officials are made, "courts should not overturn any procurement determination unless the aggrieved party demonstrates that there was not rational basis for the agency's decision." A less restrained approach would make the courts a "forum for all manner of objections to procurement decisions" and would propel them "without adequate preparation into a tangle of complex statutory and decisional rules." The district court, therefore, erred in not considering the decision to cancel the invitation and readvertise in the total context of the administrative review given to it and in deciding that the decision was arbitrary and capricious. In short, there was a rational basis for the decision.

On the question of injunctive relief pending a judicial decision on the merits,

---

[79] See note 75 supra.

[80] The court stressed the responsibility of the district court to "consider the totality of the administrative process in their review of agency action." This approach "would serve to insure the requisite judicial deference to well-reasoned judgments of agency officials acting within the confines of their statutory delegated authority and their own procurement regulations." Finally, the process of internal agency review "is a legitimate check on the decision-making process in the executive branch of government as it is in the judicial branch." 455 F.2d, at 1298.

the court manifested an even more cautious approach. The instances of judicial intervention into the procurement process must be limited, especially where difficult decisions on technical matters are required in the emergency setting which permeates the request for temporary or preliminary relief. Even though there is a probability that the decision complained of has no rational basis, "there is room for sound judicial discretion, in the presence of overriding public interest considerations, to refuse to entertain declaratory or injunctive actions in a pre-procurement context." The "public interest in the smooth flow and expeditious completion of the procurement process" combines with urgent needs on a "short delivery schedule," such as in the case at bar, to dictate restraint, particularly when the plaintiff has a damage remedy, even though limited to bid preparation costs, in the more relaxed atmosphere of the Court of Claims.

> Only when the court concludes that there has been a clear violation of duty by the procurement officials should it intervene in the procurement process and proceed to a determination of the controversy on the merits.[81]

Finally, the court, without resolving the power issue, acknowledged the expertise of GAO in these matters, reinforced the notion that a GAO decision should be afforded great respect by the court, and expressed the view that an injunction against agency action pending decision of a protest to GAO might be granted in appropriate circumstances.

As a final word the court said:

> We do not recede from our expression in *Scanwell* of the beneficial purposes served by frustrated bidders who, as "private attorney generals," can aid in furthering the public interest in the integrity of the procurement process. The courts are properly concerned that the procurement activities of the Government be carried out in accordance with the applicable statutes and agency regulations and that these governmental functions not be permitted to deteriorate into actions reflecting personal predelictions of administrative officials, whether ascribable to whim, misplaced zeal, or impermissible influence. However, the public interest in a Government procurement process that proceeds with expedition is likewise of importance. The court must refrain from judicial intervention into the procurement process unless the actions of the executive officials are without any rational basis.[82]

---

[81] *Id.* at 1303.

[82] *Id.* at 1305-06. *But see* Leventhal, *Public Contracts and Administrative Law*, 52 A.B.A.J. 35, 40 (1966):

"Beneath the surface similarities and differences between administration of the procurement and the conventional regulatory functions, there lies the rock bottom of government accountability, '[w]hatever, the form in which the Government functions.' Under our system, restraint on governmental power, fair procedures and judicial review insure the supremacy of law over administrative absolutism.

. . . .

There is much merit to the observations of critics of the conventional administrative process that it has become overjudicialized. The Government must be sure-footed, not leaden-footed. We cannot establish checks against the abuse of governmental power that inhibit the effective exercise of power. But in the soul-searching and analysis ahead ways should be sought to apply to the procurement process the fundamentals underlying administrative law without inhibiting minimum effectiveness in administration."

IV

The Problem Revisited and Some Directions for Reform

Scanwell seemingly eased the path to judicial review of award decisions by boldly employing the Administrative Procedure Act to flatten the obstacles of sovereign immunity and standing. Twenty-one months later *Steinthal*, by stressing the demands of governmental effectiveness, partially resurrected at least one of these obstacles and decorated it wtih the restrained language of judicial review. An award decision will stand unless without "any rational basis," and, even if that conclusion is probable, the court should exercise extreme caution in enjoining the award process pending judicial review.

While this result is better than the pre-*Scanwell* line of cases, the manifested reluctance to intrude into the on-going procurement process arguably preserves an alleged vice of *Larson*, that courts are permitted and even encouraged to "shirk the hard task of determining the limits of official power."[83] This reluctance will undoubtedly reinforce the volume of GAO bid protests. When this is combined with the current inability of administrative review consistently to insure that award decisions are right rather than quick, a more complete victory for the public interest in effective procurement cannot be imagined. Ignored in the purported balance is whether disappointed bidders have any distinct economic interests which require greater legal protection.[84] Assumed, is that the overriding public interest in having executive agencies follow the rules of the award game will receive adequate protection from the flow of protests by disappointed bidders wearing the armor of the private attorney general.

It is possible, of course, that GAO involvement in resolving protests and the occasional intervention of courts in cases of "shocking disproportion" will place consistent and effective pressure upon agencies to improve the procedures and standards for making contract awards. As Judge Leventhal observed in *Steinthal*, the provision of protection against "illegal" governmental action is "salutory [*sic*] not only for the relatively few cases that might result in court intervention, but also for the greater number of cases which will be handled with greater care and more diligence within the government because of the awareness of the availability of

---

[83] Byse, *Proposed Reforms in Federal "Nonstatutory" Judicial Review: Sovereign Immunity, Indispensable Parties, Mandamus*, 75 Harv. L. Rev. 1479, 1491 (1962). Even though award decisions are now reviewable, the "rational basis" test is likely to catch only those decisions which are clearly erroneous as a matter of law or involve "shocking disproportion" in the exercise of discretion. *See* Jaffe, *The Judicial Enforcement of Administrative Orders*, 76 Harv. L. Rev. 865, 870 (1963).

[84] In balancing the private and public interests thought to be necessary for sound decisions in this general area, see *Cramston, supra* note 3, at 400, Judge Leventhal, in *Steinthal*, has deleted the private interest from the equation. He identifies the "strong public interest in avoiding disruptions in procurement" and the "overriding public interest in having agencies follow the regulations which control government contracting," 455 F.2d 1289, 1300 (D.C. Cir. 1971), and indicates that he is "balancing . . . the public interest in free and fair competitive bidding against both fairness to the parties and the Government's contractual needs." *Id.* at 1304. If "fairness to the parties" is intended to identify private interests, they are equated, substantially, with the disappointed bidder's role as a private attorney general and not squarely balanced against the need for governmental effectiveness.

judicial scrutiny."[85] But even if true, the approach equates the private interest in competitive opportunity with the overriding public interest in an award system operating according to law and assumes that both will receive adequate protection under the current system. Put another way, it assumes that the regular victory of governmental effectiveness over private and overriding public interests in particular procurements is justified,[86] with any damage to those interests being remedied by constant efforts to improve the on-going process. All of this is assumed to be at no cost to the profit and other incentives necessary to develop and preserve a base of willing and able contractors or the achievement of important collateral policies, such as the small business program, which the government seeks to implement through contracts.

There are no empirical studies supporting a claim that the current system of administrative and judicial review does produce these costs.[87] There is only speculation from observing a low visibility process which spawns tales of increased concentration of firms receiving defense contracts, financial "bail outs" for "essential" contractors, small business bankruptcies, and conflicting views about who is making how much profit on public contracts.[88] Perhaps it is time to disregard award policies designed to foster equality of access and competition and take steps to establish a system of procurement that relies upon public institutions rather than private corporations as the primary sources of supply. But until this is done, it is clear that the current objectives in government procurement cannot be achieved without consistent conformity of executive award decisions to statutes and implementing regulations. Furthermore, a public award process, insulated in particular cases by a shield of governmental effectiveness, gives contracting officials an uncomfortable latitude for the exercise of discretion. Finally, this brief study indicates that contracting officials have the primary discretion in deciding whether the award process or contract performance is to stop or continue when a protest is made and

---

[85] 455 F.2d at 1301. *See The Administrative Process,* in LEGAL INSTITUTIONS TODAY AND TOMORROW 108, 138 (M. Paulsen ed. 1959) (the availability of judicial review is by far the most significant safeguard against administrative excesses which can be contrived); Berger, *Administrative Arbitrariness: A Synthesis,* 78 YALE L.J. 965 (1969).

[86] One aspect of the governmental effectiveness problem is the asserted urgency of a particular procurement. As Judge Leventhal stated in *Steinthal:* "We are not referring solely to the public interest in the smooth flow and expeditious completion of the procurement process, but more specifically to the additional public interest consideration that obtains when what is involved is an item like parachutes and a short delivery schedule. This kind of urgent matter should not arise often, but when it does arise there is discretion in the District Court to decline to consider the prayer for injunctive or declaratory relief." 455 F.2d at 1302. A recent report of the Comptroller General was highly critical of executive agencies for engaging in non-competitive procurements on dubious grounds of urgency. It was reported that these decisions were made more on the grounds of item priority rather than data based upon the urgency of the mission, the date the supplies were needed, and the effect of delay. *See* 13 GOVERNMENT CONTRACTOR ¶ 158 (1971).

[87] The meager collection of studies as of 1964 is discussed in Marcus, *Studies of the Defense Contracting Process,* 29 LAW & CONTEMP. PROB. 19 (1964). *See also,* C. DANHOF, GOVERNMENT CONTRACTING AND TECHNOLOGICAL CHANGE (1968), a study of research and development contracting sponsored by the Brookings Institute.

[88] *See The Profit Puzzle in Procurement,* BUSINESS WEEK, Mar. 6, 1971, at 44.

that no one outside the agency is able to do much about alleged illegality until it is too late to rectify the situation. The conclusion from all this is that it is time for some serious thinking about reform.

A possible direction for reform in this specialized area can be found in some fundamental ideas about administrative law. A basic question is how best to insure quality decisions by executive and administrative officers as they implement governmental programs. A general answer was provided in the 1941 Report of the Attorney General's Committee on Administrative Procedure:

> To assure enforcement of the laws by administrative agencies within the bounds of their authority, reliance must be placed on controls other than judicial review—internal controls in the agency, responsibility to the legislature or the executive, careful selection of personnel, pressure from interested parties, and professional or lay criticism of the agency's work.[89]

More recently, FCC Commissioner Nicholas Johnson has emphasized the need to develop "methods for improving the administrative process and to avoid unsound, unfair, and arbitrary decisions,"[90] and Professor Kenneth C. Davis, in a widely discussed book, has argued that the most effective restraints upon abuse of discretion must come from the administrators themselves through the development of rules which clarify and make more precise the standards for decision in particular cases.[91] Put another way, the arena for the exercise of discretion must be clearly delineated and the standards for application made more explicit through the rule-making process. Finally, executive agencies have been urged to develop more effective systems of internal administrative review. Through the power that superior officers have to control the actions of subordinates, administrative review could be achieved which would be less expensive and time-consuming than judicial review and, at the same time, achieve a better pattern of quality in the decisions made.

In sum, the review by superior officials enabled by the power of control is so flexible and broad as to satisfy all reasonable needs of the administration in this

---

[89] U.S. ATT'Y GENERAL'S COMM. ON ADMINISTRATIVE PROCEDURE, ADMINISTRATIVE PROCEDURE IN GOVERNMENT AGENCIES 76 (1968).

[90] Johnson, *Book Review*, 23 STAN. L. REV. 173, 174 (1971). For a similar perspective, see Rabin, *Book Review*, 22 STAN. L. REV. 421 (1970).

[91] DAVIS, *supra* note 16, at 220-21. *See* Clagett, *Informal Action—Adjudication—Rule Making: Some Recent Developments in Federal Administrative Law*, 1971 DUKE L.J. 51. It has been asserted that "an outstanding failure of the contemporary administrative process is the failure of the typical agency sufficiently to use the rule-making process or to clarify the standards which govern its decisions." Committee on Informal Action of the Administrative Conference of the United States, Guidelines for the Study of Informal Action in Federal Agencies 2 (Draft of Apr. 10, 1971). For an extreme reaction to this failure in the area of environmental protection, see Environmental Defense Fund, Inc. v. Ruckelshaus, 439 F.2d 584, 596-98 (D.C. Cir. 1971) (courts should require administrative officers to articulate the standards and principles that govern their discretionary decisions in as much detail as possible). For another approach to the problem, *see* Hanes, *Citizen Participation and its Impact Upon Prompt and Responsible Administrative Action*, 24 SW. L.J. 731 (1970).

respect, as well as to afford considerable protection to citizens against excesses by subordinate officers.[92]

Taken together, then, the most effective ways to control and improve the quality of administrative discretion may be further to clarify and amplify the standards for decision at the action level and to establish solid procedures for internal administrative review.

Can this approach be applied to the special problems arising in the award of public contracts? In my judgment, the answer is "yes." I will proceed on the assumption that the relationship of mutual dependence between the United States and the business community cannot afford to absorb the shocks produced by the persistent inability of anyone to insure that award decisions are made correctly rather than quickly. Whether the increased unwillingness of contractors to deal with the United States or increased pressure on contractors locked into the contracting process, the cumulative effects of this inability could impair the mix of public and private interests which underlie the existing system. Further, I will assert that any reform effort should strive for the twin objectives of improving the standards and procedures for contract award and increasing, without a substantial impairment of governmental effectiveness, the legal protection available to disappointed bidders who, in particular cases, can show that the award decision complained of was improper. This reform could be accomplished in three closely related steps:

1. By legislation, GAO could be removed from involvement in the decision of bid protests made by "interested parties," although advisory opinions on proposed awards might still be given upon agency request. Instead, GAO's role as critic and reformer of the operating award system would be strengthened by assigning it to review groups of agency award decisions made over a stated period of time and, based upon this data, to propose clearer or more complete standards and procedures for adoption by the agency involved. This role is more consistent with GAO's traditional investigation and auditing functions and would be a more efficient allocation of time and resources than waiting for evidence of impropriety to emerge from over 1,000 bid protests more or less fortuitously presented in the course of a year. Of crucial importance, the change would permit each agency to develop better procedures for internal administrative review since these procedures could no longer be suspended by direct protests to GAO. Finally, the opportunity for courts to develop a realistic theory of private "rights" in the bidding process should be greater than when the energies of disappointed bidders were directed toward persuading the Comptroller General that the proposed obligation of appropriated funds was illegal.[93]

---

[92] Zamir, *Administrative Control of Administrative Action*, 57 Cal. L. Rev. 866, 889 (1969). *See* note 29 *supra.*

[93] This recommendation rejects as inappropriate current efforts by the General Accounting Office to improve the speed of the bid protest decision process at GAO and to suspend the award process pending a final decision. See the proposed changes to 4 C.F.R., pt. 20, in 36 Fed. Reg. 8060 (1971).

2. By executive order, a uniform, internal bid protest procedure could be established within each executive agency or department and made available to disappointed bidders as a channel through which to protest award decisions. This procedure would have the following features:

(a) The responsibility for decision would be lodged with a bid protest officer, independent of and higher than the contracting officer. While a formal hearing with confrontation would not be required, the protesting bidder and other "interested parties" would be permitted to present written and oral objections to the decision which, along with agency legal, technical, and policy advice and the bid protest file, would provide the context for review. Even though the minimum standards of review would be similar to those employed by the courts, the opportunity for more control in the interest of better quality and better protection of the contractor's economic position would be available.[94] The written decision with reasons and the full review file would then be preserved for later scrutiny by GAO or the courts. A protesting bidder would be required to use the internal procedure before filing suit in the federal courts.

(b) An improved debriefing system would be developed to give each bidder or offeror maximum information about the award decision at the earliest possible time consistent with competitive bidding. The goal is to defuse protests by improved communication.[95] With better communication and internal review procedures, competing contractors should have more control over the risk of improperly losing the award.[96]

(c) Upon making a timely protest to the Bid Protest Officer within, say, five days after an award is made or an invitation cancelled, the award process or contract performance would be automatically suspended. The suspension would be effective whether the protest was made before or after award and would continue until a decision on the protest was made. To facilitate a good faith decision and to substitute certainty for discretion at this critical time, no decision adverse to the protesting bidder could be made in less than five working days beyond the date of the protest. Beyond this time, the dictates of urgency should control when the decision is made unless an advisory opinion is requested from GAO. If, before any decision is made, the award process or contract performance is permitted to continue, the protesting bidder may seek an injunction to enforce the automatic

---

[94] While similar in some respects to a recommendation by the Committee on Bids and Protests of the Section of Public Contract Law of the American Bar Association, this recommendation rejects the notion that the review process should be lodged in the agency boards of contract appeals and that decisions, while expedited, should be accompanied by notice, hearing, and confrontation, and reviewed in the federal courts under the Wunderlich Act, 41 U.S.C. § 321 (1971).

[95] This need is acknowledged by Air Force procurement officers. See note 29 supra.

[96] It has been suggested that while a dynamic model for competitive bidding must take uncontrollable risks—that is, that contracting officers will make illegal decisions—into account, that the probabilities of winning can better be calculated where the bidder has more control. The fact and cost of this control will influence rational decisions on whether to compete or not. See Stark & Mayer, supra note 13, at 470-71.

suspension i the federal courts.[97] Otherwise, there will be no access to the courts until the protest is resolved against the disappointed bidder.

3. By legislation, the following clarification could be made in the structure and powers of the federal courts in the area of bid protest litigation:

(a) As recommended by the Administrative Conference of the United States, the Administrative Procedure Act could be amended so as to clearly abolish the defense of sovereign immunity and to establish uniform standards for the review of final agency action.[98]

(b) A protesting bidder could be permitted to seek judicial review of any adverse decision by the Bid Protest Officer. The review should focus upon the documents and materials considered at the informal hearing and be governed by the "total context" approach developed in *Steinthal*. If, however, the decision were found to be "without rational basis," the plaintiff's only remedies would be a declaration of invalidity or damages. The automatic suspension while internal administrative review is underway is offered as a substitute for both the discretion of contracting officials to continue the award process in cases of urgency and the discretion of courts to enjoin the award process pending judicial review.

(c) The power both to issue appropriate injunctions and to award damages in bid protest litigation could be combined in one court, preferably the federal district court. The suggestion in *Steinthal* that one court should declare a contract invalid and another award damages is as unrealistic as the suggestion that injunctive relief should not be granted because the disappointed bidder has an adequate damage remedy in the Court of Claims. At some point, the courts must confront the question of what rights and remedies are consistent with a competitor's legitimate interests in the award process. Given the incentives and assumptions upon which government contracting is based, protection of competitive opportunity should, upon proper proof, include at the very least the net gains prevented by failing to receive the particular contract at issue.[99]

---

[97] The seeds for this form of equitable relief were planted in Wheelabrator Corp. v. Chafee, 455 F.2d 1306 (D.C. Cir. 1971), where the court was receptive to the notion that where a plaintiff was likely to succeed on the merits the administrative process might be enjoined pending resolution of a protest by GAO. See JAFFE, *supra* note 2, at 663-86. Under this recommendation, the policy decision favoring suspension of the award process pending internal administrative review would be made by the Executive Order and removed from the discretion of the court. Likelihood of success, therefore, would be irrelevant. In a post-*Steinthal* decision, the Court of Appeals for the District of Columbia has affirmed a district court injunction against proceeding with contract award pending determination of a GAO protest. General Elec. Co. v. Seamans, No. 248-72 (C.A.D.C., June 16, 1972).

[98] *See* Cramton, *supra* note 3, at 428-36.

[99] Private contract law has struggled with fitful success to resolve issues of liability and remedy arising in business relations where some reliance has been induced and some profit expectations created but an agreement enforceable under traditional doctrine has not yet emerged. Apart from restitution and cases where fraudulent intent is proved, [*see, e.g.,* Keeton, *Fraud: The Necessity for an Intent to*

In summary, these proposed changes should accomplish three basic objectives: (1) strengthen GAO's role as overall "watchdog" of the award systems in the executive departments and initiator of proposals for change; (2) provide the disappointed bidder with a short but automatic suspension of the award process in particular cases, which, combined with improved procedures for internal administrative review, should increase the chances that award decisions will be made correctly rather than quickly; and (3) clarify and redefine the role of federal courts in bid protest litigation to insure that they are the exclusive forum for the balancing of the public and private interests involved. To some, these changes will be radical or politically unrealistic. Clearly, the details for implementation have yet to be developed. However, the basic thrust of the changes—to shift the primary responsibility for the initial review of agency award decisions from GAO and the courts to the agency itself and provide for an automatic suspension while that review is underway—is sound. In my judgment, it offers the best opportunity to differentiate more plainly the private and overriding public interests involved in particular procurements and to improve their protection without unduly impairing governmental effectiveness.

EPILOGUE

As this article goes to press, a four volume Report by the Commission on Government Procurement has just been submitted to Congress. Volume Four, Part G deals with Administrative and Legal Remedies and Chapter 3 of Part G discusses and makes recommendations concerning *Disputes Related To The Award Of Contracts.* Without embellishment, the specific recommendations, taken from a Summary of the Report, are as follows:

Deceive, 5 U.C.L.A.L. REV. 583 (1958)], is there any liability when the inducer of reliance and creator of expectations terminates the relationship before the magic moment of formation? While no clear trends have emerged, recent cases have been more willing to impose some liability under the label of promissory estoppel or "good faith bargaining" and have been open to remedies that include net gains prevented by the improper termination. For disparate indicators pointing toward a more cohesive theory, see Greene v. Howard Univ., 412 F.2d 1128, 1133-34 (D.C. Cir. 1969) (university terminates non-tenured faculty); Clausen & Sons v. Theo. Hamm Brewing Co., 395 F.2d 388 (8th Cir. 1968) (brewery terminates existing franchise relationship); Coleman Eng'r Co. v. North Am. Aviation, 55 Cal. Rptr. 1, 420 P.2d 713 (1966) (subcontractor withdraws from negotiations with prime contractor); Marchiondon v. Scheck, 78 N.M. 440, 432 P.2d 405 (1967) (owner terminates listing with broker); Hoffman v. Red Owl Stores, Inc., 26 Wis.2d 683, 133 N.W.2d 267 (1965) (prospective franchisee breaks off negotiations with grocery chain); Air Technology Corp. v. General Elec. Co., 347 Mass. 613, 199 N.E.2d 538 (1964) (prime contractor terminates proposed joint venture with subcontractor); Jenkins Towel Serv., Inc. v. Fidelity-Philadelphia Trust Co., 400 Pa. 98, 161 A.2d 334 (1960) (seller refuses award to highest bidder); Locke v. United States, 283 F.2d 521 (Ct. Cl. 1960). For excellent discussion, see Slawson, *Standard Form Contracts and Democratic Control of Lawmaking Power,* 84 HARV. L. REV. 529 (1971); Knapp, *Enforcing the Contract to Bargain,* 44 N.Y.U.L. REV. 673 (1969); Henderson, *Promissory Estoppel and Traditional Contract Doctrine,* 78 YALE L.J. 343, 357-65, 376-87 (1969); Summers, *"Good Faith" in General Contract Law and the Sales Provisions of the Uniform Commercial Code,* 54 VA. L. REV. 195, 216-27, 256-58 (1968); Comment, *Once More Into the Breach: Promissory Estoppel and Traditional Damage Doctrine,* 37 U. CHI. L. REV. 559 (1970).

Recommendation 13. Promulgate award protest procedures that adequately inform protestors of the steps that can be taken to seek review of administrative decisions in the contract award process.

Recommendation 14. Continue the General Accounting Office as an award protest-resolving forum.

Recommendation 15. Establish, through executive branch and GAO corporation, more expeditious and mandatory time requirements for processing protests through GAO.

Recommendation 16. Establish in the executive procurement regulations, in co-operation with the GAO, a coordinated requirement for high-level management review of any decision to award a contract while a protest is pending with GAO.

Recommendation 17. GAO should continue to recommend termination for convenience of the Government of improperly awarded contracts in appropriate instances.

Recommendation 18. Improve contracting agency debriefing procedures.

Recommendation 19. Establish a pre-award protest procedure in all contracting agencies.

Recommendation 20. Conduct periodic reviews by GAO of agency award protest procedures and practices.

While discussing the value of judicial review and the need to clarify problems of scope and remedy, the Report made no specific recommendations regarding the role of the courts in this area.

SEC NO-ACTION LETTERS: INFORMAL ADVICE AS A DISCRETIONARY ADMINISTRATIVE CLEARANCE

WILLIAM J. LOCKHART*

The Securities and Exchange Commission has long encouraged its staff to provide to the public written advice about the need to comply, or means of complying, with the registration obligations of the 1933 Securities Act.[1] Typically, that advice is provided in the form of so-called "no-action letters," in which the staff advises a stockholder, upon inquiry, whether it would recommend Commission enforcement action if he should sell his stock, without prior registration, under the circumstances and in the manner proposed by the stockholder. The term is used loosely here to refer to all staff responses determining "no-action" requests—denial as well as approval of no-action positions.

Though neither statute nor regulation imposes an obligation to render no-action advice,[2] the no-action process has become a major staff function, particularly in the Division of Corporation Finance, which processes most of the no-action letters issued by the SEC staff.

The no-action process is performed primarily by informal written exchanges between staff and applicant, results in determinations based upon staff-developed interpretations and policies as well as upon discretionary consideration of the applicant's circumstances, and significantly affects the financial condition of applicants with little or no opportunity for agency or judicial review. For these reasons, in searching for wisdom about informal and discretionary functions of federal agencies, the Informal Action Committee of the Administrative Conference of the United States made an extensive investigation of the no-action process as administered in the Division of Corporation Finance of the SEC. This article examining those discretionary processes is drawn largely from the author's report as a consultant to the Informal Action Committee.[3]

---

* Professor of Law, University of Utah.

[1] 15 U.S.C. § 77; 3 Loss, SECURITIES REGULATION 1894-99 (2d ed. 1961); COMMISSION ON ORGANIZATION OF THE EXECUTIVE BRANCH OF THE GOVERNMENT, TASK FORCE REPORT ON LEGAL SERVICES AND PROCEDURE 189 (1955).

[2] Regulations merely inform applicants of the availability of the advisory process and the manner in which requests for advice should be submitted. 17 C.F.R. §§ 200.81, 202.1(d), 202.2 (Supp. 1971); SEC Securities Act Release No. 5127 (Jan. 25, 1971) CCH FED. SEC. L. REP. ¶ 66,481.10 (describing procedure and form for no-action requests).

[3] Administrative Conference of the United States, *Report of the Committee on Informal Action in Support of Recommendation No. 19* ("SEC No-Action Letters Under Section 4 of the Securities Act of 1933"), by William J. Lockhart, consultant, in 1 ADMINISTRATIVE CONFERENCE OF THE UNITED STATES, RECOMMENDATIONS AND REPORTS 440 (January 8, 1968—June 30, 1970). [Hereinafter cited as REPORT.]

For a study of the no-action process based on currently available, published copies of no-action requests and responses and reaffirming most recommendations of the Report, see Lowenfels, *SEC No-Action Letters: Some Problems and Suggested Approaches*, 71 COLUM. L. REV. 1256 (1971).

The staff of the Division of Corporation Finance in 1968 reported that it generated no-action letters at a rate of approximately 5000 per year, constituting approximately eighty per cent of all no-action letters generated by the entire SEC staff.[4] The objective of about four-fifths of the no-action letters rendered by the Office of Chief Counsel of the Division is to advise stockholders who have received unregistered stock whether they must register it before selling or risk SEC enforcement action. Both oral and written advice on that problem are given by the Chief Counsel's office. Oral advice tends to be general and interpretive; it assists counsel in identifying specific problems, often with a view to a more specific application for a no-action letter. Written advice in most cases is specific and conclusory; it includes little or no interpretive material but expresses the staff's conclusion whether, on a particular set of facts, it would recommend that the Commission take action if a stockholder should sell stock without registration.

The assurance provided by a no-action letter is treated as binding by the Commission, though the estoppel effect of such a letter has not been judicially determined.[5] Such an assurance may also tend to discourage private lawsuits based on sales made without registration. However, because the no-action letter is founded upon carefully constructed factual representations, it is not regarded by enforcement personnel as a bar to investigations of unregistered sales until it is determined that the sale in question conformed to the factual representations.

I

THE SUBSTANTIVE CONTEXT

This study of the no-action process in the Division of Corporation Finance (the "Division") was completed before the recent adoption of Rule 144.[6] The Commission

---

[4] Staff Memorandum to Warner W. Gardner, in REPORT, app. E.

[5] 3 L. LOSS, SECURITIES REGULATION 1843-44 (2d ed. 1961). *But see* United States v. Anzelmo, 319 F. Supp. 1106, 1117 (E.D. La. 1970).

SEC Securities Act Release No. 5098 (Oct. 29, 1970), [1970-1971 Transfer Binder] CCH FED. SEC. L. REP. ¶ 77,921, announcing a policy of public availability of no-action letters cautioned that "[i]t should be recognized that no-action and interpretative responses by the staff are subject to reconsideration and should not be regarded as precedents binding on the Commission."

The collateral effect of a no-action letter occasionally has an impact upon litigation: e.g., in determining the obligations of a transfer agent to record shares in the name of the acquiring stockholder. *See, e.g.,* Donlon Ventures, Inc. v. Avien, Inc., 158 N.Y.L.J., No. 5, p. 10, [1966-67 Decisions Transfer Binder] CCH FED. SEC. L. REP. ¶ 91,961 (1967). And in a recent case the defendant's disregard of a staff letter declining to take a no-action position may have played a role in determining the willfulness of his violation, according to a staff attorney in the Division of Trading and Markets. *See* United States v. Wolfson, 269 F. Supp. 621 (S.D.N.Y. 1967), *aff'd* 405 F.2d 779 (2d Cir. 1968), *cert. denied,* 394 U.S. 946 (1969); United States v. Wolfson, 282 F. Supp. 772 (S.D.N.Y. 1967), *rev'd & rem'd,* 437 F.2d 862 (2d Cir. 1970).

[6] Rule 144 was proposed as alternative to the recommendations of the *Disclosure Study,* note 14 *infra,* in SEC Securities Act Release No. 5087 (Sept. 22, 1970), [1970-1971 Transfer Binder] CCH FED. SEC. L. REP. ¶ 77,909. A revised proposal was published in SEC Securities Act Release No. 5186 CCH Special Report, No. 387, Extra ed., Sept. 15, 1971 (Sept. 10, 1971); and the Rule was adopted after further revisions in SEC Securities Act Release No. 5223 (Jan. 11, 1972), [1971-1972 Transfer Binder] CCH FED. SEC. L. REP. ¶ 78,487, effective April 15, 1972. [Hereinafter cited as Release 5223.] The Rule provides an exemption from "underwriter" status (see discussion in text at notes 12-31 *infra*) for

hopes, by that rule, to provide objective standards that will resolve many of the substantive uncertainties that prompted no-action requests and to reduce the burden of the no-action process.[7] Despite adoption of that rule, however, an understanding of the substantive context which prompted the demand for no-action letters—as well as the adoption of Rule 144—is essential to an understanding of the informal exercise of discretion in the no-action process. Further, that understanding may be necessary to understand the likelihood of continued demand for interpretive letters to clarify the application of Rule 144.[8]

The substantive problems resolved by the no-action process in the Division prior to Rule 144 were basically concerned with two aspects of the single question of whether the 1933 Act[9] requires that an applicant's stock be registered before sale: (1) whether the registration provisions are applicable to the applicant's proposed sale of stock, and (2) whether the applicant is relieved of the registration obligations by various exemptions created by statute and rule.

The basic purpose of the 1933 Act is to assure that public distributions of securities are accompanied by disclosure of all information material to a prospective stockholder's investment decision. The disclosure objectives are accomplished through the registration and prospectus delivery requirements of section 5 of that Act, which apply to any "sale" or "offer to sell" of a "security."[10] Failure to comply with those

---

sales of unregistered stock by control persons and others who acquired their stock from the issuer, provided sales are made under prescribed terms and conditions.

[7] SEC Securities Act Release No. 5223 (Jan. 11, 1972) CCH FED. SEC. L. REP. ¶ 78,487 *supra* note 6, announcing adoption of Rule 144 and analyzing the new rule, states at 12:

"The staff will not issue no-action letters with respect to resales of securities acquired after the effective date of the rule, but would issue interpretative letters to assist persons in complying with the new rule. In connection with securities acquired prior to the adoption of the rule, the staff would continue to issue no-action letters."

It is not clear whether the above withdraws the explicit invitation to broker-dealers to seek staff advice respecting the applicability of the 1933 and 1934 Acts to the sale of particular blocks of securities, as set forth in SEC Securities Act Release No. 5168 (July 7, 1971) CCH FED. SEC. L. REP. ¶ 22,760.

[8] Examples of potential problems which may be resolved by interpretive letters include:

(1) the definition of "affiliate," which turns on a control relationship with the issuer, and leaves the concept of "control" undefined. It further leaves unclear whether the "issuer," with which the "affiliate" shares a control relationship, refers to that term as it is defined in section 2(11) of the 1933 Act, thus including a second level of control—that is, affiliates of persons in a control relationship with the issuing company.

(2) the "brokers' transactions" by which sales are permitted under Rule 144. These are defined to require that the broker not be aware "of circumstances indicating that the person for whose account the securities are sold is an underwriter with respect to the securities." SEC Securities Act Release No. 5223, at 11 (Jan. 11, 1972). That definition seemingly reincarnates the mystique of "a view to distribution" which the rule is designed to avoid. The impression is furthered by the following comment in the explanatory portion of SEC Securities Act Release, at 13:

"In view of the objectives and policies underlying the Act, the rule shall not be available to any individual or entity with respect to any transaction which, although in technical compliance with the rule, is part of a plan by such individual or entity to distribute or redistribute securities to the public. In such case, registration is required."

[9] Securities Act of 1933, 15 U.S.C. § 77a-77aa (1970).

[10] Rule 144, however, is based, in part, on the view that adequate public information is available without registration where the issuer has, for at least 90 days, been in compliance with the reporting requirements of the 1934 Act or has otherwise made certain specified information publicly available.

requirements may subject the seller to the Commission's injunctive remedies under section 20 of the Act, the absolute liability to purchasers provided by section 12(1), and possible criminal remedies under section 24. In addition to those sanctions, a broker-dealer who participates in a sale of unregistered securities is subject to a range of sanctions including censure and denial, suspension, or revocation of his broker-dealer registration.[11]

In order to exempt regular trading transactions by persons not involved in promoting the sale of a security, persons other than an "issuer, underwriter or dealer" are exempted by section 4(1) of the Act from the registration and prospectus requirements of section 5. A further exemption, also to protect ordinary trading transactions, is given to dealers or brokers, provided they are not participating in a general public distribution of the issuer's stock.[12] Because a liberal application of these exemptions would defeat the disclosure objectives of the Act, the Commission and staff have sought to limit their availability.

A primary means by which the Act reaches general public distributions of securities is by excluding an "underwriter" from the section 4 exemption and by broadly defining that term. Thus, one who falls within the statutory definition of "underwriter" must comply with the registration and prospectus requirements of the Act. "Underwriter" is defined, in section 2(11) of the 1933 Act, as

> any person who has purchased from an issuer with a view to, or offers or sells for an issuer in connection with, the distribution of any security, or participates or has a direct or indirect participation in any such undertaking, or participates or has a participation in the direct or indirect underwriting of any such undertaking; but such term shall not include a person whose interest is limited to a commission from an underwriter or dealer not in excess of the usual and customary distributors' or sellers' commission. As used in this paragraph the term "issuer" shall include, in addition to an issuer, any person directly or indirectly controlling or controlled by the issuer, or any person under direct or indirect common control with the issuer.[13]

The interpretation and application of the "underwriter" definition is the interpretive problem presented by the bulk of the requests for no-action letters received by the Division. And the interpretive problem most frequently encountered concerns the application of the phrase "with a view to . . . distribution," which is generally acknowledged to import an extremely subjective test of "underwriter" status. Thus, the recent *Disclosure Study* conducted by the SEC staff under direction of former Commissioner Wheat, after analyzing the disclosure policies effected by the the 1933 Act, commented:

> [T]he Commission and those affected by the '33 Act soon found themselves tied to a wholly subjective test by which to determine when a person is an "underwriter." Does the person who buys from the issuer or controlling stockholder

---

[11] Securities Exchange Act of 1934, 15 U.S.C. §§ 780(b)(5) & (7) (1971).
[12] Securities Act of 1933, 15 U.S.C. §§ 77(d)(3) & (4) (1971).
[13] Securities Act of 1933, 15 U.S.C. § 77b (11) (1971).

have the "view" or "intent" of later reselling his securities to the public? How can his true "intention" be accurately determined?[14]

Although the *Disclosure Study* condemns the subjective quality of these tests and their accompanying uncertainty, it is clear that the main dimensions of the interpretive positions taken by the staff are supported by judicial interpretations of the sections in question.[15]

The following paragraphs illustrate some of the typical interpretive problems to which the 1933 Act, prior to the recent adoption of Rule 144, gave rise and particularly the magnitude of the uncertainties which generated no-action requests.[16] Much of the "law" reflected here has been displaced or modified by Rule 144 but is an essential background to the operation of that rule and to the exercise of discretion in the no-action decision-making process.

(1) X Company issues a noncontrolling block of its stock to *A*, a director and controlling shareholder, relying on the exemption from registration provided by section 4(2) of the 1933 Act for private sales that do not involve a "public offering." *A* holds the stock for six months and now seeks to sell it through a broker in the over-the-counter market. If *A* sells, the staff will ordinarily conclude that he earlier purchased the security from his company (the "issuer") "with a view to . . . distribution" of the security, or that he is "selling for" the issuer "in connection with" a distribution. Under either construction, *A* would be regarded as an "underwriter" who must comply with the registration requirements before selling his stock.[17]

The original sale by X Company to *A* may also be subject to challenge on the ground that *A*'s conduct demonstrates that his purchase contemplated a "public offering," thus compromising the original claim of a private offering exemption. The determinative question—one of "fact" in the staff's view—is whether *A*'s intent, at the time he took the stock, was to hold for investment or to distribute the stock. Even though *A*, at the issuer's insistence, may have executed a letter reciting his "investment intent" at the time he took the stock, the staff may conclude that the latter sale is a more reliable indication of *A*'s earlier state of mind. Hence, the staff would deny a request for a no-action letter.[18]

---

[14] U.S. Securities & Exchange Comm. Disclosure to Investors—A Reappraisal of Federal Administrative Policies under the '33 and '34 Acts 163 (1969). [Hereinafter cited as Disclosure Study.]

[15] *See generally*, J. Jennings & H. Marsh, Securities Regulation 271-363 (2d ed. 1968).

[16] For a more detailed description of the interpretive uncertainties that arise from the subjective tests traditionally applied, see Disclosure Study 164-77.

[17] SEC Securities Act Release No. 4445 (Feb. 2, 1962) CCH Fed. Sec. L. Rep. ¶ 3090.101; 4845.835; 22,753-759 [may be found in U.S. Securities & Exchange Comm., Compilation of Releases Dealing with Matters Frequently Arising under the Securities Act of 1933-44 (1965)] [hereinafter cited as Release 4445]; SEC Securities Act Release No. 4552 (Nov. 6, 1962) CCH Fed. Sec. L. Rep. ¶ 2770-83; 47,341.14 (Compilation, *supra* at 49) [hereinafter cited as Release 4552]; SEC v. North Am. Research & Dev. Corp., 280 F. Supp. 106, 121-22 (S.D.N.Y. 1968), *aff'd*, 424 F.2d 63 (2d Cir. 1970); *In re* Ira Haupt & Co., 23 S.E.C. 589, 596-99 (1946). *But see* example (5), *infra*, under former Rule 154.

[18] Release 4552.

Finally, A's control relationship, though suggesting a motive to distribute on behalf of his company, is not essential to the above-described application of the Act. Thus, a noncontrolling shareholder who acquired a noncontrolling block of shares in similar circumstances may also be viewed as having acquired the shares with the forbidden intent or "view to . . . distribution"; and a large number of no-action letters present just such circumstances.[19]

(2) A, in the above example, makes a further "private offering" of a noncontrolling block of X Company stock to a friend, B, who owns no other shares in X Company. B buys the stock with a representation of his investment intent, holds the stock for six months and then seeks to sell through a broker in the over-the-counter market. Section 2(11) provides (only for purposes of that definition of "underwriter") that an "issuer" includes one in a "control" relationship with the issuer. Hence, A, a controlling shareholder of X Company, is an issuer and B may be an underwriter if he bought from A "with a view to . . . distribution" rather than investment.[20] Again, the deteminative "fact" is B's state of mind at the time of his purchase from A. If he should request a no-action letter, the staff would conclude that his sale after holding only six months demonstrates that he did not have sufficient investment intent at the time of his purchase.[21] But if B suffers a severe financial setback that was not foreseeable at the time of purchase, that "change of circumstances" may support the inference that he bought for investment, despite his present desire to sell.[22]

(3) In example (1), a broker who executes a sale of A's stock will want to determine whether A is a so-called "controlling person" of X Corporation, and hence an issuer under the underwriter definition. If A is a controlling person, then the broker will be "selling for" an issuer and, under the definition, will be an underwriter.[23] The staff considers the question of control to be one of "fact," which must be determined by an analysis of all the circumstances and relationships between the person in question and the company and other controlling persons.[24]

(4) In examples (1) and (2), a broker who executes sales of stock for A or B will want to know whether either is an underwriter: whether B took from A "with a view to . . . distribution," or whether A took from the issuer with such intent. If that is the case, then, under section 2(11) of the 1933 Act, the broker may also

---

[19] *Id. See also* Release 4445; DISCLOSURE STUDY 161-62.

[20] DISCLOSURE STUDY 161-62; SEC v. North Am. Research & Dev. Corp., 280 F. Supp. 106, 121-22 (S.D.N.Y. 1968), *aff'd*, 424 F.2d 63 (2d Cir. 1970); Israels, *Checklist For Broker-Dealer Inquiry As To Customer's* Control *or* Underwriter *Relationship; Or Where Sale of Securities Proposed In* Brokerage Transaction *In Reliance Upon S.E.C. Rule 154*, 18 Bus. LAW. 94 (1962).

[21] *Re: The Crowell-Collier Publishing Co.* SEC Securities Act Release No. 3825 (Aug. 12, 1957) CCH FED. SEC. L. REP. ¶¶ 2165.15; 2850.25; 2850.81 (Compilation, *supra* note 17, at 13); Release 4552; PRACTICING LAW INSTITUTE, TRANSCRIPT OF PLI FORUM ON SEC PROBLEMS OF CONTROLLING STOCK-HOLDERS AND IN UNDERWRITINGS 27-31, 61-62 (C. Israels ed. 1962).

[22] Release 4552.

[23] Release 4445; SEC Securities Act Release No. 5168 (July 7, 1971) CCH FED. SEC. L. REP. ¶ 22, 760 [hereinafter cited as Release 5168]; PLI FORUM, *supra* note 21, at 51.

[24] *See* 2 L. Loss, SECURITIES REGULATION 770-83 (2d ed. 1961).

be an underwriter if he "participates or has a direct or indirect participation in" a sale by one who is a statutory underwriter. To avoid a charge (under section 15(b)(5)(D) or (E) of the 1934 Act) of willful violation of the Act and the accompanying possibility of disciplinary action,[25] he should conscientiously investigate any facts which suggest that his seller occupies such an underwriter status.[26]

(5) In all examples, it is possible that the seller or broker might also want to determine whether the proposed sale constitutes a "distribution" of the X Company stock. Section 2(1) of the 1933 Act, in defining "underwriter," imposes that status only where there is a "view to . . . distribution" or where a transaction is consummated "in connection with . . . the distribution" of a security. The term "distribution" has always been regarded by the Commission "as essentially synonymous with public offering."[27]

In defining the narrow exemption provided by section 4(4) of the 1933 Act for "brokers' transactions" on behalf of controlling persons, the Commission, by rule, defined a "distribution" to exclude "transactions involving an amount not substantial in relation to the number of shares or units of the security outstanding and the aggregate volume of trading in such security." The rule permits brokers' sales (for controlling persons) within certain quantitative limitations by excluding such sales from the definition of the term "distribution"; but that use of the term is applicable only for purposes of the exemption for brokers' transactions.[28] Thus, the broad statutory concept of "distribution," embracing any public sale, would be applicable to the term as it is used in the "underwriter" definition. And sales by a controlling person of stock privately acquired from the issuer, unless otherwise exempt, would involve a distribution, rendering both the seller and the broker statutory underwriters.

(6) Although one who sells for an issuing company or for a person controlling the issuer ordinarily falls within the statutory definition of underwriter, he may claim exemption under section 4(2) of the 1933 Act, which exempts "transactions by an issuer not involving any public offering." Under *SEC v. Ralston Purina Co.*,[29] the fundamental test that determines availability of the exemption is whether the offeror's relationship to the offerees in the private transaction is such that the latter "need . . . the protections afforded by registration."[30] But like the other interpretive problems described above, the question whether a transaction involves a public offering is viewed as "essentially a question of fact." And that fact question "necessitates a consideration of all surrounding circumstances, including such

[25] 15 U.S.C. §§ 78o(b)(5)(D) or (E) (1970).
[26] Release 4445; Release 5168; SEC v. North Am. Research & Dev. Corp., 280 F. Supp. 106, 126-27 (S.D.N.Y. 1968), aff'd 424 F.2d 63 (2d Cir. 1970).
[27] DISCLOSURE STUDY 161-62.
[28] SEC Rule 154, 17 C.F.R. 230.154 (1972); SEC Securities Act Release No. 4818 (Jan. 21, 1966) CCH FED. SEC. L. REP. ¶ 2920. Rule 154 is rescinded by the Release announcing adoption of Rule 144. SEC Securities Act Release No. 5223 (Jan. 11, 1972) CCH FED. SEC. L. REP. ¶ 78,478.
[29] 346 U.S. 119 (1952).
[30] *Id.* at 127.

factors as the relationship between the offerees and the issuer, the nature, scope, size, type and manner of the offering."[31]

II

THE DEMAND FOR NO-ACTION LETTERS

No ready thesis adequately explains the heavy demand for no-action letters reflected in the volume of letters generated by the Division.[32] Applicants have not been surveyed to determine the motivations which prompted their requests, but inquiry and hypothesis suggest some probable answers.

A partial explanation, of course, lies in the complications, costs, and delays incident to registration of stock for sale, which may be avoided if it is determined that registration is not required. Yet very nearly 40% of the requests appear to be from nonlawyer stockholders[33] who, presumably, would not be fully aware of the burdens of registration. And while the remaining 60% of the requests originate with counsel, the reasons for that demand are also not readily apparent. Certainly the determinations of "ultimate fact" involved in deciding whether registration is required are not unlike similar determinations typically made by counsel without agency assistance in advising clients about proposed transactions. Moreover, no-action letters are sought in the face of some substantial reasons for not doing so. Staff responses to no-action requests are frequently unfavorable—forty per cent so in one analysis[34]—and are particularly apt to be negative where the availability of an exemption from registration is for any reason doubtful.[35] Since the proposed transaction might easily have escaped regulatory attention if consummated without approval, and in view of the modest rate of success, it is apparent that other considerations prompt the large number of requests. Furthermore, though the usual delay in staff response to no-action requests is not excessive,[36] the delay is undoubtedly substantial from the viewpoint of applicants anxious to take advantage of a favorable market opportunity.

Although potential sellers of securities have good reason not to seek no-action

---

[31] Release 4552; see SEC Securities Act Release No. 5121 (Dec. 30, 1970) CCH FED. SEC. L. REP. ¶ 77,943.

[32] See text at note 4 supra.

[33] This data derives from an examination by the author of no-action requests for the months of March and July, 1969, on file in the SEC Division of Corporation Finance.

[34] This rough datum derives from an examination by the author of responses to no-action requests for the periods Feb. 14-28, 1969, and April 1-18, 1969, a total of 351 letters, on file in the SEC Division of Corporation Finance.

[35] "[T]he big practical limitation upon the utility of 'no-action' requests is the difficulty of getting a reply from the Commission. The sad truth seems to be that you get 'no-action' letters in the clear cases but have an awful time getting them—or don't even ask—in the cases where you really need them." PLI FORUM, supra note 21, at 19 (comments of Mr. Gilroy).

[36] See text following note 57, infra. Israels, in his Checklist for Assuring Broker-Dealers' Compliance with Restrictions on the Sale of Unregistered Securities, comments that the no-action procedure is "time-consuming." H. Wander & W. Grienenberger (eds.), SELECTED ARTICLES ON FEDERAL SECURITIES LAW 79 (A.B.A. Section of Corporation, Banking and Business Law, 1968).

letters, the continuing stream of applications, may be explained by a combination of factors. These include (1) issuers' fears of civil liability to ultimate purchasers of unregistered securities under section 12(1) of the 1933 Act; (2) broker-dealers' fears of disciplinary proceedings brought against them on account of sales of unregistered securities; (3) the enforcement practices of the Commission and staff; and (4) the unreliability of counsel's advice as an assurance against disciplinary proceedings.

Technically, the absolute liability imposed by section 12(1) of the 1933 Act on anyone who, without registration, "offers or sells a security" would not appear to pose a threat to the issuing company as a result of a private placement, for the violation emanates from a further sale by the recipient. On further consideration, however, several very real threats to the issuer arise: (1) The Commission may commence a formal investigation, suspend trading or bring injunctive proceedings, with serious consequences in the securities market. (2) The ultimate purchaser may claim extensive civil liabilities on the theory that the sale was made to him as part of a distribution on behalf of the issuer—a claim that is encouraged by the statutory definition of an underwriter as including one who "sells for" the issuer. (3) The practical financial consequence is enhanced by the prospect that the issuer may be required to show the potential liability on its balance sheet as a contingent claim. (4) Though it is more doubtful, it is possible that the original recipient of the private placement, if held liable to a later purchaser, would be able, in turn, to recover against the issuer because of the absolute liability imposed by section 12(1). For all of these reasons, it has been traditional for the issuer in a private sale to require an investment commitment from the purchaser to protect against a later sale which may destroy the private offering exemption—an eventuality made more likely by judicial and administrative construction. To assure that investment commitment, issuing companies are commonly advised to stamp an investment restriction on the face of the stock certificates issued in a private placement and to issue "stop transfer" orders to the transfer agent, requiring notice to company counsel if the restricted shares should be presented for transfer to a later purchaser.[37]

Similar threats of liability and disciplinary proceedings confront a broker-dealer who executes a sale found to have been made without exemption and thus in violation of registration and prospectus requirements. Division personnel uniformly agree that a large proportion of no-action requests actually originate with broker-dealers. Even before the 1964 amendments to the 1933 Securities Act, the Commission's exercise of its power over registration of broker-dealers had impressed upon them

---

[37] The Division of Corporation Finance has recently advised that it "will regard the presence or absence of an appropriate legend and stop-transfer instructions as a factor in considering whether the circumstances surrounding the offering are consistent with the exemption under Section 4(2) of the Act." SEC Securities Act Release No. 5121 (Dec. 30, 1970). *See* Israels, *Some Commercial Overtones of Private Placement*, in H. WANDER, *supra* note 36, at 125, 129-30, 135-43; Wood, *The Investment-Intent Dilemma in Secondary Transactions, id.* at 145, 169-70.

their vulnerability to sanctions for participating in distributions of securities acquired through private placements.[38] In a 1962 release, the Commission indicated that dealers would be held personally responsible for investigating the underlying facts supporting stockholders' claims of exemption, and that they are obliged "to make an appropriate investigation as to who their seller was and not simply to rely upon the opinion of the seller's attorney that no control relationship existed."[39] And in a 1971 release the Commission "reaffirmed" the broker-dealers' obligation to know their customers and the securities being sold, emphasizing the firms' obligations to develop effective supervisory procedures.[40]

The 1964 amendments significantly expanded the disciplinary powers of the SEC, giving it power to proceed against individual registered representatives as well as against broker-dealer firms, to impose a wider range of sanctions including censure and suspension, and to prohibit association of named violators with any broker-dealers.[41] In addition to seeking revocation or suspension of registration of broker-dealer firms, the Commission has enhanced the effect of such proceedings by substantial application of its new statutory power to proceed against individuals. In the fiscal years 1966 through 1969 the Commission instituted such proceedings against a total of 489 individuals.[42]

Most broker-dealer firms that are members of a registered exchange or of the National Association of Securities Dealers (NASD) have established supervisory procedures designed to minimize the risk of violations by their representatives. The procedures tend to focus upon a wide range of financial standards and rules designed to promote "just and equitable principles of trade;"[43] but if carefully followed, they would generally bring questionable transactions in "restricted" securities to the attention of supervising officers. It seems more doubtful whether ordinary supervisory procedures effectively control distributions of securities not stamped with an investment restriction, but there is a growing tendency for firms to establish compliance procedures under a supervising officer designed to focus specifically on compliance with federal securities acts.

Although the formal training of representatives in matters of federal securities law is limited,[44] the lore of the securities business supplements the formal super-

[38] See, e.g., Gilligan, Will & Co. v. SEC, 267 F.2d 461 (2d Cir. 1959), cert. denied, 361 U.S. 896 (1959); and list of revocation proceedings, e.g., 26 SEC Ann. Rep. 92-106 (1960).

[39] Release 4445, Compilation at 45.

[40] Release 5168.

[41] Securities Act of 1934, 15 U.S.C. §§ 77o(b)(5)(D), 77o(b)(7) (1971). See generally Greene, Regulation of Entry Into The Securities Business, in H. Wander, supra note 36 at 487; Sterling, National Association of Securities Dealers and the Securities Act Amendments of 1964, id. at 495.

[42] 32 SEC Ann. Rep. 58 (1966); 33 SEC Ann. Rep. 77 (1967); 34 SEC Ann. Rep. 90 (1968); 35 SEC Ann. Rep. 96 (1969).

[43] See National Association of Securities Dealers Rules of Fair Practice § 27 (1970), adopted pursuant to 1934 Act, §§ 15A(b)(8) & (9), 15 U.S.C. §§ 78o-3(b)(8) & (9) (1970), 1934 Act § 15(b)(10), 15 U.S.C. § 78o(b)(10) (1971), and Securities Exchange Act Reg. 15b10-4, 17 C.F.R. § 240.15b10-4 (Supp. 1972); SEC Securities Act Release No. 5168 (July 7, 1971).

[44] See, e.g., National Association of Securities Dealers, NASD Training Guide 96-113 (1969). See recommendations for more extensive development of compliance checklists, requirements for internal

visory structure. Both SEC enforcement personnel and NASD representatives indicate that the availability of the no-action process to clear "investment stock" is well understood by most representatives. And it seems likely that the lore of no-action letters is substantially contributed to by typical SEC investigative practices. Though a no-action letter does not assure immunity, investigations are more likely to focus upon those transactions in which a no-action letter does not appear in the file.[45] Where an investigator from a regional office is analyzing a large, questionable distribution, he is likely to inquire why a no-action letter was not obtained to support the transaction.[46]

All of these factors undoubtedly resulted in closer control of unregistered distributions in most broker-dealer firms; and, at least until Rule 144 is fully understood, supervisory or compliance officers are much more likely to insist upon either a no-action letter or the opinion of reliable counsel demonstrating the availability of an exemption from registration. However, broker-dealers to whom a proposed sale of "investment stock" is presented are not encouraged to have confidence in the opinion of private counsel. Thus, the Commission's comments in a 1962 release emphasized the unreliability of attorneys' opinions as the basis for a claimed exemption authorizing trading in unregistered securities. Reviewing a case in which reliance upon the advice of counsel had been held sufficient to insulate certain dealers from criminal liability for the sale of unregistered stock, the Commission stated that "the conduct of these dealers did not meet acceptable standards . . . . It was up to these dealers to make an appropriate investigation as to who their seller was and not simply to rely upon the opinion of the seller's attorney . . . ." The release emphasized that it is insufficient for dealers simply to obtain factual representations from the sellers and submit those representations to an attorney who supplies an opinion that an exemption is available:

> Obviously, an attorney's opinion based upon hypothetical facts is worthless if the facts are not as specified, or if unspecified but vital facts are not considered. Because of this, it is the practice of responsible counsel not to furnish an opinion concerning the availability of an exemption . . . unless such counsel have themselves carefully examined all of the relevant circumstances and satisfied themselves, to the extent possible, that the contemplated transaction is, in fact, not a part of an unlawful distribution. Indeed, if an attorney furnishes an opinion based solely upon hypothetical facts which he has made no effort to verify, and if he knows that his opinion will be relied upon as the basis for a substantial distribution of unregistered securities, a serious question arises as to the propriety of his professional conduct.[47]

---

accounting and oversight of self-regulatory systems proposed in SEC, REPORT OF THE ADVISORY COMMITTEE ON ENFORCEMENT POLICIES AND PRACTICES, at 14-16, 57-61 (1972).

[45] Interview with Mr. Ezra Weiss, then Associate Chief Counsel, Division of Trading and Markets, Securities and Exchange Commission.

[46] Id.

[47] Release 4445, COMPILATION at 45-46, discussing United States v. Crosby, 294 F.2d 928 (2d Cir. 1961). See also SEC Securities Act Release No. 5168 (July 7, 1971) CCH FED. SEC. L. REP. ¶ 22,760, indicating that any determination that an exemption exists should be made only after the broker-dealer

Responsible counsel may legitimately feel some trepidation in rendering opinions based on conclusions of "ultimate fact" about investment intent and involving extensive potential liability. Until recently, relatively few lawyers had studied or had experience with federal securities regulation. While a general understanding of the regulatory theory could be obtained from traditional sources, little material was available reflecting the concrete application of doctrine to the determination of investment intent. Thus, until the recent adoption of a policy making no-action requests and responses publicly available,[48] those materials were accessible only through private arrangements among SEC practitioners for the exchange and compilation of no-action letters as they were received. But those compilations were not generally accessible to the practitioners most in need of guidance. Furthermore, that condition prevailed in a legal context in which the *Disclosure Study*, after analyzing the substantive inconsistencies, concluded,

> In the area of statutory interpretation which is primarily involved, uncertainty and divergence of practice presently prevail to an unacceptable degree. Greater certainty and predictability are essential.
>
> . . . .
>
> Apart from the mere bulk of requests currently faced by the staff, there is a constant problem in providing reasonably consistent advice. Since the tests with which the staff must work are subjective, its reactions in given situations depend, to a degree at least, on a "feel" of the transaction conveyed by the request for "no action." Troublesome inconsistency is often the result. Yet that inconsistency, which exists within a relatively compact staff operating under a single director, pales in comparison with the inconsistency in advice given by private counsel as to when and under what circumstances securities sold in private offerings may be resold.[49]

In summary, private offerings have become increasingly popular as a means by which a company may acquire additional capital or compensate employees without undertaking the expense of registration. However, because of the potential liabilities to subsequent purchasers that may result from the sale of the unregistered stock by

---

has reviewed the facts relating to acquisition of the shares and an opinion has been obtained from "competent outside counsel having no proprietary interest in the offering . . . ." *Cf.* complaint in SEC v. National Student Marketing Corp., [1971-1972 Transfer Binder] CCH FED. SEC. L. REP. ¶ 93,360, directly charging two law firms with complicity in anti-fraud violations, including failure to advise the Commission of violations.

[48] SEC Securites Act Release No. 5098 (Oct. 29, 1970) CCH FED. L. REP. ¶ 77,921. [Hereinafter cited as Release 5098.] The new policy originated with suggestions by Professor Kenneth Culp Davis which prompted the SEC to request comments "on whether staff interpretative and no-action letters should be made available to the public." SEC Securities Act Release No. 4924 (Sept. 20, 1968) CCH FED. SEC. L. REP. ¶ 77,606. The proposal was also encouraged by Recommendation No. 19 of the Administrative Conference of the United States, adopted by the Conference at its Fourth Plenary Session, June 2-3, 1970. The text of Recommendation 19 closely follows the conclusions and recommendations of the Report from which this article is drawn. See note 3, *supra.*

Release 5098 contemplates publication of summaries of the more significant no-action letters in the Commission's News Digest; and a large number of letters have now been published in the current materials supplied with the CCH and BNA securities law loose-leaf services. See list of "No-action and Interpretative Letters" in 4 CCH FED. SEC. L. REP. ¶ 63,201.

[49] DISCLOSURE STUDY at 152, 176-77.

the immediate purchaser, the practice of stamping an investment restriction on the face of the stock certificate has increasingly been followed. That investment restriction may appear to the immediate purchaser to be a legalistic formality until he attempts to arrange for the sale of his stock through a broker-dealer. Because of the increasing frequency of Commission disciplinary and enforcement proceedings against broker-dealers, they are sensitized to the danger of selling unregistered "investment stock." When the prospective sale is brought to the attention of a supervising manager of the securities firm, he will ordinarily refuse to allow any sale to be executed until he receives a satisfactory opinion of counsel that a valid statutory exemption is available. Because of the understanding that many counsel will provide any opinion necessary to facilitate clients' sales, and because of Commission warnings that the opinion of private counsel will not necessarily insulate against disciplinary proceedings, many broker-dealers will insist upon a no-action letter unless the stockholder presents an opinion by counsel regarded as reliable. Further, it is a matter of general lore among broker-dealers and registered representatives that the safe thing to do, in any doubtful case, is to insist upon a no-action letter. And the investigation and enforcement practices of the Commission staff substantially contribute to that lore, for experience suggests to dealers that, in routine investigations, much less question is raised about transactions for which a no-action letter appears in the file.

Finally, where counsel is asked to render an opinion on the kind of "ultimate fact" questions involved in determining the availability of an exemption, he may well conclude that the uncertainty of the interpretive rules, or the unavailability of a sufficient number of concrete applications, renders it advisable to take advantage of the no-action procedure rather than risk an independent opinion.

These sources of demand for no-action letters suggest some doubt about whether the demand will diminish. Private offerings continue to produce a significant share of the total estimated gross proceeds from new securities offered.[50] Undoubtedly, the rules initiated by the *Disclosure Study* and culminating with the adoption of Rule 144[51] will reduce the uncertainty that prompts many no-action requests. But because the proposed rules are in some respects more rigidly restrictive, and somewhat uncertain with respect to unregistered sales of stock in nonreporting companies,[52] it seems possible that many transactions that are now executed without

---

[50] See SEC estimates of proceeds from private corporate offerings, *e.g.*, $2,023,789,000 in private offerings compared to $13,288,056,000 in registered public offerings in period Jan.-Ap. 1971. *Securities Offerings, Estimated Gross Proceeds from New Securities Offered for Cash in the United States*, SEC STATISTICAL BULL., June 1972, Vol. 31, No. 6, at 16.

It is possible that the substantial narrowing of the private offering exemption by SEC v. Continental Tobacco Co., 463 F.2d 137 (5th Cir. 1972), will ultimately reduce the volume of private offerings and of related no-action requests. In the shorter run, however, it seems as likely that narrowing of the exemption may result in an increase in demand for no-action or interpretive letters as counsel seek to clarify the remaining scope of the exemption.

[51] See note 6, *supra*, and accompanying text.

[52] Section (c)(2) of Rule 144, requiring certain information to be "publicly available" does not indicate what manner or extent of publicity will satisfy the rule.

notice will be more clearly identified as doubtful transactions. This, in turn, may produce additional requests for no-action letters, particularly for proposed "private transactions," which are not redefined by Rule 144. Obviously, this depends upon what proportion of the existing volume of private transactions are traceable to non-reporting companies.

Other factors may also produce additional demand for no-action letters. A more successful training program for registered representatives may be developed by the NASD, making representatives more aware of doubtful transactions, particularly as a result of the adoption of Rule 144. The expansion of relevant courses in the law schools and the continuing expansion of practice in that field by inexperienced lawyers both may add to the flow of requests for no-action letters. Continued aggressive enforcement and continuing doubt about the protection furnished by opinions of counsel will continue to induce broker-dealers to seek the security of a no-action letter where questions arise.

For these reasons, it may be desirable for the Commission, as well as other agencies, in structuring their advisory processes, to further consider the impact of enforcement practices, the role of private counsel, and the possibility of avoiding routine "clearances" in order to give more extensive consideration to questions which advance their policy and technical thought, with broader availability and fuller exposition of the grounds for their conclusions. Perhaps most of those goals will be accomplished by the Commission's announcement in connection with its recent adoption of Rule 144 that it will not issue no-action letters for transactions within the coverage of the Rule but will continue to issue interpretive letters.[53] Those letters, like no-action letters,[54] will be publicly available. Thus, the public will at least have access to a substantial collection of the staff's explanations and applications of policy.[55]

III

ORGANIZATION OF THE NO-ACTION PROCESS[56]

The no-action process administered through the Office of the Chief Counsel, Division of Corporation Finance, is a distinct facet of the organization of that Division. The Chief Counsel is assisted in administering the process by two

---

[53] Release 5223.

[54] Release 5098, announcing the policy of public availability, applies to "interpretative" as well as "no-action" letters.

[55] Staff "no-action" letters, however, seldom contain an exposition of the interpretative basis for the conclusion stated. See text at pages 113 & 120, *infra*.

[56] Much of the information in the following material was obtained by the author from a series of interviews and examinations of files and records in the SEC's Division of Corporation Finance in 1969-70, and arranged with the cooperation of the Commission and Mr. Philip A. Loomis, Jr., then General Counsel and recently appointed Commissioner, SEC. Particularly helpful and generous with their time were Mr. Courtney Whitney, Jr., then Chief Counsel of the Division of Corporation Finance, and Messrs. John J. Heneghan, William E. Toomey, assistant Chief Counsel, Edmund Shevlin, then Special Counsel, in the Division of Corporation Finance, and George P. Michaely, Jr., former Chief Counsel of the Division.

Assistant Chief Counsel (hereafter, "Assistants"), who devote at least seventy-five per cent of their time to the process. They, in turn, are assisted by approximately forty staff attorneys from the various sections of the Division who, on the average, devote slightly more than fifteen per cent of their time to the process. Two or three special counsel in the office of the Chief Counsel also assist in the process on special assignments from the Chief Counsel or his Assistants. The Division is organized into fifteen branches for the primary purpose of processing 1933 Act registration statements and letters of comment and 1934 Act reports and proxy materials. Each branch of the Division bears responsibility for processing these materials for an assigned group of companies, with new companies being assigned to the branches on a rotating basis. The branch chiefs are responsible to the Director of the Division for branch performance of these duties.

The no-action process administered by the Chief Counsel's office cuts vertically through this organizational structure; the staff attorneys in the various branches are directly responsible to the Chief Counsel's office for their performance. Assignments to prepare responses to requests for no-action letters are made to the staff attorneys by the senior Assistant through the branch chief or the senior attorney in the branch, who attempts to balance the work load.

All requests for advice respecting the need to register stock to be offered for sale, as well as other requests for information, are channeled from the branches to the Chief Counsel's office. (Exceptions are occasional calls received by a branch attorney who has previously dealt with a party or his attorney.) Verbal requests are generally handled as abstract interpretive questions, with only general guidelines stated. Conversations looking to submission of a no-action letter may become more specific in identifying key issues, and verbal disapproval of a proposal may be offered; but, as a rule, no concrete conclusions *approving* a course of action are expressed orally. Where the advice sought involves a request for approval of a specific course of action, the parties are asked to submit a written statement of all of the pertinent facts and to request a no-action letter.

All written requests for a no-action letter are initially channeled through the senior Assistant, who makes a rough appraisal of the problems they present and assigns them to a branch. (He may occasionally retain a particularly difficult problem or assign it to one of the special counsel in the Chief Counsel's office.) The letters are assigned to the various branches according to the name of the company whose stock is to be offered for sale; the branch which has previously dealt with a company in connection with a prior registration or other matter will be assigned the no-action letters involving that company's stock. Where new companies are involved, those companies and letters relating to them are assigned to the branches on a rotating basis.

After the branch chief or senior branch attorney assigns a staff attorney to the problem, he would ordinarily proceed as follows to handle the matter:

(1) analyze the apparent problems presented by the request;

(2) write (or occasionally call) to ask for a further statement of facts if essential facts are missing;

(3) conduct a file search to determine:

    (a) whether the company has filed a registration statement with the Commission;

    (b) whether the company is registered under the Securities and Exchange Act of 1934 and is currently rendering reports to the Commission pursuant to that Act;

    (c) whether the files indicate any securities violations by the companies or individuals involved, and if so, whether those violations are current;

    (d) the current price at which the stock is trading and the current trading volume, if available; and

    (e) whether the essential facts stated in the requesting letter comport with the information about the company on file with the Commission (This search generally will involve a rudimentary examination of the amount of stock issued and outstanding, the relationship of "control" persons, and a quick search of the general correspondence file on each company. If possible inconsistencies with the facts stated in the requesting letter appear, a more thorough search will be conducted);

(4) do necessary research, if any;

(5) prepare a recommended response and submit it to the Assistant, together with the requesting letter, and a form reflecting the information obtained in the file search; and

(6) in a very few cases the branch attorney may be asked to prepare a memo explaining the reason for his conclusion.

The recommended response, as submitted by the branch attorney, is then reviewed by one of the Assistants, who signs the letter (under his title) if he finds it satisfactory. In a large proportion of the cases, however, the Assistant revises the recommended letter, often (30-40 per cent of cases) reversing the conclusion recommended by the staff attorney. In other (10-20 per cent) cases, he may revise the form or content of the letter. Where the conclusion is reversed, the practices of the two Assistants diverge: unless the reason for the staff attorney's different conclusion is readily apparent (and reasonable), one Assistant discusses the matter with the originating staff attorney and explains the reason for his different conclusion; the other seldom discusses the change. In every case, however, the staff attorney is notified of the final result by receiving a copy of the responding letter in the form in which it was sent.

Where a no-action request presents a particularly difficult or unusual problem, the Assistants may discuss the matter with the Chief Counsel or Director of the Division before rendering their final determination. In some of those cases, or where the matter has been extensively discussed between the Chief Counsel and counsel for the stockholder, the Chief Counsel may sign, or prepare and sign, the letter. He also prepares some letters from time to time on a regular basis, though the total number handled by the Chief Counsel is small. One former Chief Counsel estimated that a relatively small proportion of his time (not more than 10-15 per cent) is devoted to the no-action process. His predecessor, however, estimated that he spent closer to half of his time on no-action matters. The disparity is probably explained by a recent Commission change of procedures designed to minimize the number of no-action matters brought up for Commission consideration.[57]

The no-action process appears to be administered on a substantially current basis. Relatively few cases involving significant delay appeared, and, where delay occurred, it often resulted from requests that the applicant supply more factual data. A random sampling of the letters issued in 1969 indicated that approximately half of the affirmative responses and 70 per cent of the negative responses had been pending for approximately one month or less, 30 per cent of the affirmative responses and 20 per cent of the negative responses had been pending for approximately two months, and an additional 20 per cent of the affirmative responses and 10 per cent of the negative responses had been pending longer than two months. Most of those pending more than two months had involved some additional correspondence intervening between the request and the concluding response.

The relative currency of the process is undoubtedly due to an effective check-off process maintained by the senior Assistant. He keeps track of every assignment of a no-action matter to a staff attorney and prods those who are slow in responding. While this presents some problem because the staff attorneys are primarily responsible to their branch chiefs, the system seems to be operating satisfactorily.

IV

Initiation of the Process

A. The Parties

As indicated, the applicant for a no-action letter is generally a stockholder who seeks to sell his stock without registration. In some instances, the applicant may be a promoter of a new company, seeking exemption for an initial issue, or a promoter of a merger, seeking assurance that the merged company's stockholders may receive or dispose of the surviving company's unregistered stock. And, occasionally, a pledgee seeks to realize upon pledged stock by obtaining a no-action letter authorizing sale. Although many other parties, such as broker-dealers, may be interested in particular transactions, it is not the practice for interested parties to apply or intervene;

---

[57] See text at page 115, *infra.*

and, in view of the substantive questions usually at issue, it seems doubtful that intervention would serve any purpose.

There are, however, some circumstances where the interests of third parties appear to affect staff or Commission judgments. For example, in one instance the Commission appeared to take into account the fear of administration officials that denial of an exemption and the resultant closing of the applicant's plant (for lack of funds) would produce unemployment in an already depressed area.[58]

While such informal intervention on behalf of applicants by administration officials appears to be rare, intervention by members of Congress is much more common. For example, a spot check showed responses to nine inquiries from congressmen during the period of April 1-18, 1969, a period in which 218 no-action letters were sent. Almost invariably, such an inquiry results in preparation of a memorandum for submission to the congressman, explaining the circumstances, the status of the no-action request, and the basic statutory theory supporting the staff or Commission disposition of the matter. However, intervention by members of Congress apparently has little effect on the disposition of no-action matters.[59]

B. The Form of Advice Sought

Most questions relating to registration obligations are directed to the Chief Counsel's office in the Division, and that office responds to 75-100 telephone calls per week involving requests for interpretive advice. The Chief Counsel and his Assistants give considerable oral advice about interpretive problems presented by particular transactions, but most such advice is designed to identify specific problems which are left for ultimate resolution by counsel. The staff generally will not express specific conclusions about the legal consequences of specific courses of action without a written request detailing all pertinent facts. Where the parties seek ultimate conclusions about the application of interpretive concepts to specific facts, particularly where inquiries relate to the "underwriter" problems that dominate the no-action process, the parties will be urged to submit a written request for a no-action letter. In such cases, oral advice will be directed to explaining the kinds of facts that may be helpful in submitting a no-action request.

At an earlier date, many no-action matters were handled by a conference at which the applicant's attorney appeared, bearing the form of no-action letter for which he sought staff approval. The issues presented were debated and often resolved in personal conferences, with the letter issuing immediately. Such conferences now play a considerably less significant role in the no-action process, and the responding letter is no longer negotiated and executed in the course of the conference. Personal conferences do, however, continue to provide an effective forum for advocacy on behalf of a particular application, with some apparent effect upon the outcome in some cases.

---

[58] See Commission action on no-action request, reversing the staff position, app. B, ¶ B.

[59] See text at page 127, *infra.*

There is no prescribed procedure for recording telephone or personal conferences. Some attorneys maintain a log of calls while most apparently do not. Where the information provided is material, notes are inserted in the correspondence file and generally referred to as the basis for factual recitations in a later responding letter.

As might be expected, in view of the clearance function they perform, no-action letters make up the bulk of letters processed in the Office of Chief Counsel of the Division. A sampling of 322 letters issued in the period April 1-18, 1969, revealed that 218 were no-action letters in the sense that they merely recited facts and stated conclusions respecting the obligation to register stock rather than overtly explaining the basis for the conclusions. Only seven letters in that period provided any detailed discussion of interpretative problems—but they took no position on enforcement prospects. The remaining ninety-seven letters were for general administrative or informational purposes.

V

Processing No-Action Letters

A. Defining the Questions to be Answered

The no-action process does not provide any routine method for assuring that applicants understand the factual and legal questions that may determine the result of their request. Generally the written requests for no-action letters do not pose the specific questions to be answered but merely recite facts relating to the amount of stock held, the source, date and price of the acquisition, and the extent of other holdings in the same stock, with source, date, and price of those acquisitions. A survey of the staff preparing responses indicates that the no-action requests expressly state the determinative legal or interpretive question in about 35 per cent of the applications. When the applicant identifies the question, however, he is correct (in the staff attorney's view) in about 80 per cent of the cases.[60]

Where a request for a no-action letter provides insufficient information, the staff attorney ordinarily will respond with a written request for additional facts. That inquiry, however, seldom expressly identifies the questions considered to be at issue. (And in a large number of routine requests, of course, the questions merely seek to establish the source of acquisition, the length of the holding period, and the reason for the present desire to sell.)

More often, a telephone inquiry by the staff attorney or a status inquiry by the

---

[60] A questionnaire submitted to forty-three staff attorneys in the Division of Corporation Finance. Probably because of the length and complexity of the questionnaire, only ten replies were received. Five of the replies were from attorneys who had been handling no-action matters for one year or less, and three from attorneys with experience of six months or less. On the other hand, four responses came from attorneys with experience ranging from 1½ to 3½ years. In view of the relative instability of the force of attorneys in the Division as a whole, this is probably a satisfactory cross-section.

The entire questionnaire, with a profile of the responses to each question, is set forth as app. I to Report, *supra* note 3. The 80% figure cited in the text is taken from the responses to question 13 of that questionnaire. Subsequent data drawn from the questionnaire will be cited herein as: Questionnaire, *supra* note 60, question ——.

applicant may result in a telephone or personal conversation which identifies the key issues. But staff attorneys estimate that in more than half of the cases there is no communication with the applicant that specifically identifies the determinative question.[61] In most of those cases, however, the nature of the inquiry is undoubtedly so routine that the staff assumes that the determinative issue is understood. And in many of those cases the staff's reasoning is apparent from its comment that it is unable to grant the request "in view of the short holding period."

The more sophisticated SEC practitioners, on occasion, will provide a full statement of facts, followed by a statement of their interpretive reasoning in support of the opinion which they propose to give their clients, concluding with a request that the Division indicate its concurrence. However, staff conclusions apparently do not turn on the form of application. Some staff attorneys suggest that counsel may often want to avoid committing themselves to a single rationale, or may hesitate to focus attention upon a particular problem.

Although the power to deny a no-action letter would seem to give the staff substantial power to compel modification of proposed transactions, it does not appear that the power is used extensively. Where discussion initiated by the applicant or his counsel focuses on available alternatives, staff attorneys may occasionally suggest specific modifications of a transaction. And in a few instances the Commission has suggested that a specific limiting commitment would enable it to authorize a no-action position. Ordinarily, however, where revisions are made to assure favorable treatment, the suggestion is offered by counsel for the applicant.

While discretionary factors may often play a substantial role in the staff and Commission decision, few applications address any argument to such matters. Sophisticated SEC practitioners will occasionally point out that the volume of transactions in the stock in question is sufficient to assure that the market will not be affected by the sale and that no special commission inducements will be necessary. And the relative insignificance of the holdings involved, compared to the total stock outstanding, will often be pointed out. But factors such as the difficulty of obtaining the issuer's agreement to register, or the pendency of enforcement proceedings and the applicant's relation to those proceedings, are seldom mentioned in the applicant's letter.

B. Establishing the Facts

No-action advice is usually given hypothetically in the sense that the staff does not purport to determine questions of evidentiary fact. However, the staff insists that it will not give no-action advice without a full statement from the applicant of the facts material to the transaction in question.[62] The letters essentially treat those statements as affidavits, scrupulously referring to or incorporating the factual assertions

---

[61] Questionnaire, *supra* note 60, questions 15 and 16.

[62] In a recent release outlining the procedure for "no-action" or interpretative letters, the Commission emphasized that "letters relating to unnamed companies or persons, or to hypothetical situations, will not be answered." SEC Securities Act Release No. 5127 (Jan. 25, 1971) CCH FED. SEC. L. REP. ¶ 66,481.10.

in the applicant's letter. But, with minor exceptions, no proof is required of the facts asserted by the applicant. This would seem to conflict with the Commission's own assertion that a "serious question" concerning the propriety of an attorney's conduct would arise if he "furnishes an opinion based solely upon hypothetical facts which he has made no effort to verify," knowing that his opinion will be relied upon to support distribution of unregistered securities.[63] It does appear that some of the asserted facts are verified against information available in the Commission's files. Ordinarily, however, those files would not provide means of verifying the transaction by which the shares were acquired unless they were acquired directly from the issuer. And even that information may be unavailable with respect to non-reporting companies.

It is estimated by the senior Assistant that the facts initially provided by the applicant are inadequate in about 30 per cent of the cases. In all but about 10 per cent of the cases the missing facts can be supplied from Commission files in the course of a routine check of the issuer's file.[64] But in only a negligible number of cases are the facts asserted by the applicant materially inconsistent with facts found in the routine check of the issuer's file.

Though the staff seldom requires substantiation of factual assertions, it may make routine inquiries where the applicant has not supplied sufficient information about the source or period of his holdings. And submission of an unaudited statement of the applicant's financial position, both currently and at the time that he acquired the stock in question, is frequently required. But in exceptional cases, the staff may require some further substantiation of the applicant's assertions. For example, an applicant who claims that a medical problem created a serious change of financial position may be asked to submit a doctor's certification. In other instances, applicants have been required to furnish a cancelled check to demonstrate the date of purchase of the stock in question or to furnish a copy of an employment contract on which a claimed "change of circumstances" is based.

C. Research

The available research tools, in addition to those publicly available, include the following internal sources:

(a) a monthly summary of interpretations which recites the basic facts and reasoning of the more significant no-action matters passed on each month by the staff. The summary does not include the text of the related letter, but contains considerably more explanation of the grounds for the result than do the no-action letters.

(b) a large card file containing the same summaries of interpretations, in which

---

[63] Release 4445; see also SEC Securities Act Release No. 5168 (July 7, 1971) CCH Fed. Sec. L. Rep. ¶ 22,760.

[64] Questionnaire responses suggest that it may be necessary to obtain additional facts from the applicant in 20-25% of the cases. Questionnaire, *supra* note 60, question 10.

the cumulative production of the monthly summaries is filed. The cards are indexed by subject heading and by statutory section, and are cross-referenced to the significant questions involved in each case summarized.

(c) a file of legal memos on selected problem areas is maintained in a file alongside the card file. Relatively few memos have been added to that file in recent times.

(d) "The Bible," an analytical treatise prepared for use and maintenance in the office of the Chief Counsel which analyzes the construction of each section of the 1933 Act.

(e) a file of Commission minutes which includes the related staff memos submitted to the Commission explaining the staff conclusions on no-action matters brought to the Commission for consideration.

(f) a chronological file of all letters and memoranda rendered by the Office of Chief Counsel, Division of Corporation Finance, which includes all no-action letters issued.[65]

(g) a listing of all companies for which Commission files are maintained, with a classification code keyed to identify companies in which similar disclosure problems were encountered.

The summaries of interpretations are never prepared by the originating staff attorneys. Rather, they are (or were) prepared by a law student clerk under the supervision of the senior Assistant. The usual practice is for the compiler, monthly, to select for summary a group of the more significant no-action letters sent by the Office. Occasionally letters will have been marked for summary during preparation—particularly those signed by the Director of the Division. From the selected group of letters, the Assistant Chief Counsel selects those to be summarized. The compiler summarizes the facts and reasoning underlying the letter and submits the summaries to the Assistant for review and approval. Those summaries are then utilized both in the card file of interpretations and in the monthly summary sheets distributed to the staff attorneys.

While the criterion for selection of no-action letters for summary is somewhat unclear, the general understanding of the compiler is that he is to select the cases that have "precedential value." However, he is instructed not to prepare cards on "questions of fact" such as "control" or "change of circumstances," because each case is viewed as limited to its own facts. On the other hand, he usually selects most cases which are the subject of Commission action as reflected in Commission minutes.

Responses to inquiries with the staff suggest that none of the available internal research sources are very heavily utilized. Most favored by some staff attorneys is reference to a personally-complied file of previous no-action letters, which apparently is consulted in somewhat more than half of the cases by those who use

---

[65] The no-action letters and interpretive letters have been made available for public inspection and copying as a result of a recent change of policy. See Release 5098.

such a file regularly (30 per cent of respondents). Next most frequently relied upon, in 20-30 per cent of the cases, by less than half of the respondings attorneys, are personal conferences with other staff attorneys. And the card file of interpretive summaries, running a poor third, is apparently used quite infrequently.[66]

Virtually no research use appears to be made of the monthly summaries of interpretations that are distributed to all staff attorneys. Apparently this results from the absence of any indexing system. All of the same information is available in indexed form in the card file of summaries, but use of the card file requires the staff attorney to go to the library in the offices of the Chief Counsel.

In considering the relatively infrequent use made by the staff attorneys of the available internal research sources, it should be remembered that the routine nature of most of the no-action matters invites little research. Furthermore, the ad hoc and subjective quality of the typical determinations of "ultimate fact" tend to encourage the view that conclusions are to be drawn from the facts and not from research. Thus, though the Assistant Chief Council attempts to promote a view of no-action matters as legal and interpretive questions, rather than exercises of discretion, it seems doubtful that that view is generally accepted in the staff. Questionnaire responses indicate that the less-experienced staff attorneys find their own "reservoir of experience" sufficient in 70 per cent of the cases, and the more-experienced staff attorneys in almost 90 per cent of the cases.[67]

D. Review

Internal review of staff responses to no-action requests is the primary responsibility of the two Assistant Chief Counsel of the Division, and their efforts in this regard appear to be thorough. Staff attorneys submit a proposed form of response to one of the two Assistants who, after review and any necessary revision, sends the letter over his own name and title. Review by the Assistants appears to be demanding and results in reversal of the disposition recommended by the staff attorney in 30-40 per cent of the cases.[68] To a large extent, the review process is viewed as a training opportunity, providing the Assistant Chief Counsel an opportunity to discuss the matter with the staff attorneys wherever the initial draft suggests misunderstanding or inadequate research.

Unless a specific request is made, applicants are not informed of the staff's conclusion prior to their receipt of the responding staff letter. Therefore, most opportunity for argument arises in the course of the staff attorney's preparation of a recommended response. After receiving a response and upon inquiry (but not in the

---

[66] Questionnaire, *supra* note 60, question 27.

[67] Questionnaire, *supra* note 60, question 29.

[68] Staff attorneys apparently consider the rate of reversal to be much lower: slightly less than 5%. Questionnaire, *supra* note 60, question 25. That disparity may be explained, in part, by the fact that one of the Assistants seldom discusses revisions with the staff attorneys. The other Assistant frequently discusses the matter with the originating staff attorney, suggesting areas for further inquiry, without expressly rejecting the proposed letter. In all instances, however, the originating staff attorney receives a copy of the letter in final form.

written response), applicants are advised that they may submit additional facts or argument for staff consideration. But in a large proportion of the cases (70-90 per cent), nothing further is heard from the applicant after the response is sent.

No information is volunteered to applicants about the possibility of appealing staff advice to the Commission,[69] and disclaimers by the staff of authority to speak for the Commission may lead many applicants to suppose that appeal is unavailable. However, Commission minutes indicate that it generally undertakes to dispose authoritatively of those no-action matters brought to it by the staff for consideration.[70] Upon inquiry about the possibility of appeal, an applicant will be advised that he may request the staff to bring the matter before the Commission; and all such requests are, in fact, brought to the Commission. However, the applicant is not invited to appear before the Commission or to make a written submission, and he is discouraged from requesting an appearance or making a submission in at least two ways. First, upon asking about the availability of a procedure for taking the no-action matter to the Commission, the standard response is along these lines:

> You may request to have your matter brought to the Commission for consideration. This is the procedure: We [the staff] prepare a statement of the facts and a memo in which we present your position and arguments and the staff's position and arguments, together with our recommendations to the Commission.

Second, no mention is generally made of an opportunity to appear before the Commission. And where an applicant inquires about the possibility of an appearance, the standard response is: "You have a right to request to be heard, but such requests are seldom granted." Generally the staff memo submitted to the Commission in such matters recommends against hearing the applicant or his attorney, on the ground that the staff believes he has nothing to add to the arguments submitted on his behalf by the staff.

Much of the staff resistance to appeals arises from a sense of obligation to preserve the Commission's time for more important matters. Until recently the staff had been operating under instructions to bring to the Commission all no-action matters involving a proposed offering valued at $1 million or more. As a result, though the Commission encouraged the staff not to adhere religiously to that rule, a substantial number of no-action matters were brought to the Commission at the instance of the staff in addition to those appeals arising from an applicant's persistence. However, most cases brought by the staff for Commission consideration were selected in order to obtain a clarification of policy.

The Commission has recently taken two steps in addition to Rule 144 designed

---

[69] 17 C.F.R. § 202.1(d) (Supp. 1971) advises that:

In certain instances an informal statement of the views of the Commission may be obtained. The staff, upon request or on its own motion, will generally present questions to the Commission which involve matters of substantial importance and where the issues are novel or highly complex, although the granting of a request for an informal statement by the Commission is entirely within its discretion.

[70] See text beginning at page 116, *supra.*

to reduce the burden of no-action matters reaching it for review: The "automatic appeal" rule for matters exceeding $1 million has been withdrawn, and the Commission's "duty officer," a single Commissioner on a rotating assignment, has been delegated the power "to determine whether the Commission should or should not grant a request for Commission review of a no-action request which had been denied by the Division."[71]

The urge to protect the Commission from an excessive burden of no-action matters may also be partly responsible for the "cave-in" phenomenon—the staff's reversing an earlier denial rather than complying with a request for Commission review. It is difficult to trace concrete examples of that phenomenon, but it is acknowledged by the senior Assistant that such "cave-ins" occur from time to time where the staff regards an issue as a "close question." On the other hand, it has been asserted that the reason for the "cave-in" may be the staff's reluctance to give the Commission an occasion for reversing a favored interpretive position. In any event, the "cave-in" practice is recognized among knowledgeable SEC practitioners and presents difficult ethical problems. A request for a Commission hearing is thought to consume the staff's "good will"—with the result that counsel must choose which clients are entitled to deplete his "good will" with the staff.

In most instances, the form of Commission action in reviewing no-action matters appears to involve an authoritative Commission disposition, effectively constituting an "order." A typical minute entry relating to a no-action matter may read,

> Upon the recommendation of the Division of Corporation Finance, . . . the Commission denied the request of Mr. A for a "no-action" letter with respect to his proposed sale of —— shares of X Corporation common stock and also denied his request to be heard by the Commission in the matter.

Or in another form,

> For the reasons stated in a memorandum dated ——————————, the Division of Corporation Finance recommended that the "no-action" request be granted. That recommendation was approved.

While the reasons for the Commission dispositions are seldom reflected in the minute entries, there is no doubt that the Commission takes specific action on the particular case brought before it. There is no basis for supposing that it merely gives general approval or policy direction to an informal staff process which it authorizes but does not adopt.

An examination of Commission minutes for the period May 10, 1967, through May 14, 1968, revealed that forty-five no-action matters were brought before the Commission for consideration. It is not apparent how many were brought at the instance of the applicant, but in nine instances the papers accompanying the submission to the Commission indicated that a request for appearance had been made. Five cases reflect an appearance by counsel, while four cases expressly reflect the

---

[71] Securities & Exchange Commission Minute, May 19, 1970.

Commission's refusal to hear counsel. The dispositions of these no-action matters by the Commission are reflected in the following chart drawn from a review of Commission minutes and related staff memoranda.[72]

Period: 10 May 1967—14 May 1968

No-action matters before the Commission	45
Commission reversals of staff recommendations	4
Reversals of recommended *denials* of sale	1
Reversals of recommended *approvals* of sale	3
Commission acceptance of recommended denials of sale	19
Commission acceptance of recommended approval of sale	20

E. Form of the No-Action Statement

Typically, a no-action letter makes reference to the requesting letter, recites all of the material facts supplied by the applicant (making reference to the source) or incorporates the applicant's letter by reference, and states a conclusion. The conclusions of no-action letters typically follow the conclusory and stylized patterns set forth in Appendix A, providing little or no explanation of the result.

In an effort to reduce the burdens of the no-action process, the Division at present frequently follows the practice of merely incorporating the applicant's letter without repeating the facts. Obviously this practice would make no-action letters themselves much less useful as precedent, particularly where additional facts may have been acquired from direct conversations or from internal sources. Some staff members also suggest that failure to repeat the facts renders no-action letters much less reliable as a protection for brokers who are asked to execute transactions in the unregistered stock, for it will be more difficult to satisfy their duty to investigate their seller.

VI

RELATION OF NO-ACTION LETTERS TO COMPLIANCE PROGRAMS

Former SEC Chairman Cohen has commented that the no-action process is an area "where an ounce of prevention is worth . . . a pound of enforcement."[73] That view of the compliance benefits of the no-action process is widely held among the senior administrators on the SEC staff, and is probably well-founded. Yet that conclusion seems to be based primarily upon the administrators' experienced "feel" for their subject as no available studies indicate how effectively the compliance benefits of the no-action process have reached into the securities business. Surely the results of the no-action process do not overwhelmingly favor the applicant—a fact which

---

[72] In the period from June 4—December 30, 1968, only 11 no-action matters were brought before the Commission, and in each instance it approved the staff's recommendation that sale be permitted without restriction.

[73] Panel, *Public Information Act And Interpretative And Advisory Ruling*, 20 AD. L. REV. 1, 24 (1967).

could induce many stockholders and brokers to take their chances rather than draw regulatory attention to a proposed transaction.

Earlier discussion suggests that the Division's liberal advisory practices, together with very real disciplinary threats and, until recently, the absence of dependable or helpful case law, have produced a heavy demand for no-action letters and may continue to produce that demand. But no studies indicate how extensively the educational effects of the advisory processes have pervaded the industry. Discussions with NASD personnel suggest that understanding among dealers may be limited to the view that stock with a restrictive legend may not be sold without a no-action clearance. There may be general understanding of the obligation to investigate "control" persons, but it is likely that most registered representatives make little or no effort at investigation unless they are independently aware of a seller's controlling status. And there may be little or no understanding of the need to determine whether a holder of unlegended stock may have obtained that stock from a controlling person. In any event, it is clear that nothing in the NASD training program for registered representatives deals adequately with these problems; and there is nothing in the exams for either principals or registered representatives dealing with them.[74]

There are no studies to indicate the extent of actual compliance where the staff refuses to take a no-action position. It may be inferred that most stockholders would comply. And those who understand the securities laws should, of course, be aware that a sale following the staff's refusal could provide the basis for a charge of willful violation. But neither studies nor enforcement programs have focussed upon the effect of a staff refusal, and all conclusions in this area must be based on inference.

Enforcement personnel generally regard no-action letters as an important part of the compliance program. Copies of all no-action letters are sent to the Regional (enforcement) Office nearest the city in which the proposed transaction would occur. But compliance programs are not based upon follow-up of staff refusals of no-action positions, and very few enforcement proceedings arise in that manner. Rather, no-action letters enable enforcement personnel in the Regional Offices to keep up with what is happening with particular companies and in the business generally and with the staff's thinking on particular interpretive and enforcement problems. Occasionally a letter may prompt enforcement personnel to object to a specific staff position, particularly if the same or similar transactions are under investigation in the field. To those ends, the letters are circulated among the senior personnel in the Regional Offices.

Where an investigation or enforcement proceeding is already underway, the no-action process is administered to minimize the probability of any further illegal

---

[74] See National Association of Securities Dealers, NASD Training Guide (1969); Interview with Mr. Lloyd Derrickson, then General Counsel, National Association of Securities Dealers and NASD personnel responsible for training programs. *But see* note 44, *supra.*

distributions that might prove damaging to purchasing stockholders. Thus, the processing of no-action letters routinely involves a file check to determine the pendency of any investigations. Typically, where an investigation is pending, the staff will refuse to take a no-action position via a written response that is almost totally uncommunicative. (See Appendix B, paragraph A.)

Thus, it appears that the primary compliance benefits of the advisory process are in educating the industry for, and encouraging, voluntary compliance. It remains to be demonstrated that an unconstrained advisory process, providing routine clearances for sales, is the best means of achieving that end. The Commission apparently concluded that it was not, in deciding to limit the availability of no-action letters after the effective date of Rule 144.[75]

VII

No-Action Letters As Nonpublic Public Law

In considering the status of no-action letters as "law," three different products of the no-action process should be segregated: (a) Commission "orders" determining an applicant's entitlement to a no-action letter, together with the related no-action response, staff memoranda to the Commission, and any interpretive summaries reflecting the result; (b) no-action letters which, though not reviewed by the Commission, provide the basis for internally-distributed interpretive summaries; and (c) other no-action letters rendered by the staff which are neither reviewed by the Commission nor summarized for internal distribution.

The Commission-reviewed no-action positions and accompanying statements would seem, from counsel's perspective, to constitute "law," for they involve a final official disposition of a concrete claim not unlike the mass of case law on which lawyers commonly rely for guidance. Surely such determinations are "orders" within the meaning of section 2(d) of the Administrative Procedure Act, for the agency renders "a final disposition . . . declaratory in form . . . in a matter other than rule making but including licensing."[76] And such orders may well constitute a "license" within the broad language of section 2(e) for in reality they constitute a "form of permission." Furthermore, the staff and Commission appear to treat prior Commission-approved no-action dispositions as precedent. Throughout the supporting memoranda there are frequent citations to the precedents found in prior no-action dispositions, with many general citations and frequent specific citations. Thus, in the forty-five no-action dispositions by the Commission between 10 May 1967 and 14 May 1968, there were at least fourteen specific citations to prior Commission-approved no-action dispositions.[77]

[75] See note 53 *supra*, and accompanying text.

[76] *Cf.* Medical Comm. for Human Rights v. SEC, 432 F.2d 659 (D.C. Cir. 1970), judgment vacated as moot, 401 U.S. 973, 40 L.W. 4117 (1972). *But see* First Savings & Loan Ass'n of the Bahamas, Ltd. v. SEC, 358 F.2d 358 (5th Cir. 1966); Mattson v. Medical Development Corp. v. SEC, 329 F. Supp. 304 (D. Utah 1971).

[77] See summary of staff citations to no-action dispositions compiled in App. G of REPORT, *supra* note

In considering the Commission dispositions as "law," it is important to recognize that they assume that status because they reflect Commission action and not because they are interpretive or analytical in form. The Commission minutes ordinarily do not reflect the Commission's reasons for its conclusions in particular no-action matters, and the reasons must be inferred from the facts, interpretations, and discretionary considerations set forth in the accompanying staff memoranda. While the Commission actions would seem to involve "interpretations," there is no assurance that that is the case, for often they may also reflect such other concerns as the hardship imposed by compelling rigid compliance with registration requirements, an assessment of the "quality" of the company and the probability of injury to a purchasing stockholder if the proposed sales are made, and similar "discretionary" considerations.[78]

The same considerations affect the interpretive understanding to be gleaned from no-action letters except those very few that are, in form, expressly interpretive. The former Chief Counsel of the Division of Corporation Finance has commented:

> I do not believe it is helpful . . . to attempt to make a distinction between no-action and interpretive letters . . . . By far the more numerous are those situations in which it is difficult, if not impossible, to tell whether the staff advice is intended as an interpretation, or merely as a statement that enforcement action will not be taken. . . . It is difficult for the reader to make a distinction between the two types of letters because of the rather peculiar phraseology . . . but more importantly because it is impossible for the reader to know what factors were, in the mind of the staff member who wrote the letter, determinative of the position taken. . . . Also, it is not always clear to the staff member whether he intends that the letter constitute an interpretation or merely a statement that enforcement action will not be taken. . . . It was my experience that normally when a request for advice was referred to the Commission . . . [it] considered the question as one of interpretation of the securities laws. This was true even though the person who had requested the advice may have desired nothing more than an assurance that no enforcement action would be instituted. . . . Conversely, in some instances when the staff referred matters to the Commission as interpretive questions, the Commission disposed of them as if they were nothing more than requests for assurance that no enforcement action would be instituted.[79]

The uncertainty created by the interaction of legal interpretation and discretionary enforcement policy necessitates careful appraisal of the statements of Commission and staff in order to reach a judgment about their interpretations or policies. But uncertainty about the motivations for official decisions is a problem that lawyers must continually puzzle from their days as first-year law students. That uncertainty

---

3. See the frequent citations to the authority of previous no-action positions in the memorandum supporting the staff position set forth in App. L-1 of Report, *supra* note 3. (This latter action is described in App. B, ¶ A, *infra*.)

[78] See letter of George P. Michaely, Jr., former Chief Counsel, SEC Division of Corporation Finance, App. B. of Report, *supra* note 3.

[79] *Id.*

renders the "no-action" decision no less "law," whether rendered by the Commission or by the staff.

Whether the staff interpretations, as reflected either in the original no-action letters or in those letters taken together with related interpretive summaries, are "law" must depend upon the purpose for which that question is asked. For example, it seems likely that the summaries of interpretation, together with the applicable no-action letters, may well be viewed as "instructions to staff that affect any member of the public" within the meaning of the Public Information Act.[80]

There can be little doubt that the interpretive summaries, whether based upon a Commission disposition or upon an unreviewed staff letter, provide a body of internal precedents which "affect" members of the public who request no-action letters. The senior staff counsel regard it as their function to maintain internal consistency in rendering no-action letters, and to that end the staff attorneys are urged to view the problems presented by no-action requests as legal questions to be resolved by traditional legal, interpretive techniques. The entire process of summarizing and circulating interpretive statements and maintaining a card file of interpretations can only be intended for that purpose. Thus, the senior Assistant states that he particularly expects the newer staff attorneys to "spend a lot of time in the cards," and he discourages them from basing their recommended decisions on "discretionary" factors.

Of course it is essential to recognize that both the senior counsel and the staff attorneys are agreed that a large proportion of the routine no-action letters are not of precedential value.[81] In large part this is due to the routine nature of the questions usually presented, which also results in the relatively low staff use of the internal research tools. But use of the research tools continues at a rate roughly comparable to that proportion of cases in which the staff attorneys find their experience inadequate for preparation of a no-action response.[82]

Another factor of importance which contributes to the view that many no-action matters are not of precedential importance is the widely held staff position that many no-action matters reflect only conclusions of "ultimate fact" peculiar to the facts of a particular case. Thus, the practice has developed of treating most "change of circumstance" claims as single unique cases without precedential value. Yet certain patterns of decision are surely reflected in those cases. For example, it seems likely that the worsening of a medical condition that existed at the time of purchase of the stock in question will not support a claim of "changed circumstances," though such a claim may be based upon a new medical condition that arises after purchase of the stock. But if the medical condition, though it subsisted at the time of purchase,

---

[80] 5 U.S.C.A. § 552(a)(2)(C) (1967).

[81] Questionnaire responses indicate about 7% are of precedential value. Questionnaire, *supra* note 60, question 26.

[82] See text at note 67, *supra*. Note that the use of available research tools continues at a rate roughly comparable to that proportion of cases in which the staff attorneys find their experience inadequate for preparation of no-action responses.

has grown worse, when the prognosis was that it would improve, sale may be authorized—at least, where no substantial distribution is involved. Similarly, claims of changed circumstances resulting from termination of employment are often rejected. But a recent elaboration of that position resulted in the conclusion that if the applicant can support his claim with a showing that he had a written, unqualified employment contract for a specific term, he may be successful.

While all of these applications of the "change of circumstances" concept may have been affected by the presence of other "discretionary" considerations, such concrete interpretive examples are helpful to staff counsel precisely because they indicate the quality of the "change" currently viewed as sufficient by the Assistant Chief Counsel. And probably for that reason, the more important research tools relied upon by the staff counsel are their own copies of previous no-action letters and consultation with their colleagues.[83]

The effect of discretionary considerations upon ostensible "interpretations" is not to be discounted, however. A good example is found in the no-action matter considered by the Commission in Appendix B, paragraph C, and reported on a summary card. The summary card reflecting this action is marked "card only" because it is considered too unique—as a "change of circumstance" matter—to be included in the summaries distributed monthly to the staff counsel. The card provides an interpretation of the Commission decision which appears to demonstrate that the Commission routinely found no "changes" of circumstance that could not have been anticipated by the stockholder at the time of his purchase. But the card also recognizes at least one of the typical "discretionary" types of considerations that affect judgment in noting that the applicant's investment intent was compromised by the fact that he had made earlier repeated attempts to obtain a no-action letter. Furthermore, yet another "discretionary" consideration is found in examining the staff's supporting memorandum to the Commission, though the card indicates nothing about it. That memorandum shows that one of the applicants had been counsel for the president of the issuer and that he was currently under investigation and was thought to have been aware of the president's illegal activities. On that account, one of the Regional Offices had indicated that, under the circumstances, a no-action letter should not be granted. While it is uncertain what effect such additional considerations may have had on the outcome in this instance, availability of that information is helpful to a full appraisal of the Commission action in denying the application, and in that sense is a part of the "law" of the case.

Another aspect of the file of interpretive summaries which may render it unreliable as a basis for determining current interpretive positions is the fact that it includes an historical accumulation of cards reflecting positions taken at various times in the past, many of which may have been superseded by new positions also

---

[83] See note 66, *supra*, and accompanying text.

summarized in the cards. Informed researchers approach the cards with caution, frequently consulting one of the Assistants on apparent conflicts of position. That movement and conflict, however, do not diminish the status of no-action and interpretive positions as law; as with most legal sources, it merely requires thorough research to discern current positions and to resolve conflicting positions.

Finally, the inadequacy of many no-action letters as guides to interpretation is illustrated by comparing the no-action matters summarized in Appendix B, paragraph F: the staff simply offers no explanation for conflicting results in circumstances that appear substantially identical.

VIII

THE ROLE OF DISCRETION

As suggested above, the body of law found in the staff and Commission interpretive positions may be heavily influenced by various discretionary considerations that are brought to bear on specific no-action determinations. Those discretionary factors, together with the ad hoc nature of many "fact" determinations, have created a body of interpretive law in which "uncertainty and divergence of practice presently prevail to an unacceptable degree."[84]

While many discretionary considerations undoubtedly contribute to the uncertainty, others reflect staff efforts to provide means of protecting investors within a clumsy statutory and interpretive structure. Many of the concepts and distinctions required by currently-accepted interpretations of the 1933 Act have no real relevance to the protection of investors. The *Disclosure Study* commented:

> The most casual inquiry into the effects of prevailing interpretative pattern discloses its grave shortcomings . . . . Sale without registration may turn on events wholly unconnected with the needs of investors. . . .
>
> . . . .
>
> An obvious question may be asked: in what possible way is . . . "change of circumstances" relevant to the needs of public investors, so as to justify the sale of . . . shares without appropriate disclosure? The easy answer to the question is "none."
>
> . . . .
>
> In application, the present "fungibility concept" bears little relationship to the needs of investors for disclosure. It has never been formalized as a Commission rule or interpretative release, and hence introduces an additional element of uncertainty into an already clouded situation.[85]

It is apparent from the *Disclosure Study* discussion of these problems that many interpretive positions were taken and many discretionary factors taken into account, in order to prevent the formal structure of registration from choking off legitimate

---

[84] DISCLOSURE STUDY at 152.
[85] DISCLOSURE STUDY at 155-56, 170, and 174.

securities transactions intended to be exempted from the Act. The framework of subjective "ultimate fact" judgments provided the flexibility necessary to reach doubtful distributions, while permitting sales which appeared to be prompted by the financial needs of an innocent shareholder. But focusing on such subjective considerations often made confident judgment impossible precisely because theory focussed upon shareholder's motivations.

It is little wonder that under such circumstances, often involving a determination which might as well be decided by a flip of the coin, various other factors more obviously pertinent to the protection of shareholders should be taken into account. Many of those factors, mentioned at various times in discussion with staff personnel, were listed in responses to the questionnaire submitted to staff attorneys together with appraisals of their relative importance. The frequency with which such discretionary considerations were instrumental in decision is reported to be between 37 and and 45 per cent.[86]

There have been occasional suggestions that political factors play a large role in obtaining a favorable no-action response from the staff or Commission. And in at least one instance, available records seem to reflect "political" considerations. (See Appendix B, paragraph B.) But a careful analysis of many cases in which congressmen made written "status" inquiries with the Commission failed to demonstrate any substantial effect, except possibly a more prompt review of the matter and the preparation of an explanatory memorandum for the congressman.

Undoubtedly the most signifiant "discretionary" factor that plays a role in the outcome of no-action requests is the pendency of an investigation or an enforcement proceeding. Where a Regional Office or the Division of Trading and Markets indicates that a "hold" should be placed on no-action letters concerning stock of a particular issuer, a no-action request ordinarily will be met by a simple uncommunicative rejection. That practice seems often to be followed regardless of whether the immediate applicant appears to be involved in the potential proceedings.[87] And it also seems that the staff is much more reluctant to authorize a no-action position for the benefit of a stockholder who has previously been found to be a securities violator.

Various other "discretionary" considerations which appear to play a part in decision reflect a desire to assure protection of the investor. Thus, particularly in close cases, the staff is more likely to look favorably on proposed sales of stock of a reporting company, or of the same class as that recently registered by the issuer, or sales which are within the ordinary trading volume of the stock in question. A variety of other discretionary considerations and their effect upon particular no-action requests are summarized in Appendix B.

---

[86] Questionnaire, *supra* note 60, questions 30 and 14.
[87] See SEC "No-Action" Letters: Some Problems and Suggested Approaches, 71 COLUM. L. REV. 1256, 1270 (1971).

IX

CONCLUSIONS AND RECOMMENDATIONS

The no-action process as administered by the Division of Corporation Finance appears to be a sophisticated and effective system of providing informed and specific staff advice under active agency supervision. The basic conclusion of the Task Force On Legal Services and Procedure, Second Hoover Commission, appears to remain sound:

> By practice and precedent, letters of advice and staff opinions are given limited validity . . . [by several agencies.] This excellent practice in administrative procedure has been most effectively used by the Securities and Exchange Commission, which issues several thousand such opinion letters annually . . . . The satisfactory experience of agencies which have . . . followed the practice . . . suggests the advisability of a more general use of the advisory opinion by all agencies of the executive branch.[88]

That accolade is justly cited with pride by Division personnel; and the accessibility and pragmatism of Division personnel, as reflected in the no-action process, is an outstanding example of an agency making government work effectively within the inevitably rigid confines of governing statutes. By exercising discretion to modify statutory rigidity and grant advisory assurance concerning enforcement intentions, the staff and Commission enable businessmen, in compliance with law, to execute legitimate securities transactions, while restraining transactions that may appear to offend the basic policy objectives of the 1933 Act. But as the demand for advisory assistance grew, the emphasis on accessability and service to the industry began to overshadow the major objectives of the advisory processes.

The major objectives of the no-action advisory processes are set forth as follows in a Division memorandum:

> The no-action letter procedure is used to assist persons to comply with the law in prospective transactions, to discourage unlawful transactions, and to assist in effectuating transactions that do not appear to be contrary to the intent of the statutes and rules.[89]

To this statement of objectives should be added the further objectives of "advising the staff in advance of activities that might be questionable,"[90] and encouraging a flow of information about financial and regulatory problems to assist the staff and Commission in developing, elaborating, and testing concepts and policies for current and future application.

The former policy of granting advisory clearances for specific transactions, in-

---

[88] COMMISSION ON ORGANIZATION OF THE EXECUTIVE BRANCH OF THE GOVERNMENT, TASK FORCE REPORT ON LEGAL SERVICES AND PROCEDURE 189-90 (1955).

[89] Staff Memorandum to Warner W. Gardner, in REPORT, *supra* note 3, app. E at 2.

[90] *Id.*

cluding a mass of routine transactions, appeared to operate on the implicit assumption that the best way to "assist persons to comply with the law in prospective transactions" was to run a clearinghouse for those transactions. That "clearinghouse" concept of the staff's advisory role consumed the time of some of the best-informed and most experienced attorneys in the Division of Corporation Finance and seriously interfered with their effectiveness in exploring new regulatory problems and developing sound interpretative positions and rules. While experience with some problems presented for advisory assistance can add to the staff's insight, the bulk of the no-action problems heretofore considered by the staff involved routine questions, unrewarding for development of policies or interpretations.

Recognizing that its objectives will be better served by a broadened public understanding of staff and Commission interpretations and policies, the Commission has sought, by Rule 144, to clarify the restrictions on secondary sales[91] and has made publicly available its no-action and interpretive letters.[92] Some interpretative problems in the application of Rule 144 will remain, of course; and there will be continuing requests for no-action letters in areas beyond the scope of the Rule.[93] Nevertheless, these developments substantially expand public access to Commission policies and interpretations, while promising the staff a reduced burden of no-action requests. Additional Commission action along the lines begun in the release announcing Rule 144 could further reduce the burden of routine no-action or interpretative letters, leaving the staff more time for considered responses to inquiries presenting new or unique fact situations or interpretative problems. In order to derive maximum benefit from the public availability of no-action requests and responses, the Commission should encourage the staff to include in the public materials an adequate statement of facts and reasons.[94] Where inquiries present matters fully covered by available interpretative materials, the staff should be encouraged to respond with a form letter or to decline any substantive response. And where continued administration of routine no-action requests is prompted by doubt about the reliability of the advice of private counsel,[95] the Commission should develop and adopt rules of

---

[91] Release 5223, *supra* note 6.

[92] Release 5098, *supra* note 48. Provision has not yet been made to comply with the recommendation of the Report that public availability should extend to agency minutes and monthly interpretative summaries, interpretative staff memoranda "and all such statements by the staff which are of significant importance as a guide to interpretation. . . ." REPORT, *supra* note 3 at 490. But the importance of making available systematic statements of the staff's interpretive positions has again been emphasized in the recent study of enforcement policy instituted by the Commission. SEC, REPORT OF THE ADVISORY COMMITTEE ON ENFORCEMENT POLICIES AND PRACTICES, at 17 (1972).

[93] Although the bulk of no-action letters relate to questions that Rule 144 attempts to resolve, examination of representative samples of the summaries of interpretations distributed monthly among the staff of the Division indicates that more than half of the no-action letters summarized deal with other problems.

[94] Inclusion of a statement of facts and reasons will also provide the applicant with an understanding of the factual and legal issues posed by his request, which is not assured by the existing procedures for processing no-action requests. See pages 113-14, *supra*. Where additional understanding suggests the pertinence of additional available facts, the applicant can request reconsideration.

[95] See note 47, *supra* and accompanying text.

practice which will permit greater reliance on counsel by discouraging rendition of opinions on the basis of inadequate legal or factual investigation or in disregard of available interpretative positions.

The no-action process has been administered by the SEC staff with an unnecessarily broad conception of its discretionary power to grant or deny clearance. While the area of broadest discretion will be significantly narrowed by Rule 144, a more fundamental approach to the problem of unnecessary discretion is required. The key to that approach is adoption of a new policy respecting public disclosure of the agency's operating interpretations, standards, and policies. That new policy should assure the public availability of those positions, at least on a tentative basis, when they are first applied in no-action or other informal proceedings, rather than awaiting definitive development and formal pronouncement. It should encourage public statements of those operating interpretations, standards, and policies in as much generality as their current and projected applications permit, going well beyond conclusory "no-action" determinations wherever possible. Where general statements are not feasible, hypotheticals may be used to illustrate the application of narrower interpretative positions.[96] And where discretionary factors are commonly considered in ameliorating or stiffening the informal application of established interpretations, standards, or policies, a list of those factors should be made publicly available with a general explanation of their pertinence to the informal determination and, where feasible, of their specific application.

Obviously, these recommendations raise issues about the control of discretion which go well beyond the no-action process. How much room should there be for discretionary staff judgments to temper the rigid limitations of law and established interpretations? Should that discretion be exercised openly with full public disclosure and the attendant risk of compromising the authority or enforceability of the law?[97] Should it be exercised in secret with the attendant risks of discriminatory and abusive manipulation of power? Will open exercise of discretion produce demands for consistency which reduce the administrator's willingness to exercise needed and available discretion? Are there legal or administrative devices which will permit administrators to maintain the authority and enforceability of the law despite open exercise of discretion?

The recommendation that the thinking of the staff and Commission respecting interpretations, standards, policies, or discretionary factors be fully disclosed does not imply any illusions about the difficulty of the above questions. Rather, it is based on the assumption that pragmatic resolution of these problems can be achieved and that full disclosure will produce greater compliance benefits, as well as greater

---

[96] K. DAVIS, DISCRETIONARY JUSTICE 62 (1969).

[97] For a statement of the need for a wide and uncertain range of administrative discretion in order to prevent "imaginative fraud" in the field of securities regulation "where publicly stated rules are one of the instruments of fraud . . . ," see Mason, *Administrative Law—Reality or Red Tape*, 40 REV. JUR. U.P.R. 91 (1971).

fairness, than retention of an uncertain and unneeded range of discretion. As Professor Davis has demonstrated, we have too long operated on the opposite assumption.

APPENDIX A: TYPICAL FORMATS OF SEC NO-ACTION RESPONSES

"Based on the facts presented, we are not able to conclude that the sale of ——— shares of ——— Corporation to the public at this time would be exempt from the registration requirements of the Securities Act of 1933."

* * *

"On the basis of the facts submitted, this Division will not recommend any action to the Commission, if ——— sells the ——— shares of ——— Corporation without compliance with the registration requirements of the Securities Act of 1933."

* * *

"Based on the facts presented, this Division is unable to conclude that the ——— shares of ——— Corporation may be sold by ——— without complying with the registration requirements of the Securities Act of 1933."

* * *

"Based upon the facts presented and particularly in view of the short holding period by the present owner and preceding owner, and the medical circumstances that arose before the purchase of the shares, this Division is unable to conclude that the shares which your client owns may be sold without compliance with the registration requirements of the Securities Act of 1933, as amended, or Regulation A, if available."

* * *

"Based on the facts presented, including counsel's opinion that Mr. ———'s continued need for medical attention is a new and unanticipated circumstance, although an exemption from the registration requirements of the Securities Act of 1933 is not free from doubt, in view of the small amount of your client's holdings, this Division will not recommend any action to the Commission if the ——— shares of ——— Corporation stock are sold without compliance with such requirements."

* * *

"Based on the facts presented, this Division will not recommend any action to the Commission if your client sells the shares in question without prior compliance with the registration requirements of the Securities Act of 1933 in reliance upon your opinion as counsel that the proposed transaction is exempt therefrom."

* * *

"Based upon the above facts, as more fully set forth in your (counsel's) letter, we are unable to concur in your opinion. Accordingly, no public offer or sale of the shares of X Company by Mr. B should be made without compliance with the registration requirements of the Securities Act of 1933."

APPENDIX B: SUMMARY OF DISCRETIONARY FACTORS CONSIDERED IN PARTICULAR NO-ACTION MATTERS

The following summaries reflect discretionary considerations taken into account by the staff or Commission in making particular no-action determinations. It is not feasible to provide detailed explanations of the particular cases, but detailed statements by the staff or Commission explaining the particular determinations are set forth in Appendices L-1 through L-10 to the Report, *supra* note 3. Those statements are relied upon and cited here as the source of the particular case in which the various discretionary factors were considered.

A. *Refusal of No-Action Position Where Administrative or Enforcement Proceedings Are Pending (Appendix L-2)*

In this instance, the applicant had held the stock in question for what would ordinarily be an adequate "holding period" before seeking permission to sell. With respect to the interpretation by which he sought to justify his sale, the Division *expressly* agreed that his "conclusion of law is correct." But because the Division of Trading and Markets suggested that the issuing company may be merely a shell, that some of the promoters of the company had been involved in prior securities violations, and that the applicant had served the company as counsel, a no-action letter was denied. In this case, after receiving three responses from the staff that were totally uncommunicative about the reasons for the denial, the applicant threatened to make a sale of a portion of his holdings and to invite Commission enforcement personnel to witness the sale. (See also the staff memorandum in Appendix L-1, Report, *supra* note 3, at n. 3, indicating that a no-action position was denied in a previous matter because "the Division of Trading and Markets was at that time conducting an informal market quiz to determine the causes for a price rise in the company's stock . . . .")

B. *Extensive Losses by Large Employer, With Resulting Prospect of Reducing Employment and Intervention by Commerce Department (Appendices L-3 and L-4)*

This involves comparison of two similar matters, which should be considered together. The first matter demonstrates a routine denial of a request based upon a claimed "change of circumstances" arising out of pressing financial and business circumstances. The staff generally views such circumstances as ordinary financial risks which the stockholder should have anticipated.

Similar considerations might have produced a similar result in the second matter (Appendix L-4). Indeed, the staff memorandum so recommends because an accident and engineering difficulties put the applicant behind schedule in developing a prototype and created his claimed "change of circumstances" requiring additional capital. In the staff's view, those contingencies would reasonably be expected as a part of the risks of developing a prototype. But the Commission was obviously swayed by the extent of the losses involved, by the possible increase in local unemployment that would result from discharge of the applicant's many employees, or by the intervention of administration officials pressing the latter argument. This no-action matter does not appear to have been made the subject of an interpretive summary.

C. *"Investment Intent" Compromised by Premature Attempts to Obtain No-Action Letter (Appendix L-5)*

In this matter, the interpretive summary card expressly asserts and relies on the view that early and repeated attempts to obtain a no-action letter may compromise any claim of original investment intent. Further, though not reflected on the summary, it demonstrates that enforcement considerations may play a part in decision—in this case, the pendency of an investigation of the issuer and the applicant's possible involvement in the matter under investigation. For that reason, it leaves some doubt whether the interpretive summary reflects all of the reasons for the result.

D. *Refusal of No-Action Position Based On Internally-Adopted Rules (Appendices L-1 and L-8)*

One no-action request (in Appendix L-1) proposes a sale of stock acquired on warrants by an underwriter of an issuer's earlier registered distribution. Although alternative reasons for denial are offered, one substantial explanation appears to be the staff's development of a presumption that warrants received by underwriters in connection with an earlier distribution are invariably taken for sale and not for investment. Here, the underwriter-applicant appears to have held the stock for more than three years, after holding the warrants for a year and a half—more than adequate to satisfy the usual holding period applied in other no-action cases. The staff, however, contends that where warrants have been issued as additional underwriting compensation, stock acquired on the exercise of those warrants must be presumed to have been acquired for sale rather than investment.

A similar hard-and-fast but unpublished rule is reflected in Commission action on the second matter (in Appendix L-8). This case involved an apparently legitimate claim on the part of a former member of a controlling family group that family friction, and his resulting expulsion from any policy-making position in the company, constituted a "change of circumstances" which could justify sale. Though such claims had been approved not infrequently, the Commission here disapproves because of a policy decision to deny no-action letters to all members of controlling family groups.

E. *Conditional Grants of No-Action Letters (Appendix L-10)*

Although the practice is not common, the Commission will occasionally extract a condition as the basis for granting a no-action letter. In this instance, the Commission approved a no-action position on the condition that the applicant agree not to buy a certain class of shares in the future—presumably because of the applicant's affiliations with those companies. In another instance, a variation on this theme, the Commission "concluded that, under the special facts here involved, the staff might take a 'no-action' position after the expiration of two years" from the date on which the applicant had acquired the stock in question—an authorization to the staff somewhat at odds with the theory that investment intent is proved *after* an appropriate holding period. And in a third instance, the Commission rejected a request to sell 692,050 shares, constituting 22.6% of the issuer's outstanding shares, but indicated that if the applicant and his counsel "of their own volition withdrew that request and made a new request relating to 100,000 shares, it would grant the latter request." (The latter two examples are drawn from Commission minutes and staff memoranda made available to the author but not a matter of public record.)

F. Absence of Any Apparent Explanation For Diverse Results in Similar Cases (Appendices L-6 and L-7)

In these matters, one applicant is permitted to sell 225,000 shares representing 14.5% of the issuer's outstanding stock, the last 75,000 shares of which were acquired 14½ months earlier; but the other applicant is denied the right to sell 5,006 shares (presumably less than 14.5% of outstanding) which were acquired in an exchange effective approximately 16 months earlier. Both applications appear to be based upon a claim of unanticipated discharge from employment, and neither staff letter includes any explanatory rationale. While some theories might be elaborated to explain the difference, no adequate explanation appears on the face of the letters.

PRESIDENTIAL SPENDING DISCRETION AND CONGRESSIONAL CONTROLS

Louis Fisher*

On the basis of the Constitution and traditional legislative prerogatives, Congress lays claim to exclusive control over the purse. Nevertheless, while it is up to Congress to appropriate funds, it is also true that the President and the executive branch enjoy considerable discretion as to how those funds are spent. Existing studies tell us how the President formulates the budget and how Congress acts on the budget requests he submits. Surprisingly, we know relatively little about how the money, once appropriated, is actually spent. A notable exception in this field is a work by Lucius Wilmerding, Jr., published three decades ago.[1]

The purpose of this article is to present a more contemporary account of executive spending discretion, to show its impact on public policy, and to point to some of the techniques and procedures used by Congress to preserve its power of the purse. Although the President's spending discretion may seem essentially a twentieth century phenomenon, resulting primarily from the Budget and Accounting Act of 1921,[2] it has been a problem since George Washington's first administration. A number of early examples underscore that fact and add historical perspective and balance to this presentation.

The material is organized under seven main headings: lump-sum appropriations, covert financing, transfers between classes, reprogramming, transfers in time, impoundment, and unauthorized commitments. Within those broad categories are smaller sections on such topics as contingency funds, military assistance, no-year money, accelerated procurement, and coercive deficiencies. A number of these categories overlap, resulting in a certain arbitrariness in organization.

I

LUMP-SUM APPROPRIATIONS

A. History

Executive spending discretion produced sharp partisan clashes during the early years of the national government. We are told that the Federalists advocated executive discretion while the Jeffersonian Republicans insisted on legislative restraint. That kind of distinction is quite artificial, fabricated more from party rhetoric than from administrative practice.

---

* Analyst, Congressional Research Service, The Library of Congress. Author, PRESIDENT AND CONGRESS: POWER AND POLICY (1972).

The views expressed in this article are those of the author, not of the Congressional Research Service. This article is based on the author's paper presented at the 1971 annual meeting of the American Political Science Association.

[1] L. WILMERDING, JR., THE SPENDING POWER (1943).

[2] Act of June 10, 1921, ch. 18, 42 Stat. 20.

For instance, after Jefferson's election as President in 1801, he told Congress that it would be prudent to appropriate "specific sums to every specific purpose susceptible of definition."[3] Hamilton promptly denounced that recommendation as "preposterous," declaring that nothing was "more wild or of more inconvenient tendency." He was indeed correct. Jefferson's Secretary of the Treasury, Albert Gallatin, admitted that it was impossible for Congress to foresee, "in all its details, the necessary application of moneys, and a reasonable discretion should be allowed to the proper executive department." Jefferson himself, as President, recognized that "too minute a specification has its evil as well as a too general one," and thought it better for Congress to appropriate in gross while trusting in executive discretion.[4]

Lump-sum appropriations become particularly noticeable during emergency periods of war and national depression. During the Civil War, an act provided for $50 million to pay two- and three-year volunteers; $26 million for subsistence; another $14 million to cover transportation and supplies; and $76 million for an assortment of items, to be divided among them "as the exigencies of the service may require...."[5] During World War I, President Wilson received $100 million for "national security and defense" (to be spent at his discretion) and $250 million to be applied to construction costs under the Emergency Shipping Fund.[6]

Emergency relief programs during the Great Depression set aside billions to be spent at the President's discretion. An act of 1934 appropriated $950 million for emergency relief programs and the Civil Works Program, making the money available "for such projects and/or purposes and under such rules and regulations as the President in his discretion may prescribe...."[7] The Emergency Relief Appropriation Act of 1935 appropriated $4 billion for eight general classes of projects, the money to be used "in the discretion and under the direction of the President."[8] A study published in the June-July 1937 issue of *The Congressional Digest* estimated that Congress, since March 4, 1933, had given President Roosevelt discretionary spending authority over $15,428,498,815. That compared with a total of $1,687,112,500 in discretionary spending power given to *all* Presidents in the periods from 1789 to 1933.[9]

B. Budget Itemization

Lump-sum figures do not always reflect the actual scope of Presidential spending discretion. For instance, legislative control over lump-sum appropriations can be exercised by holding the President to his itemized budget requests, even though that itemization is not included in the appropriation bill. The Budget and Account-

---

[3] I U.S. President, A Compilation of Messages and Papers of the Presidents 329 (J. Richardson ed. 1896).

[4] 7 The Works of Alexander Hamilton 256-57 (H. Lodge ed. 1904); 3 The Writings of Albert Gallatin 117 (H. Adams ed. 1879); 4 The Writings of Thomas Jefferson 529-30, 533 (H. Washington ed. 1854).

[5] Act of Feb. 25, 1862, ch. 32, 12 Stat. 344.

[6] Act of Apr. 17, 1917, ch. 3, 40 Stat. 28; Act of June 15, 1917, ch. 29, 40 Stat. 182.

[7] Act of Feb. 15, 1934, ch. 13, 48 Stat. 351.

[8] Act of Apr. 8, 1935, ch. 48, 49 Stat. 115.

[9] 16 Cong. Dig. 172 (1937).

ing Act of 1921 provided that estimates for lump-sum appropriations "shall be accompanied by statements showing, in such detail and form as may be necessary to inform Congress, the manner of expenditure of such appropriations and of the corresponding appropriations for the fiscal year in progress and the last completed fiscal year."[10]

The use of executive budget estimates as a substitute for line-item appropriations is illustrated by the public works appropriations act of 1971. A lump sum of $1.9 billion was made available to the Atomic Energy Commission for "operating expenses."[11] Theoretically, the money could be spent for just about anything, and yet there exists a moral understanding between the Commission and the appropriations subcommittees that the money will be spent in accordance with the Commission's budget estimates, as amended by congressional actions and directives included in committee reports. This kind of nonstatutory control depends on a "keep the faith" attitude among agency officials and a trust by subcommittees in the integrity of administrators. If the AEC were to violate that trust and abuse its discretionary powers, it would face the prospect the next year of budget cutbacks and line-item appropriations.

C. Contingency Funds

Since future events cannot be anticipated, or anticipated with great precision, Congress has had to provide special funds to cover contingencies and emergencies. Emergency funds were particularly large during World War II. In statutes from June 13, 1940, to October 26, 1942, Congress appropriated a total of $425 million in funds for "emergencies affecting the national security and defense,"[12] plus another $320 million in funds for temporary shelters in areas suffering from the housing shortage brought about by the war.[13]

To cite a contemporary example of emergency funding, President Johnson decided in July 1965 to increase American fighting forces in Vietnam. This decision resulted in a $1.7 billion Emergency Fund for Southeast Asia over which the executive branch enjoyed complete discretion. Upon determination by the President that such action was necessary in connection with military activities, the Secretary of Defense could transfer the money to any appropriation available to the Defense Department for military functions.[14]

The Defense Department also receives money for a separate Emergency Fund,

---

[10] Act of June 10, 1921, ch. 18, § 204(b), 42 Stat. 21.

[11] Pub. L. No. 92-134, tit. I, 85 Stat. 365 (Oct. 5, 1971). *See* M. KIRST, GOVERNMENT WITHOUT PASSING LAWS (1969).

[12] Act of June 11, 1940, ch. 313, 54 Stat. 297; Act of June 13, 1940, ch. 343, 54 Stat. 377; Act of Apr. 5, 1941, ch. 40, 55 Stat. 94; Act of Dec. 17, 1941, ch. 591, 55 Stat. 818; Act of July 25, 1942, ch. 524, 56 Stat. 705; Act of Oct. 26, 1942, ch. 629, 56 Stat. 995.

[13] Act of Mar. 1, 1941, ch. 9, 55 Stat. 14; Act of May 24, 1941, ch. 132, 55 Stat. 198; Act of Dec. 17, 1941, ch. 591, 55 Stat. 818.

[14] Act of Sept. 29, 1965, Pub. L. No. 89-213, 79 Stat. 872. *See* 2 U.S. PRESIDENT, PUBLIC PAPERS OF THE PRESIDENTS: LYNDON B. JOHNSON, 1965, at 794-96 (1966); S. Doc. No. 45, 89th Cong., 1st Sess. (1965).

used primarily to support the exploitation of new scientific developments and technological breakthroughs. The House and the Senate appropriations committees have both criticized the use of the fund for other than emergency purposes. In 1963 the House Appropriations Committee complained that the Emergency Fund "has been resorted to in too many instances when no scientific or technical breakthrough was involved. It seems that the Emergency Fund has been considered by some as a general purpose fund from which to finance low priority or unbudgeted programs."[15] Two years later the Senate Appropriations Committee observed that the fund was tapped frequently during the closing weeks of the fiscal year: "Such action lends credence to the suspicion that the fund is being employed for other than emergency purposes which would tend to subvert the congressional review and appropriation process."[16] From a level of $150 million in fiscal 1963, the Emergency Fund for the Department of Defense dropped to $50 million by fiscal 1972.

Other sources of emergency funds are found in statutes that provide for disaster relief. The Federal Disaster Act of 1950 and subsequent statutes offer financial assistance to state and local governments whenever the President declares a major disaster. From 1951 through 1970, the President issued 338 declarations and allocated $857 million from the disaster relief fund.[17]

Contingency funds are sometimes used for purposes not even vaguely contemplated by Congress when it appropriated the money. For instance, on March 1, 1961, President Kennedy issued an executive order establishing the Peace Corps.[18] Not until seven months later did Congress appropriate funds for the agency.[19] In the meantime, the President financed the Peace Corps by using more than a million dollars in contingency funds from the Mutual Security Act.[20] Several years later, the sum of $450,000 was taken from the Defense Department's contingency fund to pay a portion of the expenses of the President's Commission on Civil Disorders.[21]

When the executive branch abuses its authority over contingency funds, Congress can reassert its control over the purse by passing more stringent legislation. As an example, in a 1959 report the Foreign Operations Subcommittee of the House Appropriations Committee specifically denied funds for an Incentive Investment Program which the Administration had proposed. The subcommittee's denial was omitted from the final appropriation bill passed by Congress, at which point the Administration proceeded to use money from the President's contingency fund to initiate the program. The House Appropriations Committee, charging that the contingency fund was being used to nullify the actions of Congress, recommended

---

[15] H.R. REP. No. 439, 88th Cong., 1st Sess. 63 (1963).

[16] S. REP. No. 625, 89th Cong., 1st Sess. 53 (1965).

[17] Act of Sept. 30, 1950, ch. 1125, 64 Stat. 1109; Act of Nov. 6, 1966, Pub. L. No. 89-769, 80 Stat. 1316; Act of Dec. 31, 1970, Pub. L. No. 91-606, 84 Stat. 1744. The number of declarations and total allocations were obtained from the Office of Emergency Preparedness. Figures include actions by the Housing and Home Finance Agency in 1951-52 when it administered disaster relief programs.

[18] Exec. Order No. 10,924, 3 C.F.R. 447 (1961).

[19] Act of Sept. 30, 1961, Pub. L. No. 87-329, tit. V, 75 Stat. 72.

[20] See H.R. REP. No. 1115, 87th Cong., 1st Sess. 66 (1961).

[21] S. REP. No. 1576, 90th Cong., 2d Sess. 28 (1968).

language the next year to curb this executive practice. The resulting appropriation bill stipulated that none of the funds appropriated for the President's special authority and contingency fund "shall be used for any project or activity for which an estimate has been submitted to Congress and which estimate has been rejected." The Act also prohibited the use of any of the funds to finance any of the activities under the Investment Incentive Program.[22]

II

COVERT FINANCING

Appropriations during World War II were often lumped together under a general heading to prevent analysis by the enemy. The atomic bomb project, for instance, was financed for several years from funds set aside for "Engineer Service, Army" and "Expediting Production." When larger sums for manufacturing the bomb could no longer be concealed by such methods, a few legislative leaders were told of the project and asked to provide funds without letting other legislators know how the money would be spent. Accordingly, the money was tucked away unnoticed in an appropriation bill. Total appropriations for the Manhattan Project came to over $2 billion. Members of the House Appropriations Committee told Elias Huzar that about $800 million had been spent on the project before they knew about it.[23]

According to the Budget and Accounting Procedures Act of 1950, it is the policy of Congress that the accounting of the government shall provide "full disclosure of the results of financial operations, adequate financial information needed in the management of operations and the formulation and execution of the Budget, and effective control over income, expenditures, funds, property, and other assets."[24] Despite that general policy, it has been estimated that, in a fiscal 1972 budget of $229.2 billion, secret funds may amount to as much as $15-20 billion.[25]

A. Free World Forces

The financing of the war in Vietnam illustrates how billions can be spent for programs known to relatively few Congressmen.[26] In September 1966, President Johnson expressed his "deep admiration as well as that of the American people for the action recently taken by the Philippines to send a civic action group of 2,000 men to assist the Vietnamese in resisting aggression and rebuilding their country."[27] Other announcements from the White House created the impression

---

[22] H.R. REP. No. 712, 86th Cong., 1st Sess. 8 (1959); H.R. REP. No. 1798, 86th Cong., 2d Sess. 13 (1960). Act of Sept. 2, 1960, Pub. L. No. 86-704, § 106, 74 Stat. 777. *See also* S. REP. No. 1849, 86th Cong., 2d Sess. 10 (1960) and W. MORROW, CONGRESSIONAL COMMITTEES 165-67 (1969).

[23] E. HUZAR, THE PURSE AND THE SWORD 338 (1950). See J. MARTIN, MY FIRST FIFTY YEARS IN POLITICS 100-01 (1960); L. GROVES, NOW IT CAN BE TOLD 360-61 (1962).

[24] Act of Sept. 12, 1950, ch. 946, § 111, 46 Stat. 834.

[25] CONG. Q. WEEKLY REP., Aug. 21, 1971, at 1786.

[26] Most of the material in the following sections on covert financing first appeared in Fisher, *Executive Shell Game: Hiding Billions From Congress*, THE NATION, Nov. 15, 1971, at 486. This article is reprinted in 117 CONG. REC. S18,232 (daily ed. Nov. 11, 1971) (inserted by Senator Fulbright).

[27] 2 U.S. PRESIDENT, PUBLIC PAPERS OF THE PRESIDENTS: LYNDON B. JOHNSON, 1966, at 1029 (1967).

that not only the Philippines but also Thailand, South Korea, and other members of the "Free World Forces" had volunteered their assistance.

1. Congressional Investigations

However, hearings held by the Symington subcommittee in 1969 and 1970 revealed that the United States had offered sizable subsidies to these countries. It was learned that the Philippines had received river patrol craft, engineer equipment, a special overseas allowance for their soliders sent to Vietnam, and additional equipment to strengthen Philippine forces at home. It cost the United States $38.8 million to send one Filipino construction battalion to Vietnam. Senator Fulbright remarked that it was his own feeling that "all we did was go over and hire their soldiers in order to support our then administration's view that so many people were in sympathy with our war in Vietnam."[28]

The Philippine Government denied that U.S. contributions represented a subsidy or a fee in return for the sending of the construction battalion, but an investigation by the General Accounting Office (GAO) confirmed that "quid pro quo assistance" had indeed been given. Moreover, there was evidence that the Johnson Administration had increased other forms of military and economic aid to the Philippines for its commitment of a battalion to Vietnam.[29]

The Symington subcommittee also uncovered an agreement that the Johnson Administration had made with the Royal Thai Government in 1967 to cover any additional costs connected with the sending of Thai soldiers to Vietnam. The State Department estimated that U.S. support to Thai forces—including payment of overseas allowances—came to approximately $200 million. A number of other expenses were also involved, such as modernization of Thai forces and the deployment of an anti-aircraft Hawk battery in Thailand.[30] The Foreign Ministry of Thailand denied that the United States had offered payments to induce Thailand to send armed forces to Vietnam. Nevertheless, GAO investigators reported that U.S. funds had been used for such purposes as the training of Thai troops, payment of overseas allowances, and payment of separation bonuses to Thai soldiers who had served in Vietnam. An interim GAO report estimated that the U.S. government had invested "probably more than $260 million in equipment, allowances, subsistence, construction, military sales concessions, and other support to the Thais for their contribution under the Free World Military Assistance program to Vietnam."[31]

U.S. subsidies were used once again to support the sending of South Korean forces to Vietnam. Assistance included equipment to modernize Korean forces at home,

[28] Hearings on United States Security Agreements and Commitments Abroad: The Republic of the Philippines (part 1) Before the Senate Comm. on Foreign Relations, 91st Cong., 1st Sess. 261, 358 (1969).

[29] N.Y. Times, Nov. 20, 1969, at 13 col. 1; 116 CONG. REC. S4453 (daily ed. Mar. 25, 1970).

[30] Hearings on United States Security Agreements and Commitments Abroad: Kingdom of Thailand (part 3) Before the Senate Comm. on Foreign Relations, 91st Cong., 1st Sess. 625-57 (1969).

[31] N.Y. Times, Dec. 16, 1969, at 10, col. 1; 116 CONG. REC. S19,743 (daily ed. Dec. 9, 1970).

equipment and all additional costs to cover the deployment of Korean forces in Vietnam, additional loans from the Agency for International Development, and increased ammunition and communications facilities in Korea. To assure that the sending of Korean forces to Vietnam would not weaken the defensive capabilities of the Republic of Korea, the Johnson Administration agreed to finance the training and replacement of forces deployed in Vietnam and to improve South Korea's anti-infiltration capability. From fiscal 1965 to fiscal 1970, U.S. costs resulting from the dispatch of Korean forces to Vietnam were estimated at $927.5 million.[32]

2. Legislative Authority and Restrictions

The legal basis for this assistance to Free World Forces in Vietnam goes back to authorization and appropriation statutes of 1966. Funds were made available to support Vietnamese "and other free world forces in Vietnam, and related costs . . . on such terms and conditions as the Secretary of Defense may determine." Assistance was broadened in 1967 to include local forces in Laos and Thailand.[33] Reports on such expenditures were submitted only to the armed services and appropriations committees of each house. One would not know from the general language of the statutes what type of financial arrangements the Administration might enter into, or with what country. Staff people, who had access to the reports, told me they did not know the nature and dimension of financing the Free World Forces until hearings were held by the Symington subcommittee.

Legislation in 1969 and 1970 tightened up the language of the statutes somewhat by placing a ceiling on the funds that could be given to Free World Forces. Standards were also established for payments of overseas allowances.[34] The ceiling of $2.5 billion, which exceeded the amounts spent in previous years, did not constitute much of a restriction. The fiscal 1971 appropriation bill for the Defense Department included a proviso stating that nothing in the Act should be construed as authorizing the use of funds "to support Vietnamese or other free world forces in actions designed to provide military support and assistance" to the governments of Cambodia and Laos. The force of that restriction was diluted by another provision which declared that nothing in the Act should be construed "to prohibit support of actions required to insure the safe and orderly withdrawal or disengagement of U.S. Forces from Southeast Asia, or to aid in the release of Americans held as prisoners of war."[35] On February 8, 1971, after the United States had provided support for South Vietnam's intervention in Laos, the State Department justified the U.S. support partly on the ground that it "will protect American lives."[36]

---

[32] *Hearings on United States Security Agreements and Commitments Abroad: Republic of Korea (part 6) Before the Senate Comm. on Foreign Relations*, 91st Cong., 2d Sess. 1529-47 (1970).

[33] Act of Mar. 15, 1966, Pub. L. No. 89-367, § 401, 80 Stat. 37; Act of Mar. 25, 1966, Pub. L. No. 89-375, § 102, 80 Stat. 82; Act of June 5, 1967, Pub. L. No. 90-22, § 301, 81 Stat. 53; Act of Sept. 29, 1967, Pub. L. No. 90-96, § 639, 81 Stat. 248.

[34] Act of Nov. 19, 1969, Pub. L. No. 91-121, § 401, 83 Stat. 206; Act of Oct. 7, 1970, Pub. L. No. 91-441, § 502, 84 Stat. 905.

[35] Act of Jan. 11, 1971, Pub. L. No. 91-668, § 838(a), 84 Stat. 2037.

[36] N.Y. Times, Feb. 9, 1971, at 17, col. 6.

The fiscal 1972 authorization bill for the Defense Department repeated the ceiling of $2.5 billion for Free World Forces, along with the restriction on actions by Vietnamese and other Free World Forces in Cambodia and Laos.[37] Despite those restrictions, the Administration had provided funds to support thousands of Thai forces in Laos. The State Department denied that this support represented a violation of legislative restrictions. The State Department explained to Senator Symington that the "Thai forces in Laos are composed exclusively of volunteers, most of whom have served in the Thai Army, but have been discharged."[38] Another explanation rested on the theory that the soldiers were not really Thais but rather ethnic Lao from northwest Thailand. After a trip to Vietnam, Congressman Jerome Waldie said that Souvanna Phouma, in the presence of Ambassador Godley, told him " 'those troops aren't Thais—they are really Laotians living in Thailand.' And he told us this with a straight face!"[39]

The theories of "volunteers" and "ethnic Lao" were not supported by newspaper accounts. Reports in the *Washington Post* and in the Washington *Evening Star* described the Thai soldiers serving in Laos as regular army troops of Thailand who had been asked to accept special assignment in Laos for extra pay.[40]

B. CIA Financing

Covert financing has been used to finance, through the Central Intelligence Agency, such diverse activities as military operations in Laos and the broadcasting of U.S. information to Eastern Europe and Russia. The CIA can do this because of its extraordinary authority over the transfer and application of funds. The Central Intelligence Act of 1949 provides that the sums made available to the CIA "may be expended without regard to the provisions of law and regulations relating to the expenditure of Government funds . . . ." For objects of a confidential nature, such expenditures are accounted for solely on the certificate of the CIA Director, with each certificate deemed a sufficient voucher for the amount certified.[41] The Act also authorizes the CIA to transfer to and receive from other government agencies "such sums as may be approved by the Bureau of the Budget" for the performance of any functions or activities authorized by the National Security Act of 1947. Other government agencies are authorized to transfer to or receive from the CIA such

---

[37] Act of Nov. 17, 1971, Pub. L. No. 92-156, § 501, 85 Stat. 427 (repeated in the fiscal 1972 appropriations bill for the Defense Department, Pub. L. No. 92-204, § 738, 85 Stat. 734 [Dec. 18, 1971]).

[38] 117 CONG. REC. S15,769 (daily ed. Oct. 4, 1971).

[39] 117 CONG. REC. E4910 (daily ed. May 24, 1971).

[40] Newspaper accounts by D. E. Ronk in the Washington Post, Aug. 9, 1971, and Tammy Arbuckle in the Washington Evening Star, Sept. 23, 1971, appear in 117 CONG. REC. S15,768-69 (daily ed. Oct. 4, 1971). Staff members of the Senate Foreign Relations Committee reported in 1972 that Thai irregulars were "recruited by the Royal Thai Army from all over Thailand" and that "no special effort was made to recruit ethnic Lao as distinct from other Thai." The cost of maintaining the Thai irregular force for a year in Laos was estimated at approximately $100 million. STAFF OF THE SENATE FOREIGN RELATIONS COMM., 92d CONG., 2d SESS., THAILAND, LAOS, AND CAMBODIA: January 1972, at 19-20 (Comm. Print 1972).

[41] 50 U.S.C. § 403j(b) (1970).

sums "without regard to any provisions of law limiting or prohibiting transfers between appropriations."[42]

1. Radio Free Europe and Radio Liberty; Laos

Early in 1967 it was reported in the press that the CIA had been secretly subsidizing religious organizations, student groups, labor unions, universities, and private foundations. President Johnson appointed a three-member committee, headed by Under Secretary of State Katzenbach, to review the relationships between the CIA and private American voluntary organizations. On March 29 the committee reported that covert CIA assistance had been made available by the last four administrations, dating back to October 1951. The committee recommended that "[no] federal agency shall provide any covert financial assistance or support, direct or indirect, to any of the nation's educational or private voluntary organizations." President Johnson accepted the committee's statement of policy and directed all agencies of the government to implement it fully.[43]

A footnote to the committee's report explained that its statement of policy did not entirely close the door to covert financing of private voluntary organizations. Exceptions might be necessary: "Where the security of the nation may be at stake, it is impossible for this committee to state categorically now that there will never be a contingency in which overriding national security interests may require an exception—nor would it be credible to enunciate a policy which purported to do so."[44]

The CIA continued to finance the broadcasting that had been conducted by Radio Free Europe to Eastern Europe and by Radio Liberty to Soviet Russia. The continuation could have been justified either on the ground of national security or by identifying RFE and RL as foreign-based institutions—as distinct from "any of the nation's educational or private voluntary organizations." The latter had been the thrust of the Katzenbach report.

In an address delivered in January 1971, Senator Case said that several hundred million dollars had been expended from CIA budgets over the previous two decades for RFE and RL broadcasting. He introduced a bill to require that future broadcasting of the two stations be subject to annual authorizations passed by Congress.[45] President Nixon recommended in May 1971 that Congress create a tax-exempt nonprofit corporation to finance and supervise the two stations.[46] The Senate Foreign Relations Committee rejected the President's recommendation, and on August 2 the full Senate upheld the committee.[47] During subsequent months the House and the Senate differed on the precise means of supporting the radio stations, but the

[42] 50 U.S.C. § 403f (1970).

[43] "CIA Support to Private Organizations," 3 WEEKLY COMP. PRES. DOC. 556-57 (1967). See also 23 CONG. Q. ALMANAC 358-61 (1967).

[44] 3 WEEKLY COMP. PRES. DOC. 557 (1967).

[45] S. 18, 92d Cong., 1st Sess. (1971); 117 CONG. REC. S130 (daily ed. Jan. 25, 1971).

[46] N.Y. Times, May 24, 1971, at 5, col. 1.

[47] S. REP. No. 319, 92d Cong., 1st Sess. (1971); 117 CONG. REC. S12,756 (daily ed. Aug. 2, 1971).

form of interim financing was no longer covert. A supplemental appropriations act, for example, provided a conditional $32 million grant to Radio Free Europe and Radio Liberty.[48]

Senator Case, who sits on both the Appropriations and the Foreign Relations Committees, apparently had to rely on an article in the *Christian Science Monitor* to learn that the Administration had agreed to finance Thai troops in Laos.[49] Further investigation by Senate staff members disclosed that the CIA was covertly financing 4,800 Thai troops fighting in northern Laos in support of the Laotian government. The cost of the operation was initially estimated at between $10 million to $30 million a year, but a staff report prepared for the Senate Foreign Relations Committee later disclosed that the CIA had spent at least $70 million in Laos during fiscal 1971.[50] During debate on the military authorization bill for fiscal 1972, Senator Symington offered an amendment to establish, with one exception, a ceiling of $200 million on U.S. expenditures in Laos during the fiscal year 1972. The exception was the costs connected with combat air operations by U.S. forces over the Ho Chi Minh trail area in southern Laos. He later raised that ceiling to $350 million. The Senate adopted his amendment by a vote of 67 to 11, and it was included in the bill signed into law.[51]

2. *Congressional Controls*

There appears to be little legislative supervision of CIA expenditures. Senator Symington is a member of a five-man Armed Services subcommittee responsible for reviewing CIA programs. On November 10, 1971, he said that the subcommittee had yet to meet during the year.[52] The other subcommittee in the Senate charged with overseeing the CIA is in the Appropriations Committee. With regard to the CIA operation in Laos, Senator Ellender, former chairman of that committee, said that he "did not know anything about it." He did not ask whether CIA funds were being used to carry on the war in Laos: "It never dawned on me to ask about it."[53] This frank exchange then took place between Senators Cranston and Ellender:

> Mr. Cranston. . . . I am sure I never would have thought to ask such a question. But it appeared in the press that perhaps that was happening. I would like to ask the Senator if, since then, he has inquired and now knows whether that is being done?
> Mr. Ellender. I have not inquired.
> Mr. Cranston. You do not know, in fact?

---

[48] Pub. L. No. 92-184, 85 Stat. 640 (Dec. 15, 1971).

[49] 117 CONG. REC. S7503 (daily ed. May 20, 1971).

[50] Washington Post, May 22, 1971, at A17, col. 1; STAFF OF THE SENATE FOREIGN RELATIONS COMM., 92d CONG., 1ST SESS., LAOS: APRIL 1971, at 3 (Comm. Print 1971). The $70 million figure is not cited directly; it represents the balance after deducting military assistance and AID figures from the fiscal 1971 total.

[51] 117 CONG. REC. S15,762-82 (daily ed. Oct. 4, 1971); Pub. L. No. 92-156, § 505, 85 Stat. 428 (Nov. 17, 1971).

[52] 117 CONG. REC. S17,996 (daily ed. Nov. 10, 1971).

[53] 117 CONG. REC. S19,527 (daily ed. Nov. 23, 1971).

Mr. Ellender. No.

Mr. Cranston. As you are one of the five men privy to this information, in fact you are the No. 1 man of the five men who would know, then who would know what happened to this money?

The fact is, not even of the five men, and you are the chief one of the five men, know the facts in the situation.

Mr. Ellender. Probably not.[54]

Senator McGovern introduced a bill on July 7, 1971, to require that proposed appropriations, estimated expenditures, and appropriations for the CIA shall appear in the budget as a single item. His bill would also prohibit the use of funds appropriated to other departments or agencies from being spent by the CIA. McGovern explained that a single sum in the budget would permit members of Congress to judge whether that amount was too small, too large, or fully adequate to meet the needs of intelligence gathering. It would, in short, enable Congress to do what it is supposed to do, decide priorities. Moreover, Congress and the taxpayer would know for the first time the exact amount of money going into other government programs. The current practice is to inflate certain agency and departmental budgets in order to conceal CIA money. "As a result," McGovern observed, "we are led to believe that some programs are better financed than, in fact, they are. We have no way of knowing what these programs and agencies might be."[55] During a recent debate on a bill to provide funds for military intelligence, Senator Fulbright commented: "When you look at an item in this bill you wonder if it is really the amount of money for the A-14, for example, or if it is for the NSA. One cannot tell what it is."[56]

C. Military Assistance

On the basis of a GAO report, Senator Edward Kennedy charged that money appropriated for refugee programs, public health, agriculture, economic and technical projects, and for the "Food for Peace" program, had been diverted to pay for CIA-directed paramilitary operations in Laos. The term "refugee" was a euphemism used by the Agency for International Development to cover the development and support of these operations. Hearings in 1972 confirmed that AID funds had been used to supply Lao military and paramilitary forces with food and medical care and supplies.[57] AID continues to supply these services as before, but funds are now advanced by the CIA and the Defense Department to cover the costs.

[54] *Id.* at S19,529. House supervision of the CIA does not appear to be much better. Rep. Lucien N. Nedzi, chairman of one of the two subcommittees in the House responsible for overseeing intelligence work, suggested that only the Budget Bureau and the Kremlin had a full understanding: "Perhaps they are the only ones. We simply don't have that kind of detailed information. . . . I have to be candid and tell you I don't know whether we are getting our money's worth." Washington Post, Dec. 21, 1971, at A28, col. 1.

[55] S. 2231, 92d Cong., 1st Sess. (1971); 117 CONG. REC. S10,527 (daily ed. July 7, 1971).

[56] 117 CONG. REC. S19,526 (daily ed. Nov. 23, 1971).

[57] *Hearings on Problems of War Victims in Indochina* (Part II: Cambodia and Laos) *Before the Senate Comm. on the Judiciary,* 92d Cong., 2d Sess. 38-39, 41 (1972). *See* Washington Post, Feb. 7, 1971, at A2, col. 8; Washington Sunday Star, Feb. 7, 1971, at A1, col. 1.

This is simply one example of how funds can be appropriated for economic and social programs and yet end up financing a secret war.

During hearings held in January 1971, the Joint Economic Committee discovered that nearly $700 million in Food for Peace funds had been channeled into military assistance programs over the past six years. Since 1954, in fact, when Public Law No. 480 was enacted, $1.6 billion of funds generated by Food for Peace have been allocated to military assistance.[58] Statutory authority exists for this use,[59] but few members of Congress were aware that Food for Peace was such a capacious vehicle for military assistance. Nor could they have gained that understanding by reading the budget, which describes Food for Peace in these terms: "The United States donates and sells agricultural commodities on favorable terms to friendly nations under the Agricultural Trade Development and Assistance Act (Public Law 480). This program combats hunger and malnutrition, promotes economic growth in developing nations, and develops and expands export markets for U.S. commodities."[60]

Senator Proxmire castigated this use of rhetoric to conceal the full scope of the Food for Peace program. "This seems to me," he said, "to be kind of an Orwellian perversion of the language; food for peace could be called food for war."[61] He joined with Senators Humphrey, McGovern, and Mansfield in introducing a bill to repeal a provision which presently bars military aid to any country receiving Food for Peace surplus unless that country agrees to permit the use of U.S.-held foreign currencies for military procurement.[62]

No one can determine from a present-day budget how much is spent for military assistance. The budget for fiscal 1972 estimates 1971 outlays for military assistance at $1.175 billion in Defense Department funds, plus an additional $504 million in supporting assistance.[63] The total is apparently $1.679 billion. In January 1971, however, Senator Proxmire obtained from the Defense Department its estimates for the Military Assistance Program (MAP) and foreign military sales. The amount of military assistance for fiscal 1971 was as follows: (1) $3.226 billion in MAP, "military assistance service funded," and related programs; (2) $600 million in supporting assistance; (3) $7 million in additional public safety programs; (4) $143 million for Food for Peace funds for common defense purposes; and (5) $2.339 billion in military export sales. The total: $6.317 billion.[64]

---

[58] *Hearings on Economic Issues in Military Assistance Before the Joint Economic Comm.*, 92d Cong., 1st Sess. 2, 293 (1971) [hereinafter cited as *Economic Issues*].

[59] 7 U.S.C. § 1704(c) (1970).

[60] U.S. OFFICE OF MANAGEMENT AND BUDGET, THE BUDGET OF THE UNITED STATES GOVERNMENT, FISCAL YEAR 1972, HOUSE DOC. No. 15, pt. 1, 92d Cong., 1st Sess., 101 (1971) [hereinafter cited as THE BUDGET (FISCAL 1972)].

[61] *Economic Issues* 61.

[62] S. 905, 92d Cong., 1st Sess. (1971). The substance of this bill was included in the Foreign Assistance Act of 1971, enacted into law on Feb. 7, 1972, as Pub. L. No. 92-226, § 201(c), 86 Stat. 25. Enactment does not affect the basic authority to use Food for Peace funds for military purposes, but such use would be more voluntary. *See* note 59 *supra*.

[63] THE BUDGET (FISCAL 1972) 36, 96.

[64] *Economic Issues* 203. The total is $2 million higher than the sum of its parts, since the latter are rounded off.

Prior to 1965, the scope of military assistance was essentially defined by the Military Assistance Program, which was administered by the State Department and authorized by the Foreign Relations and Foreign Affairs committees. With the build-up in Vietnam, however, military aid to Saigon was taken out of MAP and placed under a category called military assistance service funded (MASF). The effect was to transfer budget control to the Pentagon and place authorization decisions under the jurisdiction of the armed services committees. In 1966, military assistance to Laos and Thailand was also switched from MAP to MASF. Service-funded assistance to South Vietnam, Laos, and Thailand totaled more than $10 billion for the period from fiscal 1966 to fiscal 1971.[65]

On March 8, 1971, Senator Proxmire introduced a bill to remove from the Defense Department its present involvement in service-funded military aid. All remaining military assistance programs would be put under the Department of State. The object would be to return to the Foreign Relations and Foreign Affairs committees the responsibility for authorizing military assistance funds.[66]

III

TRANSFERS BETWEEN CLASSES

A. History

Specific Congressional authorization sometimes permits the President to take funds that have been appropriated for one class of items and to re-apply those funds elsewhere. This practice has been the source of dispute for almost 180 years. In 1793, Representative Giles of Virginia offered a number of resolutions that charged Hamilton with improper use of national funds. The first resolution stated that "laws making specific appropriations of money should be strictly observed by the administrator of the finances thereof." Representative Smith of South Carolina proceeded to refute Giles point by point, arguing that the Administration ought to be free to depart from Congressional appropriations whenever the public safety or credit would thereby be improved. When exercised for the public good, executive spending discretion would "always meet the approbation of the National Legislature."[67] The Giles resolutions were subsequently voted down by the House.

This appears to be a typical collision between the legislative and executive branches, but the dispute was not as much constitutional as it was partisan and personal. It was Hamilton's colleague in the Cabinet, Thomas Jefferson, who had

---

[65] *Id.* at 190. *See* Kaufmann, *Double-Talk Bookkeeping*, THE NATION, Nov. 1, 1971, at 429.

[66] S. 1129, 92d Cong., 1st Sess. (1971); 117 CONG. REC. S2566-71 (daily ed. Mar. 8, 1971). The Foreign Assistance Act of 1971 (not enacted until February 7, 1972) shifted Thai military assistance from the armed services committees to the Foreign Relations and Foreign Affairs committees. Pub. L. No. 92-226, § 513, 86 Stat. 25. The Foreign Assistance Act of 1972, as reported out by Foreign Relations, attempted to do the same thing for military assistance to South Vietnam and Laos. S. REP. No. 823, 92d Cong., 2d Sess., p. 10 (1972). The Senate rejected the bill by a 42-48 roll-call vote. 118 CONG. REC. S11, 672 (daily ed. July 24, 1972).

[67] 3 ANNALS OF CONG. 902 (1793).

drafted the resolution for Giles. The author of Smith's effective rebuttal was none other than Hamilton himself.[68]

Jefferson's strictures against transfers were excessively narrow and failed to halt the practice. During his own Administration, one Congressman explained that it was sometimes necessary to allow expenditures to deviate from appropriations by taking funds from one account and applying them to another. Such transfers were technically illegal, but "its being the custom palliates it."[69] Proposals to abolish transfers altogether were countered by two arguments. Secretary of the Treasury Crawford told Congress in 1817 that legislators, in receiving reports of transfers, automatically learned where appropriations had been redundant and where deficient, thus providing a convenient guide for future appropriation bills. Furthermore, removal of transfer authority would encourage executive departments to submit inflated estimates as a cushion against unexpected expenses. Crawford warned Congress: "The idea that economy will be enforced by repealing the provision will, I am confident, be found to be wholly illusory. Withdraw the power of transfer, and the Departments will increase their estimates."[70]

Statutes over the next few decades permitted transfers under various circumstances.[71] Beginning in 1868, Congress repealed all previous acts authorizing transfers and stipulated that "no money appropriated for one purpose shall hereafter be used for any other purpose than that for which it is appropriated."[72]

Nevertheless, during periods of great emergency, Congress delegates broad transfer authority to the executive branch. The 1932 Economy Act cut federal spending so indiscriminately that Congress permitted the Administration to transfer funds from one agency to another to repair the damage.[73] The Lend Lease Act of 1941 appropriated $7 billion for ordnance, aircraft, tanks, and for other categories of defense articles. The President could transfer as much as twenty per cent of the appropriations from one category to another, provided that no appropriation would be increased by more than thirty per cent.[74] In 1943 the Budget Director was authorized to transfer ten per cent of military appropriations made available for fiscal 1944, subject to certain conditions. Appropriations in that particular act came to about $59 billion.[75] Contemporary examples of this transfer authority include the Defense Department appropriation act for fiscal 1971, which permitted the Secretary

---

[68] 6 THE WRITINGS OF THOMAS JEFFERSON 168 (P. Ford ed. 1899); 2 B. MITCHELL, ALEXANDER HAMILTON 260-63 (1957).

[69] 11 ANNALS OF CONG., 320 (1801) (remarks of Congressman Bayard).

[70] 30 ANNALS OF CONG. 421 (1817).

[71] Act of May 1, 1820, ch. 52, § 5, 3 Stat. 568; Act of July 3, 1832, ch. 154, 4 Stat. 558; Act of June 30, 1834, ch. 171, 4 Stat. 742; Act of July 2, 1835, ch. 268, § 2, 5 Stat. 78; Act of Apr. 6, 1838, ch. 54, 5 Stat. 223; Act of Aug. 26, 1842, ch. 202, § 23, 5 Stat. 533; Act of Aug. 10, 1846, ch. 177, § 5, 9 Stat. 101; Act of Mar. 3, 1847, ch. 48, 9 Stat. 171.

[72] Act of Feb. 12, 1868, ch. 8, § 2, 15 Stat. 36.

[73] Act of June 30, 1932, ch. 314, § 317, 47 Stat. 411; see L. WILMERDING, supra note 1, at 180-84.

[74] Act of Mar. 27, 1941, ch. 30, § 1(c), 55 Stat. 54.

[75] Act of July 1, 1943, ch. 185, § 3, 57 Stat. 367.

of Defense to transfer up to $600 million.[76] That authority was increased to $750 million for fiscal 1972 as a means of giving the Secretary of Defense greater flexibility in coping with Congress's $3 billion reduction in the defense budget.[77]

B. Aid to Cambodia

Current law states that "Except as otherwise provided by law, sums appropriated for the various branches of expenditures in the public service shall be applied solely to the objects for which they are respectively made, and for no others."[78] Exceptions to that general rule are fairly common, however, as evidenced by the use of transfer authority by President Nixon in extending financial assistance to Cambodia after his intervention there in the spring of 1970.

At the end of 1970 the President appealed to Congress for $255 million in military and economic assistance for Cambodia. Of that amount, $100 million was to restore funds which the President had *already* diverted to Cambodia from other programs. Operating under the authority of Section 610 of the Foreign Assistance Act of 1961,[79] the Nixon Administration borrowed $40 million from aid programs originally scheduled for Greece, Turkey, Taiwan, and the Philippines; took another $50 million from funds that had been assigned largely to Vietnam; and diverted still other funds until a total of $108.9 million in military assistance had been given, or committed, to Cambodia.[80]

In the waning days of the Ninety-first Congress, legislators tried to place two restrictions on Presidential actions in Cambodia. The Special Foreign Assistance Act of 1971 barred the use of funds to finance the introduction of U.S. ground troops into Cambodia or to provide U.S. advisers to Cambodian forces in Cambodia.[81] Those restrictions were blunted by the remarks of House conferees, who accepted the restrictions only on the understanding that (1) U.S. troops could be used in border sanctuary operations designed to protect the lives of American soldiers, (2) U.S. military personnel could be provided to supervise the distribution and care of U.S. military supplies and equipment deliveries to Cambodia, and (3) U.S. military advisers could train Cambodian soldiers in South Vietnam.[82] Moreover, in the Administration's bombing operations in Cambodia, air power was interpreted in such broad terms as to circumvent much of the legislative restriction. When

---

[76] Act of Jan. 11, 1971, Pub. L. No. 91-668, § 836, 84 Stat. 2036.

[77] Pub. L. No. 92-204, § 736, 85 Stat. 733 (Dec. 18, 1971); *see* 117 CONG. REC. H12,567 (daily ed. Dec. 14, 1971). Transfers made under this authority are to be submitted to the Committees on Appropriations as "reprogramming actions" (to be explained in the next section of this article) requiring prior approval; H.R. REP. No. 754, 92d Cong., 1st Sess. 16 (1971).

[78] 31 U.S.C. § 628 (1970).

[79] 22 U.S.C. § 2360 (1970). Under this section, the President may transfer up to ten per cent of the funds from one program to another, provided that the second program is not increased by more than twenty per cent.

[80] *Hearings on Supplemental Foreign Assistance Authorization, 1970, Before the Senate Comm. on Foreign Relations*, 91st Cong., 2d Sess. 2, 78 (1970).

[81] Pub. L. No. 91-652, § 7(a), 84 Stat. 1943 (Jan. 5, 1971).

[82] H.R. REP. No. 1791, 91st Cong., 2d Sess. 5 (1970).

helicopter gunships have the capability of patrolling at treetop level, the distinction between air power and "ground troops" begins to disappear.[83]

Some restrictions do remain on the extent of Presidential discretion under the Special Foreign Assistance Act of 1971. For example, the President is prohibited from exercising certain transfer authorities granted to him for the purpose of providing additional assistance to Cambodia unless he notifies the Speaker and the Foreign Relations Committee in writing at least thirty days prior to the date he intends to exercise his authority, or ten days if he certifies in writing that an emergency exists requiring immediate assistance to Cambodia. The notification to the Speaker and the Foreign Relations Committee would include the authority under which he acts and the justification for, and the extent of, the exercise of his authority.[84] A more recent act, the Foreign Assistance Act of 1971 contains a provision which prevents the President from exercising his transfer authority under certain sections of the Foreign Assistance Act of 1961, as amended, unless he gives the Congress advance notice prior to the date he intends to exercise those authorities.[85]

IV

REPROGRAMMING

Reprogramming is a term used to describe the shifting of appropriated funds from the original purpose to a new purpose. Unlike transfers, reprogramming does not depend on statutory authority. Instead, it operates on an informal clearance and reporting procedure worked out by executive agencies and Congressional committees. Furthermore, reprogramming does not involve the shifting of funds from one appropriation account to another (as with transfers), but rather the shifting of funds *within* an account. For instance, if an appropriation bill provides a billion dollars for a single account, that figure could be broken down into perhaps a hundred separate subaccounts on budget justification sheets or in committee reports. Thus when funds are shifted from an original purpose to a new purpose, the shift would take place between these nonstatutory subaccounts rather than between statutory accounts.

The reprogramming procedure is partly a remedy for the long period of time that exists between an agency's justification of programs and its actual expenditure of funds. During that interval new and better applications of funds come to light. New factors arise to prompt the use of funds in a manner different from that called for in the appropriations act or committee report. The House Appropriations Committee has explained that reprogrammings are effectuated for a number of reasons

---

[83] Another provision in the Special Foreign Assistance Act of 1971 stipulated that military and economic assistance to Cambodia "shall not be construed as a commitment by the United States to Cambodia for its defense." *Id.* § 7(b). The discussion in the final section of this article, regarding unauthorized commitments, makes it clear that a commitment nonetheless exists.

[84] *Id.* § 8.

[85] Pub. L. No. 92-226, § 652, 86 Stat. 28 (Feb. 7, 1972).

including "unforeseen requirements, changes in operating conditions, incorrect price estimates, wage rate adjustments, legislation enacted subsequent to appropriation action, and the like."[86] Reprogramming takes place in such areas and agencies as public works, the Atomic Energy Commission, foreign assistance, the District of Columbia, and the Defense Department.

In recent years military reprogramming has run to more than a billion dollars a year. During fiscal 1970, for instance, the House Appropriations Committee received reprogramming requests from the Defense Department for a total dollar change of more than $4.7 billion (299 increases totaling $2.4 billion and 422 reductions totaling $2.3 billion).[87] Although defense reprogramming at the multibillion-dollar level is relatively recent, the transition from the Eisenhower to the Kennedy Administrations resulted in heavy use of reprogramming. Budget revisions by the Kennedy Administration brought the fiscal 1961 reprogramming figure for the Defense Department to at least $3.8 billion.[88]

A. Clearance Procedures

The appropriations committees, while recognizing the need for some degree of flexibility for the executive branch, are also aware that excessive reliance on reprogramming can downgrade the appropriation process. In 1955 the House Committee on Appropriations requested the Defense Department to submit semi-annual reports on all reprogramming actions. The Pentagon responded by issuing a set of instructions to define the scope of reporting requirements and to set forth criteria for what would constitute a "major reprogramming" action.[89] The following year the House Appropriations Committee expressed its dissatisfaction with certain reprogrammings. This dissatisfaction arose from such Defense Department practices as describing backlogs in maintenance and repair work and then taking funds appropriated for those purposes and using them for something else. As a result, the committee directed that there be no diversion in the future of funds appropriated for repair and maintenance.[90]

A 1959 report by the House Appropriations Committee observed that while the semi-annual reports had been helpful, they had not been sufficiently timely. Moreover, the practice of having the military services advise the committee informally of major reprogrammings had become "virtually inoperative." As a result, the committee directed that the Defense Department report periodically—but in no case less than thirty days after departmental approval—the approved reprogramming actions involving $1 million or more for operation and maintenance, $1 million or

---

[86] H.R. REP. No. 493, 84th Cong., 1st Sess. 8 (1955).

[87] H.R. REP. No. 1570, 91st Cong., 2d Sess. 6 (1970).

[88] HOUSE COMM. ON ARMED SERVICES, 89TH CONG., 1ST SESS., DEPARTMENT OF DEFENSE REPROGRAMMING OF APPROPRIATED FUNDS: A CASE STUDY 32 (Comm. Print 1965).

[89] H.R. REP. No. 493, 84th Cong., 1st Sess. 8 (1955); DOD instructions are included in *Hearings on Budgeting and Accounting Before the Senate Comm. on Government Operations*, 84th Cong., 2d Sess. 13-19 (1956).

[90] H.R. REP. No. 2104, 84th Cong., 2d Sess. 13 (1956).

more for research, development, test, and evaluation, and $5 million or more for procurement. New instructions were prepared by the Pentagon to accommodate the Committee's request.[91]

A report by the House Appropriations Committee in 1962 noted "with some concern" that there had been no revision of Defense Department instructions for reprogrammings since 1959, although "significant changes based on mutual understandings" had occurred since that time. The committee asked that the instructions be revised immediately.[92] The revised DOD directive called for prior approval by the committees, not only by the appropriations committees, but also by the authorizing committees. Prior approval of selected items and programs was required of the armed services and the appropriations committees from both houses. In situations where prior approval was not required, the committees were to be "promptly notified" (that is, within two working days) of approved reprogramming actions.[93]

Current DOD practices include calling for semi-annual reports, obtaining prior committee approval on certain items and programs, and making prompt notification to the committees on other reprogrammings. A DOD directive describes "prior approval" by the committees in the following way: in the event the Secretary of Defense is not informed of approval or disapproval within fifteen days of receipt by the committees of a reprogramming request, it would be assumed that there was no objection to implementing the proposed reprogramming.[94] In actual fact, prior approval means *explicit* approval, whether it takes the committees fifteen days, a month, or longer.

B. Circumventing Committee Control

It is evident that reprogramming can become a convenient means of circumventing the normal authorization and appropriation stages. Instead of obtaining approval from Congress as a whole, agency officials need only obtain approval from a few subcommittees. An agency could request money for a popular program, knowing that Congress would appropriate the funds, and then try to use the money later for a program that might not have survived scrutiny by the full Congress.

Reprogramming is used on occasion to undo the work of Congress and its committees. A recent example concerns the Defense Intelligence Agency. DIA had requested $66.8 million for fiscal 1971. The House Appropriations Committee cut that request by $2 million, in large part on the conviction that DIA was heavily overstaffed. DIA reduced its budget by only $700,000, having successfully prevailed upon the Defense Department to request reprogramming for $1.3 million to make

---

[91] H.R. REP. No. 408, 86th Cong., 1st Sess. 20 (1959); DEPARTMENT OF DEFENSE REPORT ON REPROGRAMMING OF APPROPRIATED FUNDS, DEPARTMENT OF DEFENSE INSTRUCTION No. 7250.5 (Oct. 23, 1959).

[92] H.R. REP. No. 1607, 87th Cong., 2d Sess. 21 (1962).

[93] DEPARTMENT OF DEFENSE REPROGRAMMING OF APPROPRIATED FUNDS, DEPARTMENT OF DEFENSE DIRECTIVE No. 7250.5 (Mar. 4, 1963).

[94] DEPARTMENT OF DEFENSE REPROGRAMMING OF APPROPRIATED FUNDS, DEPARTMENT OF DEFENSE DIRECTIVE No. 7250.5, at 3 (May 21, 1970). See S. HORN, UNUSED POWER 192-95 (1970).

up the difference. Representative Jamie L. Whitten was incensed by this maneuver: "Am I to understand that after Congress developed the record and made reductions on that basis, we are to have them come in here and ask for restoration, which is what it amounts to, of funds that the Congress saw fit to eliminate?"[95] House Appropriations allowed the Defense Department to reprogram $700,000 for DIA.

Another extraordinary use of reprogramming involved the Defense Special Projects Group (DSPG). The Defense Department wanted to initiate a research project that would cost $4 million. On any new research project of $2 million or more, the Defense Department must submit the request for committee review. In this case, however, DSPG was advised by the Defense Department to use $1 million to begin the project. The Pentagon would then supplement that later by transfering $3 million from the Emergency Fund. By the time the reprogramming request reached Congress, the project was three months underway. Representative Whitten described the attempted circumvention of the $2 million threshold in these terms: "You took a million dollars and got it started, and now you come up here and we are caught across the barrel. You have already started with a million dollars, but the million dollars was part of something which cost more than $2 million and clearly comes within the reprograming agreement."[96]

The House Appropriations Committee rejected this reprogramming request. Not only that, the request helped pique the committee's interest. DSPG was a new name for the Defense Communications Planning Group (DCPG). Congress was under the impression that DCPG—having been responsible for the electronic battlefield ("McNamara Line")—would be disbanded and the program transferred to the military services. Instead, DCPG adopted a new name and dreamed up new research projects to keep itself alive. To the question "what in the world are they doing over there?" the legislative answer was not favorable. The House Appropriations Committee characterized the attempt to perpetuate DSPG as "a classic example of bureaucratic empire building and of the bureaucratic tendency to never end an organization even after the work for which it was created has been concluded."[97] Appropriations committees in both houses agreed to terminate the agency.[98]

C. Broader Legislative Control

Reprogramming procedures, as they have evolved over the past few decades, now include a larger number of legislators in the review role. In earlier years requests for defense reprogramming were handled by the chairmen and ranking minority members of the defense appropriations subcommittees. At the present time, in House

---

[95] *Hearings on Department of Defense Appropriations for 1972 (part 2) Before the House Comm. on Appropriations*, 92d Cong., 1st Sess. 331 (1971).

[96] *Id.* at 610.

[97] H.R. REP. No. 666, 92d Cong., 1st Sess. 118-19 (1971).

[98] *Id.* at 118; S. REP. No. 498, 92d Cong., 1st Sess. 197 (1971); H.R. REP. No. 754, 92d Cong., 1st Sess. 14 (1971).

Appropriations, approval is granted by the full defense subcommittee. In Senate Appropriations, reprogrammings for minor matters were formerly decided by the chairman and ranking minority member of the defense subcommittee. The full subcommittee was brought together only for major reprogrammings. Beginning in 1972, all prior-approval reprogrammings—whether major or minor—were brought before the full subcommittee during regular hearings on the defense budget.

With regard to authorizing committees, the full House Armed Services Committee acts on reprogramming requests. In earlier years the Senate Armed Services Committee used to delegate such decisions to the committee chairman, ranking minority member, and committee counsel. In 1970 a separate Subcommittee on Reprogramming of Funds was established. Depending on the issue involved, this five-member subcommittee may decide the request or else pass it on to the full committee. The tendency has been toward greater involvement by the full committee.

Legislative efforts to monitor reprogramming occasionally go beyond the review responsibilities of designated committees. For instance, early in 1971 Secretary Laird expressed interest in obtaining funds to begin a fourth nuclear-powered carrier (CVAN-70). If it became necessary to submit a budget amendment or initiate a reprogramming request, he would be willing to give up $139.5 million that had been requested for an oil tanker and three salvage ships.[99] Senators Case and Mondale were able to enlist the support of Senator Ellender, chairman of the Appropriations Committee, and of Senator Stennis, chairman of Armed Services. The two chairmen agreed that reprogramming would be an improper technique for providing funds. The Administration would have to follow normal budgetary procedures: a budget request from the President followed by Congressional authorization and appropriation. The Administration decided to postpone making that request until a subsequent fiscal year.[100]

Thus, in the case of controversial reprogramming requests, the review role extends beyond the designated committees to involve Congress as a whole. To take another example, the Defense Department submitted a reprogramming request in 1971 for an additional $61.2 million for the Cheyenne helicopter. That covered approximately $35 million to reimburse the contractor for services performed, $9.3 million to continue the development program during fiscal 1972, and approximately $17 million to continue it during fiscal 1973. Since the Cheyenne had been under attack by members of Congress in recent years, only the reimbursement portion of the reprogramming request was approved. The House Appropriations Committee denied the request for fiscal 1973 development on the ground that "it did not seem

[99] *Hearings on Fiscal Year 1972 Authorization for Military Procurement, Research and Development, Construction and Real Estate Acquisition for the Safeguard ABM and Reserve Strengths (part 1) Before the Senate Armed Services Comm.*, 91st Cong., 1st Sess. 97, 258-59, 978 (1971).

[100] N.Y. Times, Apr. 18, 1971, at 40, col. 3; Washington Post, Apr. 28, 1971, at A8, col. 5. The correspondence between Senators Case and Mondale and Senator Ellender is reprinted in *Hearings on Department of Defense Appropriations for Fiscal Year 1972 Before the Senate Comm. on Appropriations*, 92d Cong., 1st Sess. 1344-45 (1971).

proper to anticipate the will of Congress with respect to the Cheyenne program that far in advance."[101] With regard to fiscal 1972 development, $9.3 million was placed in the appropriation bill as a separate and identifiable item so that the full Congress could work its will on the request.[102]

A still broader review by Congress over the reprogramming of funds is contemplated in a bill introduced by Senator Lawton Chiles in March 1971.[103] His bill would require the Comptroller General to compile information on reprogramming and to furnish such information to all committees and to all members of Congress.

V

TRANSFERS IN TIME

In addition to being transferred from one class of appropriations to another, or within a class, funds may be transferred from one year to the next. Congress enacted legislation in 1795 to restrict this practice. With certain exceptions, any unexpended funds remaining in the Treasury for more than two years were to be transferred to a surplus fund. At that point the appropriation would lapse.[104] Nevertheless, administrative actions could nullify the law's intent. For instance, Congress passed legislation in 1819 to suppress the slave trade and to punish crimes of piracy. In so doing, it neglected to appropriate funds to pay for these new responsibilities. President Monroe supplied the necessary vessels by using old balances remaining on the books of the Navy Department. When legislators protested that this violated the two-year limit, they were told that the balances were exempt from the law because they had been in the hands of the *Treasurer* (who acted as agent for the military departments), rather than being in the Treasury itself.[105]

An 1820 statute directed the Secretary of the Treasury to place funds that had been left unexpended by the departments of War and Navy into a surplus fund. Implementation of that statute, however, depended on a statement from the secretary of the department that "the object for which the appropriation was made has been effected."[106] By failing to make such a declaration the department could have access to those funds in future years.

A more stringent provision appeared in 1852. Congress directed that any moneys unexpended after two years be carried immediately to a surplus fund, with the appropriation regarded as having ceased. Decisions by the Attorney General quickly diluted the force of that restriction. In cases of contracted items, personal service, or other claims on the government, appropriations would remain available from

---

[101] H.R. REP. No. 666, 92d Cong., 1st Sess. 105 (1971).

[102] S. REP. No. 498, 92d Cong., 1st Sess. 18 (1971); H.R. REP. No. 754, 92d Cong., 1st Sess. 13 (1971).

[103] S. 1333, 92d Cong., 1st Sess. (1971). A similar bill (H.R. 10429) was introduced by Representative Fascell on August 5, 1971.

[104] Act of Mar. 3, 1795, ch. 45, § 16, 1 Stat. 437.

[105] 35 ANNALS OF CONG. 807-09 (1819); see L. WILMERDING, supra note 1, at 83-94.

[106] Act of May 1, 1820, ch. 52, § 1, 3 Stat. 567.

year to year until the obligation was fully discharged. In such situations "un-expended" came to mean "unobligated," and the appropriation did not lapse into the surplus fund.[107] In a second decision, the Attorney General held that it was proper for a department to begin a year by first expending old balances. Since old money would be used first, the Attorney General explained that it would be im-possible for a balance of two or more years to exist "unless the balance of a previous year exceed in amount the whole expenditure of the present year . . . ."[108]

A. No-Year Money

New statutes appeared in 1870 and 1874 to restrict the use of unexpended balances. Specifically excluded from those restrictions, however, were appropriations for projects funded by permanent or indefinite appropriations, such as rivers and harbors, lighthouses, fortifications, and public buildings.[109] Current law permits appropriations to "remain available until expended" for public works under the Bureau of Yards and Docks and for public buildings.[110] Such appropriations are referred to as no-year money. Appropriations in this form permit the President to release funds when he determines that they can be spent in the most effective manner, depending on the availability of labor and materials and on the state of technical development.

According to article I, section 8, of the Constitution, appropriations to raise and support armies shall not be for a longer term than two years. Yet no-year financing for military procurement has been upheld in several opinions by the Attorney General. A 1904 opinion argued that to raise and support an army was one thing; to equip it was another. The constitutional prohibition applied only to the former. That sounds a little like a distinction without a difference, but the opinion also argued that the power to arm and equip armies followed from the constitutional power to declare war, to raise and support armies, to provide forts, magazines, and arsenals and to levy and collect taxes to provide for the common defense.[111]

In the Department of Defense, appropriations for procurement and for research, development, test, and evaluation (R.D.T. & E.) have generally been made available on a no-year basis. For fiscal 1970, the amount of no-year funds for those categories came to $25.5 billion.[112] In an effort to bring carryover balances under closer legislative control, the fiscal 1971 appropriation bill for the Defense Department adopted a multi-year approach. Appropriations for major procurement became avail-able for only three fiscal years (except for shipbuilding, which requires a five-year term), while appropriations for R.D.T. & E. were made available for only a two-year period.[113]

---

[107] Act of Aug. 31, 1852, ch. 108, § 10, 10 Stat. 98; 7 OP. ATT'Y GEN. 1 (1854).
[108] 7 OP. ATT'Y GEN. 14 (1854).
[109] Act of July 12, 1870, ch. 251, § 5, 16 Stat. 251; Act of June 20, 1874, ch. 328, § 5, 18 Stat. 110.
[110] 31 U.S.C. §§ 635, 682 (1970).
[111] 25 OP. ATT'Y GEN. 105 (1904); see also 40 OP. ATT'Y GEN. 555 (1948).
[112] Act of Dec. 29, 1969, Pub. L. No. 91-171, tits. IV & V, 83 Stat. 475-79.
[113] Act of Jan. 11, 1971, Pub. L. No. 91-668, § 842(a), 84 Stat. 2037.

B. Carryover Balances

When the Administration accumulates large unobligated balances, the traditional Congressional response is to treat this as a sign of poor financial planning and a threat to legislative control. To a certain extent, the executive branch thereby in fact becomes independent of legislative action. As a result, the appropriations committees have tended to take into account these "carryover balances" in their decisions on new funding requests.

It is to the advantage of the executive branch to report as low a figure as possible for carryover balances, and several techniques have been tried, not always successfully, toward this end. For example, an executive department may try to obligate as much of the funds as possible. Sometimes this means prematurely obligating funds before testing or developmental work has been completed. In the case of weapons systems such as the Sheridan armored vehicle and Cheyenne helicopter, this tactic can prove embarrassing if not counter-productive for the Administration. The House Appropriations Committee has remarked that "Budgetary considerations based on fear of losing funding authority have often dictated such decisions rather than sound technical judgment."[114] Large obligations become especially suspicious when they take place in the closing months of a fiscal year ("June buying"), or when emergency and contingency funds are used at the end of a fiscal year.

Carryover balances can also be minimized by the executive departments by under-estimating the amount of unobligated funds that will be carried forward into the next fiscal year. For example, the Army estimated that $30.1 million in unobligated funds for R.D.T. & E. would be carried forward into fiscal 1962; the actual amount carried forward was more than $89 million. For this same period, the comparable figures for R.D.T. & E. in the Navy was $26.7 million estimated and $134.3 million actual. Where there is a pattern of underestimating unobligated balances, the appropriations committees may make budget reductions to avoid overfunding.[115] Budget cutbacks may also be made when there is too much unobligated money being carried forward from year to year. One such action occurred in 1967 when the House Appropriations Committee ordered a decrease in weapons procurement funds (primarily Navy) because the military services were maintaining excessive unobligated balances.[116]

Despite these legislative actions, a huge volume of funds continues to flow from one year to the next. The budget for fiscal 1973 shows an estimated 266.7 billion in unspent authority available from prior years. Of that amount, only $98.3 billion was expected to be spent in fiscal 1973, with the remainder carried forward once

---

[114] H.R. REP. No. 698, 91st Cong., 1st Sess. 48 (1969).
[115] H.R. REP. No. 1607, 87th Cong., 2d Sess. 48-49, 51 (1962).
[116] H.R. REP. No. 349, 90th Cong., 1st Sess. 35-36 (1967).

again to later years.[117] All of the $266.7 billion is appropriated money or the equivalent. Some of it consists of authorization to borrow from the Treasury; some of it is authority to incur obligations without further action by Congress, as with the Highway Trust Fund. Hence, whether in the form of appropriated money or the equivalent, the amount of $266.7 billion was available for expenditure without further Congressional action.[118] In justifying this discretion budget officials maintain that "full funding"—even though it results in large unobligated balances—leads to better management of public funds than appropriating for projects and programs in bits and pieces.

C. Accelerated Procurement

The Eisenhower Administration used "accelerated procurement" as an antirecession measure in 1958. Public works were accelerated, Housing and Home Finance programs speeded up, and government supply levels raised, all in an effort to pump more money into the economy and to stimulate recovery. This technique was not without its drawbacks. Advance procurement adds to the cost of storage space and inventory checks. It also creates administrative complications by forcing agencies to depart from prior schedules and long-term contractual commitments.[119] Moreover, with a fixed amount appropriated for these programs, acceleration at some point must be balanced by deceleration unless new funds are provided. Thus, at the very moment when the recovery phase needs reinforcement, the depletion of alloted funds has a retarding effect. That is especially serious since the automatic stabilizers, in the recovery phase, reverse direction and have a retarding effect of their own.

In 1961, President Kennedy also relied on accelerated procurement to combat recession. He directed the Veterans Administration to speed up the payment of $258 million in life insurance dividends, making that amount available in the first quarter instead of spread over the entire year. A special dividend payment of $218 million was made later, thereby reinforcing the speed-up with new funds and contributing a permanent boost to the economy. Kennedy also directed the heads of each department to accelerate procurement and construction wherever possible; he hastened payments to farmers under the price support program, increased the annual rate of free food distribution to needy families from about $60 million to more than $200 million, and made immediately available to the states the balance of federal-aid highway funds ($724 million) that had been scheduled for the entire fiscal year.[120]

---

[117] U.S. OFFICE OF MANAGEMENT AND BUDGET, THE BUDGET OF THE UNITED STATES GOVERNMENT, FISCAL YEAR 1973, at 42 (1972).

[118] U.S. OFFICE OF MANAGEMENT AND BUDGET, SPECIAL ANALYSES OF THE UNITED STATES GOVERNMENT, FISCAL YEAR 1973, at 97-105 (1972).

[119] W. LEWIS, JR., FEDERAL FISCAL POLICY IN THE POSTWAR RECESSIONS 221-27 (1962).

[120] Id. at 250-72. See also, U.S. PRESIDENT, PUBLIC PAPERS OF THE PRESIDENTS: JOHN F. KENNEDY, 1961, at 41 (1962); U.S. PRESIDENT, ECONOMIC REPORT OF THE PRESIDENT, 1962, at 97-98 (1962).

VI

IMPOUNDMENT

Impoundment of funds is a "transfer in time" that deserves separate treatment. During the past three decades, Presidents have withheld funds from such programs as the B-70 bomber, Air Force groups, antimissile systems, flood control projects, highways, supercarriers, urban renewal projects, and Model Cities. By refusing to spend appropriated funds, the President provokes the charge that he is obligated under the Constitution to execute the laws, not hold them in defiance—obligated to interpret appropriation bills not as mere permission to spend but as a mandate to spend as Congress directed. Otherwise, the argument runs, he encroaches upon the spending prerogatives of Congress, violates the doctrine of separated powers, and assumes unto himself a power of item veto that is neither sanctioned by the Constitution nor granted by Congress.

A number of authors of law journal articles, in advancing this line of argument, invoke phrases from Supreme Court decisions to bolster their case. Examination of those decisions, however, suggests that they have only the most tenuous relationship to the issue of impoundment and offer little hope of resolving the dispute.[121] The decisive appeal over the years has not been to legal principles and court decisions but to constituencies and agency support. In the words of one author, the President "can and may withhold expenditure of funds to the extent that the political milieu in which he operates permits him to do so."[122]

Political leverage is maximized, of course, by claims of constitutional support, and both sides therefore invoke the separation doctrine and the "intent of the framers" to their own advantage. The efforts largely cancel one another. When Congress appropriates and the President refuses to spend, legislators chastise him for encroaching upon their spending prerogatives. Yet if Congress tried to compel the President to spend the funds, he could charge usurpation of administrative responsibilities.

A. Basis for Impoundment

Instead of introducing into this discussion pieces of evidence from prior court decisions, I think it is more instructive to understand the larger political, economic, and legal framework within which impoundment takes place. It has long been the practice of the executive branch to treat appropriations as permissive rather than mandatory. President Jefferson, for example, notified Congress in 1803 that the sum of $50,000 appropriated for gunboats remained unexpended: "The favorable and peaceable turn of affairs on the Mississippi rendered an immediate execution of that law unnecessary . . . ."[123] An opinion by the Attorney General in 1896 main-

---

[121] Fisher, *Funds Impounded by the President: The Constitutional Issue*, 38 GEO. WASH. L. REV. 124 (1969).

[122] Miller, *Presidential Power to Impound Appropriated Funds: An Exercise in Constitutional Decision-Making*, 43 N.C.L. REV. 502, 533 (1965).

[123] I A COMPILATION OF MESSAGES AND PAPERS OF THE PRESIDENTS, *supra* note 3, at 360.

tained that an appropriation was not mandatory "to the extent that you are bound to expend the full amount if the work can be done for less . . . ."[124] The Hoover Commission report in 1949 recommended that the President should have authority to impound funds, provided that "the purposes intended by the Congress are still carried out."[125]

When the President impounds funds on that basis, few legislators are likely to challenge him. George Mahon, chairman of the House Appropriations Committee, has said that "the weight of experience and practice bears out the general proposition that an appropriation does not constitute a mandate to spend every dollar appropriated. . . . I believe it is fundamentally desirable that the Executive have limited powers of impoundment in the interests of good management and constructive economy in public expenditures."[126]

Not only is the President permitted limited powers of impoundment to be exercised at his discretion; in some cases he is required by law to withhold expenditures. By law, the President is expected to set aside funds for contingencies or to effect savings whenever they are made possible "by or through changes in requirements, greater efficiency of operations, or other developments" that take place after funds have been appropriated.[127] The vague and undefined terms of this provision obviously give the President wide latitude to impound funds: what, for example, constitutes "changes in requirements," or "greater efficiency of operations," or "other developments"?

Other statutes require that funds be withheld under conditions and circumstances spelled out by Congress. The 1964 Civil Rights Act empowers the President to withhold funds from federally financed programs in which there is discrimination by race, color, or national origin.[128] On the basis of that provision, special desegregation grants may be terminated when school districts violate civil rights requirements. A 1968 act requires states to update their welfare payment standards to reflect cost-of-living increases.[129] Failure to comply with the act can lead to a cutoff of federal welfare assistance. The Revenue and Expenditure Control Act of 1968 required expenditure reductions, most of which were achieved by administrative action.[130] The spending ceilings adopted by Congress for fiscal years 1969, 1970, and 1971 pro-

---

[124] 21 OP. ATT'Y GEN. 415 (1896). Similar statements appear at 21 OP. ATT'Y GEN. 392, 422 (1896).

[125] THE COMMISSION ON ORGANIZATION OF THE EXECUTIVE BRANCH OF THE GOVERNMENT, BUDGETING AND ACCOUNTING, A REPORT TO THE CONGRESS 17 (1949).

[126] Letter from Representative George Mahon to Senator Sam J. Ervin, Jr., Feb. 25, 1969 (copy obtained from Mr. Eugene B. Wilhelm, staff assistant, House Committee on Appropriations).

[127] 31 U.S.C. § 665(c)(2) (1970).

[128] 42 U.S.C. § 2000d-1 (1970).

[129] 42 U.S.C. § 602(a)(23) (1970). For accounts of threats made by HEW during 1971 to cut off relief funds from Calif., Ind., Neb., and Ariz., see the Washington Post, Jan. 9, 1971, at A2, col. 1; N.Y. Times, Jan. 20, 1971, at 15, col. 1; Washington Post, Jan. 28, 1971, at A18, col. 1; N.Y. Times, Mar. 29, 1971, at 19, col. 1; and N.Y. Times, Apr. 1, 1971, at 24, col. 3.

[130] 31 U.S.C. § 11 (1970). See L. FISHER, PRESIDENT AND CONGRESS: POWER AND POLICY 107-08 (1972).

vided the executive branch with additional authority to withhold funds.[131] Foreign assistance acts have directed the President to withhold economic assistance in an amount equivalent to the amount spent by any underdeveloped country for the purchase of sophisticated weapons systems, unless he informs Congress that the withholding of such assistance would be detrimental to the national security.[132]

1. Military Procurement

Presidents have also withheld funds on their own initiative after determining that it would be wasteful or unwise to spend money on weapons systems. President Eisenhower, for instance, impounded funds for the production of antiballistic missiles, insisting that funds should not be released until developmental tests were satisfactorily completed.[133] A major clash between legislative directives and executive discretion occurred in 1961 when Congress added $180 million to the $200 million requested by the Kennedy Administration for development of the B-70 bomber (later designated RS-70). Defense Secretary McNamara, after stressing the U.S. advantage over the Soviets in bombers and the deterrent capability of American missile strength, refused to release the unwanted funds. The House Armed Services Committee threatened to "direct" the Administration to spend money for production, but later removed the language at the urging of President Kennedy.[134] Even if Congress had followed through with its threat to mandate expenditures, the President could well have argued that there were too many developmental unknowns, too many technical problems unresolved, and therefore no justification for proceeding beyond the prototype stage.

In such situations it is contended that the President thwarts the will of Congress. It is not always easy, however, to know what that will is. President Truman's impoundment of Air Force funds in 1949 would appear to be a clear denial of legislative intent, and yet the issue was not at all that simple. The House had voted to increase Air Force funds, while the Senate sided with the President in opposing the increase. The matter lay deadlocked in conference committee, with adjournment close at hand and the military services in need of funds to meet their payrolls. A Senate motion to vote continuing appropriations was rejected by the House. To break the impasse, the Senate reluctantly accepted the extra Air Force funds, but with the understanding, as Senator Thomas said, that "if the money is appropriated it may not be used" by the President.[135] In light of that legislative history, it is clearly an oversimplification to say that Truman's impoundment of funds represented a denial of "the will of Congress."

---

[131] See FISHER, PRESIDENT AND CONGRESS: POWER AND POLICY, supra note 130, at 106-10.

[132] See, e.g., Act of Feb. 9, 1970, Pub. L. No. 91-194, § 119, 84 Stat. 10.

[133] U.S. PRESIDENT, PUBLIC PAPERS OF THE PRESIDENTS: JOHN F. KENNEDY, 1960-61, at 54-55, 414 (1961).

[134] For discussion on this dispute and other impoundment controversies, see Fisher, The Politics of Impounded Funds, 15 AD. SCI. Q. 361 (1970).

[135] 95 CONG. REC. 14,355 (1949). Note also the exchange between Senators Ferguson and Salstonstall at 95 CONG. REC. 14,855 (1949); Fisher, The Politics of Impounded Funds, supra note 134, at 366-67.

2. *Impounding Funds to Promote Executive Domestic Priorities*

In the cases cited thus far, funds were withheld in response to statutory directives or justified as good management of funds for weapons procurement. A different situation developed under the Nixon Administration; funds were withheld from domestic programs because the President considered those programs incompatible with his own set of budget priorities. Priorities and impoundment were at issue in 1969 when President Nixon announced plans to reduce research health grants, defer Model Cities funds, and reduce grants for urban renewal. During that same period he proceeded with his own preferences, such as the supersonic transport, a new manned bomber, a larger merchant marine fleet, and the Safeguard ABM system.[136]

In the spring of 1971 the Nixon Administration announced that it was withholding more than $12 billion, most of which consisted of highway money and funds for various urban programs. When Secretary Romney appeared before a Senate committee in March, he explained that funds were being held back from various urban programs because there was no point in accelerating programs that were "scheduled for termination." He was referring to the fact that Congress had added funds to grant-in-aid programs, whereas the Administration wanted to consolidate those programs and convert them into its revenue-sharing proposal.[137] To impound funds in this prospective sense—holding on to money in anticipation that Congress will enact an Administration bill—is a new departure for the impoundment technique. Money is not being withheld to avoid deficiencies, or to effect savings, or even to fight inflation, but rather to shift the scale of budget priorities from one Administration to the next, prior to Congressional action.

Another example of how the Nixon Administration used impoundment to promote its domestic priorities involved public works projects. The Administration went ahead with the projects it had recommended to Congress but deferred, without exception, all of the additional projects that Congress had wanted. The Deputy Director of the Office of Management and Budget offered this explanation to a House subcommittee: "Given the necessity for retrenchment in some areas, I think it is inevitable that the President would feel that the items he included were items that should be released first."[138] The subcommittee did not ask the Administration to identify its authority for giving priority to its programs while deferring Congressional add-ons.

B. Legislative Remedies

As a partial remedy for the withholding of funds by the President, Congress has adopted "floors," or minimum levels, below which the Administration could not go

[136] Fisher, *The Politics of Impounded Funds, supra* note 134, at 372.

[137] *Hearings on The Withholding of Funds for Housing and Urban Development Programs, Fiscal Year 1971, Before the Senate Comm. on Banking, Housing and Urban Affairs,* 92d Cong., 1st Sess. 163, 165 (1971).

[138] *Hearings on Public Works for Water and Power Development and Atomic Energy Commission Appropriations (part 6) Before the House Comm. on Appropriations,* 92d Cong., 1st Sess. 22 (1971) [hereinafter cited as *Public Works*].

In 1958, for instance, the Eisenhower Administration wanted to reduce the strengths of the Army Reserve and the Army National Guard, both of which had strong support in the local communities. Congress retaliated by providing mandatory language to maintain the strengths at higher levels.[139]

Political pressure has also been used to pry loose impounded funds. After the November 1966 elections, President Johnson announced a $5.3 billion reduction in federal programs. Sensitive to criticism from the states, he released some of the money in February 1967 and, on the eve of a conference the following month with governors, released additional amounts.[140] Pressure also came into play in the fall of 1970 after President Nixon had withheld some education funds. Two weeks before the November elections, in the midst of widespread criticism from school districts, the Administration announced that the money was being released. When a Cabinet officer was asked whether the pending elections had prompted the Administration to reverse its position and free the funds, he replied, smiling, that there was "no connection whatsoever."[141]

These pressure tactics and confrontations, even when successful, are not wholly satisfactory to the mayors of large cities dependent on federal funds. They must take time from their busy schedules to come to Congress in support of authorization bills for urban programs. They testify a second time in behalf of an appropriation bill. Now they must come to Congress and to the Administration a third time to see that the money, having already been authorized and appropriated, is actually spent.

In March 1971, the Senate Subcommittee on Separation of Powers held hearings for the purpose of establishing better legislative control over impounded funds. Senator Sam J. Ervin, Jr., chairman of the subcommittee, introduced a bill several months later to require the President to notify Congress within ten days whenever he impounds funds appropriated for a specific purpose or project. The President's message would include the amount of funds impounded, the specific projects or functions affected, and the reasons for impounding the funds. Congress would then have sixty days to pass a joint resolution disapproving the impoundment.[142] Senator Ervin introduced a subsequent bill in September to provide that an impoundment action by the President shall cease at the end of sixty calendar days unless Congress approves the action by concurrent resolution.[143] This bill is stronger than its predecessor in two respects: it provides for affirmative approval instead of a resolution of disapproval, and it relies on a concurrent resolution (which cannot be vetoed) instead of a joint resolution (which must be presented to the President).

[139] Act of Aug. 22, 1958, Pub. L. No. 85-724, 72 Stat. 715. See S. REP. No. 1578, 87th Cong., 2d Sess. 5 (1962).
[140] Fisher, *The Politics of Impounded Funds, supra* note 134, at 370-71.
[141] Washington Post, Oct. 23, 1970, at A6, col. 1 (remarks of HEW Secretary Richardson).
[142] S. 2027, 92d Cong., 1st Sess. (1971); *Hearings on Executive Impoundment of Appropriated Funds Before the Senate Comm. on the Judiciary,* 92d Cong., 1st Sess. (1971).
[143] S. 2581, 92d Cong., 1st Sess. (1971).

This kind of legislation assumes that Congress has the power to compel expenditures. While it is true that a legal memorandum issued by an official in the Nixon Administration affirms the power of Congress to mandate expenditures for the impacted areas program,[144] the President could exert his prerogatives elsewhere. In the area of defense procurement, in particular, the President could take the position that Congress cannot deprive him of his judgment and discretion in the administration of programs and management of funds.

Another approach for legislative control is to take back from the Administration some of its reasons for impounding funds. As a result of the spending ceilings adopted by Congress in recent years, the Administration has argued that certain funds have to be withheld in order to avoid the risk of exceeding the ceiling. Congress did not adopt a spending ceiling for fiscal 1972. Rep. Joe L. Evins explained to a budget official that "the Congress feels that they don't want to give you a flexible ceiling which you could use as a tool to freeze and impound funds as you did in the past."[145]

During debate on the Revenue Act of 1971, the Senate considered an amendment by Senator Humphrey to require the President to transmit to Congress and to the Comptroller General a report on impounded funds. The report would include such features as the amount of funds impounded, the date of impoundment, the departments affected, the reasons for impoundment, and the period of time during which the funds are to be impounded. The Senate adopted the amendment by a vote of 48 to 18,[146] but the amendment was not considered in conference because of questions raised regarding its germaneness under House rules.[147]

The Foreign Assistance Act of 1971 contained a provision which made the obligation or expenditure of funds available under the Foreign Assistance Act and the Foreign Military Sales Act contingent upon the release of certain impounded funds. The Comptroller General would have to certify that the Administration had released, by April 30, 1972, a little over $2 billion in funds for programs administered by the Department of Agriculture, the Department of Health, Education, and Welfare, and the Department of Housing and Urban Development.[148]

VII

UNAUTHORIZED COMMITMENTS

Article 1, section 9, of the Constitution provides that "No money shall be drawn from the Treasury but in consequence of appropriations made by law." Presidents have nevertheless found it expedient at times to enter into financial

---

[144] Memorandum by William H. Rehnquist, Assistant Attorney General, Office of Legal Counsel, Dec. 1, 1969, reprinted at 116 CONG. REC. S158 (daily ed. Jan. 20, 1970).

[145] Public Works, supra note 138, at 13.

[146] 117 CONG. REC. S18,485 (daily ed. Nov. 13, 1971).

[147] H.R. REP. No. 708, 92d Cong., 1st Sess. 59 (1971).

[148] Pub. L. No. 92-226, § 658, 86 Stat. 32 (Feb. 7, 1972). See 117 CONG. REC. S21,903 (daily ed. Dec. 17, 1971). The GAO subsequently reported that these funds, as of the deadline, had been released. See 118 CONG. REC. H4098 (daily ed. May 3, 1972).

obligations not authorized by Congress. Jefferson, for instance, agreed to accept France's offer to sell the whole of Louisiana for $11,250,000—plus an additional $3,750,000 to cover private claims against France—even though the offer exceeded instructions set forth by Congress.[149] Jefferson also relied on the executive prerogative in June 1807, after a British vessel had fired on the American ship *Chesapeake*. Without statutory authority, Jefferson ordered military purchases for the emergency and disclosed his actions to Congress when it came back in session. "To have awaited a previous and special sanction by law," he said, "would have lost occasions which might not be retrieved."[150]

In 1861, after the firing on Fort Sumter, and while Congress was adjourned, Lincoln directed his Secretary of the Treasury to advance $2,000,000 to three private citizens, the money to be used for "military and naval measures necessary for the defense and support of the Government . . . ."[151] Also in this category of unauthorized commitments was the decision by Theodore Roosevelt to send an American fleet around the world, despite Congressional threats not to finance the expedition. Roosevelt answered that he had enough money to take the fleet halfway around the world. "[I]f Congress did not choose to appropriate enough money to get the fleet back, why, it would stay in the Pacific. There was no further difficulty about the money."[152]

The Supreme Court has occasionally reviewed some of the finanical initiatives taken by executive officers. In one case, decided in 1833, the Court addressed itself to the question of whether the head of an executive department could allow payments not authorized by law. A unanimous decision observed that "A practical knowledge of the action of any one of the great departments of the government, must convince every person that the head of a department, in the distribution of its duties and responsibilities, is often compelled to exercise his discretion. He is limited in the exercise of his powers by the law; but it does not follow that he must show a statutory provision for every thing he does. No government could be administered on such principles."[153] Another Court decision involved an agreement made between a government contractor and Buchanan's Secretary of War, John B. Floyd. The contractor, lacking sufficient funds to complete the order, was allowed to draw time-drafts and have them purchased by his suppliers as a means of providing interim assistance. The government subsequently accepted drafts of $5 million, but over a million dollars remained unpaid. Holders of the unpaid drafts contended that Secretary Floyd's acceptances were binding on the

---

[149] I A COMPILATION OF MESSAGES AND PAPERS OF THE PRESIDENTS, *supra* note 3, at 357. Congress initially appropriated $2,000,000 to be applied toward the purchase of New Orleans and the Floridas. 12 ANNALS OF CONG. 370-71 (1803); Act of Feb. 26, 1803, ch. 8, § 1, 2 Stat. 202. Supplemental appropriations: Acts of Nov. 10, 1803, ch. 2 and 3, 2 Stat. 245, 247.

[150] I A COMPILATION OF MESSAGES AND PAPERS OF THE PRESIDENTS, *supra* note 3, at 428.

[151] 6 *id.* at 78.

[152] 20 THE WORKS OF THEODORE ROOSEVELT 540 (rev. ed. 1927).

[153] United States v. Macdaniel, 32 U.S. (7 Pet.) 1, 14 (1833).

government. The Court, however, dismissed their claim, denying that Floyd possessed either constitutional or statutory authority to enter into his agreements.[154]

In trying to prevent unauthorized commitments, Congress has had to soften statutory language at times in order to allow army and navy supply agencies to sign contracts in advance of appropriations. Otherwise, the material would not have been available on time. Thus, when Congress prohibited unauthorized commitments in 1820, an exception was allowed for contracts for subsistence and clothing for the army and navy, as well as for contracts by the Quartermaster's Department. Legislative delays in passing appropriation bills (enacted after one-fourth to one-third of the year had elapsed) forced departments to make commitments and expenditures not legally authorized. The Secretary of the Navy reported to Congress in 1825 that his department, for nearly half the year, acted in "perfect ignorance of the law under which it is bound to act." As a result "The law is, necessarily, not complied with, because it is passed after the act is performed."[155]

Administrative discretion in the handling of funds regularly provoked the ire of Congress. The Gilmer Committee reported in 1842 "Under color of what are termed regulations, large amounts of money are often applied to purposes never contemplated by the appropriating power, and numerous offices are sometimes actually created in the same way."[156] Funds generated from such governmental activities as the postal service or customs collection invited executive discretion as to their use. William T. Barry, Postmaster General from 1828 to 1835, borrowed large sums of money on the credit of the Post Office. His practice was defended on the grounds that the Post Office Department "created its own funds" and that bank loans were therefore simply a claim on future postal revenues.[157] A Senate report in 1834 roundly condemned such practices and justifications.[158] In 1842 the House Committee on Public Expenditures complained that the Secretary of the Treasury was using customs revenue to finance a naval force for the collection of revenue. "He appropriates and pays," the committee said, "without the sanction of Congress, and even without its knowledge."[159]

A. Coercive Deficiencies

A statute passed in 1870 prohibited executive departments from spending in a fiscal year any sum in excess of appropriations for that year; nor could any department involve the government in any contract for the future payment of money

---

[154] The Floyd Acceptances, 74 U.S. (7 Wall.) 666 (1868).

[155] Act of May 1, 1820, ch. 52, § 6, 3 Stat. 568. Secretary of the Navy, *Report to the U.S. Congress*, in 2 AMERICAN STATE PAPERS: NAVAL AFFAIRS 101 (1860). The 1820 contract authority evolved into the "Feed and Forage" Law, passed in 1861 and still part of the U.S. Code. In advance of authorizations or appropriations, the Departments of the Army, Navy, and Air Force are permitted to make contracts or purchases for clothing, subsistence, forage, fuel, quarters, transportation, or medical and hospital supplies, to cover the necessities of the current year. 41 U.S.C. § 11(a) (1970).

[156] H.R. REP. No. 741, 27th Cong., 2d Sess. 17-18 (1842).

[157] *See* L. WHITE, THE JACKSONIANS 265-66 (1954).

[158] S. REP. No. 422, 23d Cong., 1st Sess. (1834).

[159] H.R. REP. No. 756, 27th Cong., 2d Sess. 6 (1842).

in excess of such appropriations.[160] The thrust of that law was regularly blunted by the incurring of deficiencies. If the departments ran out of money before the end of the fiscal year there was little that Congress could do except pass a supplementary appropriation. The fault was not entirely that of the departments, however. James A. Garfield, who had been chairman of the House Appropriations Committee from 1871 to 1875, made this observation: "One of the vicious party devices too often resorted to for avoiding responsibility for extravagance in appropriations is to cut down the annual bills below the actual amount necessary to carry on the government, announce to the country that a great reduction has been made in the interest of economy, and after the elections are over, make up the necessary amount by deficiency bills."[161]

The Antideficiency Act of 1905 introduced the technique of monthly or other allotments to prevent "undue expenditures in one portion of the year that may require deficiency or additional appropriations to complete the service of the fiscal year . . . ."[162] In the Antideficiency Act of 1906, Congress stipulated that apportionments could be waived or modified in the event of "some extraordinary emergency or unusual circumstance which could not be anticipated at the time of making such apportionment . . . ."[163] That constituted an admission by Congress that regardless of spending patterns anticipated when passing appropriation bills— or even after apportioning the funds—changing conditions might necessitate a different course for expenditures.

Contemporary regulations on unauthorized commitments are far more explicit than the Constitution. The U.S. Code contains the following admonition:

No officer or employee of the United States shall make or authorize an expenditure from or create or authorize an obligation under any appropriation or fund in excess of the amount available therein; nor shall any such officer or employee involve the Government in any contract or other obligation, for the payment of money for any purpose, in advance of appropriations made for such purpose, unless such contract or obligation is authorized by law.[164]

Despite the rigorous nature of that language, there are a number of cases where the Administration has presented Congress with a *fait accompli* and in effect compelled it to appropriate the necessary funds.

The commitments of troops to Korea by President Truman is one postwar example. Military intervention began prior to the second United Nations resolution of June 27, 1950, and, despite the provisions of the United Nations Participation Act of 1945, no attempt was made to obtain Congressional approval for the venture.[165] The war in Southeast Asia—notwithstanding the adoption of

---

[160] Act of July 12, 1870, ch. 251, 16 Stat. 251.
[161] L. WILMERDING, *supra* note 1, at 141.
[162] Act of Mar. 3, 1905, ch. 1484, § 4, 33 Stat. 1257-58.
[163] Act of Feb. 27, 1906, ch. 510, § 3, 34 Stat. 49.
[164] 31 U.S.C. § 665(a) (1970). *But see* "Feed and Forage" Law, *supra* note 155.
[165] L. FISHER, *supra* note 130, at 194-95.

the Tonkin Gulf Resolution—has been another case of Presidential commitment first and Congressional support second. The executive branch initiated the covert war carried out prior to the Tonkin Gulf incident. Executive decisions were also responsible for filling out the scope of the commitment, including the bombing of North Vietnam and the introduction of American ground forces. Executive commitments are evident even in peace negotiations. Dr. Henry A. Kissinger, Assistant to the President for National Security Affairs, told reporters on January 26, 1972, that the Administration had offered North Vietnam "a massive reconstruction program for all of Indochina in which North Vietnam could share to the extent of several billion dollars."[166] It was later reported that the plan contemplated a five-year aid program of $5 billion for South Vietnam, Laos, and Cambodia, and $2.5 billion for North Vietnam.[167]

B. Cambodian Intervention

Another executive-inspired commitment resulted from the Cambodian intervention of the spring of 1970. Following his intervention there, President Nixon asked Congress for $255 million in military and economic assistance for Cambodia. The executive branch clearly involved the government in an obligation in advance of appropriations, not only for the expenses resulting from the Cambodian operation itself, but for future expenses as well. As Secretary of State Rogers explained to the Senate Foreign Relations Committee, on December 10, 1970: "I think it is true that when we ask for military assistance and economic assistance for Cambodia we do certainly take on some obligation for some continuity."[168] In an interview with a Washington, D.C., reporter, the Cambodian foreign minister said that he felt there was an unwritten treaty between the two countries: "I am convinced that there really is a moral obligation of the United States to help. We are confident that the United States will continue to help us."[169]

The extent of this support was indicated in October 1971 when the Senate debated an amendment to the Foreign Assistance Act which would limit the total expenditure in Cambodia to $250 million for fiscal 1972. The Administration opposed the restriction, contending that it would threaten the capacity of the Cambodian Government to defend itself. John N. Irwin, III, Acting Secretary of State, offered Senator Fulbright this appraisal: "We believe that with continued United States assistance at the levels requested by the Administration, the Cambodians with some external logistics and maintenance support will continue to make progress in defending their country from foreign invasion."[170]

On October 29, during debate on the Foreign Assistance Act of 1971, the Senate

---

[166] 8 WEEKLY COMP. PRES. DOC. 128 (1972).

[167] Washington Post, Jan. 28, 1972, at A1, col. 2.

[168] *Hearings on Supplemental Foreign Assistance Authorization, 1970, Before the Senate Comm. on Foreign Relations*, 91st Cong., 2d Sess. 27 (1970).

[169] Interview with Henry Bradsher, Washington Sunday Star, May 23, 1971, at A5, col. 1.

[170] 117 CONG. REC. S16,390 (daily ed. Oct. 19, 1971).

voted to increase the ceiling on expenditures in Cambodia from $250 million to $341 million. The latter was the figure requested by the Administration. Thus, while the Senate agreed to give the Administration what it wanted, it also asserted the right of Congress to set limits on expenditures. The ceiling could not be circumvented by special powers and authorities, such as the ability of the Pentagon to declare defen'se articles "excess" and give them to Cambodia, or the broad authority of the Defense Department and the CIA to transfer funds from one area to another. If it turned out that more than $341 million was required, this provision required the Administration to return to Congress for additional authorization.[171]

The $341 million ceiling did not apply to combat air operations over Cambodia. Moreover, the House accepted the ceiling in conference, but only with amendments which specifically excluded the obligation or expenditure of funds attributable to South Vietnamese operations in Cambodia.[172] The President signed the Foreign Assistance Act on' February 7, 1972.[173]

C. GAO Controls

It is generally assumed that the General Accounting Office is empowered to decide the legality of a payment of public funds and that such decisions are binding on the Administration. Several decisions have indeed been issued by the Comptroller General to disapprove expenditures by the executive branch.[174] However, it is also possible for the executive branch to invoke its own prerogatives and oppose a GAO decision. Thus, in a letter directed to the Secretary of State on December 13, 1960, the Comptroller General advised that program funds under the Mutual Security Act would no longer be available because of the Secretary's failure to forward certain documents and records to the GAO or to Congress, as required by the Act. The Attorney General rejected that opinion on the ground that Congress could not infringe on the right of "executive privilege" by forcing the President to release information which he considers to be injurious to the national security or the public interest.[175]

As another example, in 1960 the Defense Department entered into a written agreement with a consortium of five NATO countries formed to produce Hawk surface-to-air missiles in Europe. The Pentagon, lacking sufficient funds to fulfill its part of the agreement, inserted a clause stating that the U.S. commitment was "subject to availability of funds." GAO took the positon that no express authorization existed in law allowing DOD to enter into the purchase agreement, the commit-

---

[171] 117 CONG. REC. S17,169-75 (daily ed. Oct. 29, 1971).

[172] S. REP. No. 590, 92d Cong., 1st Sess. 28 (1971).

[173] Pub. L. No. 92-226, § 655, 86 Stat. 29 (Feb. 7, 1972).

[174] See, e.g., 42 COMP. GEN. 226 (1962). A GAO report states that decisions of the Comptroller General "are final and conclusive on the executive branch and are binding on the General Accounting Office in its audit." Functions of the General Accounting Office, S. Doc. No. 96, 87th Cong., 2d Sess. 21 (1962).

[175] 41 OP. ATT'Y GEN. 507 (1960).

ment did not comply with the intent of the Antideficiency Act, and that the Pentagon had firmly committed the United States to buy four missile systems at an unknown cost. Although GAO advised the Pentagon to take certain actions, the Defense Department in December 1970 stated that it did not agree that there had been any violation of law and that it did not consider any corrective action necessary.[176]

The GAO also clashed with the executive branch over the legality of the "Philadelphia Plan." In order to work on federally assisted projects, contractors had to set specific goals for hiring members of minority groups. On August 5, 1969, the Comptroller General issued a decision in which he held that the Plan conflicted with the 1964 Civil Rights Act, which prohibited the setting up of any kind of preferential treatment on the basis of race, color, or national origin. The Comptroller General said it did not matter whether one designated the hiring commitment as a "goal" or a "quota."[177] The Secretary of Labor promptly announced that the Administration would continue to press ahead with the Philadelphia Plan. He said that interpretation of the Civil Rights Act had been vested by Congress in the Department of Justice and that the Department had approved the plan as consistent with the Act.[178] Moreover, the Secretary of Labor said that the Comptroller General had ignored the President's Executive Order "as an independent source of law."[179] The U.S. Court of Appeals for the Third Circuit later upheld the legality of the Philadelphia Plan. The court justified this use of Presidential power partly on the Chief Executive's implied power—as it relates to economical procurement policy—to assure that "the largest possible pool of qualified manpower be available for the accomplishment" of federal projects.[180]

GAO reviews, as in the case of payments to Free World Forces, have been hampered by administrative delays and by refusals on the part of executive agencies to allow GAO investigators access to future planning information, routine evaluative reports, and program evaluation group reports.[181] To offset such difficulties, it has been proposed that the Comptroller General should have subpoena authority to compel agencies to make available books, accounts, and other contractor records required for a GAO investigation. At least forty executive agencies, independent boards, and commissions have subpoena powers now.[182]

---

[176] GENERAL ACCOUNTING OFFICE, REPORT TO THE SENATE COMM. ON FOREIGN RELATIONS ON UNITED STATES ECONOMIC AND MILITARY FOREIGN ASSISTANCE PROGRAMS 36-37 (Comm. Print 1971).

[177] 49 COMP. GEN. 59 (1969), reprinted at 115 CONG. REC. S9176-79 (daily ed. Aug. 5, 1969).

[178] 42 OP. ATT'Y GEN. 37 (1969), reprinted at 115 CONG. REC. S11,318 (daily ed. Sept. 25, 1969).

[179] 115 CONG. REC. S9954 (daily ed. Aug. 13, 1969).

[180] Contractors Ass'n of E. Pa. v. Secretary of Labor, 442 F.2d 159, 171 (3rd Cir. 1971), cert. denied, 404 U.S. 854 (1971).

[181] Hearings on Executive Privilege: The Withholding of Information by the Executive Before the Senate Comm. on the Judiciary, 92d Cong., 1st Sess. 303-15 (1971).

[182] Hearings on the Capability of GAO to Analyze and Audit Defense Expenditures Before the Senate Comm. on Government Operations, 91st Cong., 1st Sess. 105-06 (1969). During the fall of 1970 the Senate passed a bill (S. 4432, 91st Cong., 2d Sess.) designed to strengthen GAO access to departmental records, but the bill was not acted upon by the House.

CONCLUSION

We know from other studies, with a fair amount of detail, the discrepancies that exist between the President's budget requests and the amounts authorized by Congress. Comparable gaps exist between what is authorized and what is appropriated. On these areas of the budget process we know a great deal. In contrast, we know embarrassingly little about the expenditure phase. Why are there discrepancies between what is appropriated and what is spent? What, if anything, should be done about it?

The information supplied in this paper should provide advocates of reform with a little better understanding of what the problem is and why past efforts at reform have not always produced beneficial and predictable results. It frequently happens that the adoption of a reform proposal, intended to drive out one evil, simply creates another that proves harder to extirpate. Take away the power to make transfers, and agency officials pad their budgets. Eliminate discretionary authority altogether, and agency officials incur deficiencies. Give the President the power to allot funds—as a means of preventing deficiencies—and he uses that power to impound funds and further his own policies.

The reform advocate is therefore advised to regard executive spending discretion as an essential, ineradicable feature of the budget process. Expenditures deviate from appropriations for a number of reasons. Appropriations are made many months, and sometimes years, in advance of expenditures. Congress acts with imperfect knowledge in trying to legislate in fields that are highly technical and constantly undergoing change. New circumstances will develop to make obsolete and mistaken the decisions reached by Congress at the appropriation stage. It is not practicable for Congress to adjust to these new developments by passing large numbers of supplemental appropriation bills. Were Congress to control expenditures by confining administrators to narrow statutory details it would perhaps protect its power of the purse but it would not protect the purse itself. Discretion is needed for the sound management of public funds.

While there no doubt exists a need for executive flexibility, that is an abstract term capable of hiding much mischief. The executive branch complains about the vast amount of "uncontrollables" in the budget and yet somehow comes up with a hundred million dollars to finance the Cambodian intervention. It is evident that in a number of areas, including covert financing, impoundment, reprogramming, transfers, and unauthorized commitments, Congress has yet to discover a satisfactory means of controlling expenditures. Public policy is then decided by administrators rather than by elected representatives and the funds they provide.

The results are often incongruous. Congress goes through the formality of authorizing and appropriating funds but the money is never spent. On the other hand, Congress can find itself locked into paying for administrative commitments it never authorized. The expenditure process is one in which administrators must enjoy substantial discretion in exercising judgment and in taking responsibility for their actions, but those actions ought to be directed toward executing Congressional, not administrative, policy. It is up to Congress to make that policy clear and consistent.

SOME COMMENTS ON THE ROLE OF DISCRETION IN MILITARY JUSTICE

ROBINSON O. EVERETT*

An unpopular war has produced vehement criticism of the military establishment; and military justice, a pillar of that establishment, has not been immune from that criticism. According to a book title, "Military Justice is to Justice as Military Music is to Music."[1] From the more lofty position of the Supreme Court, Mr. Justice Douglas has referred to "so-called military justice" and to "the travesties of justice perpetrated under the 'Uniform Code of Military Justice.'"[2] Legislative proposals for reform of military justice have appeared from many quarters.[3] And distrust of military justice has led to judicial constriction of court-martial jurisdiction.[4]

Central to many of the complaints against military justice is the great discretion granted to military commanders in its administration. The following discussion has as its purpose the identification of the diverse areas in which discretion is a pivotal part of the military justice system. While the general approach here is descriptive, attention is given to newly emerging limitations on discretion in the military.

I

DISCRETION OF THE COMMANDER IN CHIEF

A. Sources of Presidential Discretion

1. Article II of the Constitution

Under Article II of the Constitution the President is vested with the "executive power" and is "Commander in Chief of the Army and Navy of the United States, and of the Militia of the several States, when called into the actual Service of the United States."[5] It is unnecessary to decide to what extent these constitutional provisions would suffice of themselves to confer broad discretion upon the President in the administration of military justice,[6] since Congress has delegated extensive

---

* Professor of Law, Duke University School of Law; Lt. Col., USAFR.

[1] R. SHERRILL, MILITARY JUSTICE IS TO JUSTICE AS MILITARY MUSIC IS TO MUSIC (1969).

[2] O'Callahan v. Parker, 395 U.S. 258, 266 (1969).

[3] E.g., Bayh, The Military Justice Act of 1971: The Need for Legislative Reform, 10 AM. CRIM. L. REV. 9 (1971); Sherman, Congressional Proposals for Reform of Military Law, 10 AM. CRIM. L. REV. 25 (1971); U.S. COURT OF MILITARY APPEALS AND THE JUDGE ADVOCATES GENERAL, 1971 ANNUAL REPORT 1-2.

[4] O'Callahan v. Parker, 395 U.S. 258 (1969); Reid v. Covert, 354 U.S. 1 (1957); Toth v. Quarles, 350 U.S. 11 (1955); Latney v. Ignatius, 416 F.2d 821 (D.C. Cir. 1969).

[5] U.S. CONST. art. II, §§ 1, 2.

[6] See Youngstown Sheet & Tube Co. v. Sawyer, 343 U.S. 579 (1952). For an argument that the President has a very broad constitutional power to regulate military justice, see Fratcher, Presidential Power to Regulate Military Justice: A Critical Study of Decisions of the Court of Military Appeals, 34 N.Y.U.L. REV. 861 (1959).

power to the President. The scope of the power delegated depends, in part, on the basis for his exercise of military jurisdiction in a particular case.

2. *The Law of War*

One source of military jurisdiction is the law of war—a branch of international law. Thus, in *Ex parte Quirin*[7] the Supreme Court permitted trial by military commission of eight spies who disembarked on the East Coast from German submarines during World War II. Even though one of the spies claimed American citizenship and the civil courts were available, the Court concluded that Congress had authorized such trial pursuant to its constitutional power "to define and punish Piracies and Felonies committed on the high Seas, and offenses against the Law of Nations."[8] By order, President Roosevelt had both appointed a military commission to try the accused and prescribed regulations governing the trial procedure and review of the case. The presidential order did not conform to the provisions of the Articles of War for trial and appellate review in courts-martial.[9] Even so, the Court upheld the President's regulations.[10]

Similarly, the Supreme Court sustained the jurisdiction of a military commission which the Commanding General of the United States Army Forces, Western Pacific, appointed in 1945 to try General Yamashita for alleged war crimes in the Philippine Islands.[11] Here again jurisdiction was predicated on the law of war and on Congress' constitutional power to define and punish offenses against the Law of Nations. Hostilities had terminated; but a state of war continued, since peace had not yet been proclaimed.[12] The regulations prescribed by military authorities for Yamashita's trial permitted use of affidavits and depositions under circumstances when such evidence would not be admissible in a court-martial. However, in the Court's opinion the military establishment had been left free by Congress to use the rules of evidence it believed most appropriate.[13]

Courts created in connection with American military government of occupied Germany were considered by the Supreme Court in *Madsen v. Kinsella*.[14] Mrs. Madsen, who was an American citizen and the dependent wife of an Air Force lieutenant, was tried and found guilty of murder by a United States Military Government Court. This occupation court was deemed to be in the nature of a military commission, and its jurisdiction stemmed from the law of war. According to the

---

[7] 317 U.S. 1 (1942).

[8] U.S. CONST. art. I, § 8, cl. 10.

[9] 317 U.S. at 22.

[10] *Id.* at 47. Some members of the Court considered that Congress did not intend the Articles of War to govern the procedures of a military commission convened by the President to determine questions relating to admitted enemy invaders. Other Justices concluded that although the trial was subject to whatever provisions of the Articles of War Congress had made applicable to "military commissions," the Articles cited by the defense counsel did not foreclose the procedures which the President prescribed or which the military commission was shown to have employed.

[11] *In re* Yamashita, 327 U.S. 1 (1946).

[12] *Id.* at 12.

[13] *Id.* at 18-23.

[14] 343 U.S. 341 (1952).

Court, military commissions "have been called our common-law war courts. They have taken many forms and borne many names. Neither their procedure nor their jurisdiction has been prescribed by statute."[15] With respect to military commissions the Supreme Court also noted:

> In the absence of attempts by Congress to limit the President's power, it appears that, as Commander-in-Chief of the Army and Navy of the United States, he may, in time of war, establish and prescribe the jurisdiction and procedure of military commissions, and of tribunals in the nature of such commissions, in territory occupied by Armed Forces of the United States. His authority to do this sometimes survives cessation of hostilities. . . . The policy of Congress to refrain from legislating in this uncharted area does not imply its lack of power to legislate. That evident restraint contrasts with its traditional readiness to "make Rules for the Government and Regulation of the land and naval Forces; . . . ." Under that clause Congress has enacted and repeatedly revised the Articles of War which have prescribed, with particularity, the jurisdiction and procedure of United States court-martial.[16]

The Court ruled that Article of War 15, as it then existed, provided a concurrent jurisdiction for courts-martial and military commissions with respect to violations of the law of war; and military commanders had the discretion to choose which type of tribunal they would employ.[17]

In *Quirin, Yamashita,* and *Madsen* the Supreme Court was applying the law of war in connection with a declared war, and perhaps these decisions might be limited by that fact.[18] However, in those situations where the law of war can properly be invoked, Congress has continued to provide military commanders with a choice between courts-martial, which are subject to the procedures and safeguards of the Uniform Code of Military Justice and the Manual for Courts-Martial, and military commissions, for which the President as Commander-in-Chief and his subordinate commanders can make rules of evidence and provide for trial procedure on an ad hoc basis.

Under Article 18 of the Uniform Code, general courts-martial "have jurisdiction to try any person who by the law of war is subject to trial by a military tribunal and may adjudge any punishment permitted by the law of war."[19] Article 21[20]—in wording almost identical to that of the corresponding Article of War 15 which was

---

[15] *Id.* at 346-47.

[16] *Id.* at 348-49.

[17] *Id.* at 345-55. *Cf.* United States v. Schultz, 1 U.S.C.M.A. 512, 4 C.M.R. 104 (1952).

[18] *Cf.* United States v. Averette, 19 U.S.C.M.A. 363, 41 C.M.R. 363 (1970), discussed in 49 N.C.L. REV. 188 (1970). There the Court of Military Appeals ruled that Article 2(10), which "in time of war" extends military jurisdiction to civilians "serving with or accompanying an armed force in the field," applied only in the event of a declared war. *See also* Lee v. Madigan, 358 U.S. 228 (1959).

[19] Uniform Code of Military Justice, art. 18, 10 U.S.C. § 818 (1970) [hereinafter referred to as U.C.M.J.]. Since this express provision invoking the law of war appears only in the article concerning the jurisdiction of general courts-martial and is not contained in the comparable articles of the Uniform Code which deal with the jurisdiction of special and summary courts-martial (U.C.M.J., arts. 19-20, 10 U.S.C. §§ 819, 820 [1970]) there may arise a negative implication that special and summary courts-martial were not intended to possess any jurisdiction under the law of war.

[20] U.C.M.J., art. 21, 10 U.S.C. § 821 (1970).

in effect at the time of *Quirin* and *Yamashita*[21]—provides that the jurisdiction of courts-martial does "not deprive military commissions, provost courts, or other military tribunals of concurrent jurisdiction with respect to offenders or offenses that by statute or by the law of war may be tried by" such courts. Under Article 36 the President may prescribe rules for the "procedure, including modes of proof, in cases before courts-martial, courts of inquiry, military commissions and other military tribunals."[22] Refusal to appear or to testify "before a court-martial, military commission, court of inquiry or any other military court or board" is made punishable by Article 47 of the Code;[23] and a "court-martial, provost court, or military commission may punish for contempt any person who uses any menacing word, sign, or gesture in its presence or who disturbs its proceedings by any riot or disorder."[24] Under certain circumstances the sworn testimony contained in the record of proceedings of a court of inquiry may "be read in evidence by any party before a court-martial or military commission."[25] Moreover, both Article 104,[26] which proscribes aiding the enemy, and Article 106,[27] which concerns spies in time of war, authorize trial by court-martial or military commission. Each article clearly is based on the law of war; and unlike the other punitive articles of the Uniform Code, each applies to "any person" and not merely to persons subject to the Uniform Code.[28]

3. *Martial Law*

The broad discretion available to the Commander-in-Chief and his subordinates in dealing with offenses against the law of war—offenses for which even civilians can be tried by military tribunals—involves the atypical situation. Also atypical is the exercise of military jurisdiction pursuant to martial law, when civil courts cannot carry on their functions.[29] Martial law is a doctrine of necessity; and if the necessity exists, the use of military personnel and military tribunals is permissible to maintain order. However, the imposition of martial law must have some basis in fact.[30]

4. *Congressional Delegation*

Military jurisdiction is usually based on the Uniform Code of Military Justice,[31] which Congress enacted pursuant to its constitutional power "to make Rules for

---

[21] *See* 327 U.S. at 19-20.

[22] U.C.M.J., art. 36, 10 U.S.C. § 836 (1970). Similar wording was contained in Article of War 38 which was in effect when *Quirin* and *Yamashita* arose. Act of June 4, 1920, ch. 227, ¶ II, § 1, 41 Stat. 794. Apparently it left the President free to provide quite different rules for military commissions than those which he prescribed to regulate trials by court-martial.

[23] U.C.M.J., art. 47, 10 U.S.C. § 847 (1970).

[24] U.C.M.J., art. 48, 10 U.S.C. § 848 (1970).

[25] U.C.M.J., art. 50, 10 U.S.C. § 904 (1970).

[26] U.C.M.J., art. 104, 10 U.S.C. § 904 (1970).

[27] U.C.M.J., art. 106, 10 U.S.C. § 906 (1970).

[28] U.C.M.J., arts. 77-134, 10 U.S.C. §§ 877-934 (1970).

[29] *See* Duncan v. Kahanamoku, 327 U.S. 304 (1946); *Ex parte* Milligan, 71 U.S. (4 Wall.) 2 (1866).

[30] Sterling v. Constantin, 287 U.S. 378 (1932).

[31] The Code was originally enacted on May 5, 1950, and was contained in ch. 169, § 1 (Arts. 1-140), 64 Stat. 108-45. In 1956, it was recodified, 70A Stat. 36-78, 10 U.S.C. §§ 801-940 (1970).

the Government and Regulation of the land and naval Forces."[32] In Article 36 of the
Code, Congress has made a broad delegation of power to the President in these terms:

(a) The procedure, including modes of proof, in cases before courts-martial,
courts of inquiry, military commissions, and other military tribunals may be prescribed by the President by regulations which shall, so far as he considers practicable,
apply the principles of law and the rules of evidence generally recognized in the
trial of criminal cases in the United States district courts, but which may not be
contrary to or inconsistent with this chapter.

(b) All rules and regulations made under this article shall be uniform insofar
as practicable and shall be reported to Congress.[33]

In exercising this power delegated by Article 36 and its predecessor statutory provisions, various Presidents have issued Executive Orders which prescribed Manuals
for Courts-Martial.[34] Similarly, from time to time Presidents have, in their discretion, amended a Manual for Courts-Martial by Executive Order.[35] The term
"modes of proof" that appears in Article 36 might be interpreted to mean only rules
of evidence. However, since the same article also uses the phrase "rules of evidence,"
it is arguable that "modes of proof" has a broader scope. And this probably has been
the view of the military establishment.[36]

For decades, successive Manuals for Courts-Martial have contained discussions
of the various punitive articles—first as they were in the Articles of War and more
recently as the punitive articles appear in the Uniform Code. If "modes of proof,"
as used in Article 36, is intended to include these discussions of the punitive articles,

---

[32] U.S. CONST. art. I, § 8, cl. 14.

Up to this point the Supreme Court has refused to permit the Code's application to persons who
were not members of the armed forces both at the time of the offense and the time of trial. Toth v.
Quarles, 350 U.S. 11 (1955), held unconstitutional Article 3(a) of the Code, 10 U.S.C. § 803(a) (1970),
insofar as it sought to retain military jurisdiction to try a former serviceman for offenses committed
while he was on active duty. McElroy v. United States *ex rel.* Guagliardo, 361 U.S. 281 (1960); Wilson
v. Bohlender, 361 U.S. 281 (1960); Grisham v. Hagan, 361 U.S. 278 (1960); Kinsella v. United States
ex. rel. Singleton, 361 U.S. 234 (1960); and Reid v. Covert, 354 U.S. 1 (1957), established that military
jurisdiction does not extend to either civilian dependents or employees who accompany the armed
forces overseas in time of peace. The Court has not yet expressly considered the constitutionality of
Article 2(10), 10 U.S.C. § 802(10) (1970), which subjects to trial by court-martial civilians who accompany the armed forces in the field in time of war. *See* note 18, *supra.* Nor has the Court yet overruled its 1920 holding that discharged military prisoners may be amenable to military jurisdiction. Kahn
v. Anderson, 255 U.S. 1 (1920).

[33] U.C.M.J., art. 36, 10 U.S.C. § 836 (1970). A predecessor of the article was enacted in 1916 as
part of the Articles of War, applicable to the Army. *See* Fratcher, *supra* note 6, at 864.

[34] Exec. Order No. 11476, 34 Fed. Reg. 10502 (1969) (prescribing the MANUAL FOR COURTS-MARTIAL,
UNITED STATES [rev. ed. 1969]); Exec. Order No. 11430, 33 Fed. Reg. 13502 (1968) (prescribing the
MANUAL FOR COURTS-MARTIAL, UNITED STATES [1969]); Exec. Order No. 10214, 16 Fed. Reg. 1303
(1951). Pursuant to the Articles of War the President issued Manuals for Courts-Martial in 1917, 1921,
1928, and 1949, which were reported to Congress. Fratcher, *supra* note 6, at 865.

[35] *See, e.g.,* Exec. Order No. 10247, 16 Fed. Reg. 5035 (1951) (suspending the limitations for violations
of Articles 82, 85, 86(3), 87, 90, 91(1) and (2), 113, and 115 of the U.C.M.J.); Exec. Order No. 10628,
20 Fed. Reg. 5741 (1955) (restoring limitations upon punishments); Exec. Order No. 10565, 19 FED.
Reg. 6299 (1954) (amending certain maximum punishments); Exec. Order No. 10652, 21 Fed. Reg. 235
(1956) (amending provisions concerning automatic reduction in certain sentences).

[36] The Court of Military Appeals has taken the position that "modes of proof" in Article 36 means
only "rules of evidence." United States v. Worley, 19 U.S.C.M.A. 444, 445, 42 C.M.R. 46, 47 (1970).

then the President has been delegated some discretion to choose between competing rules of substantive criminal law concerning the offenses proscribed in those articles.

Since the Constitution confers on Congress, not the President, an express power "to make Rules for the Government and Regulation of the land and naval Forces," a question arises as to Congress' right to delegate this power to the President. In several instances the question has been rendered moot by judicial rulings that the Manual's discussion of a particular offense was contrary to the legislative intent revealed by the Uniform Code.[37] Three different Manuals for Courts-Martial have been promulgated by Presidential Executive Order since enactment of the Uniform Code.[38] As contemplated by Article 36 of the Code, Congress has been informed of the existence of these Manuals, which have remained relatively constant in their discussions of the various punitive articles. The failure of Congress to repudiate the Manual interpretations of those articles might be considered as implied ratification of the President's action, in which event it would be unnecessary to determine if the President had been properly delegated authority in the first instance to interpret the punitive articles.

This issue of presidential authority to participate in defining crimes is especially important with respect to two punitive articles which—as various critics have complained[39]—are especially sweeping in their terms. Article 133, which applies only to commissioned officers, cadets, and midshipmen, proscribes conduct unbecoming an officer and gentleman.[40] Article 134—codified under the heading "General Article"— applies to all military personnel and prohibits "all disorders and neglects to the prejudice of good order and discipline in the armed forces, all conduct of a nature to bring discredit upon the armed forces, and crimes and offenses not capital."[41] Although the point has sometimes been misunderstood,[42] the third category of mis-

---

[37] United States v. Horton, 9 U.S.C.M.A. 469, 26 C.M.R. 249 (1958) (larceny); United States v. Welker, 8 U.S.C.M.A. 647, 25 C.M.R. 151 (1958) (larceny); United States v. Johnson, 7 U.S.C.M.A. 488, 22 C.M.R. 278 (1957) (unauthorized absence and desertion); United States v. Jenkins, 7 U.S.C.M.A. 261, 22 C.M.R. 51 (1956) (fraudulent enlistment); United States v. Huff, 7 U.S.C.M.A. 247, 22 C.M.R. 37 (1956) (desertion); United States v. Rushlow, 2 U.S.C.M.A. 641, 10 C.M.R. 139 (1953) (desertion). These decisions are criticized in Fratcher, *supra* note 6, at 871-78.

[38] In 1951, by President Truman; in 1968, by President Johnson; and in 1969, by President Nixon. See note 34, *supra*.

[39] *See, e.g.,* O'Callahan v. Parker, 395 U.S. 258, 265-66 (1969); Gaynor, *Prejudicial and Discreditable Military Conduct: A Critical Appraisal of the General Article*, 22 Hast. L.J. 259 (1971). *But see* Wiener, *Are the General Military Articles Unconstitutionally Vague?*, 54 A.B.A.J. 357 (1968). For a criticism of some of the applications of Article 134, see Everett, *Article 134, Uniform Code of Military Justice—A Study in Vagueness*, 37 N.C.L. Rev. 142 (1959). The 1971 Annual Report of the Court of Military Appeals and the Judge Advocates General proposed that Congress consider legislation to "restrict the scope of Article 134 by enacting separate punitive articles of the code covering selected offenses now dealt with by Article 134, and by limiting the maximum punishment for other conduct prejudicial to good order and discipline or service-discrediting conduct to confinement and forfeitures for 6 months." 1971 Annual Report, *supra* note 3, at 2.

[40] U.C.M.J., art. 133, 10 U.S.C. § 933 (1970).

[41] U.C.M.J., art. 134, 10 U.S.C. § 934 (1970).

[42] A Senate Report erroneously assumed that a violation of the law of a foreign country would automatically constitute a violation of the Uniform Code. *See* R. Everett, Military Justice in the Armed Forces of the United States 41 (1956).

conduct—"crimes and offenses not capital"—is deemed to incorporate by reference conduct which would constitute a violation of criminal provisions of federal statutes other than the Uniform Code itself.[43] As to this category the President has no opportunity to participate in defining the crime.

On the other hand, the first two categories of misbehavior—disorders and service-discrediting conduct—are so inexact that they even raise the specter of unconstitutional vagueness.[44] The Manual for Courts-Martial, prescribed by Presidential Executive Order, has been employed as a means for imparting greater specificity to these two broad statutory standards, as well as to the standard of "conduct unbecoming an officer and gentleman," which is utilized in Article 133. The specificity is obtained in two ways—first through the Manual discussion of the two punitive articles[45] and also by setting out in a Manual appendix form specifications indicating how various offenses should be alleged under Articles 133 and 134.[46] In substance, then, various Presidents in promulgating different Manuals for Courts-Martial have made determinations of substantive law as to the types of conduct which should be punishable under the broad wording of these two punitive articles.

Up to this point Congress has not interfered overtly with the President's prerogative in this regard; indeed, in enacting the Uniform Code in 1950 and the Military Justice Act of 1968,[47] that body revealed no desire to change the use of Articles 133 and 134. On the other hand, the Court of Military Appeals, while sometimes permitting extensions of these two articles,[48] developed a doctrine of preemption to the effect that Article 134 may not be employed to punish areas of conduct which were the subject of other punitive articles in the Uniform Code.[49]

Article 92 of the Uniform Code makes punishable the failure to obey "any lawful general order or regulation."[50] As Commander-in-Chief the President may himself issue such an order or regulation, or he may direct that it be issued by one of his subordinate commanders. By promulgating orders and regulations, the President may add substantially to those rules which military personnel may disobey only at their peril. In a sense, Article 92 delegates to the President and other military commanders a part of Congress' constitutional power to "make Rules for the Government and Regulation of the land and naval Forces."[51]

Article 36 directs the President to apply, "so far as he considers practicable," the

---

[43] MANUAL FOR COURTS-MARTIAL, UNITED STATES (rev. ed. 1969), ¶ 213e [hereinafter cited as MANUAL].

[44] As to possible vagueness of Article 134, see United States v. Frantz, 2 U.S.C.M.A. 161, 7 C.M.R. 37 (1953); Dynes v. Hoover, 61 U.S. (20 How.) 65 (1857); Everett, supra note 39.

[45] MANUAL, ¶¶ 212, 213.

[46] MANUAL, app. 6c. Forms 122-25 concern Article 133; forms 126-88 are for use under Article 134.

[47] Act of Oct. 24, 1968, Pub. L. 90-632, 82 Stat. 1335-43.

[48] See, e.g., United States v. Hooper, 9 U.S.C.M.A. 637, 26 C.M.R. 417 (1958); United States v. Berry, 6 U.S.C.M.A. 609, 20 C.M.R. 325 (1956). See generally, Everett, supra note 39.

[49] United States v. Norris, 2 U.S.C.M.A. 236, 8 C.M.R. 36 (1953); United States v. Johnson, 3 U.S.C.M.A. 174, 11 C.M.R. 174 (1953).

[50] U.C.M.J., art. 92, 10 U.S.C. § 892 (1970).

[51] U.S. CONST. art. I, § 8, cl. 14.

rules of evidence used in the federal district courts.[52] However, the President's determination of practicability seems nonreviewable, unless it clashes with a specific provision of the Uniform Code or the Constitution. Thus, the President was upheld in his choice of a rule governing corpus delicti—corroboration of confessions—which proved to be different from that utilized in the federal district courts and more favorable to the accused.[53] It is illustrative of the President's discretion to amend Manual provisions that the 1969 edition of the Manual for Courts-Martial changed this rule of evidence governing corroboration to bring it into line with the federal practice.[54] Ironically, in dealing with self-incrimination, the Court of Military Appeals concluded that a Manual rule of evidence which later proved to be in accord with the federal rule[55] was invalid because of conflict with provisions in the Uniform Code.[56]

The rules of character evidence prescribed by the President differ from those applied in many courts, since they permit proof of a person's character not only by testimony as to his reputation but also by testimony about the witness's own opinion of his character.[57] No privilege is recognized by the Manual for Courts-Martial with respect to communications of a patient either to a military or a civilian physician.[58] A certificate or statement concerning a comparison of fingerprints may be introduced in evidence without calling as a witness the person who made the comparison.[59]

For the military establishment one of the most helpful rules of evidence prescribed by the President in the Manual for Courts-Martial authorizes admission of official records as an exception to the hearsay rule.[60] Proof of unauthorized absence—probably the offense most frequently tried by court-martial—is usually accomplished by introduction in evidence of official personnel records reflecting the absence. However, admissibility of an official record of a fact or event depends on the existence of an official duty to record that fact or event.[61] The President as Commander-in-

---

[52] U.C.M.J., art. 36, 10 U.S.C. § 836 (1970).

[53] United States v. Smith, 13 U.S.C.M.A. 105, 32 C.M.R. 105 (1962) (extensive discussion of power delegated to the President under Article 36); United States v. Mims, 8 U.S.C.M.A. 316, 24 C.M.R. 126 (1957); United States v. Villasenor, 6 U.S.C.M.A. 3, 19 C.M.R. 129 (1955).

[54] MANUAL, ¶ 140a(5). Similarly the Manual was changed in 1969 to allow presentencing consideration of nonjudicial punishments the accused received. MANUAL, ¶ 75c(4). See United States v. Worley, 19 U.S.C.M.A. 444, 42 C.M.R. 46 (1970); United States v. Johnson, 19 U.S.C.M.A. 464, 42 C.M.R. 66 (1970).

[55] Gilbert v. California, 388 U.S. 263 (1967); United States v. Wade, 388 U.S. 218 (1967); Schmerber v. California, 384 U.S. 757 (1966).

[56] United States v. Musguire, 9 U.S.C.M.A. 67, 25 C.M.R. 329 (1958); United States v. Rosato, 3 U.S.C.M.A. 143, 11 C.M.R. 143 (1953); United States v. Eggers, 3 U.S.C.M.A. 191, 11 C.M.R. 191 (1953); United States v. Greer, 3 U.S.C.M.A. 576, 13 C.M.R. 132 (1953).

[57] MANUAL, ¶ 138f(1). Proposed Federal Rule of Evidence 405(a) adopts the same view as the military rule. 93 S.Ct. 37 (1973).

[58] MANUAL, ¶ 151c(2). Proposed Federal Rule of Evidence 504 provides only for a psychotherapist-patient privilege and does not provide a privilege generally. 93 S.Ct. 55 (1973).

[59] MANUAL, ¶ 143a(2)(f).

[60] MANUAL, ¶ 144b.

[61] Id. See also United States v. Kitchen, 5 U.S.C.M.A. 541, 18 C.M.R. 165 (1955); United States

Chief is empowered to impose duties to record various facts and events. By creating a duty to prepare a record, he makes that record admissible in evidence. On various occasions the power to change record-keeping requirements has been utilized by military commanders to facilitate proof of certain offenses.[62]

A striking feature of the Uniform Code is the provision in most of its punitive articles that upon conviction an accused "shall be punished as a court-martial may direct."[63] Since a few of the punitive articles state that the accused "shall be punished by death or such other punishment as a court-martial may direct,"[64] it would appear on their face that most of the punitive articles would permit imposition of life imprisonment. Congress, however, has specifically authorized the President to prescribe limits on the punishment for an offense;[65] and undoubtedly it contemplated that such limits would be imposed by the President for many types of offenses. The Manual for Courts-Martial contains a detailed Table of Maximum Punishments;[66] and so the President, rather than Congress, possesses the discretion to prescribe the maximum punishments imposable for most offenses. Furthermore, especially with respect to combat areas, a President has sometimes removed the limitations on maximum punishments for certain offenses.[67] In that event, the maximum punishment reverts to confinement for life.

Although it would be unusual for him to do so, the President is empowered by the Uniform Code to convene a court-martial.[68] His approval of certain sentences is required;[69] he may commute sentences;[70] he possesses a constitutional authority "to grant Reprieves and Pardons for Offenses against the United States"[71]—which would include violations of the Uniform Code of Military Justice. With the advice and consent of the Senate, the President appoints all "Officers of the United States"[72]— among them the officers of the military establishment and the civilian judges of the Court of Military Appeals.

B. Practical and Legal Limitations of Presidential Discretion

To complete the survey of the President's discretion with respect to military justice, some of the practical and legal limitations of that discretion should be men-

---

v. Bennett, 4 U.S.C.M.A. 309, 15 C.M.R. 309 (1954); United States v. Wilson, 4 U.S.C.M.A. 3, 15 C.M.R. 3 (1954).

[62] See United States v. Simone, 6 U.S.C.M.A. 146, 19 C.M.R. 272 (1955); United States v. Kitchen, 5 U.S.C.M.A. 541, 18 C.M.R. 165 (1955).

[63] U.C.M.J., arts. 77-134, 10 U.S.C. §§ 877-934 (1970).

[64] See U.C.M.J., arts. 85, 90, 94, 99, 100, 101, 102, 104, 113, 118, 120, 10 U.S.C. §§ 885, 890, 894, 899, 900, 901, 902, 904, 913, 918, 920 (1970). Article 106, 10 U.S.C. § 906 (1970), which concerns spies, provides a mandatory death sentence.

[65] U.C.M.J., art. 56, 10 U.S.C. § 856 (1970). See also U.C.M.J., art. 36, 10 U.S.C. § 836 (1970).

[66] Manual, ¶ 127b.

[67] See, e.g., Exec. Order No. 10247, 16 Fed. Reg. 5035 (1951).

[68] U.C.M.J., arts. 22-24, 10 U.S.C. §§ 822-24 (1970).

[69] Manual, ¶¶ 98, 100c(2).

[70] Manual, ¶ 105a.

[71] U.S. Const. art. II, § 2.

[72] Id.

tioned. For example, Congress may amend the Uniform Code and, in so doing, may set aside rules which the President in his discretion has provided in the Manual for Courts-Martial. Furthermore, even with respect to offenses against the law of war, Congress apparently would be perfectly free to impose limitations on the President's discretion—for example, his discretion to use military commissions rather than courts-martial. Congress' constitutional power over the military budget also serves as a powerful restraint on presidential discretion in all matters pertaining to the military establishment.[73]

Congress has well-staffed committees whose existence facilitates its efforts to impose reins on the Commander-in-Chief and his military subordinates. In fact, the extensive inquiries made by the Senate Subcommittee on Constitutional Rights into the rights of military personnel caused it to be likened to a military ombudsman, as that post exists in West Germany.[74] To maintain its access to information, Congress has specifically prohibited any effort by the military establishment to restrict communication by service personnel with members of Congress.[75]

Judicial decisions have also limited the potential role of presidential discretion in the administration of military justice. Thus, the Court of Military Appeals has established that military personnel do possess constitutional rights.[76] Therefore, the President and his subordinate military commanders may not take action which denies those rights.

Furthermore, the Supreme Court has restricted military jurisdiction both as to persons and offenses. Ex-servicemen are not subject to court-martial for offenses prior to discharge.[77] And civilian dependents and employees also fall outside the scope of military jurisdiction.[78] Of special importance is *O'Callahan v. Parker*,[79] which held that even as to military personnel military jurisdiction was lacking over offenses that were not service-connected.

The full impact of *O'Callahan* remains unknown. For example, the concept of service-connection has not yet been fully clarified, although the Supreme Court has since ruled that an offense committed on a military post is service-connected.[80] The opinion of the Court in *O'Callahan* placed great emphasis on the unavailability

---

[73] U.S. CONST. art. I, § 8, cl. 12, 13.

[74] *See Hearings on S. Res. 260 Before the Subcomm. on Constitutional Rights of the Senate Comm. on the Judiciary*, 87th Cong., 2d Sess. 822 (1962) (testimony of Frank E.G. Weil) [hereinafter cited as *1962 Hearings*].

[75] 10 U.S.C. § 1034 (1970). *See also* United States v. Schmidt, 16 U.S.C.M.A. 57, 36 C.M.R. 213 (1966).

[76] The Court of Military Appeals is a court composed of three civilian judges appointed by the President with the advice and consent of the Senate and was provided for by Article 67 of the Uniform Code, 10 U.S.C. § 867 (1970). More than a decade ago it proclaimed that "the protections in the Bill of Rights, except those which are expressly or by necessary implication inapplicable, are available to members of our armed forces." United States v. Jacoby, 11 U.S.C.M.A. 428, 430, 29 C.M.R. 244, 246 (1960). *See also* United States v. Tempia, 16 U.S.C.M.A. 629, 37 C.M.R. 249 (1967).

[77] Toth v. Quarles, 350 U.S. 11 (1955).

[78] *See* note 32 *supra*.

[79] 395 U.S. 258 (1969).

[80] Relford v. Commandant, 401 U.S. 355 (1971).

of the protections of jury trial and grand jury indictment in courts-martial.[81] In light of that rationale, it is unclear whether *O'Callahan* applies to offenses committed in other countries where jury trial and grand jury indictment are unavailable in the civil courts.[82] Similarly, petty offenses have been held not to fall within the rule of *O'Callahan*, since there is no constitutional right to jury trial or grand jury indictment for such crimes.[83] Furthermore, a question remains as to whether *O'Callahan* would have reached a different result in time of war, declared or undeclared.

The opinion in *O'Callahan* was also concerned with the interpretation of Congress' constitutional power to "make Rules for the Government and Regulation of the land and naval Forces."[84] Therefore, it is arguable that, regardless of the presence or absence of jury trial and grand jury indictment, Congress lacks the power to regulate the conduct of military personnel if that conduct is not service-connected. Under this view Congress is constitutionally powerless to prohibit the acts that were involved in the *O'Callahan* case. Even if there had been legislative provision for prosecution of such acts in a federal tribunal where jury trial and grand jury indictment were available, jurisdiction of the offense would be lacking because Congress has no authority to regulate conduct that is not service-connected. Of course, if Congress lacked such authority, it could not be delegated to the President or to military commanders by Congress; nor would the Commander-in-Chief and his subordinate commanders appear to possess such authority in their own right. Furthermore, even if the President issued military orders that all personnel should refrain from certain conduct, the existence of such orders would not establish that the conduct was service-connected. Otherwise, the military establishment would be free to evade *O'Callahan* by issuing orders which prohibited conduct that in itself was not service-connected, relying on the orders to establish service-connection of the prohibited conduct, and prosecuting for disobedience of the prohibitory orders.[85] Of course, if *O'Callahan* intended only to denounce the lack of jury trial and grand jury indictment as to conduct that is not service-connected, then an entirely different result would obtain. Congress could cure the defect by providing that misconduct of military personnel, if not service-connected, could nonetheless be prosecuted in a federal district court, where jury trial and grand jury indictment are available. Similarly, the President and his subordinate military commanders could be authorized to issue orders regulating conduct that lacked service-connection, and prosecutions for disobedience of these orders would also take place in the federal courts.

---

[81] 395 U.S. at 261, 273.

[82] The Court of Military Appeals has ruled that *O'Callahan* does not apply to offenses committed overseas. United States v. Keaton, 19 U.S.C.M.A. 64, 41 C.M.R. 64 (1969). *See also* Blumenfeld, *Court-Martial Jurisdiction Over Civilian-Type Crimes*, 10 AM. CRIM. L. REV. 51, 72 (1971); Everett, *O'Callahan v. Parker—Milestone or Millstone in Military Justice?*, 1969 DUKE L.J. 853, 890.

[83] United States v. Sharkey, 19 U.S.C.M.A. 26, 41 C.M.R. 26 (1969); Blumenfeld, *supra* note 82, at 71; Everett, *supra* note 82, at 893.

[84] U.S. CONST. art. I, § 8, cl. 14.

[85] The Court of Military Appeals seems to have rejected the view that the giving of the order provides service-connection. United States v. Castro, 18 U.S.C.M.A. 598, 40 C.M.R. 310 (1969).

In addition to restricting the jurisdiction of courts-martial, the courts have some-times opened wider the doors for successful collateral attack on court-martial juris-diction.[86] The availability of added opportunities for successful collateral attack on military action also has a limiting practical effect on the discretion available to the President and his subordinate commanders in the administration of military justice.

II
MILITARY DISCRETION TO EMPLOY ALTERNATIVES TO TRIAL BY COURT-MARTIAL

A. Assignment of Duties

In civilian life criminal prosecutions are not the only means whereby govern-mental authorities may seek to deter disapproved conduct. Revocation of a license to practice a profession,[87] conduct a business, or operate a vehicle,[88] as well as de-portation of undesirable aliens,[89] blacklisting of government contractors,[90] and civil penalties[91] illustrate, but do not exhaust, the possibilities.

Similarly, military commanders have many alternatives to the use of trial by court-martial. The very authority to give orders and promulgate regulations—an authority fortified by severe criminal penalties for disobedience[92]—provides the com-mander with an important disciplinary tool. He may order a subordinate to take, or not take, some action, and disobedience of the order could then be punished by court-martial. Of course, if the order is given for the sole purpose of increasing the penalty for an offense which it is expected the recipient of the order will com-mit, then disobedience of the order is not punishable.[93] Similarly, a commander may not order a subordinate to perform additional duties for punitive purposes with-out complying with the Uniform Code.[94] However, the commander is free to

---

[86] See, e.g., Parisi v. Davidson, 405 U.S. 34 (1972); Kauffman v. Secretary of the Air Force, 415 F.2d 991 (D.C. Cir. 1969); but see Noyd v. Bond, 393 U.S. 1048 (1969); United States v. Augenblick, 393 U.S. 348 (1969); Burns v. Wilson, 346 U.S. 137 (1953). The leading precedents are discussed in Weckstein, Federal Court Review of Courts-Martial Proceedings: A Delicate Balance of Individual Rights and Military Responsibilities, 54 MIL. L. REV. 1 (1971); Everett, Collateral Attack on Court-Martial Convictions, 11 A.F. JAG L. REV. 399 (1969); Sherman, Judicial Review of Military Determinations and the Exhaustion of Remedies Requirement, 55 VA. L. REV. 483 (1969). The courts have also proved more receptive to collateral attacks on military administrative action. Harmon v. Brucker, 355 U.S. 579 (1958); Everett, Military Administrative Discharges—The Pendulum Swings, 1966 DUKE L.J. 41, 67.

[87] For example, an attorney may be disbarred from practice of his profession. 7 AM. JUR. 2D Attorneys at Law §§ 12-72 (1963).

[88] Suspension or revocation of a driver's license because of traffic convictions is a familiar part of motor vehicle codes. See, e.g., N.C. GEN. STAT. § 20-16 (Supp. 1965).

[89] See 8 U.S.C. § 1251 (1970).

[90] See, for example, 41 U.S.C. §§ 10(b), 37, 276a(2)(a) (1970), authorizing the debarment of bidders who have violated the Davis-Bacon, Walsh-Healy, and Buy American Acts.

[91] Civil penalties often are authorized without regard to the results of criminal proceedings which arise from the same facts. Rex Trailer Co. v. United States, 350 U.S. 148 (1956); United States ex. rel. Marcus v. Hess, 317 U.S. 537 (1943); Helvering v. Mitchell, 303 U.S. 391 (1938); Various Items v. United States, 282 U.S. 577 (1931).

[92] U.C.M.J., arts. 90-92, 10 U.S.C. §§ 890-92 (1970); MANUAL, ¶ 127b.

[93] MANUAL, ¶ 169b.

[94] U.C.M.J., art. 13, 10 U.S.C. § 813 (1970).

require performance of additional duties for training purposes,[95] and misconduct on the part of a member of his organization may properly alert the commander to that member's need for additional training. Many onerous duties in the armed forces— such as kitchen police—have either disappeared or become less prevalent. Other duties may vanish in the near future as part of the program to make the military service more attractive to prospective volunteers. Yet the residue of unpleasant chores still seems sufficient to provide commanders with an important disciplinary tool.

In combat areas the commander's discretion in assigning hazardous duties is coupled with frightening penalties for failure to perform the assignments.[96] Commanders in charge of confinement installations may use administrative segregation and close order drill to correct inmates.[97] And commanders generally have a broad administrative power to deny passes and leave to their personnel or to impose restrictions to specified areas or limits.[98]

While it is true that the Code limits the imposition of an order which imposes additional duties for punitive purposes,[99] the order will enjoy the benefit of a presumption of legality.[100] And, unless a commander is very ill-informed, proof that he intended his order as a punishment will be hard to come by, for he will usually have some other explanation for giving the order. Moreover, there is considerable judicial reluctance to undertake review of the assignments of military duties.[101] Thus, an order assigning extra duties or restricting the recipient to specified limits can be challenged only at considerable peril to the subordinate who disobeys the order.

---

[95] United States v. Trani, 1 U.S.C.M.A. 293, 3 C.M.R. 27 (1952).

[96] See U.C.M.J., art. 99, 10 U.S.C. § 899 (1970).

[97] United States v. Phillips, 18 U.S.C.M.A. 230, 39 C.M.R. 230 (1969); United States v. Vaughan, 3 U.S.C.M.A. 121, 11 C.M.R. 121 (1953); United States v. Trani, 1 U.S.C.M.A. 293, 3 C.M.R. 27 (1952); but cf. United States v. Williams, 10 U.S.C.M.A. 615, 28 C.M.R. 181 (1959); United States v. Bayhand, 6 U.S.C.M.A. 762, 21 C.M.R. 84 (1956).

[98] Cf. United States v. Petroff-Tachomakoff, 5 U.S.C.M.A. 806, 19 C.M.R. 120 (1955); United States v. Teague, 3 U.S.C.M.A. 317, 12 C.M.R. 73 (1953); but cf. United States v. Gentle, 16 U.S.C.M.A. 437, 37 C.M.R. 57 (1966); United States v. Haynes, 15 U.S.C.M.A. 122, 35 C.M.R. 94 (1964). See also MANUAL, ¶ 128c.

[99] Article 13 of the U.C.M.J., 10 U.S.C. § 813 (1970), prohibits punishment before trial; and Article 15 of the Code, 10 U.S.C. § 815 (1970), appears to provide the sole method for legally imposing non-judicial punishment. Cf. United States v. Gentle, 16 U.S.C.M.A. 437, 37 C.M.R. 57 (1966); United States v. Haynes, 15 U.S.C.M.A. 122, 35 C.M.R. 94 (1964); United States v. Williams, 10 U.S.C.M.A. 615, 28 C.M.R. 181 (1959); United States v. Bayhand, 6 U.S.C.M.A. 762, 21 C.M.R. 84 (1956). Moreover, an order may not be "given for the sole purpose of increasing the penalty for an offense which it is expected the accused may commit." MANUAL, ¶ 169b.

[100] The Manual now provides that "an order requiring the performance of a military duty or act may be inferred to be lawful and it is disobeyed at the peril of the subordinate." MANUAL, ¶ 169b. The corresponding wording of the 1951 Manual was that "an order requiring the performance of a military duty or act is presumed to be lawful and is disobeyed at the peril of the subordinate." MANUAL FOR COURTS-MARTIAL, UNITED STATES (1951), ¶ 169b. The full impact of the change from presumption to inference is not yet clear. Among the cases relying on the presumption of legality under the prior Manual wording are United States v. Coombs, 8 U.S.C.M.A. 749, 25 C.M.R. 253 (1958), and United States v. Trani, 1 U.S.C.M.A. 293, 3 C.M.R. 27 (1952).

[101] See, e.g., Orloff v. Willoughby, 345 U.S. 83 (1953).

B. Promotions

Pay and assignments have a very direct relationship to rank. Accordingly, by means of their discretion in determining promotions, military commanders possess an important tool for controlling the conduct of their personnel. With respect to enlisted personnel, commanders have a very direct control over promotions. Moreover, under some circumstances administrative demotions for inefficiency may be ordered. Promotions of officers hinge on the decisions of selection boards, which consider the military records of the various officers eligible for promotion. However, the most relevant part of these records for promotion purposes are the various ratings which, pursuant to service regulations, are periodically given to officers by their superiors. Low ratings of an officer by his commander may preclude his promotion. Furthermore, having been passed over when eligible for promotion may lead to an officer's separation from the service. Thus, especially for a career officer, fear of a low rating from his commander may have a very inhibiting influence on his conduct, and a commander is free to exploit that fear for disciplinary purposes.[102]

C. Administrative Discharges

Often a commander's primary concern is to remove permanently from his unit—and perhaps from the armed services—a serviceman who is suspected of serious or repeated misconduct or who is a sexual deviant or a drug addict. One avenue to this goal is by preferring criminal charges, referring them to a court-martial for trial, and seeking a sentence which includes punitive discharge—a bad conduct discharge if the accused is tried by special court-martial or either a dishonorable or bad conduct discharge if he is tried by general court-martial.[103] If, however, such a discharge is adjudged, then the Uniform Code provides for extensive and rather time-consuming appellate review. Furthermore, the safeguards provided to the accused by the Code —such as the presence of a military judge and trained defense counsel, rules of evidence, and proof of guilt beyond reasonable doubt—may prevent the court-martial's returning a finding of guilty. However, a commander may have another means for separating undesirable personnel, since the Uniform Code does not apply directly to administrative discharges—discharges which do not result from the sentence of a court-martial. At the present time five kinds of discharge are in use: (1) honorable; (2) general—which is under honorable conditions but differs from an honorable

---

[102] There have occasionally been indications that low efficiency ratings may be used by superior military officers to "punish" defense counsel for distateful tactics. *See, e.g.,* United States v. Kitchens, 12 U.S.C.M.A. 589, 592, & n.3, 31 C.M.R. 175, 178, & n.3 (1961). Congress has now specifically prohibited the use of efficiency ratings to influence court-martial personnel. U.C.M.J., art. 37(b), 10 U.S.C. § 837(b) (1970). Military personnel may seek to attack unfavorable efficiency ratings through the Board for Correction of Military Records, established in each military department under 10 U.S.C. § 1552 (1970).

[103] Articles 18 and 19 of the Uniform Code, 10 U.S.C. §§ 818, 819 (1970), deal respectively with the jurisdiction of general and special courts-martial. Dismissal of an officer, which can only be adjudged by a general court-martial, is equivalent to a dishonorable discharge of enlisted personnel.

discharge; (3) undesirable; (4) bad conduct; and (5) dishonorable.[104] The first three kinds can only result from administrative action and are not considered to be punishment; the last two must be adjudged by a court-martial as punishment. Regardless of the theoretical difference between them, the bad conduct discharge and the undesirable discharge, which is administrative, have almost the same effects on benefits. Moreover, each carries considerable stigma for the recipient.[105] And the administrative undesirable discharge may be based on an unfitness demonstrated by acts for which the perpetrator could be tried by court-martial.[106]

Thus, a military commander often finds that he has discretion to choose between two methods for achieving separation of a misbehaving serviceman—namely, trial

---

[104] See Everett, *Military Administrative Discharges–The Pendulum Swings*, 1966 Duke L.J. 41, 43. The Task Force on the Administration of Military Justice believes "that the administrative discharge has impacted to the detriment of minority group servicemen. In all services, black service members received in Fiscal Year 1971 a lower proportion of honorable discharges and a higher proportion of general and undesirable discharges than whites of similar aptitude and education." 1 Task Force on the Administration of Military Justice in the Armed Forces, Report 109 (1972) [hereinafter cited as Task Force Report]. Accordingly,

half the members of the Task Force recommend that the present characterization of administrative discharges be eliminated. The other half believe that the honorable discharge should be retained, although some would accept a course of action that would retain the honorable discharge but substitute the furnishing of an uncoded certificate of service in all administrative separations not meriting an honorable discharge. A majority of the members of the Task Force believe that if the honorable discharge is eliminated, the manner in which that would be accomplished would require serious and intensive study and that, pending completion of such a study, uncoded certificates of service should be furnished in all separations not meriting an honorable discharge.

The procedure for processing service personnel for elimination with other than an honorable discharge [should] be revised to:

a. Ensure that the prospective dischargee is fully advised as to the potential consequences of the receipt of a discharge other than an honorable discharge, with an accurate and realistic appraisal of the possibility that such a discharge would never be changed to a a discharge of a more creditable nature; and

b. Strengthen the administrative due process safeguards presently accorded in the administrative discharge system by:

(1) Requiring a legally-qualified officer to sit as a member of any administrative elimination board, ruling on all legal questions.

(2) Requiring that the serviceman consult with counsel at the outset of any processing for elimination.

(3) Giving the respondent a right to legal counsel furnished by the government throughout the proceedings.

(4) Providing for participation by legally-qualified officers in review procedures.

c. Provide to the extent practicable that the composition of administrative elimination boards be designed to include minority membership.

d. Provide for the conditional suspension of administrative discharges and a probationary period, including reassignment to a new unit, for persons recommended for an administrative discharge, requiring the discharge authority, when he does not suspend the discharge and place the serviceman on probation, to state in writing his reasons therefor.

Id. 118-19.

[105] *Id.* at 45 n.21. Because of the stigma, the Task Force also recommended that the Defense Department encourage legislation and other appropriate means that would prohibit civilian employers' inquiries as to the character of a serviceman's or servicewoman's discharge from the service. One means suggested was that the Equal Employment Opportunity Commission declare such an inquiry to be a discriminatory practice. The Task Force also recommended exploring the feasibility of establishing a procedure of substituting an uncoded certificate of service after an appropriate period of time for those who have, in the past, been awarded other than honorable discharges. *Id.* at 119.

[106] *Id.* at 45.

by court-martial, which sometimes proves lengthy and laborious, and undesirable discharge, issued administratively and thus not subject to the Uniform Code and its procedural safeguards. The methods are not mutually exclusive; and so a commander may court-martial an accused for his infractions and, if the court-martial does not adjudge a punitive discharge, apparently may initiate administrative action based on essentially the same misconduct.[107]

At one point the armed services apparently abused their discretion to choose between court-martial and administrative discharge. As the Court of Military Appeals noted in its annual report for 1960:

> The unusual increase in the use of the administrative discharge since the code became a fixture has led to the suspicion that the services were resorting to that means of circumventing the requirements of the code. The validity of that suspicion was confirmed by Maj. Gen. Reginald C. Harmon, then Judge Advocate General of the Air Force, at the annual meeting of the Judge Advocates Association held at Los Angeles, Calif., August 26, 1958. He there declared that the tremendous increase in undesirable discharges by administrative proceedings was the result of efforts of military commanders to avoid the requirements of the Uniform Code. Although he acknowledged that men thereby affected were deprived of the protection afforded by the code, no action to curtail the practice was initiated.[108]

As I have discussed elsewhere, this discretion has now been considerably limited by regulations of the armed services themselves and by various judicial decisions.[109] Furthermore, Senator Ervin, the Chairman of the Senate Subcommittee on Constitutional Rights, has for many years made legislative proposals to regulate more closely the issuance of administrative discharges.[110] However, a considerable residue of discretion still remains with the commander to choose between court-martial, administrative discharge proceedings, or a combination of the two.

D. Nonjudicial Punishment

Up to this point the discussion has concerned a commander's discretion to take action which, although not labelled punitive, may have much the same effect as would punishment. However, a commander also has the discretion to initiate action which is designated punishment but does not utilize trial by court-martial. Under Article 15 of the Uniform Code and subject to any more restrictive departmental

---

[107] *Id.* at 78-80. A court-martial has a different burden of proof for the Government—namely, proof beyond reasonable doubt. However, it is arguable that failure of a court-martial to impose a punitive discharge should limit the authority of the Government to discharge administratively for what is basically the same misconduct.

[108] Quoted in *1962 Hearings* 2.

[109] In Harmon v. Brucker, 355 U.S. 579 (1958), the Supreme Court ruled that administrative discharges were judicially reviewable. Since then various cases have arisen which involved attacks on administrative discharge action. *See* Everett, *supra* note 104. Among the most fruitful grounds of attack has been failure by the armed services to follow their own regulations. *See, e.g.*, Roberts v. Vance, 343 F.2d 236 (D.C. Cir. 1964); Murray v. United States, 154 Ct. Cl. 185 (1961); Clackum v. United States, 296 F.2d 226 (Ct. Cl. 1960). *Cf.* Vitarelli v. Seaton, 359 U.S. 535 (1959).

[110] *See* Everett, *supra* note 104, at 41.

regulations, "any commanding officer" may impose certain nonjudicial punishment.[111] The maximum punishment imposable is to some extent related to the rank of the commander who imposes the punishment. For example, if it is imposed on an enlisted accused by an officer of the grade of at least major or lieutenant commander, then nonjudicial punishment may include up to thirty consecutive days of "correctional custody";[112] but otherwise it is limited to seven consecutive days.

An Air Force squadron commander or Army company commander would normally lack power to convene a court-martial of any type; thus, if he chooses not to utilize Article 15, or if the accused refuses to accept nonjudicial punishment, the unit commander must either drop the charges or refer them to a superior commander for consideration. The captain of a naval vessel not only may impose nonjudicial punishment but also is empowered to convene a summary or special court-martial to try the accused. The traditionally wide discretion belonging to the captain of a naval vessel is also reaffirmed in Article 15's provision that as to enlisted persons "attached to or embarked in a vessel," a commander may impose "confinement on bread and water or diminished rations for not more than three consecutive days."[113] Ironically, even a general court-martial is subject to this same limitation in adjudging the punishment of confinement on bread and water, which in the view of the Court of Military Appeals involves cruel and unusual punishment.[114]

Not only the rank of the commander imposing nonjudicial punishment but also

---

[111] U.C.M.J., art. 15, 10 U.S.C. § 815 (1970). See also United States v. Mackie, 16 U.S.C.M.A. 14 36 C.M.R. 170 (1966), which analogized Article 15 to the procedures available under 18 U.S.C. §§ 1(3), 3401 (1970). The Task Force made a number of recommendations concerning nonjudicial punishment under Article 15—among them the following: nonjudicial punishment procedures be standardized among the services, insofar as practicable; servicemen be given the right to obtain the advice of legally-qualified military counsel before deciding whether to demand trial in lieu of nonjudicial punishment (except in those situations when the exigencies of the service limit the availability of counsel); an individual receive a personal hearing before the commander contemplating the imposition of punishment (except, again, when prevented by the exigencies of the service); a person at an Article 15 hearing have the right to be accompanied by an available personal representative—who may but need not be a lawyer—to advise him and to make a statement on his behalf; all Article 15 hearings be open to spectators, except where security interests dictate otherwise, but that the individual have the right to confer privately with the commander imposing punishment, to relate matters of a personal nature; when there are controverted questions of fact, witnesses be called if present on the same ship, post, or otherwise available; forfeitures and reduction not be imposed at a single Article 15 action since both carry a loss of income; commanders take into consideration the effect which any monetary loss will have upon the offender or his family; commanders who impose a reduction in grade upon a first offender as a part of nonjudicial punishment, and who do not suspend that reduction, state for the record their reasons for not doing so; the increased use of correctional custody as a form of nonjudicial punishment be encouraged, with the necessary funding for manpower and facilities being provided; punishment under Article 15 be stayed upon the filing of an appeal, provided the appeal is made at the time of imposition of punishment or within a reasonable time thereafter; every person receiving nonjudicial punishment be properly advised of his right to appeal; the length of time an Article 15 conviction remains in an individual's field personnel file be standardized; periodic monitoring of the administration of nonjudicial punishment be provided. TASK FORCE REPORT 120-21. In January, 1973, many of these recommendations were administratively implemented by Secretary of Defense Laird.

[112] "Correctional custody" is defined in MANUAL, ¶ 131c(4).

[113] U.C.M.J., art. 15(b)(2)(A), 10 U.S.C. § 815(b)(2)(A) (1970).

[114] United States v. Wappler, 2 U.S.C.M.A. 393, 9 C.M.R. 23 (1953).

the rank or grade of the accused affects the maximum punishment imposable. An officer is subject to entirely different nonjudicial punishments than those which a commander may impose on enlisted personnel.[115] Further, an enlisted member in a pay grade above E-4 may not be reduced more than two pay grades.[116]

Although Article 15 provides for appeal from nonjudicial punishments, the greatest restraint on use of nonjudicial punishment is the option of an accused who has been offered such punishment to demand trial by court-martial.[117] Until recently the case of an accused who rejected nonjudicial punishment might be referred to a summary court-martial for trial—where procedural protections are, at best, minimal—and he would have no right to refuse such trial. The Military Justice Act of 1968 created an absolute right to refuse trial by summary court-martial—even if the accused had initially been offered nonjudicial punishment.[118] Accordingly, in exercising his discretion in the first instance either to deal with an offense nonjudicially under Article 15 or to prefer charges for trial by court-martial, a commander must consider the possibility that, even if initiated under Article 15, the case may, by the accused's exercise of his statutory rights, ultimately reach a special or general court-martial.

At one time it seemed arguable that if a case were initiated under Article 15 or by reference of charges to a summary court-martial but later was transferred to a special or general court-martial as a result of the accused's election not to receive nonjudicial punishment or not to be tried by summary court-martial, then the punishment imposable by the special or general court-martial should be limited to that which initially would have been imposable nonjudicially or by summary court-

---

[115] U.C.M.J., art. 15(b)(1), 10 U.S.C. § 815(b)(1) (1970), as to officers; U.C.M.J., art. 15(b)(2), 10 U.S.C. § 815(b)(2) (1970), as to other personnel. An officer may not be subjected to correctional custody or confinement, demoted in grade, or assigned extra duties as nonjudicial punishment; under some circumstances such punishments may be imposed on enlisted personnel pursuant to Article 15.

[116] U.C.M.J., art. 15(b)(2)(H)(iv), 10 U.S.C. & 815(b)(2)(H)(iv) (1970). The power to demote depends on the promotion authority of the commander who is imposing nonjudicial punishment. *See also* U.C.M.J., art. 15(b)(2)(D) (1970).

[117] "[E]xcept in the case of a member attached to or embarked in a vessel, nonjudicial punishment may not be imposed upon any member of the armed forces if he has, before the imposition of such punishment, demanded trial by court-martial in lieu of such punishment." U.C.M.J., art. 15(a), 10 U.S.C. § 815(a) (1970). As originally enacted, the Uniform Code did not grant a right to demand trial by court-martial in lieu of nonjudicial punishment, although it did grant the secretary of a department power, by regulation, to place limitations on the applicability of nonjudicial punishment to an accused who demands trial by court-martial. Pursuant to this provision, the Army and the Air Force granted an absolute right to demand trial by court-martial in lieu of nonjudicial punishment. The Navy and the Coast Guard gave no such right. MANUAL FOR COURTS-MARTIAL, UNITED STATES (1951), ¶ 132. In 1962, when the powers of a commander under Article 15 were strengthened, Congress also gave a statutory basis for the right to demand trial by court-martial except for personnel "attached to or embarked in a vessel." The current Manual follows the statutory wording. MANUAL, ¶ 132.

[118] U.C.M.J., art. 20, 10 U.S.C. § 820 (1970). Previously an accused could object to trial by summary court-martial unless "he has been permitted and has elected to refuse punishment under Article 15." MANUAL FOR COURTS-MARTIAL, UNITED STATES (1951), ¶ 79d(1). Undoubtedly the right to object to nonjudicial punishment was significantly less valuable when the likelihood remained that the case could be referred to a summary court-martial and that the accused could not object to trial by that court-martial. This problem never existed for officers and warrant officers who have not been subject to trial by summary court-martial under the Uniform Code. U.C.M.J., art. 20, 10 U.S.C. § 820 (1970).

martial. However, the recent Supreme Court ruling which upheld increased sentences after a de novo trial upon appeal from an inferior court would suggest a different result.[119] Accordingly, an accused who declines nonjudicial punishment under Article 15 or elects not to be tried by a summary court-martial must reckon with the possibility that, when tried by a special or general court-martial, which has greater authority to punish, he may receive a sentence far greater than the maximum imposable either nonjudicially or by summary court-martial. Furthermore, in the instance of nonjudicial punishment, he does not carry the stigma of court conviction that would result from being found guilty by any kind of court-martial.[120]

E. Trial by Civil Court

Frequently a serviceman's conduct may involve not only violation of the Uniform Code but also of federal or state statutes or, if occurring overseas, the laws of a foreign country. In that instance, a military commander may have discretion to determine whether the accused is tried by a civil court, by a court-martial, or under some circumstances, by both. Within the United States, if military authorities institute court-martial proceedings, they are entitled to proceed and have no obligation to delay in order to permit trial in the civil courts.[121] Conversely, if the jurisdiction of a state or federal civil court first attaches, it cannot be ousted by the commencement of court-martial proceedings. Trial by court-martial will preclude trial in a federal district court for the same offense, and vice versa.[122] Whether a court-martial creates double jeopardy with respect to trial in a state court, or the converse, seems more doubtful.[123]

Although American military authorities seem free under the Constitution to waive their jurisdiction over a serviceman in order to permit his trial by a foreign country,[124] American policy does not favor such waivers.[125] The NATO Status of

---

[119] Colten v. Kentucky, 407 U.S. 104 (1972).

[120] Contrary to the provisions under the 1951 Manual, nonjudicial punishments may be considered by a court-martial in determining an appropriate sentence. Manual, ¶ 75d. United States v. Johnson, 19 U.S.C.M.A. 464, 42 C.M.R. 66 (1970). However, it remains true that an "Article 15 punishment is not a conviction; it does not empower a court-martial to adjudge permissible additional punishments under Section B of the Table of Maximum Punishments." Id. at 467, 42 C.M.R. at 69.

[121] Concerning the relationship between courts-martial and civil courts, see R. Everett, supra note 42, at 38-40.

[122] Grafton v. United States, 206 U.S. 333 (1907).

[123] Bartkus v. Illinois, 359 U.S. 121 (1959); Abbate v. United States, 359 U.S. 187 (1959); United States v. Lanza, 260 U.S. 377 (1922); but cf. Murphy v. Waterfront Comm'n., 378 U.S. 52 (1964). Regardless of constitutional limitations, trial by court-martial for a crime for which the serviceman has already been tried in a state court is infrequent. 1962 Hearings 848, 874, 909, 945, 961.

[124] Wilson v. Girard, 354 U.S. 524 (1957).

[125] Cf. J. Snee & A. Pye, Status of Forces Agreement: Criminal Jurisdiction 117-19 (1957); R. Everett, supra note 42, at 44-45. With respect to the Status of Forces Agreement, the Task Force recommended that when a case involves the exercise of jurisdiction by a foreign government a military advisor be provided to the accused, necessary action be taken to pay the accused who is in pretrial confinement, and all services be encouraged to use to the extent practicable a form of restraint other than pretrial confinement. Task Force Report 126-27.

Forces Agreement[126] and other jurisdictional agreements modelled thereon[127] prescribe very detailed rules concerning primary and secondary jurisdiction where the misconduct of a serviceman violates both the Uniform Code and the laws of the host country.[128] Thus, they limit the military commander's discretion to choose between trial by court-martial and trial in the civil courts. Also, the Status of Forces Agreement provides a double jeopardy protection that seems unavailable to an accused who is tried both by court-martial and by state court.[129]

In determining whether to try by court-martial or to defer to trial in the civil courts, military commanders may be limited by agreements between the Defense Department and the Department of Justice[130] and by local understandings with civil authorities. They may also be influenced by the circumstance that a serviceman who is convicted of a felony by a civil court may be administratively discharged as undesirable.[131] Thus, trial and conviction of a serviceman in a civil court may provide an easy means for separating him from the armed services.

F. Reserve Personnel

If reserve personnel on extended active duty engage in conduct distasteful to their commanders, the result may be release from active duty.[132] This discretion to release from active duty may have serious financial consequences for the reservist—especially for the career reserve officer. Thus, a reservist may have a strong inducement to behave in the manner least likely to prompt a decision by his commander that he be returned to civilian life.

For reserve personnel not on active duty, the discretion of military commanders may be adversely exercised in just the opposite way—by action that will bring such personnel from civilian life into uniform. Sometimes a poorly performing reservist has been ordered to extended active duty pursuant to his obligations as a member of the reserve forces; in other instances, he has been dropped from his reserve

---

[126] NATO Status of Forces Agreement, June 19, 1951, art. VIII, [1953] 2 U.S.T. 1792, T.I.A.S. No. 2846. *See also Status of Forces Policies and Information*, Department of Defense Directive No. 5525.1, Jan. 20, 1966.

[127] For example, an executive agreement of Oct. 29, 1953, with Japan, contained criminal jurisdictional provisions like those of the NATO Status of Forces Agreement. *See* [1953] 4 U.S.T. 1846, T.I.A.S. No. 2848. The agreement with West Germany modifies the jurisdictional scheme significantly. Supplementary Agreement to NATO Status of Forces Agreement for Federal Republic of Germany, Aug. 3, 1959, [1963] 14 U.S.T. 531, T.I.A.S. No. 5351 (effective July 1, 1963).

[128] Generally the host country will have primary jurisdiction unless the offense was committed in the performance of official duty or involved only the security or property of the sending state or the person or property of other nationals of the sending state. NATO Status of Forces Agreement, art. VIII, ¶ 3.

[129] NATO Status of Forces Agreement, art. VII, ¶ 8. For cases involving this protection see United States v. Cadenhead, 14 U.S.C.M.A. 271, 34 C.M.R. 51 (1963); United States v. Sinigar, 6 U.S.C.M.A. 330, 20 C.M.R. 46 (1955).

[130] *1962 Hearings* 847, 909, 945.

[131] *See* Everett, *supra* note 104, at 58.

[132] See, for example, Roberts v. Vance, 343 F.2d 236 (D.C. Cir. 1964), where, however, the release from active duty of the reserve Army officer was set aside because the Army failed to abide by applicable Army regulations governing such releases.

unit and thereby made subject to draft induction. Thus, one reservist was in danger of induction because he had not received credit for attending the training periods of his reserve unit. Under Army directives, credit was precluded since the reservist had appeared at such periods in long hair, which he claimed was necessitated by his employment as agent for "rock and roll" bands. Upholding the military establishment, a Court of Appeals observed that applicable statutes required reserve personnel to "satisfactorily participate in scheduled drills and training periods as prescribed by the Secretary of Defense"; and it concluded that, unless extraordinary circumstances existed, courts should not review a military determination that participation had been unsatisfactory.[133] Existence of this administrative means to discipline reserve personnel not on active duty is all the more important because of severe limitations on military jurisdiction to try such personnel by court-martial.[134]

III

INVESTIGATION AND PRETRIAL PROCEDURES

A. Searches and Seizures

Although the Uniform Code does not purport to limit unreasonable searches and seizures, the Manual for Courts-Martial has long contained a prohibition against the reception of evidence obtained by an unreasonable search and seizure.[135] However, the determination of what constitutes reasonableness still leaves considerable room for a commander's discretion to operate. At one time it was the position of the military establishment that searches on a military installation could be undertaken by authorization of a suitable commander without any showing of probable cause. The commander was analogized to a property-owner inspecting his own property. The Court of Military Appeals did not accept this view and has long required that probable cause exist even for a search on post.[136] However, the military commander remains free to determine probable cause, rather than submit the facts to a neutral, detached magistrate.[137] Nor has there been a requirement that an affidavit be prepared which would set forth the circumstances believed to establish probable cause.[138]

[133] Raderman v. Kaine, 411 F.2d 1102 (2d Cir. 1969), cert. denied 396 U.S. 976 (1969).

[134] See U.C.M.J., Article 2(3), 10 U.S.C. § 802(3) (1970), which restricts such jurisdiction to those reservists who have voluntarily accepted written orders specifying that they are subject to the Uniform Code of Military Justice. See also United States v. Schuering, 16 U.S.C.M.A. 324, 36 C.M.R. 480 (1966); but see Wallace v. Chafee, 451 F.2d 1374 (9th Cir. 1971).

[135] MANUAL, ¶ 152. See also MANUAL FOR COURTS-MARTIAL, UNITED STATES (1951), ¶ 152.

[136] United States v. Brown, 10 U.S.C.M.A. 482, 28 C.M.R. 48 (1959).

[137] As to the requirement of a neutral, detached magistrate, see Coolidge v. New Hampshire, 403 U.S. 443 (1971); Aguilar v. Texas, 378 U.S. 108 (1964); Giordenello v. United States, 357 U.S. 480 (1958).

[138] For applications of this requirement in the federal courts, see, e.g., Spinelli v. United States, 394 U.S. 410 (1969); United States v. Ventresca, 380 U.S. 102 (1965). In United States v. Martinez, 16 U.S.C.M.A. 40, 36 C.M.R. 196 (1966), it is suggested that authority to search be in writing and set out the facts upon which the authorization is based and the articles to be seized. See also United States v. Penman, 16 U.S.C.M.A. 67, 69, 36 C.M.R. 223, 225 (1966). The Air Force seems to have accepted this suggestion. See AF Form 1176 "Authority to Search and Seize."

The Manual for Courts-Martial appears to allow "administrative inspections."[139] In so doing, it has given greater legitimacy to the shakedown inspections so often used in the armed forces—inspections of a barracks or similar area to determine its cleanliness and the presence of contraband.[140] These inspections provide an obvious tool for harassment, and they are hard to reconcile with the Supreme Court's emphasis on the need for court orders even in connection with health inspections.[141] However, recently the Court has granted greater leeway for administrative inspections without court orders.[142]

The armed services have themselves begun to encourage the preparation of written statements of reasons for a search[143]—statements somewhat paralleling the affidavits used in civil courts for establishing probable cause. Also, the military judge is sometimes being utilized as a magistrate to determine whether probable cause exists.[144] Just as warrants issued by a magistrate upon an affidavit are given greater weight than the determination of probable cause by a police officer, so too, the warrants for search issued by the military judges will probably fare better in the courts than determinations of probable cause made by a commander. It seems likely that control of authorizations to search will ultimately be concentrated in the hands of the military judiciary, in which event the courts may be more willing to decide borderline cases in favor of the Government.

B. Apprehension and Confinement

Apprehension—the military equivalent of arrest in civilian life[145]—requires "reasonable belief that an offense has been committed and that the person apprehended committed it."[146] However, the Code does not provide either for the issuance of arrest warrants or for preliminary hearings to determine if probable cause exists. Thus, the discretion of military authorities in taking a serviceman into custody as a suspect is virtually non-reviewable.[147]

---

[139] See Manual, ¶ 152. After setting forth a restriction on permissible objects of search, the Manual provides that, "[t]his restriction does not apply to administrative inspections or inventories conducted in accordance with law, regulation, or custom." In the corresponding paragraph of the 1951 Manual there is no reference to "administrative inspections," but an exception is recognized for the legality of searches made by military personnel "in accordance with military custom." Manual for Courts-Martial, United States (1951), ¶ 152.

[140] The Court of Military Appeals has been willing to uphold "shakedown" inspections under some circumstances. United States v. Gebhart, 10 U.S.C.M.A. 606, 28 C.M.R. 172 (1959); United States v. Swanson, 3 U.S.C.M.A. 671, 14 C.M.R. 89 (1954). For a recent case holding that, under the particular facts, the shakedown was a search and not an inspection, see United States v. Lazerus, C.M. 426877 (Army Court of Military Review, Aug. 15, 1972).

[141] Camara v. Municipal Court, 387 U.S. 523 (1967); See v. Seattle, 387 U.S. 541 (1967).

[142] Wyman v. James, 400 U.S. 309 (1971).

[143] See note 138, supra.

[144] The Army has empowered its military judges to issue search warrants. See 1971 Annual Report, supra note 3, at 3, 21.

[145] In military justice, "arrest is the restraint of a person by an order, not imposed as punishment for an offense, directing him to remain within certain specified limits." Manual, ¶ 18a.

[146] U.C.M.J., art. 7, 10 U.S.C. § 807 (1970).

[147] If a search has been made incident to apprehension, the legality of the apprehension may be reviewed in determining the admissibility of evidence seized in connection therewith. See, e.g., United States v. Ball, 8 U.S.C.M.A. 25, 23 C.M.R. 249 (1957).

Pretrial confinement of persons charged with offenses is authorized by the Uniform Code "as circumstances may require."[148] The Manual for Courts-Martial limits this authority to situations where such confinement is "deemed necessary to insure the presence of the accused at the trial or because of the seriousness of the offense charged."[149] The military's right to confine before trial because of the seriousness of the offense charged may go beyond the power of civil authorities.[150] Moreover, in civilian life bail is available so that an accused may obtain his release prior to trial, and an unreasonably high bail may be contested by appeal.[151] In the military system of justice bail is not allowed, and judicial remedies are not readily available to contest an unreasonable denial of freedom pending trial.[152] In some military commands, however, local regulations have been promulgated to prevent unnecessary pretrial confinement.[153] Moreover, in civilian life there has been considerable criticism of reliance on bail as a means of assuring the accused's presence at trial.[154] Thus, the unavailability of bail in the military establishment may be less significant than might first appear. Furthermore, military justice insists on a speedy trial so that pretrial confinement may prove much shorter for a military accused than for his civilian counterpart who fails to make bail.[155] Even so, military commanders have a degree of discretion as to pretrial confinement unrivaled in civilian life.

C. Statements and Reports

Often military authorities will be in an advantageous position to obtain admissions from a suspect. For one thing, the suspect will frequently be young, in-

---

[148] U.C.M.J., art. 10, 10 U.S.C. § 810 (1970).

[149] MANUAL, ¶ 20c. The Task Force has recommended that

[p]rocedures concerning the admission of an accused into pretrial confinement and retention therein in each service be standardized with a view towards limiting the opportunity for the abuse of discretion and enhancing the perception of fairness, such procedures to include the appointment of both a qualified judge advocate defense counsel to talk with each accused prior to his entry into pretrial confinement or shortly thereafter, and a legal officer, independent of the confining command, authorized to review the pretrial confinement and release the accused from confinement as the circumstances warrant; the confinee be served with a copy of any letter requesting or granting permission for pretrial confinement in excess of thirty days; persons placed in pretrial confinement for less serious offenses be segregated from those placed in pretrial confinement for more serious offenses; and the accused, if found guilty, be credited for time spent in pretrial confinement.

TASK FORCE REPORT 122.

[150] Cf. Stack v. Boyle, 342 U.S. 1 (1951), where assuring the defendant's presence seems to be the sole permissible purpose of bail.

[151] Id.

[152] See Levy v. Resor, 17 U.S.C.M.A. 135, 37 C.M.R. 399 (1967).

[153] See 1962 Hearings 847, 873, 909, 925, 944, 961. Pretrial confinement contrary to local regulations is illegal. United States v. Gray, 6 U.S.C.M.A. 615, 20 C.M.R. 331 (1956). The Army has authorized certain "military magistrates" to release persons in pretrial confinement. See 1971 ANNUAL REPORT, supra note 3, at 321.

[154] See, e.g., D. FREED & P. WALD, BAIL IN THE UNITED STATES (1964); Rankin, The Effect of Pretrial Detention, 39 N.Y.U.L. REV. 641 (1964); Foote, The Coming Constitutional Crisis in Bail, 113 U. PA. L. REV. 960, 1125 (1965). Criticism of bail as the determinant of pretrial confinement gave rise to the Bail Reform Act of 1966, 80 Stat. 214, codified in 18 U.S.C. §§ 3146-50 (1970).

[155] See, e.g., U.C.M.J., arts. 10, 33, 98, 10 U.S.C. §§ 810, 833, 898 (1970); MANUAL, ¶¶ 68i, 215e; United States v. Williams, 16 U.S.C.M.A. 589, 37 C.M.R. 209 (1967).

experienced, and far away from family and friends; and so he may feel especially isolated and powerless. He may be more subject to pretrial confinement than a suspect would in civilian life. He has been conditioned during his military service to obey an order from his superiors, and a request for a statement regarding an offense may be interpreted by the military suspect as an order to talk. The total effect of these factors may be a strong pressure on a suspect to make admissions. Probably to counteract this pressure, Congress has enacted in Article 31 of the Code a specific requirement that any suspect requested to make a statement must be informed both of the nature of the offense, and that any statement he does make may be used in evidence against him.[156] This requirement, which preceded the warning requirement of *Miranda* and which was relied on in that case in Chief Justice Warren's opinion,[157] does not depend on custodial interrogation. Thus, in one way the discretion of military authorities in obtaining statements is limited by this broad statutory requirement.

Grants of immunity are often a valuable tool for investigators in obtaining statements. Although the Uniform Code does not deal with this subject, the Manual for Courts-Martial provides that "an authority competent to order a person's trial by general court-martial may grant or promise him immunity from trial."[158] Thus, grants of immunity are within the discretion of military commanders without judicial review.

Various types of reporting requirements are found in civilian life—such as reports of accidents and reports of certain business transactions.[159] In some manner the duty to report usually derives from a statute. The military commander may also impose requirements on his personnel to report certain events or transactions, but in this instance the requirement stems from military regulation, rather than from statute.[160]

D. Article 32 Investigation and Staff Judge Advocate's Advice

For charges that may be referred to a general court-martial, Article 32 of the Uniform Code requires that a thorough and impartial investigation be made.[161] Provision is made for appointment of an investigator who must inquire into the form and truth of the charges and make a recommendation "as to the disposition

---

[156] U.C.M.J., art. 31, 10 U.S.C. § 831 (1970).

[157] *See* Miranda v. Arizona, 384 U.S. 436, 498 (1966).

[158] MANUAL, ¶ 68*h*; United States v. Kirsch, 15 U.S.C.M.A. 84, 35 C.M.R. 56 (1964). Apparently the immunity authorized is a transactional immunity and not merely the immunity from use of testimony provided under 18 U.S.C. § 6002 (1970). *See also* Kastigar v. United States, 408 U.S. 931 (1972). The convening authority and his staff judge advocate are disqualified from reviewing and taking action as to a record of trial in which a government witness has testified under an immunity grant. *See* United States v. Diaz, 22 U.S.C.M.A. 52, 46 C.M.R. 52 (1972).

[159] See California v. Byers, 402 U.S. 425 (1971); Grosso v. United States, 390 U.S. 62 (1968); Marchetti v. United States, 390 U.S. 39 (1968); Shapiro v. United States, 335 U.S. 1 (1948), with respect to constitutional limitations on reporting requirements.

[160] Prosecutions for failure to comply with the reporting requirements of military regulations were involved in United Stataes v. Kauffman, 14 U.S.C.M.A. 283, 34 C.M.R. 63 (1963); United States v. Smith, 9 U.S.C.M.A. 240, 26 C.M.R. 20 (1958). *See also* Kauffman v. Secretary of the Air Force, 415 F.2d 991 (D.C. Cir. 1969).

[161] U.C.M.J., art. 32, 10 U.S.C. § 832 (1970).

which should be made of the case in the interest of justice and discipline."[162] Thus, the discretion of a military commander is limited by the requirement of this Article 32 investigation, which has sometimes been compared to an inquiry by a civilian grand jury. However, while the return of an indictment is a prerequisite to further proceedings in the federal courts and in those state courts which employ a grand jury, trial by court-martial in the military system can be ordered in the discretion of a military commander regardless of a contrary recommendation by the officer who conducted the pretrial investigation.[163]

As a prerequisite to trial by general court-martial, the convening authority—the commander who convenes the court-martial—must obtain advice from his staff judge advocate or legal officer.[164] This legal advice must state whether there has been adequate pretrial investigation, whether each charge alleges an offense, and whether the allegations are supported by the evidence in the pretrial investigation.[165] However, the discretion of the convening authority is not limited by the staff judge advocate's advice; he may still refer for trial any charge that he finds alleges a violation of the Uniform Code and is warranted by evidence indicated in the Article 32 pretrial investigation.[166]

E. Referring Charges for Trial

Charges under the Uniform Code may be signed by any member of the armed forces who swears that he has investigated or has personal knowledge of the matters alleged and that they are true to the best of his knowledge and belief.[167] However, preferring charges is not especially significant in itself, since military commanders are not required to refer them to a court-martial for trial.[168] A military commander

---

[162] Id.

[163] The statute speaks only of a "recommendation" by the investigating officer. See U.C.M.J., art. 32(a), 10 U.S.C. § 832(a) (1970). See also MANUAL, ¶ 34e. If a charge is referred to a general court-martial for trial, the convening authority must find "that the charge alleges an offense under this chapter and is warranted by evidence indicated in the report of investigation." U.C.M.J., art. 34(b), 10 U.S.C. § 834(b) (1970).

[164] U.C.M.J., art. 34(a), 10 U.S.C. § 834(a) (1970).

[165] MANUAL, ¶ 35c. The staff judge advocate also provides "a signed recommendation of the action to be taken by the convening authority" and this "recommendation will accompany the charges if they are referred for trial." Id.

[166] U.C.M.J., art. 34, 10 U.S.C. § 834 (1970).

[167] U.C.M.J., art. 30, 10 U.S.C. § 830 (1970). However, a "person subject to the code cannot be ordered to prefer charges to which he is unable truthfully to make the required oath on his own responsibility." MANUAL, ¶ 29c.

[168] The statutory obligation is that "[u]pon the preferring of charges, the proper authority shall take immediate steps to determine what disposition should be made thereof in the interest of justice and discipline, and the person accused shall be informed of the charges against him as soon as practicable." U.C.M.J., art. 30, 10 U.S.C. § 830 (1970). The Manual requires a "preliminary inquiry into the charges"; but this inquiry can be informal. MANUAL, ¶ 32b. On the basis of this preliminary inquiry, the accused's immediate military commander may determine to dismiss the charges that have been preferred, unless he is directed to the contrary by competent superior authority. Id., ¶ 32d. If the commander dismisses all the charges, he may—but apparently is not required to—"notify the accuser of the action taken and the reasons therefor." Id., ¶ 32d. Even for serious charges, there is no requirement that a formal investigation be conducted under Article 32 as a prerequisite for dismissal.

The convening authority's discretion to determine whether to refer charges for trial and, if so, to what grade of court-martial is a personal discretion and cannot be delegated. United States v. Simpson,

has full discretion to refuse to prosecute, subject to being overruled by a military superior and ordered to take action on the charges. There is, however, no military grand jury that can indict against his wishes.[169] Nor is it likely that a military commander could be himself prosecuted successfully for dereliction of duties by reason of his failure to refer charges for trial.[170]

There are three types of court-martial: (a) the general court-martial, which may impose any punishment authorized by the Code and the Manual for Courts-Martial;[171] (b) the special court-martial, which may adjudge no punishment greater than a bad conduct discharge, confinement for up to six months, and forfeiture of up to two-thirds pay for up to six months;[172] and (c) the summary court-martial, which may not adjudge punishment greater than confinement for one month and forfeiture of two-thirds pay for one month.[173] Basically the authority to convene a particular type of court-martial and refer cases to it for trial depends on the position of a commander in the military hierarchy of command. Thus, a general court-martial may be convened by the President, the secretary of the military department concerned, or the commander of a division, a fleet, a naval station, an Air Force or Marine Corps wing.[174] A special court-martial may be convened by any person who may convene a general court-martial and various commanders at lower echelons, such as the commanders of an Air Force base or an Army or Marine Corps brigade or regiment and the captain of a naval or Coast Guard vessel.[175] A summary court-martial may be convened by any person who may convene a general or special court-martial, the commanding officer of a detached company or other detachment of the Army, and the commanding officer of a detached squadron or other detachment of the Air Force.[176] With respect to all three types of courts-martial, Congress granted the secretary of a military department the power to designate other commanding officers who might act as convening authorities;[177] and the same power was given the President as to general courts-martial.[178]

---

16 U.S.C.M.A. 137, 36 C.M.R. 293 (1966); United States v. Robert, 7 U.S.C.M.A. 322, 22 C.M.R. 112 (1956); United States v. Bunting, 4 U.S.C.M.A. 83, 15 C.M.R. 84 (1954).

[169] United States v. Cox, 342 F.2d 167 (5th Cir. 1965), seems to hold that a federal grand jury cannot return a valid indictment without the cooperation of the United States attorney, who must sign an indictment before it may become a basis for prosecution.

[170] A military commander has certain duties with respect to the maintenance of discipline among his troops. *See In re* Yamashita, 327 U.S. 1 (1946). Thus, if a commander repeatedly dismissed charges that had been preferred against members of his command and that clearly had merit, he might be subject to prosecution under U.C.M.J., Article 92, 10 U.S.C. § 892 (1970), for dereliction of duties as a commander. However, a factual situation that would permit successful prosecution on this basis is unlikely. The repeated dismissal of charges would probably not constitute a violation of Article 98, which proscribes noncompliance with procedural rules. U.C.M.J., art. 98, 10 U.S.C. § 898 (1970).

[171] U.C.M.J., art. 18, 10 U.S.C. § 818 (1970).

[172] U.C.M.J., art. 19, 10 U.S.C. § 819 (1970).

[173] U.C.M.J., art. 20, 10 U.S.C. § 820 (1970).

[174] U.C.M.J., art. 22, 10 U.S.C. § 822 (1970).

[175] U.C.M.J., art. 23, 10 U.S.C. § 823 (1970).

[176] U.C.M.J., art. 24, 10 U.S.C. § 824 (1970).

[177] U.C.M.J., arts. 22(a)(6), 23(a)(7), 24(a)(4), 10 U.S.C. §§ 822(a)(6), 823(a)(7), 824(a)(4) (1970).

[178] U.C.M.J., art. 22(a)(7), 10 U.S.C. § 822(a)(7) (1970).

If a commander is not authorized to convene a court-martial which would have jurisdiction to adjudge the punishment which, in his opinion, is suitable for the offense charged, he may transmit the charges to a commander of higher rank for determination of the action to be taken. For example, a company commander in the Army would usually not have authority to convene any type of court-martial; his only method for imposing punishment would be by means of nonjudicial punishment under Article 15 of the Uniform Code. Therefore, if the company commander did not feel that the case was suitable for disposition under Article 15 but that further action should be taken, he could transmit the charges to the Army regimental or brigade commander, who would have power to convene either a summary or special court-martial. If that commander felt that the charges might warrant trial by general court-martial, he could take steps to transmit the case to the division commander or some other higher commander with authority to convene a general court-martial. In the Air Force, the progression might be from the squadron commander to a group or base commander, and then to the commander of a separate wing or of some other higher command. In the Navy, fewer steps would be involved, for the captain of a vessel would have the authority either to mete out nonjudicial punishment or to convene a summary or a special court-martial.

The broad discretion conferred upon military commanders with respect to referring charges for trial by court-martial is limited in two important ways. Neither a general nor a special court-martial may be convened by a commanding officer who is an "accuser"[179]—a term which has been broadly defined by the Code[180] and by the Court of Military Appeals. For example, a general whose home had been burglarized could not convene a court-martial to try the accused;[181] and in one case it was held that a general who attempted to convene a court-martial for disobedience of an order issued in his name was disqualified by his personal interest in the result.[182]

Even an accuser can convene a summary court-martial. Thus, the second limitation on the commander's discretion is especially important. Article 20 provides an absolute right to object to trial by summary court-martial.[183] However, this right itself contains some peril since the accused who objects to trial by summary court-martial, which is limited in jurisdiction to the imposition of no more than one month's confinement, may thereby risk trial by general or special court-martial, which may adjudge a more serious punishment.[184]

---

[179] U.C.M.J., arts. 22(b), 23(b), 10 U.S.C. §§ 822(b), 823(b) (1970).

[180] Article 1(9) of the U.C.M.J., 10 U.S.C. § 801(9) (1970), defines accuser as "a person who signs and swears to charges, any person who directs that charges nominally be signed and sworn to by another, and any other person who has an interest other than an official interest in the prosecution of the accused."

[181] United States v. Gordon, 1 U.S.C.M.A. 255, 2 C.M.R. 161 (1952).

[182] United States v. Marsh, 3 U.S.C.M.A. 48, 11 C.M.R. 48 (1953); *but cf.* United States v. Teel, 4 U.S.C.M.A. 39, 15 C.M.R. 39 (1954); United States v. Keith, 3 U.S.C.M.A. 579, 13 C.M.R. 135 (1953).

[183] Prior to the effective date of the Military Justice Act of 1968 an accused could object to trial by summary court-martial only if he had not been offered nonjudicial punishment pursuant to Article 15.

[184] At one time it seemed arguable that the determination of military authorities to refer the charges

IV

APPOINTMENT OF COURT-MARTIAL PERSONNEL

Considerable invective has been directed against military justice because of the opportunities for a military commander as convening authority of a court-martial to influence the outcome of a case tried by that court. While these opportunities were significantly curtailed by the Military Justice Act of 1968, they have not completely been eliminated.

A. General Courts-Martial

Prior to the effective date of the 1968 legislation, only one type of general court-martial existed, and it was composed of a "law officer" and not less than five members.[185] In the Army and later in the Navy and Marine Corps, the law officers were members of a trial judiciary which performed only duties in connection with general courts-martial and which was considerably insulated from the influence of military commanders.[186] In the Air Force full-time law officers were not utilized and the military lawyers who acted as law officers were much less protected from the possibility of command influence. The Military Justice Act of 1968 redesignated the law officers as military judges,[187] provided a statutory basis for the trial judiciary, and attempted to safeguard their independence.[188] Furthermore, a general court-martial might consist of "only a military judge, if before the court is assembled the accused, knowing the identity of the military judge and after consultation with defense counsel, requests in writing a court composed only of a military judge and the military judge approves."[189] Here then is authorized waiver of jury—and without the consent of the Government, which is required in the federal courts.[190] Such a waiver is especially significant since in the traditional general court-martial with lay members, the "military jury" not only returns the verdict but also imposes the sentence.

---

to a summary court-martial for trial would have the practical effect of limiting the punishment imposable to that which could be adjudged by a summary court-martial, even if the accused objected to trial by summary court-martial and the charges were then referred to a special or general court-martial. Otherwise the possibility of greater punishment would have a "chilling effect" on the accused's statutory right to object to trial by court-martial. *Cf.* United States v. Jackson, 390 U.S. 570 (1968). A similar argument can be made with respect to the punishment imposable if an accused objects to nonjudicial punishment and charges are referred for trial by court-martial. However, the Supreme Court has now made this position seem almost untenable. *Cf.* Colten v. Kentucky, 407 U.S. 104 (1972).

[185] *See* R. EVERETT, *supra* note 42, at 145-57.

[186] *See 1962 Hearings* 838-40, 904-05, 936-37.

[187] U.C.M.J., arts. 1(10), 26, 10 U.S.C. §§ 801(10), 826 (1970). The redesignation of the "law officer" to "military judge" is paralleled by the recent change of title from "hearing examiner" to "administrative law judge." 41 U.S.L.W. 2115.

[188] U.C.M.J., arts. 26(c), 37, 10 U.S.C. §§ 826(c), 837 (1970). The officer certified for duty as military judge of general courts-martial is "directly responsible to the Judge Advocate General, or his designee."

[189] U.C.M.J., art. 16(1)(B), 10 U.S.C. § 816(1)(B) (1970).

[190] FED. R. CRIM. P. 23(a); Singer v. United States, 380 U.S. 24 (1965).

B. Special Courts-Martial

Before the Military Justice Act of 1968 special courts-martial could only consist of not less than three members. Now alternative arrangements are possible. The court-martial may consist of a military judge and not less than three members. Or, it may be staffed by a military judge if one has been detailed to the court and the accused, knowing his identity and after consultation with defense counsel, so requests in writing, and the military judge approves.[191] In the instance of the special court-martial the military judge may be, but is not required to be, a member of the trial judiciary whose duties are solely of a judicial nature. Moreover, he is subject to the influence of military commanders in the field through their power over his assignments and through their control of his performance ratings.[192] Thus, for special courts-martial there remains the possibility that a military commander—if he is willing to achieve his end despite an express statutory prohibition in the Uniform Code[193]—may influence the military judge's performance of duties. Also, for the special court-martial the military commander in the field may have some ability to control what military judge will be assigned to a particular case.

The commander who serves as convening authority may also determine if the special court-martial will have a military judge, since there is no statutory requirement that a special court-martial have a military judge. His discretion is, however, severely limited in practice. For one thing, a special court-martial without a military judge cannot impose a bad conduct discharge "except in any case in which a military judge could not be detailed to the trial because of physical conditions or military exigencies."[194] Furthermore, in any such case the convening authority must "make a detailed written statement, to be appended to the record, stating the reason or reasons a military judge could not be detailed."[195] It is perfectly clear that Congress intended for few cases, indeed, to be disposed of under this exception. Since many of the cases referred to special court-martial would be those where the convening authority would wish the court to be free to impose a bad conduct discharge, he will be under considerable compulsion to appoint a military judge to the court-martial.

---

[191] U.C.M.J., art. 16(2)(C), 10 U.S.C. § 816(2)(C) (1970).

[192] *See* U.C.M.J., art. 26(c), 10 U.S.C. § 826(c) (1970). Article 37(b) provides that, in preparing an effectiveness, fitness, or efficiency report, no one may "consider or evaluate the performance of duty . . . as a member of a court-martial." U.C.M.J., art. 37(b), 10 U.S.C. § 837(b) (1970). In this context the word "member" may not include the "military judge" who has been detailed to a special court-martial and who is not certified to serve as military judge of general courts-martial. However, any omission in the statutory wording is remedied by the Manual provision that "a convening authority shall not prepare or review any report concerning the effectiveness, fitness, or efficiency of a military judge detailed to a special court-martial which relates to his performance of duty as a military judge." MANUAL, ¶ 38e(2). The ratings in these reports are a major factor in determining an officer's assignments, promotion, qualification for a regular commission, and retention in the service.

The Air Force has recently expanded its Trial Judiciary to provide 28 full-time military judges for special courts-martial. These officers will be assigned directly to the Office of the Judge Advocate General and thus will not be subject to efficiency ratings by commanders in the field. AFJAG REPORTER, Aug., 1972, at 21.

[193] U.C.M.J., art. 37, 10 U.S.C. § 837 (1970).

[194] U.C.M.J., art. 19, 10 U.S.C. § 819 (1970).

[195] *Id.*

A second practical consideration is created by the increased presence of legally-trained defense counsel in special courts-martial. Prior to the Military Justice Act of 1968, there was no requirement that a military lawyer be assigned to represent the accused, unless the prosecutor was a lawyer. Although the Air Force generally provided lawyers both to prosecute and defend in special courts-martial, this was not true in the Army and Navy.[196] The 1968 legislation required that the accused be provided legally-trained counsel in special courts-martial "unless counsel having such qualifications cannot be obtained on account of physical conditions or military exigencies."[197] Moreover, the convening authority must make a "detailed written statement, to be appended to the record, stating why counsel with such qualification could not be obtained."[198] The result has been the appointment of military lawyers as defense counsel in almost all special courts-martial tried since the 1968 Act took effect.[199] If a lawyer is to defend, then generally the convening authority wishes to have a lawyer as trial counsel—prosecutor—to protect the Government's interests. In turn, experience has demonstrated that trial by a special court-martial composed only of lay members in a case where lawyers are prosecuting and defending is often very unsatisfactory. The members are frequently confused by legal issues as to which they have available no impartial source of advice. Thus, another very strong practical pressure exists for a convening authority to appoint a military judge to a special court-martial.

Before the requirement existed that lawyers be appointed to defend an accused tried by a special court-martial, a convening authority had considerable leeway to influence the quality of the defense, for among the non-legally-trained officers appointed as defense counsel in special courts-martial the aptitude for court-martial practice and the zeal displayed might vary markedly. Even today the convening authority is in a position to affect the quality of defense representation by his decisions concerning which lawyers in his command will be appointed or made available as defense counsel. However, the accused is assured at least a minimal level of skill on the part of his counsel, for the lawyer must be a licensed attorney or the graduate of an accredited law school and must also be certified by the Judge Advocate of his armed force as being competent to defend general courts-martial.[200] Moreover, the Air Force has undertaken a pilot program for trial teams composed of full-time trial and defense counsel to prosecute and defend general and special courts-martial.

---

[196] *1962 Hearings* 837-38, 903, 935. The Court of Military Appeals did not consider legally-trained defense counsel to be constitutionally required in a special court-martial, even when a bad conduct discharge was adjudged. *See* United States v. Culp, 14 U.S.C.M.A. 199, 33 C.M.R. 411 (1963).

[197] U.C.M.J., art. 27(c)(1), 10 U.S.C. § 827(c)(1) (1970).

[198] *Id.*

[199] The Military Justice Act of 1968, 82 Stat. 1355, took effect on Aug. 1, 1969. The requirement that legally-trained counsel be provided in connection with special courts-martial created an added need for lawyers in the Army and the Navy.

[200] U.C.M.J., art. 27, 10 U.S.C. § 827 (1970).

In addition to their greater experience, the members of the trial team are insulated more fully from command influence on their performance.[201]

C. Summary Courts-Martial

In a summary court-martial the convening authority, who is not disqualified by any personal interest, appoints a commissioned officer who serves as the summary court-martial. While neither the Code nor the Manual contemplate the appointment of counsel for such a court-martial, the recent ruling of the Supreme Court in *Argersinger v. Hamlin*[202] requires a reassessment in this regard. However, the military establishment may take the position that the absolute right to object to trial by summary court-martial—in which event the case will only be tried by special or general court-martial where legally-trained counsel are provided—distinguishes the *Argersinger* case.[203]

---

[201] On June 1, 1971, the pilot project for the Air Force Judiciary Trial Division officially began its test period. This project, which was discussed in the January 1, 1970-December 31, 1970 report, is one in which some 15 judge advocates were assigned as fulltime trial and defense counsel and special court-martial military judges within geographical districts within the 2d Circuit of the eastern U.S. Judiciary Region. They work out of offices at Maxwell AFB, Ala., Keesler AFB, Miss., MacDill AFB, Fla., and Shaw AFB, S.C. All report directly to the Judge Advocate General rather than field commanders. The test period was concluded on November 30, 1971, and is currently undergoing an evaluation with a view toward determining its feasibility for worldwide adoption. 1971 ANNUAL REPORT, *supra* note 3, at 33. A similar approach was suggested in 1962 by Dean A. Kenneth Pye. *See 1962 Hearings* 548-49. The pilot program has apparently been successful and is being expanded. *See* AFJAG REPORTER, Aug., 1972, at 21. With respect to counsel, the Task Force has recommended that there be provided:

[a]dequate legal facilities and services to military judges and military counsel, including proper office equipment, adequate legal libraries, private offices for defense counsel and trial counsel, separated so that they will not appear to be working out of the same organization, and necessary logistical and administrative support (*e.g.*, paralegal representation and enlisted investigative assistants). . . . [t]he senior circuit judge appoint members of court and detail the military judge and defense counsel made available to him. Members of the trial judiciary be placed under the direction of the appropriate Judge Advocate General. All judge advocate defense counsel be placed under the direction of the appropriate Judge Advocate General or, in the case of the Marine Corps, the Director, Judge Advocate Division, Headquarters, United States Marine Corps. In view of the critical need for more minority lawyers, the feasibility of contracting for a pool of minority civilian defense counsel from which the military could draw, as needed, be explored; and adequate funds be made available to the services for the express purpose of expanding their efforts in recruiting minority lawyers. Military counsel be provided with additional training in human relations and in communicating with minority persons.

TASK FORCE REPORT 124-25.

[202] 407 U.S. 25 (1972).

[203] U.C.M.J., art. 20, 10 U.S.C. § 820 (1970). In four summary court-martial cases the Judge Advocate General of the Army has set aside the confinement portion of the sentence since the accused were neither represented by lawyer counsel at trial nor did the accused knowingly and intelligently waive their right to representation by lawyer counsel. 72-14 JUDGE ADVOCATE LEGAL SERVICE § III(3) (DA Pam 27-72-14). For a federal district court holding that *Argersinger* applies to summary courts-martial, see Daigle v. Warner, 348 F. Supp. 1074 (D. Hawaii 1972). Under the same reasoning, does *Argersinger* apply to nonjudicial punishment involving correctional custody?

The Task Force has recommended a decrease in the use of the summary court-martial with a view toward its eventual abolishment. Pending this, the Task Force suggests several modifications to ensure the appearance of fairness in the operation of summary courts-martial. These include: only judge advocates should be appointed to sit as summary court-martial officers; counsel should be detailed to represent the accused and the Government; the nature of the summary court-martial should be an

D. Determining the Number of Court Members

Neither a general court-martial nor a special court-martial need contain a pre-scribed number of members—only a minimum number. Thus, the convening au-thority can determine the number of members to serve on the court-martial, subject to the right of the accused to reduce this number by use of peremptory challenge or challenge for cause. The number appointed may be significant, since military justice does not require a unanimous verdict and findings of guilty may be returned by a two-thirds vote.[204] From the standpoint of an accused contesting guilt, a court-martial composed of five or eight members is preferable to one composed of six or nine members.[205]

E. Pretrial Instruction

Prior to the Military Justice Act of 1968 a convening authority could instruct or lecture prospective court-martial members, and if the instructions were sufficiently astute, they would not fall within the proscription of unlawful influence on a court-martial.[206] Article 37 of the Code now markedly limits this practice.[207] It also im-poses other limitations on actions of the convening authority that might tend to influence court members. However, he still retains the power to appoint the mem-bers; and, so the criticism goes, he can manipulate his appointments in a way that will stack the court. Furthermore, the court members are still usually the military subordinates of the commander who appoints them.

F. Enlisted Membership

In the instance of enlisted accused, the commander's discretion is limited by the right of an enlisted man to request in writing that the membership of his court-

---

adversary proceeding; the evidence of conviction by summary court-martial should be removed from an accused's field file upon reenlistment or release from active duty; and summary courts-martial should be empowered to impose correctional custody.

Although a minority of the Task Force felt that the summary court-martial still serves a valid purpose and provides a useful array of options for the benefit of the accused, the majority believed that elimination of the summary court would achieve three important results: the ends of justice would be better served; fewer persons would have their records marred by court-martial convictions; and trial by special court-martial would involve adequate procedural protection of the rights of the individual accused. TASK FORCE REPORT 76-77.

[204] U.C.M.J., art. 52, 10 U.S.C. § 852 (1970). *Cf.* Apodaca v. Oregon, 406 U.S. 404 (1972) (unanimous verdict is not required as part of the constitutional right to a jury trial); Williams v. Florida, 399 U.S. 78 (1970) (right to jury trial does not require twelve-member jury).

[205] *See* R. EVERETT, *supra* note 42, at 179.

[206] *See, e.g.,* United States v. Danzine, 12 U.S.C.M.A. 350, 30 C.M.R. 350 (1961). Paragraph 38 of the 1951 Manual for Courts-Martial authorized the convening authority to give "general instruction to the personnel of a court-martial which he has appointed, preferably before any cases have been referred to the court for trial. . . . Such instruction may relate to the rules of evidence, burden of proof, and presumption of innocence, and may include information as to the state of discipline in the command, as to the prevalence of offenses which have impaired efficiency and discipline, and of command measures which have been taken to prevent offenses." Because of complaints about the practice of giving pretrial instruction to prospective court-martial members, the Army discontinued this practice in 1962. See *1962 Hearings* 869, 923 ("Handbook for Court Members" sponsored by the Navy to obviate the need for special instructions to court members).

[207] U.C.M.J., art. 37, 10 U.S.C. § 837 (1970).

martial be comprised of at least one-third enlisted personnel.[208] As this right is implemented by the Manual for Courts-Martial, it applies throughout the trial, so that, if by challenges, illness, or otherwise, the enlisted membership of the court-martial is reduced below one-third, then the trial cannot proceed.[209] The one-third requirement can be valuable to an enlisted accused whose defense counsel foresees that enlisted members of a court-martial would probably vote to acquit. By peremptorily challenging an officer member of the court-martial, the defense can increase the enlisted membership above one-third and thereby prevent the Government from obtaining the two-thirds vote required for conviction. Such cases, however, do not arise in practice. Instead, many experienced defense counsel have found that when an accused requests enlisted membership, those appointed are typically senior non-commissioned officers with a predisposition toward the prosecution. Military commanders have found authorization for such appointments in the Uniform Code's mandate that a convening authority detail as members persons "who are best qualified for the duty by reason of age, education-training, experience, length of service, and judicial temperament."[210] Many military commanders seem to believe that no enlisted man could be better qualified within these guidelines than a top sergeant or a chief petty officer. The Court of Military Appeals permits this view.[211] Thus, provisions for enlisted court membership have become almost a dead letter because of defense reluctance to utilize this option.

G. Selection of Court Members

The Uniform Code directs that "when it can be avoided, no member of an armed force may be tried by a court-martial any member of which is junior to him in rank or grade."[212] To some extent this standard may reflect the deference afforded rank by military custom. It may also be grounded on very practical concerns that a subordinate of the accused might be influenced by fear, resentment, or some other improper motive. In any event, it provides no serious limitation on the discretion of a convening authority who wishes to "stack" membership of a court-martial to achieve a particular result.

Various legislative proposals have been made to limit the discretion of military commanders in the appointment of court members. Some would remove completely the power of the military commander to appoint the members of a court-martial to which he refers charges.[213] Other proposals would require random selection of court members from a predesignated roster, appointment of court members from

---

[208] U.C.M.J., art. 25(c), 10 U.S.C. § 825(c) (1970).

[209] Manual, ¶ 62h(4).

[210] U.C.M.J., art. 25(d)(2), 10 U.S.C. § 825(d)(2) (1970). Cf. Carter v. Jury Comm'r, 396 U.S. 320 (1970).

[211] United States v. Crawford, 15 U.S.C.M.A. 31, 35 C.M.R. 3 (1964), discussed in 1965 Duke L.J. 633. For criticism of this case and of prevailing practice in the selection of court-martial members, see Remcho, *Military Juries: Constitutional Analysis and the Need for Reform*, 47 Ind. L.J. 193 (1972). *See also* United States v. Greene, 20 U.S.C.M.A. 232, 43 C.M.R. 72 (1970).

[212] U.C.M.J., art. 25(d)(1), 10 U.S.C. § 825(d)(1) (1970).

[213] Bayh, *supra* note 3, at 19; Sherman, *supra* note 3, at 45.

the lower enlisted grades for the trial of enlisted personnel, or appointment of court members from different military commands.[214] Although such proposals would eliminate some of the opportunities for abuse that have been complained of, none would completely remove every possibility of abuse, since the court members would still be military personnel who might feel subject to the possibility of military reprisal by a disgruntled commander.

While several of these proposals would require enabling legislation, some of them could be implemented administratively. For example, by agreement between military commanders, court-martial members could be appointed who were not under the command of the convening authority. Of course, even in that instance the possibility of reprisal pursuant to agreement between the commanders involved would still exist; and, in practice, commanders would probably be reluctant to spare members of their own organization to help solve the disciplinary problems of another organization. Similarly, random selection could be utilized by a commander. With the aid of his personnel officers he could appoint members of his command who were selected on a random basis from the officers in his command.[215] Conceivably, however, under the existing provisions of the Code, random selection might be regarded as inconsistent with the exercise of the commander's discretion in choosing the "best qualified," as contemplated by the statutory wording.[216]

V

TRIAL

As has already been explained, the convening authority determines if charges will be referred for trial by court-martial, and his determination may be at odds with the recommendations of an Article 32 investigating officer or of the convening authority's own staff judge advocate. Furthermore, it appears from the Manual for Courts-Martial that a trial counsel has no independent power to refuse to prosecute a case which the convening authority wishes tried. According to the Manual, a trial counsel who, while preparing a case for trial, discovers that trial would be inadvisable is directed to "inform the convening authority at once."[217]

---

[214] Id. See also Remcho, supra note 211, at 223-29.

[215] In one case random selection was apparently used by a convening authority in appointing court-martial members. See Remcho, supra note 211, at 219. The Task Force has recommended selection of court members on a random basis and that "[a]dditional peremptory challenges to the court members be permitted by both prosecution and defense, with the defense having a greater number than the prosecution." TASK FORCE REPORT 125.

[216] The language of Article 25 seems to contemplate that the commander who convenes a court-martial will use his personal discretion in choosing court members. U.C.M.J., art. 25(d)(2), 10 U.S.C. § 823(d)(2) (1970). In one sense random selection is the antithesis of conscious selection by a commander of the persons whom he deems best qualified to perform duties as court members pursuant to the standards prescribed in Article 25(d)(2). On the other hand, there is a rational exercise of discretion in a commander's choice to utilize the principle of random selection. United States v. Kemp, No. 25,893 (U.S.C.M.A., filed Nov. 20, 1972), now pending in the Court of Military Appeals, raises the question of the extent to which the convening authority must be personally involved in the various aspects of selecting court members.

[217] MANUAL, ¶ 44f(5).

Obviously the convening authority is to make the final determination whether trial will proceed.

Unlike civil courts where venue is an important concept, military justice does not designate the place where a trial by court-martial may be conducted. Thus, a convening authority has some discretion as to the place at which an accused may be brought to trial. Change of venue is authorized but only when "there exists at the place of trial so great a general atmosphere of prejudice against him that he cannot obtain a fair and impartial trial in that place."[218]

A convening authority may direct that an offense that otherwise would be capital shall be tried as noncapital.[219] By so doing, he may affect the rules of evidence applicable to the case, especially with respect to depositions, which are not admissible in behalf of the prosecution in capital cases.[220] Also, the convening authority may be involved in a decision concerning the right of the defense to subpoena a civilian witness[221]—although the matter may be reopened at trial. He may forbid the taking of depositions before trial.[222] At the trial, if a charge has been held to be defective and inadequate to allege an offense, the matter is referred to the convening authority for action.[223]

Plea bargaining is a prevalent feature of civilian criminal justice. Similarly it is employed within the military establishment, although not in all the armed forces. For a decade the Army, Navy, and Marine Corps have utilized plea bargaining; the Air Force, on the other hand, forbids it.[224] In the military procedure for plea bargaining, the convening authority who has referred a case for trial plays a major role. Upon the initiative of the defense counsel, a written agreement is entered between the accused and the convening authority that, if the accused pleads guilty, the convening authority will approve no sentence in excess of that which is agreed upon. The agreement sets only a ceiling, but not a floor. The defense counsel is still under a duty to seek the lowest possible sentence from the court-martial, the members of which are unaware of the agreement between the accused and the convening authority. If the sentence imposed proves to be greater than that which has been agreed upon, then the convening authority reduces the sentence as required. On the other hand, if the sentence adjudged is below that which has been

---

[218] MANUAL, ¶ 69e.

[219] MANUAL, ¶ 15a(3).

[220] U.C.M.J., art. 49, 10 U.S.C. § 849(a) (1970); MANUAL, ¶ 145a.

[221] MANUAL, ¶ 145a. The convening authority may also be involved in determining whether certain confidential and secret evidence is made available to defense counsel. MANUAL, ¶ 151b(3).

[222] See U.C.M.J., art. 49(a), 10 U.S.C. § 849(a) (1970).

[223] MANUAL, ¶¶ 67f; 69b; U.C.M.J., art. 62(a), 10 U.S.C. § 862(a) (1970); Priest v. Koch, 19 U.S.C.M.A. 293, 41 C.M.R. 293 (1970). Under Article 62, the convening authority may review a military judge's ruling favorable to the accused on a motion to dismiss; however, he cannot make findings of fact contrary to those of the judge. U.C.M.J., art. 62, 10 U.S.C. § 862 (1970). See United States v. Frazier, 21 U.S.C.M.A. 444, 45 C.M.R. 218 (1972).

[224] For a discussion of the plea bargaining practices in the various armed services, see 1962 Hearings 843, 870, 905, 923, 937, 957. See also the judges' view on the negotiated guilty plea program as expressed in United States v. Watkins, 11 U.S.C.M.A. 611, 29 C.M.R. 427 (1960). See McMenamin, Plea Bargaining in the Military, 10 AM. CRIM. L. REV. 93 (1971).

agreed upon, there is no procedure for increasing it and the accused receives a windfall of sorts. This procedure, which conforms to all constitutional require-ments,[225] gives the convening authority a discretion and responsibility that many judges do not possess. However, unlike plea bargaining in some civil courts, the bargained plea in the military is embodied in a document before trial.[226]

VI

APPELLATE REVIEW

The military commander who convenes a court-martial has considerable dis-cretion in the review of its decision. While he is expected to rely upon the advice of his staff judge advocate,[227] he retains final responsibility. It is in his power to review the facts, law, and sentence, but his discretion can be exercised only in behalf of the accused.[228] The discretion to grant clemency is an absolute one, and can be predicated upon information, such as lie detector results, which would be inadmissible in a trial.[229] The convening authority can determine whether to suspend all or part of a sentence;[230] he may defer confinement under certain circumstances;[231] and he designates the place of confinement, subject to applicable regulations of his military department.[232] Thus, the initial determination as to rehabilitation is that of the convening authority.

It has been suggested that the broad discretion of the commander is so great that it may sometimes produce an adverse effect on the accused at the trial. Court mem-bers may conclude that they should impose a severe sentence and rely on the discretion of the convening authority to reduce it to a suitable level. Obviously such reasoning by court members would violate their sworn responsibility.[233]

Perhaps in response to the possibilities of abuse at the trial level, Congress has provided for extensive appellate review of courts-martial. For example, in addition to initial review by the convening authority, a Court of Military Review must review any case in which there is a punitive discharge or confinement for a year or

---

[225] In United States v. Care, 18 U.S.C.M.A. 535, 40 C.M.R. 247 (1969), the Court of Military Appeals acted to assure that military pleas of guilty would conform to the requirements of Boykin v. Alabama, 395 U.S. 238 (1969), and McCarthy v. United States, 394 U.S. 459 (1969).

[226] See McMenamin, *supra* note 224, at 95, who favors the visibility of the written pretrial agreement. The military procedure tends to avoid problems like those present in Santobello v. New York, 402 U.S. 994 (1971).

[227] See MANUAL, ¶ 85c. However, if he disagrees with his staff judge advocate, the convening authority should state the reasons for that disagreement. See also *id.*, ¶ 91a. The Task Force has recommended that "[i]n other than capital cases, automatic review of all general courts-martial and special courts-martial in which a bad conduct discharge is approved by the convening authority be eliminated, except for a clemency review by the convening authority, providing instead for review by the appellate judiciary of only those cases appealed by the accused." TASK FORCE REPORT 125-26.

[228] Cf. U.C.M.J., arts. 62-64, 10 U.S.C. §§ 862-64 (1970).

[229] United States v. Massey, 5 U.S.C.M.A. 514, 18 C.M.R. 138 (1955).

[230] U.C.M.J., art. 71(d), 10 U.S.C. § 871(d) (1970).

[231] U.C.M.J., art. 57(d), 10 U.S.C. § 857(d) (1970).

[232] MANUAL, ¶ 89c(5).

[233] Cf. United States v. Ellis, 15 U.S.C.M.A. 8, 34 C.M.R. 454 (1964).

more.[234] In other cases, the Judge Advocate General of the appropriate service may act to correct error prejudicial to the substantial rights of the accused.[235] A petition for new trial is available.[236] And further relief may be secured through certain administrative boards.[237]

The Court of Military Appeals may review cases which have been reviewed by a Court of Military Review. For the most part the grant of review is discretionary and is upon an accused's petition for review.[238] Like a Supreme Court denial of certiorari, the denial of a petition for review by the Court of Military Appeals is without a formal opinion. Thus, the criteria for the exercise of its discretion to review can only be surmised.[239]

CONCLUDING COMMENTS

Traditionally American military commanders, from the Commander-in-Chief down to the company commander, have enjoyed considerable discretion in disciplining their troops. Not surprisingly, the scope of the discretion committed to a a commander frequently depends on his rank, his position in the chain of command, and sometimes on his service. Thus, some of the nonjudicial punishments permissible under Article 15 depend on the rank of the commander who administers the punishment.[240] An Army company commander or Air Force squadron commander generally has no authority to convene any sort of court-martial; he can simply transmit charges, with his recommendations, to a higher echelon of command. The captain of a naval or Coast Guard vessel can convene a summary or special court-martial, and as to personnel "attached to or embarked in" his vessel, he may even impose confinement on bread and water, without any election on the part of the accused to elect trial by court-martial.[241]

To some extent the rank of a commander may affect the quality of the justice he administers. Usually there will be some correlation between rank on the one hand, and experience and training on the other. Hopefully, therefore, a seasoned colonel will be able to administer justice more impartially and beneficially than a new lieutenant. However, the converse may be true, and the years of experience may simply reinforce existing prejudices.

The rank of the accused may also affect the scope of the discretion available

---

[234] U.C.M.J., art. 66, 10 U.S.C. § 866 (1970).

[235] U.C.M.J., art. 69, 10 U.S.C. § 869 (1970). *See also* Everett, *Collateral Attack on Court-Martial Convictions*, 11 A.F. JAG L. REV. 399 (1969).

[236] U.C.M.J., art. 73, 10 U.S.C. § 873 (1970).

[237] 10 U.S.C. § 1553 (1970) (Discharge Review Boards) and 10 U.S.C. § 1552 (1970) (Correction Boards).

[238] U.C.M.J., art. 67(b), 10 U.S.C. § 867(b) (1970). However, mandatory review is provided for capital cases and those involving general or flag officers. Also, the Judge Advocate General of an armed service can certify to the court for decision questions arising in cases decided by the Court of Military Review.

[239] The court's most recent annual report reveals that as of June 30, 1971, it had granted 2,845 petitions for review and had denied 20,793. 1971 ANNUAL REPORT, *supra* note 3, at 15.

[240] U.C.M.J., art. 15(b), 10 U.S.C. § 815(b) (1970).

[241] U.C.M.J., art. 15(a), 10 U.S.C. § 815(a) (1970).

to his commander in administering justice. For example, officers may be prosecuted for certain conduct that would not be an offense on the part of an enlisted man.[242] With respect to nonjudicial punishments, the limitations applicable to officers and enlisted personnel are quite distinct; and as to enlisted personnel the grade of the accused is important in determining the reduction in grade that may be imposed.[243] No commander—whatever his rank or position—has the power to refer charges against an officer to a summary court-martial for trial.[244] No officer may be sentenced to hard labor without confinement.[245] An officer dismissed by order of the President has a right to a trial by general court-martial,[246] and a sentence extending to dimissal of an officer must be approved by the secretary of the military department.[247] Cases involving general and flag officers bring into play additional requirements of review.[248]

Congress has sought to limit the discretion of commanders in administering military justice by providing some unique safeguards for service personnel. The detailed appellate review of findings and sentence—which extends to the weight of the evidence and the appropriateness of the sentence,[249] the Article 31 warning required in pretrial interrogation,[250] and the Article 32 pretrial investigation which must precede trial by general court-martial,[251] are among these safeguards. Another protection is afforded by the privilege granted any member of the armed forces to make a complaint of wrongs against his commanding officer.[252]

In shielding service personnel against abuses of discretion, military justice has placed great reliance on the numerous elections and options offered to an accused. Unless attached to or embarked in a vessel, he may refuse nonjudicial punishment.[253] He possesses an absolute right to object to trial by summary court-martial.[254] In a

---

[242] See, e.g., Articles 88 (contempt toward officials) and 133 (conduct unbecoming an officer and gentleman), U.C.M.J., 10 U.S.C. §§ 888, 933 (1970).

[243] U.C.M.J., art. 15(b)(2)(H)(iv), 10 U.S.C. § 815(b)(2)(H)(iv) (1970).

[244] U.C.M.J., art. 20, 10 U.S.C. § 820 (1970).

[245] MANUAL, ¶ 126d. The 1951 Manual for Courts-Martial had provided that an officer could not be sentenced to confinement or total forfeitures of pay unless he was also sentenced to dismissal; but this provision was held to be contrary to the Uniform Code. See United States v. Madison, 14 U.S.C.M.A. 655, 34 C.M.R. 435 (1964); United States v. Smith, 10 U.S.C.M.A. 152, 27 C.M.R. 227 (1959).

[246] U.C.M.J., art. 4, 10 U.S.C. § 804 (1970).

[247] U.C.M.J., art. 71(b), 10 U.S.C. § 871(b) (1970).

[248] U.C.M.J., art. 67(b)(1), 10 U.S.C. § 867(b)(1) (1970) (mandatory review by Court of Military Appeals); U.C.M.J., art. 71(a), 10 U.S.C. § 871(a) (1970) (approval by the President). The mandatory review for general and flag officers was held to be based upon a reasonable classification. See United States v. Gallagher, 15 U.S.C.M.A. 391, 35 C.M.R. 363 (1965).

[249] U.C.M.J., arts. 64, 66, 69, 10 U.S.C. §§ 864, 866, 869 (1970).

[250] U.C.M.J., art. 31, 10 U.S.C. § 831 (1970).

[251] U.C.M.J., art. 32, 10 U.S.C. § 832 (1970).

[252] U.C.M.J., art. 138, 10 U.S.C. § 938 (1970). The Court of Military Appeals has recognized Article 138 as a proper means to question the legality of pretrial or post-trial confinement. Dale v. United States, 19 U.S.C.M.A. 254, 41 C.M.R. 254 (1970); Walker v. United States, 19 U.S.C.M.A. 247, 41 C.M.R. 247 (1970). However, the armed services apparently take the position that, except as to confinement, the Article does not concern matters involving discipline. See OpJAGAF 1972/111 (Oct. 17, 1972); OpJAGAF 1972/53 (Apr. 26, 1972).

[253] U.C.M.J., art. 15(a), 10 U.S.C. § 815(a) (1970).

[254] U.C.M.J., art. 20, 10 U.S.C. § 820 (1970).

special or general court-martial the accused may, with the military judge's consent, waive trial by the military jury and elect to be tried and sentenced by the judge alone.[255] An enlisted accused may require that the jury of a special or general court-martial which tries him contain at least one-third enlisted personnel at all times.[256] The creation of these various rights and the customary requirement that a waiver of the rights be knowing and intelligent has necessitated the increasing availability of military lawyers to advise accused persons concerning the alternatives available to them.

In addition to the more obvious limitations that the Uniform Code has placed on a commander's discretion, there are others which are less visible. For example, if a commander fails, under some circumstances, to assign a military judge or a legally qualified military defense counsel to a special court-martial, he must attach to the record of trial his explanation of the necessities which required the use of laymen.[257] Similarly, if he fails to accept the post-trial recommendation of his staff judge advocate, the commander must attach to the record the reasons for this disagreement.[258] The necessity of the explanation and the possibility that it might later be scrutinized judicially and found wanting, undoubtedly induce considerable reluctance in a commander to take the action that might appear to be within his discretion.

A commander still retains the authority to refer cases to a special court-martial that consists only of lay members and has no military judge.[259] However, by limiting the punishment which such a court-martial could impose and by providing for the presence of legally-trained defense counsel in almost all special courts-martial,[260] Congress has created a situation where a commander would seldom feel that it was practical to appoint a special court-martial that had no military judge. Similarly, while the Uniform Code does not require that the trial counsel—prosecutor—in special courts-martial must be an attorney, the provision that legally-trained defense counsel be provided in such courts compels the commander to appoint a lawyer to prosecute in order to avoid a mismatch of legal skills that might be disastrous for the Government's case.

Just as the alternatives available to a commander may be less meaningful than at first appears, so to, the choices available for an accused may have some restrictions not at first apparent. For example, the opportunity of an accused to elect trial by an enlisted court-martial is diminished in significance by the right of the commander to appoint as enlisted members senior non-commissioned officers who usually would be oriented to the prosecution.[261]

Since 1951 when the Uniform Code of Military Justice took effect, there have

[255] U.C.M.J., art. 16, 10 U.S.C. § 816 (1970).
[256] U.C.M.J., art. 25(c), 10 U.S.C. § 825(c) (1970).
[257] U.C.M.J., arts. 19, 27(c)(1), 10 U.S.C. §§ 819, 827(c)(1) (1970).
[258] MANUAL, ¶¶ 85c, 91a.
[259] U.C.M.J., art. 16(2)(A), 10 U.S.C. § 816(2)(A) (1970).
[260] U.C.M.J., arts. 19, 27(c)(1), 10 U.S.C. §§ 819, 827(c)(1) (1970).
[261] United States v. Crawford, 15 U.S.C.M.A. 31, 35 C.M.R. 3 (1964).

emerged many new limitations on the discretion of commanders in administering military justice. Many of those limitations were imposed by the decisions of the Court of Military Appeals, a civilian tribunal created by the Code. For example, this court expanded pretrial safeguards,[262] helped transform the "law officer" of a general court-martial into a "military judge,"[263] required detailed instructions concerning the evidence and the offenses,[264] gave new meaning to appellate review,[265] and created extraordinary remedies.[266] The court deprived the Manual for Courts-Martial, prescribed by the President, of its stature as a "bible" for the military lawyer.[267]

The various military departments promulgated regulations and developed policies which limited the discretion of commanders in the field. For example, the Army, Navy, and Marine Corps, while authorizing a commander to accept or decline a proposed negotiated guilty plea, have required that the bargain be embodied in a written pretrial agreement, so that it is visible and will not be subject to misunderstanding concerning the terms.

The Army's initiative in developing a trial judiciary—law officers who were allowed to specialize in military justice and were insulated from possible command influence in the field—has had a major impact on military justice. Together with the decisions of the Court of Military Appeals, this innovation, swiftly adopted by the Navy and Marine Corps, led to congressional provision for "military judges" in both general and special courts-martial.[268] In turn, creation of this new position—and the prestige, independence, and power provided for it—has had the practical effect of reducing the discretion available to military commanders in administering military justice. Various types of decisions previously made by commanders are gradually being transferred to military judges. In a similar manner, the Army has now provided for "military magistrates," who are authorized to make determinations concerning searches and seizures and pretrial confinement that previously were entrusted solely to commanders.[269]

The enactment of the Military Justice Act of 1968 reflected a congressional intent

---

[262] See, e.g., United States v. Tempia, 16 U.S.C.M.A. 629, 36 C.M.R. 249 (1967); United States v. Wilson, 2 U.S.C.M.A. 248, 8 C.M.R. 48 (1953).

[263] For different opinions concerning this transformation, see Quinn, Courts-Martial Practice: A View from the Top, 22 HAST. L.J. 201, 208-10 (1971); Miller, Who Made the Law Officer a "Federal Judge"?, 4 MIL. L. REV. 39 (1959).

[264] See, e.g., United States v. Amie, 7 U.S.C.M.A. 514, 22 C.M.R. 304 (1957); United States v. Clay, 1 U.S.C.M.A. 74, 1 C.M.R. 74 (1951).

[265] See, e.g., United States v. Chandler, 22 U.S.C.M.A. 73, 46 C.M.R. 73 (1972); United States v. Massey, 5 U.S.C.M.A. 514, 18 C.M.R. 138 (1955); United States v. Coulter, 3 U.S.C.M.A. 657, 14 C.M.R. 75 (1954).

[266] See, e.g., United States v. Synder, 18 U.S.C.M.A. 480, 40 C.M.R. 192 (1969); United States v. Bevilacqua, 18 U.S.C.M.A. 10, 39 C.M.R. 10 (1968); Everett, supra note 235.

[267] As to the change in the court's attitude toward the Manual, compare United States v. Hemp, 1 U.S.C.M.A. 280, 3 C.M.R. 14 (1952), with United States v. Rinehart, 8 U.S.C.M.A. 145, 23 C.M.R. 369 (1957). See also Quinn, supra note 263, at 203-08.

[268] U.C.M.J., art. 26, 10 U.S.C. § 826 (1970).

[269] See 1971 ANNUAL REPORT, supra note 3, at 3, 21.

to curtail in certain ways the discretion of military commanders. Thus, the strengthening of prohibitions on command influence was intended to remove a commander's discretion to take certain action that might influence the outcome of a trial by court-martial.[270] The requirement that legally-trained counsel be assigned in special courts-martial was designed to lessen significantly the scope of the commander's discretion in appointing defense counsel for such courts.[271]

However, the Uniform Code and the 1968 amendments thereof limited commanders' discretion in one way that probably was not fully appreciated. By making military justice far more technical and complicated, Congress—together with the Court of Military Appeals—has created a situation where a commander feels far more dependent on his legal advisers. At least as to serious offenses, the alternatives for commanders have become so much more complicated that, regardless of the discretion provided them by statute, they can hardly feel much confidence in disregarding recommendations of their legal advisers. In short, for purposes of military justice, as in many other areas, the military commander has become much more dependent on the technician; and so, in practical effect, his discretion has been reduced.

Another result of the increasing complexity of military justice is the use by commanders of alternatives other than court-martial in maintaining discipline. Assignments of duty, promotions or demotions, administrative discharge, release from active duty or call to duty have been among the means available. Use of these alternatives was often more attractive because of a traditional judicial reluctance to review assignments of military duties and similar matters.[272] However, in some instances the federal courts found authority to correct abuses of discretion involved in disciplinary measures other than trial by court-martial. Especially with respect to administrative discharges,[273] the courts have acted to limit the discretion of military commanders—sometimes by finding violations of the regulations of the military department involved.

Of much greater impact in limiting military discretion was the Supreme Court's decision in *O'Callahan v. Parker*,[274] which ruled that—subject to some possible exceptions—even offenses committed by servicemen could not be tried by court-martial unless those offenses were service-connected. The rationale of *O'Callahan* is especially noteworthy since it transcends questions of court-martial jurisdiction and concerns the substantive power of military commanders to regulate the conduct of their personnel in matters not clearly service-connected.

From one direction or another, further inroads may be anticipated on the discretion of military commanders in administering military justice. Probably the

---

[270] U.C.M.J., art. 37, 10 U.S.C. § 837 (1970).
[271] U.C.M.J., art. 27(c)(1), 10 U.S.C. § 827(c)(1) (1970).
[272] Orloff v. Willoughby, 345 U.S. 83 (1953).
[273] Harmon v. Brucker, 355 U.S. 579 (1958); Everett, *supra* note 104, at 41.
[274] 395 U.S. 258 (1969).

summary court-martial will disappear from the scene—at least in its present form.[275] The role and power of the military judge will increase, and with it will come a diminution of the authority of military commanders. It seems likely that soon the military judge will be empowered to issue all the writs authorized by the All Writs Act,[276] will be ruling on search and arrest questions and the issuance of warrants, will be granting releases from pretrial and post-trial confinement, and will become even more involved in the sentencing process, even without specific waiver by the accused of his right to be tried by military jury.

The incessant complaints about composition and selection of courts-martial may soon diminish sharply as changes occur in the procedures for selecting court members. Greater use of random selection of such members seems increasingly probable, but the high percentage of waivers of trial by jury may reduce the importance of the entire issue. Furthermore, recent Supreme Court decisions which have altered prevailing conceptions of the constitutional right to "trial by jury" tend to reduce criticisms that military justice deprives an accused of his right to jury trial.

Whatever the commander's role may become in the selection of court-martial members, he will probably retain a major role in determining which offenses are tried by court-martial. Thus, he will continue to share in that discretion usually enjoyed by prosecuting attorneys. His role in the process of appellate review may become more limited—partly in response to the more technical nature of the issues presented during this review and partly because of the desirability of transferring clemency and rehabilitation decisions to experts in penology and corrections.

In response to complaints in Congress and elsewhere that racial discrimination occurs in the administration of military justice, a task force established by the Department of Defense has recently been studying military justice. Its report deals both with intentional discrimination[277] and systemic discrimination;[278] and the recommendations extend to preservice educational factors, equal opportunity programs, job assignments and testing, regulation of personal appearance, updating racial and ethnic identity codes, and administrative discharges. As to the military justice system, the Task Force Report recommends various changes in nonjudicial punishment,[279] decreased use of summary courts-martial,[280] increased stature for military judges and counsel, random selection of court members, reduction of the convening

---

[275] Over the years there have been many recommendations for abolition of summary courts-martial. Now, as a result of the decision in Argersinger v. Hamlin, 407 U.S. 25 (1972), their continued use may be unfeasible. See note 203, supra.

[276] 28 U.S.C. § 1651(a) (1970).

[277] The Task Force has defined intentional discrimination as "a policy of an authority—especially in the context of our study, a military authority—or action of an individual or group of individuals which is intended to have a negative effect on minority individuals or groups without having such an effect on others." TASK FORCE REPORT 18-19.

[278] Systemic discrimination has been defined as "policies or practices which appear to be neutral in their effect on minority individuals or groups but which have the effect of disproportionately impacting upon them in harmful or negative ways." Id.

[279] Supra note 105.

[280] Supra note 227. Summary courts-martial have very minimal use currently in the Air Force.

authority's role in appellate review, codification of offenses currently tried under Article 134,[281] and better military justice training.[282] Aside from the recommendations concerning nonjudicial punishment, as to which the effects are hard to predict, the Report does not seem to call for drastic revision in the military justice system.

Perhaps—but not probably—some new task force or investigative group will bring to light some abuses not previously suspected. In that event drastic new restrictions may be imposed administratively or legislatively on the discretion of commanders in maintaining discipline and punishing crime.

For example, jurisdiction of all offenses committed within the United States by service personnel might be transferred from courts-martial to federal district courts, so that the United States Attorney, rather than a military commander, would make the decision as to which offenses would be prosecuted. And even as to offenses committed overseas, greater civilian influence might be provided—perhaps replacing the "military judges" with civilian judges.

Up to this point, the case for new major changes in military justice does not seem to have been proved. Indeed, Congress will probably wish to allow further opportunity for evaluation of the existing system, as substantially amended by the Military Justice Act of 1968 and by various innovations and pilot programs that have been initiated by the armed services. Thus, for the foreseeable future it seems likely that military commanders will continue to enjoy broad discretion in the administration of justice.

---

[281] This specificity has also been recommended by the Court of Military Appeals and the Judge Advocates General. 1971 ANNUAL REPORT, *supra* note 3, at 1-2.

[282] The Task Force Report also has recommendations concerning Status of Forces agreements. *Supra* note 125.